Illuminating the Narrow Gate

The Writing on the Wall for the Mainstream Western Religions

Volume I

Karl R. Luther

Illuminating the Narrow Gate:
The Writing on the Wall for the Mainstream Western Religions
Volume I

Published by
Peerseen Truth Publishing
Scottsdale, AZ

Copyright 2022 by Karl R. Luther

All rights reserved. No part of this book may be reproduced or transmitted in any form without the prior written permission from the publisher except brief quotations embodied in critical reviews. For permission requests, contact the publisher at PeerseenTruth@gmail.com.

All Scripture quotations, unless otherwise indicated, are taken from the Holy Bible, New International Version®, NIV®. Copyright 1973, 1978, 1984, 2011 by Biblica, Inc.™ Used by permission of Zondervan. All rights reserved worldwide. www.zondervan.com. The "NIV" and "New International Version" are trademarks registered in the US Patent and Trademark Office by Biblica, Inc.™

*"Pulling Rank," by Frank Koch (*Proceedings, *November 1987), reprinted by permission of the US Naval Institute.*

Book cover design by JD&J LLC

Library of Congress Control Number: 2020915825

ISBN Hardcover: 978-1-7356347-0-8
ISBN Paperback: 978-1-7356347-1-5
ISBN E-book: 978-1-7356347-2-2

First Edition

To the two greatest leaders of the 20th century, who boldly lived with unconditional love and spiritual power in the societal and political arenas of life and thereby changed the world:

Mohandas K. Gandhi
Martin Luther King Jr.

Contents

Volume I

Preface (p. xi)

Introduction
Supplementing Information (p. xv) ◆ The Book's Nature and Length (p. xv) ◆ Overview of the Book's Content (p. xvi) ◆ The Essence of the Book (p. xxi)

Chapter 1. The Search for Truth
1.1. Introduction (p. 1) ◆ 1.2. Suffering and the Path to Liberation (p. 1) ◆ 1.3. The Truth and Consequences of Free Will (p. 5) ◆ 1.4. The Stages of Spiritual Growth (p. 11) ◆ 1.5. Spiritual Evolution at the Collective Level (p. 19) ◆ 1.6. Conclusion (p. 21)

Chapter 2. The Trustworthy Horse of Science
2.1. Introduction (p. 23) ◆ 2.2. The Nature of Pure Science (p. 23) ◆ 2.3. The Egoic Trouble With Scientism (p. 25) ◆ 2.4. Prelude to the Great Paradigm Shift (p. 30) ◆ 2.5. Empirical Data Supporting a Spiritual Paradigm (p. 33) ◆ 2.6. Conclusion (p. 45)

Chapter 3. The Frozen Pillars of Religion
3.1. Introduction (p. 47) ◆ 3.2. The Nature of Western Religious Truth (p. 47) ◆ 3.3. The Foundational Errors of Judaism and Christianity (p. 50) ◆ 3.4. A "New" Christianity (p. 60) ◆ 3.5. A Question of Deception: Not If, but How (p. 62) ◆ 3.6. Souls Existing in Hell: Not If, but Why (p. 66) ◆ 3.7. Conclusion (p. 69)

Chapter 4. Judaism, the Messiah and the Hybrid Religion
4.1. Introduction (p. 71) ◆ 4.2. The Prophesied Messiah (p. 71) ◆ 4.3. The Revolutionary Messiah (p. 72) ◆ 4.4. Recording the Life and Teachings of Jesus (p. 79) ◆ 4.5. The Heated Debate Among the Christians (p. 91) ◆ 4.6. Cementing the Power of the Holy People (p. 105) ◆ 4.7. Conclusion (p. 113)

Chapter 5. Egoic Pride and the Book of Job
5.1. Introduction (p. 115) ♦ 5.2. The Nature of Evil (p. 115) ♦ 5.3. Modern Interpretations of Job (p. 121) ♦ 5.4. Shining the Light Upon Job (p. 123) ♦ 5.5. The Wisdom and Deceptive Covering of Job (p. 129) ♦ 5.6. The Devil and the Old Testament (p. 136) ♦ 5.7. Conclusion (p. 138)

Chapter 6. The Book of Daniel
6.1. Introduction (p. 139) ♦ 6.2. The Great Debate About Daniel (p. 139) ♦ 6.3. Why Daniel's Prophecies Remained a Mystery (p. 144) ♦ 6.4. Conclusion (p. 148)

Chapter 7. Daniel's Prophecies
7.1. Introduction (p. 149) ♦ 7.2. The Grouping and Purpose of Daniel's Prophecies (p. 149) ♦ 7.3. The Four Prophecies About the Four Kingdoms (p. 151) ♦ 7.4. Crown Jewel #1: The 70 "Sevens" and ACD-2 (p. 169) ♦ 7.5. Crown Jewel #2: The Great Awakening (p. 180) ♦ 7.6. Conclusion (p. 191)

Chapter 8. Triangulating the Great Awakening
8.1. Introduction (p. 193) ♦ 8.2. Freedom, Prosperity and Mass Communication (p. 193) ♦ 8.3. The Maya Calendar (p. 194) ♦ 8.4. The Life and Messages of Edgar Cayce (p. 195) ♦ 8.5. Saint Malachy's Prophecy (p. 198) ♦ 8.6. An Atheist Learns About the Spiritual Revolution (p. 210) ♦ 8.7. The "Conversations with God" Material (p. 211) ♦ 8.8. Conclusion (p. 212)

Chapter 9. The Little Apocalypse
9.1. Introduction (p. 213) ♦ 9.2. Guiding Principles (p. 213) ♦ 9.3. The Little Apocalypse in Mark (p. 214) ♦ 9.4. Additional Perspectives in Matthew and Luke (p. 220) ♦ 9.5. The Unparalleled Distress of the Great Awakening (p. 225) ♦ 9.6. Conclusion (p. 231)

Chapter 10. The Vision of Revelation
10.1. Introduction (p. 233) ♦ 10.2. Guiding Principles (p. 234) ♦ 10.3. Global Story, Slice #1: Darkness and Awakening (p. 238) ♦ 10.4. Global Story, Slice #2: The Divine Kingdom (p. 253) ♦ 10.5. Global Story, Slice #3: Religion's Dark Reign (p. 256) ♦ 10.6. Global Story, Slice #4: Physical Seductions (p. 279) ♦ 10.7. The Grand Future (p. 294) ♦ 10.8. Conclusion (p. 296)

Chapter 11. The Broad Road That Led to Destruction

11.1. Introduction (p. 299) ♦ 11.2. The Formative Undercurrent of Hatred and Fear (p. 299) ♦ 11.3. The Convergence of the Darkness (p. 303) ♦ 11.4. The Churches Empower the Nazi Regime (p. 307) ♦ 11.5. Christianity Creates the Energetic Tsunami (p. 317) ♦ 11.6. A Fiendish Impact and a Devilish Denial (p. 331) ♦ 11.7. Conclusion (p. 335)

Chapter 12. The Time Is Now

12.1. Introduction (p. 337) ♦ 12.2. The Spiritual Thesis About the Western Religions (p. 337) ♦ 12.3. Taking the Next Step (p. 343) ♦ 12.4. Healing Ourselves and the World (p. 347) ♦ 12.5. Martin Luther King Jr., Christianity and Slavery (p. 350) ♦ 12.6. Conclusion (p. 364)

Postscript (p. 369)

VOLUME II

Appendix A. Reincarnation

A.1. Introduction (p. 371) ♦ A.2. Conflicting Biblical Teachings About the Afterlife (p. 371) ♦ A.3. New Age Falsehoods About Church History (p. 380) ♦ A.4. Past-Life Regression Therapy (p. 382) ♦ A.5. Overwhelming Scientific Data (p. 384) ♦ A.6. Conclusion (p. 397)

Appendix B. Spirit Possession

B.1. Introduction (p. 399) ♦ B.2. Professionals Discover the Phenomenon (p. 399) ♦ B.3. Clinical Accounts of Demons and the Devil (p. 420) ♦ B.4. Pertinent Wisdom (p. 427) ♦ B.5. Conclusion (p. 430)

Appendix C. The Septuagint and Daniel

C.1. Introduction (p. 433) ♦ C.2. The Septuagint's History (p. 433) ♦ C.3. The Additional Text in Daniel (p. 436) ♦ C.4. Apocrypha and Pseudepigraphy (p. 438) ♦ C.5. Conclusion (p. 441)

Appendix D. Redirecting the Debate About Daniel

D.1. Introduction (p. 443) ♦ D.2. Three Sides to the Story (p. 445) ♦ D.3. Archaeological Evidence (p. 459) ♦ D.4. The Ancient Historians (p. 478) ♦ D.5. Finishing the Debate About the Date (p. 500) ♦ D.6. Storytelling and Later Editing (Not Inerrancy) (p. 504) ♦ D.7. The Redirected Debate (p. 512) ♦ D.8. Conclusion (p. 541) ♦ D.X. Literary Endnotes (p. 542)

Appendix E. The Egregious Error in Ezra
E.1. Introduction (p. 557) ♦ E.2. Chronicles, Ezra and Nehemiah (p. 557) ♦ E.3. The Compiler's Error (p. 558) ♦ E.4. The Warped Chronology of Persian Kings (p. 566) ♦ E.5. The Scribal Editing Theory (p. 570) ♦ E.6. Conclusion (p. 574)

Appendix F. The Beast With Ten Horns
F.1. Introduction (p. 575) ♦ F.2. Foretelling the Roman Empire (p. 575) ♦ F.3. Nero: The Little Boastful Horn (p. 578) ♦ F.4. Conclusion (p. 581)

Appendix G. Constantine the Great
G.1. Introduction (p. 583) ♦ G.2. Constantine's Rise to Power (p. 584) ♦ G.3. Constantine and the Church (p. 587) ♦ G.4. Constantine Fulfills the Prophecy (p. 595) ♦ G.5. Conclusion (p. 600)

Appendix H. The Numbering of Days
H.1. Introduction (p. 603) ♦ H.2. Historical Sources and Calendars (p. 604) ♦ H.3. Relevant Events of the Maccabean Era (p. 605) ♦ H.4. The Daniel Prophecies' Numbering of Days (p. 615) ♦ H.5. Conclusion (p. 622)

Appendix I. The Angel's Prophecy of Ancient History
I.1. Introduction (p. 623) ♦ I.2. The Omniscient Angel Foretells Ancient History (p. 623) ♦ I.3. Conclusion (p. 627)

Appendix J. The King of the End Times
J.1. Introduction (p. 629) ♦ J.2. A Character Profile (p. 629) ♦ J.3. A Military and Political Profile (p. 635) ♦ J.4. Conclusion (p. 641)

Appendix K. Understanding the 69 "Sevens"
K.1. Introduction (p. 643) ♦ K.2. The Prophecy's Starting and Ending Points (p. 643) ♦ K.3. Dating the Baptism and Crucifixion of Jesus (p. 645) ♦ K.4. Interpreting the Prophecy (p. 651) ♦ K.5. Conclusion (p. 655)

Appendix L. The Catholic Church in the 20th Century
L.1. Introduction (p. 657) ♦ L.2. The Vatican Empowers Fascist Aggression (p. 658) ♦ L.3. Illuminating the Darkness of the Vatican's Choices (p. 702) ♦ L.4. The Vatican's Financial World (p. 717) ♦ L.5. Conclusion (p. 751)

Appendix M. The Crashing of the Great Star
M.1. Introduction (p. 753) ♦ M.2. The Great Star of Science and Technology (p. 753) ♦ M.3. Conclusion (p. 759)

Appendix N. The Wolf in Sheep's Clothing
    N.1. Introduction (p. 761) ♦ N.2. The Crusades, Inquisition and Witch Hunts (p. 761) ♦ N.3. Conclusion (p. 768)

Appendix O. The Impact on Islam
    O.1. Introduction (p. 769) ♦ O.2. The World of Islam (p. 769) ♦ O.3. The Foundational Flaws of Islam (p. 779) ♦ O.4. The Essence of the Islamic Darkness (p. 785) ♦ O.5. The Path Out of the Islamic Darkness (p. 795) ♦ O.6. Conclusion (p. 798)

Endnotes (p. 801)

Bibliography (p. 825)

Index (p. 851)

Acknowledgments (p. 871)

About the Author (p. 873)

Preface

This book challenges the assumptions of the Western religions and unravels the Bible's apocalyptic prophecies. The spiritual messages hidden within Daniel and Revelation will shock the world, for they contradict what has been confidently preached for all these centuries. These mysterious prophecies are like a challenging riddle that cannot be solved although the answer is obvious in hindsight. Only the blinding power of a paradigm can explain how we missed it for so long.

Although the book will profoundly impact Judaism and Islam, it is primarily focused on Christianity. Given how sharply it cuts through those beliefs while promoting the teachings of Jesus and even proving he was the Anointed One (Messiah), its Christian readers will probably have a wide range of reactions. Some will fearfully denounce it as a satanic assault upon their religion. Others will courageously embrace it as the inevitable completion of the Reformation.

In any case, the book will most likely trigger a theological earthquake. I thus feel compelled to offer some additional guidance for navigating the turmoil.

Eastern and Western Religion

I am not undercutting the Western religions in favor of unilaterally embracing the Eastern mystical teachings. To the contrary, the healthiest and truest spirituality is one that embraces both sides of the universe's grand paradoxes.

[Note: A paradox is when two contradictory suppositions defy logic to somehow both be true. For example, light behaves with the incompatible properties of both an oscillatory wave and a stream of particles that tracks as straight as an arrow.]

Consider the paradox of individuality and unity. Many of the Eastern mystical teachings embrace only the unity pole with a doctrine known as anatta, or "no self." While correctly teaching there is no distinctly independent and separate self, these philosophies go overboard by voiding all essence of individuality.

The problem is that many seekers are led to renounce their unique loci of individual consciousness and free will. In this ill-fated attempt to blank out the immortal individuation of the divine (the soul), spiritual power and co-creative responsibility are often denied or repressed.

Case in point: Where would we be if Winston Churchill and Franklin D. Roosevelt had instructed their nations that there is no evil in this illusory world and to blissfully accept what is? Moreover, these philosophies inherently blaspheme God by implying the existence of only a single will. The ideology means the deplorable state of our world is the best this unitary will could create, and this solitary creator only enlightens a few lucky people while leaving the rest of us to flounder in suffering.

The underlying unity of all things and beings is a universal truth. It is essential to embrace and eventually transform into the fullest expression of this reality though meditation and an inward journey. Yet it is just as essential to also embrace and eventually transform into the fullest expression of the truth of individuality. This means owning our free will, spiritual power and co-creative responsibility for the state of our communities, nations and planet.

By all means dissolve the defensiveness, ignorance, shame and fear that constitute the ego, but do not forsake an inescapable essence of self and its individual will and creative power. Buddhist monk and psychologist Jack Kornfield expresses this wisdom: "There are two parallel tasks in spiritual life. One is to discover selflessness, the other is to develop a healthy sense of self. Both sides of that apparent paradox must be fulfilled for us to awaken."[1]

Additional Resources

Although the book deepens our understanding of universal truth, its primary value comes from revealing the errors of the West's most popular conceptions. Just as importantly, it will help alleviate the fear of challenging the hallowed teachings about a wrathful God of judgment and punishment.

As it has its hands full with those matters, it is well beyond its scope to fully articulate a case for the best answer. For that I recommend the *Conversations with God* books, by Neale Donald Walsch, which present a dialogue he had with a transcendental source of information that identified itself as God.

Blindly accepting information from an otherworldly source can be dangerous, yet we should not make the opposite mistake of blindly rejecting it all either. For if we categorically dismiss what God purportedly communicated to us through Walsch, we need to do likewise with Moses and the rest of the Old Testament prophets, the apostle Paul and everybody else who conveyed what they received from an otherworldly source.

We are best served, then, by applying our critical discernment to all such information. For what it is worth, I believe the *Conversations with God* material offers an excellent explanation of universal truth. I will gladly share my foremost reasons for this opinion.

First, the material articulates numerous paradoxical truths and does so with clarity and grace. Second, it dovetails the teachings of Jesus, Buddha and many other spiritual masters. Third, it includes the core insights of psychology. Fourth, it conveys a beautifully symmetrical and integrated philosophy that resonates with the deepest fibers of my being. Finally, it details a profound purpose and meaning behind the existence of the universe, a most spectacular and uplifting explanation for all that we are experiencing.

However, God makes it clear the entire picture has not been revealed in this material, nor should it be deemed a third-millennium Bible.[2] Moreover, it would be impossible for Walsch or anybody else to be a perfect receiver of the transmission, so distorting effects are surely present.[3]

For those who feel like their emotional worlds are being ripped apart at the seams, I recommend the book *Oneness*. Written by a spiritual channel named Rasha, it dovetails the *Conversations with God* material but focuses on guiding us through the turbulence of our collective awakening.

Yet if I could only have a single book to guide my spiritual growth, it would be *The Way of Mastery*. It was purportedly communicated by Jesus and is about transforming to be and live like him.

Let the Adventure Begin

I've made these recommendations because many readers may suddenly find themselves swimming in the wake of an ancient ship of religious security that just started sinking below the waves. In any case, find and live your own truth, and see where it takes you. That is what this eternal journey of life is all about.

To spiritually grow, we have to courageously embrace the unknown and sail into uncharted waters. That means leaving the safe harbor of our religious past and going through a hurricane of fear on the high seas, all because we were created to embark on this sacred journey to our spiritual promised land.

We simply need to venture forth in surrendered trust that God's love will guide us through. We will eventually be able to calm the waves of our personal and societal storms as we heal and grow toward manifesting our divine essence.

Even if we never have the pleasure of meeting, know that I deeply honor you and your courage to consider the book. I hope and pray it serves you and your journey well.

Namaste,
Karl Luther
Scottsdale, Arizona

Introduction

Part 1. Supplementing Information

You do not have to read any of the appendixes to get the book's primary insights and revelations. If you do not purchase Volume II, you can make this volume akin to a self-standing book by downloading a PDF document of the end matter published in Volume II (the Endnotes, Bibliography, Index, Acknowledgments and About the Author) from the book's website (www.narrowgatebook.com).

You can also download "The Book's Diagrams" if you would like to print the diagrams in Appendixes D, E and H to assist your reading. Finally, the "Additional Endnotes" document preserves 457 endnotes that were not required and removed to improve readability. If a fact went uncited and you are interested in the source, you may find it there.

All biblical text in Volume I is from the New International Version (NIV). Volume II includes apocryphal text from Catholic and Eastern Orthodox Bibles that is sourced from the New American Bible (NAB).

Certain phrases within biblical quotes are occasionally underlined for emphasis. Unless noted otherwise, the italics and underlining in all quotes from nonbiblical sources are the reproduction of that author's formatting.

Part 2. The Book's Nature and Length

The Big Picture

Based on the pioneering work of psychiatrist Carl Jung, the Myers-Briggs Type Indicator system differentiates ways of perceiving information between the poles of the N (Intuitive) and S (Sensing). The N-versus-S continuum is one of four personality components in the system.

N's gravitate to the unseen dynamics that drive the world and thrive on explanatory abstractions. S's prefer gathering observable, factual knowledge about the world and thrive on experiential details. Research indicates that 73 percent of American adults gather information more along the lines of the S.[1]

This is important because N's will be right at home with this big-picture book about the foremost questions of our existence. It delves into a wide range of topics to render an accurate panorama.

The book does not forsake the S's, though, for it would be powerless if it was not built upon a litany of facts and scholarly assessments. One of its guiding principles has been to empower you to arrive at independent conclusions. Another has been to greatly strengthen your intellectual position in the face of certain challenges. As Francis Bacon long ago observed, "Knowledge is power."

Purpose and Value of the Book's Length

Another guiding principle has been to deliver both efficiency and effectiveness. The two-volume book could have been divided and fluffed out into at least five different books of normal size and excellent value, four of which could have been deemed seminal works for rendering quantum leaps in their respective domains.

A trio of books could have framed and delivered the new and astonishing interpretations of Job (Chapter 5), Daniel (Chapter 7) and Revelation (Chapter 10), and the fourth could have trumped the prevailing scholarship about dating the Book of Daniel (Appendix D). Although the fifth potential book would not have rendered any more revolutionary insights, it still would have been a fresh and innovative treatment of Christianity's deadly role in the Holocaust (Chapter 11 and Appendix L) and Civil War (Chapter 12).

Instead, these insights have all been condensed and integrated into a single book. The reason has been to gain a vital synergy (a result that is greater than the sum of its parts), deliver exceptional value, and make as powerful an impact as possible.

The book weaves them all together to answer the foremost question about any particular insight: What is its ultimate meaning? Since the answer is so profound and shocking, many readers will feel like their souls are on the line. If they are to release their core beliefs, they need a book that is both compelling and complete. It thus covers all the important bases in helping such readers go all in with a far more spectacular and amazing God.

All in all, the book efficiently serves those who want reliable answers to the most vital questions of life. The cost of the two volumes is much lower than a series of five books, and you will need less time to read them. If you do not desire the supporting and enhancing information of Volume II, you can further cut those costs of money and time in half.

Because so many facts and concepts have been distilled, the book is naturally dense. Although every effort has been made to make it a smooth and easy read, it is not a quick read. So please take your time with it, for you will be assimilating a lot more information than normal.

Part 3. Overview of the Book's Content

Volume I: The 12 Chapters

Chapter 1 ("The Search for Truth") motivates our journey and introduces concepts that foreshadow the later revelations. The principles of free will, responsibility and spiritual power are especially important and surface throughout the book. The stages of spiritual growth provide an orienting map and help explain why the religious earthquake was inevitable.

The next two chapters explore the West's two major approaches to understanding the universe. Chapter 2 ("The Trustworthy Horse of Science") differentiates a pure version of science from the religion of scientism. It also explains science's limitations, introduces the blinding power of paradigms, and presents scientific evidence of a greater spiritual reality.

Chapter 3 ("The Frozen Pillars of Religion") examines the traditional religious approach to truth. After explaining how this mindset is solidified upon fear and repressed doubt, the chapter surfaces and debunks core assumptions as the book begins unearthing the erroneous roots of the Judeo-Christian paradigm. It also introduces a more enlightened version of Christianity and addresses questions about the devil, deception and hell.

Chapter 4 ("Judaism, the Messiah and the Hybrid Religion") continues the spiritual gardening by clarifying Jesus's ministry and showing how the gospels were significantly distorted by human processes. It explains how the version of Christianity that developed in his wake failed to make the paradigm shift, thereby resulting in a hybrid religion of unrenounced tenets and traditions (from the Old Testament), unacknowledged errors and fabrications (from the New Testament), and unchallenged theologies and authorities (from the splintered fusion).

The book abruptly shifts gears with Chapter 5 ("Egoic Pride and the Book of Job"), which shines the light of consciousness upon the nature of evil and its well-cloaked ways. Drawing from the wisdom of Jesus and modern psychology, it reveals the true colors of Job in a new and stunning interpretation. This pivotal chapter is the backbone of the book, for clarity about the metaphysical darkness is essential for understanding the shocking meaning of the apocalyptic prophecies.

Although the first five chapters deliver great value, the best is yet to come as the book turns to the Bible's apocalyptic prophecies. The next five chapters unravel them in their entirety by progressing through Daniel, the gospels and Revelation.

Since so much is riding on Daniel's prophecies, Chapter 6 ("The Book of Daniel") introduces the great debate about their dating and references the appendix that conclusively resolves it. The chapter also reviews the Reformation, as this history helps explain the reason for the spiritual realm's communication.

Chapter 7 ("Daniel's Prophecies") is the heart of the book. The chapter and its accompanying appendixes reveal how prophecies long believed to be forewarning an antichrist were instead foretelling ancient kingdoms, emperors and events that have long been forgotten. Far more importantly, an astonishing set of spiritual messages are laced within this matrix of interwoven references. Shrouded in mystery for over 2,500 years, these revelations will be obvious in hindsight.

The prophecies are a buried treasure that includes a priceless gem for the world of science. Their accuracy and precision about ancient history render some amazing empirical data that the future can be foretold. This practically proves the nature of time is paradoxical: it both exists and does not exist. Although a linear progression of past-present-future exists from our physical perspective, the nonexistence of time is also a reality for the spiritual realm and its otherworldly dimensions.

To substantiate the interpretation of a key part of Daniel's prophecies, Chapter 8 ("Triangulating the Great Awakening") explores some corroborating sources. The highlight of this material is the ominous prophecy of Saint Malachy. Tendered to the Vatican in 1140 and published in 1595, it pinpointed the Catholic Church's demise to the reign of Pope Francis (2013–present)!

Chapter 9 ("The Little Apocalypse") deciphers Jesus's sermon about the end times. It also explains why we are and will be living amid the "days of distress unequaled from the beginning…and never to be equaled again" (Mk 13:19).

Leveraging the answer key from Daniel, Chapter 10 ("The Vision of Revelation") delivers another dramatic set of surprises with its unraveling of Revelation. It shows that a spiritual awakening paradigm provides an almost infinitely better interpretation to the bizarre imagery than a cataclysmic destruction paradigm.

Although nothing can match Daniel's mastery of forthcoming history, Revelation is just as impressive in foretelling the metaphysical story of humanity. Because so many people are familiar with Revelation and what it means to Christian theology, the chapter may be the most impactful of them all.

At this point, the book has traveled two independent paths to the same destination. The third and fourth chapters integrated the scholarly insights and evidence to arrive at this ironic conclusion: the religion based upon the man who came to uproot Judaism must itself be uprooted. Then the seventh through tenth chapters showed how the apocalyptic prophecies are proclaiming the same shocking truth.

In case that is not enough to awaken humanity, the final two chapters blaze a third truth-seeking trail to the same destination. This path applies Jesus's advice for seeing through the deceptions of false prophets. As he was quoted, "A good tree cannot bear bad fruit" and "by their fruit you will recognize them" (Mt 7:18–20).

Chapter 11 ("The Broad Road That Led to Destruction") explains the three independent dynamics that converged like a perfect storm to generate the Holocaust and how Christianity created or enabled all of them. While showing how this ancient religious tree bore its poisonous fruit in Nazi Germany, the chapter also surfaces some vital lessons for the future.

With the writing on the wall shining like the sun for all to see, Chapter 12 ("The Time Is Now") pulls it all together in a powerful synopsis of the spiritual thesis. The concluding chapter also shows how Christianity was the primary reason America experienced the nightmare of slavery and the Civil War.

Volume II: The 15 Appendixes

Although the appendixes are not required reading, they make important contributions. Appendix A ("Reincarnation") and Appendix B ("Spirit Possession") present scientific and clinical evidence that will be new to most readers. They also deliver insights regarding Christian theology, especially Appendix B's paradoxical answer to the question of the ages about the devil's existence. In addition, Appendix B presents vital wisdom from the clinical evidence so you can avoid a traumatic experience after you die.

The next three appendixes pertain to dating the Book of Daniel. Appendix C ("The Septuagint and Daniel") introduces the ancient translation of the Jewish scriptures into Greek and the different biblical versions of Daniel.

Appendix D ("Redirecting the Debate About Daniel") is akin to a doctoral thesis and close to being its own book. Its main objective is proving Daniel's prophecies were indeed penned in the sixth century BCE as advertised. Since a solid majority of scholars have dated them to the second century BCE and thereby deemed them fraudulent, a formidable parade of data and logic is needed to debunk each and every argument behind their erroneous conclusion. There is, however, one glaring exception.

The wealth of archaeological and historical data also serves the secondary objective of demonstrating the ancient book has some gross errors. Therein resides the exception, for the fraudulence theory's arguments are still in full effect for two of Daniel's chapters. To reconcile the contorted mess, the appendix presents a rigorous hypothesis to explain Daniel's developmental history.

Appendix E ("The Egregious Error in Ezra") reveals a major gaffe in Ezra that appears to be intimately linked to the anomalies in Daniel, much like DNA evidence links the same perpetrator to two different crimes. It also completes the theory of how the majority of Daniel could be written in the sixth century BCE yet be so absurdly erroneous with its secular history.

These three appendixes have been written for the newcomer to the scholarly fray. However, they are only worth reading if you are interested in the proof of Daniel's dating, obvious examples of biblical errors and fabrications, or fascinating insights about the developmental history of Daniel and Ezra.

The next six appendixes present the historical data for, and explain the fulfillment of, key passages in Daniel's prophecies. Although summarized in Chapter 7, Appendix F ("The Beast With Ten Horns"), Appendix G ("Constantine the Great"), Appendix J ("The King of the End Times") and

Appendix K ("Understanding the 69 'Sevens'") deliver the spine-tingling details of how the spiritual realm accurately and precisely foretold history that occurred centuries after the era when all scholars agree Daniel was on the historical record (160s BCE).

Appendix H ("The Numbering of Days") also brings new insights to the table but addresses a red-herring problem and can be skipped without much loss in value. Appendix I ("The Angel's Prophecy of Ancient History") simply renders material that can be found in a decent study Bible.

Appendix L ("The Catholic Church in the 20th Century") shows that although the Church no longer champions crusades, sequesters Jews in ghettos, or tortures and kills those who believe differently, its underlying darkness has continued unabated. The majority of this other book within a book details how the Vatican helped Benito Mussolini and Adolf Hitler gain dictatorial power and then made strategic alliances with them, sanctioned their predatory aggression, and turned a blind eye to the Holocaust.

After illuminating the essence of the papal choices before and during World War II, the appendix exposes the dark nature of the Vatican's financial affairs. It shows how the sudden death of Pope John Paul I in 1978 was most likely a blackmail-enabled murder by the Vatican Bank's nefarious partners.

The next two appendixes support the interpretation of Revelation. Appendix M ("The Crashing of the Great Star") delves into a passage that foretold the damage we would be inflicting upon our environment and health. Appendix N ("The Wolf in Sheep's Clothing") overviews the Crusades, Inquisition and witch hunts.

The book is focused on the Judeo-Christian paradigm, and its length prohibits a similar study of Islam. Nevertheless, Appendix O ("The Impact on Islam") shows how its insights are also inscribing the writing on the wall for that religion.

[Note: Because the appendix may tempt more Westerners into pinning the blame for modern evil upon Islam or its radical extremists, a forthcoming book will provide the counterbalance. *Illuminating the Reinforcing Cycle of Darkness: The Path to Reclaim the Soul of America* shows how the United States and its enabling allies are not engaged in a battle of good versus evil, if you will, but rather are trapped in one of evil versus evil. Both sides are attacking the evil they only see in their enemy. Shining the light of consciousness upon our own evil is the first step toward an enlightened foreign policy that can resolve a host of problems in this win-win universe.]

Part 4. The Essence of the Book

Reconsidering the Path to Salvation

Judaism, Christianity and Islam render differing maps about the path to salvation. Billions of people have followed them with hopes of escaping the suffering of the human experience. Like thundering herds of buffalo that roamed the prairies of native America, each religious exodus has trampled a swath of land stretching hundreds of miles wide.

The weary travelers are plodding along because they accepted the indoctrination of their religious herd and found safety in numbers. Having assumed it is in sole possession of the highest truth, they have bet the farm on the ancient men who blazed the trail and scrawled out the map.

Believing an incredibly aloof God only communicated in earnest with their founding fathers, they think nothing humanity might learn over time could change anything. They have thus shut their minds and hearts to an infinitely loving God who is trying to redirect them onto a path that would truly take them home.

If you are plodding along with a religious herd, perhaps it is time to reconsider your assumption. Perhaps it is time to consider what Jesus purportedly advised: "Enter through the narrow gate. For wide is the gate and broad is the road that leads to destruction, and many enter through it. But small is the gate and narrow the road that leads to life, and only a few find it" (Mt 7:13–14).

Jesus thus forewarned that the popular religious roads would all lead to destruction. With Western history having transpired as predicted, perhaps it is finally time to admit we are lost and ask for directions.

The Time Has Come

There is great wisdom to the view that all problems are ultimately spiritual issues.[2] The book delves into their roots by candidly examining our religious beliefs.

The time has come to address them with intelligence, attention, courage and deep intuition. The time has come to embrace an enlightened spirituality that will enable us to solve the problems we face at individual to global levels. As Albert Einstein explained, "A new type of thinking is essential if mankind is to survive and move toward higher levels."[3]

The time has come for us to become aware of the nature of the universe and the purpose of our existence. The time has therefore come for hundreds of millions of people to leave the broad road that has led to destruction and to begin finding the narrow gate that leads to true life. The book reveals what until now has been hidden from all but a small percentage of people—and thus its title.

To make way for the new, though, we must release our viselike grip on the old. Doing so is a frightening process and an inescapable part of spiritual growth.

Clearly seeing the founding errors of our religions will help with transcending this prodigious fear. Therefore, the book does not bow to any sacred cows or refrain from calling it like it is because such uncompromising language might offend somebody. Too much is at stake to not be as clear and sharp as possible, for the sword of truth was meant to cut through the deceptive web of the entrenched darkness.

The time has come for an epic breakthrough of personal awakenings amid a great global awakening. As substantiated by the prophecies, the divine intention for humanity is a far greater spirituality than what has been taught by Judaism, Christianity and Islam. As the world awakens to and embraces a far more spectacular and amazing God, the traditional religions will eventually fade into the history books of the third millennium CE.

Meanwhile, the "mainstream" in the book's subtitle extends beyond the three traditional Western religions. Although a pure version of science is an essential part of a healthy spirituality, the worldview of far too many scientists is also a religion. Their atheistic paradigm is built upon unproven assumptions that have been taken on faith, such as consciousness being produced by the brain and requiring that organ to exist. This religion is often referred to as scientism and will eventually succumb to the ever-increasing volumes of empirical data.

Ready or not, the end times are upon us. As may already be suspected, though, they are not the apocalyptic horror that has been taught by mainstream Christianity.

Rather, it is the time of the end of a very long era when only a fringe minority could find the narrow gate. It is also the time of the end for the fearful belief about a wrathful and judgmental God and the unenlightened teachers who have been indoctrinating such dogma. As an omniscient angel disclosed the historic milestone that would mark the fulfillment of all prophesied events, "When the power of the holy people has been finally broken, all these things will be completed" (Dn 12:7).

While many will side with their self-righteous pride and fight the spiritual process, rest assured it cannot be stopped. The eternal force of divine love will eventually awaken us all.

The greatest barrier is the stagnation of organized religion, but that is about to be blown away by a tsunami of truth. Like the last grains of sand about to fall through an hourglass, the time is just about up for the holy people. As this happens, the dark night of ignorance we have been living amid will be giving way to a morning dawn of clarity.

All in all, the time has come for us to forge ahead with our search for truth. As each of us steps up to embrace it, we will be collectively taking an unprecedented step of spiritual evolution toward manifesting the divine intention of heaven on earth.

Chapter 1

The Search for Truth

1.1. Introduction

We are about to journey onto the hallowed terrain of our beliefs about God and the essence of life. As the world's religions are the feudal lords who have ruled this land for so long, our expedition will proceed straight into their well-cultivated estates. Since our search for truth will gravely threaten them, friendly hospitality can hardly be expected. Given all they have to lose, the holy people of religious power will most likely attack our entourage.

Our quest will also threaten the masses who have been serving and are being cared for by their feudal lord. Billions of people have assumed their religion has answered life's ultimate questions, and any challenge to that bond will probably stir a strong blend of emotions. As many folks have a primal need for their sacred beliefs to hold firm, this journey may provoke intense anger, fear and anxiety. Only some will be able to forge through it.

This book, then, is for those who are ready to challenge the powers that be to learn what most would rather not know. It is for those who are willing to pay the psychological price to uncover the truth about God and the essence of life.

After discussing the importance of embracing this truth, this chapter explores the correlated dynamics of free will, responsibility and power. It then introduces theory about the stages of spiritual growth, which will provide orienting guidance for the rest of our journey.

1.2. Suffering and the Path to Liberation

Searching for the truth about a subject is a sacred passion at the heart of science, history, journalism, the legal system, education and psychotherapy. It is an innate desire that may be as deep as any other.

1.2.a. The Human Predicament

Jesus supposedly said that by living his teachings, we would know the truth, and it would set us free (Jn 8:31–32). While testifying to the truth's incomparable value, he conveyed that most of us are not free. He implied we are trapped. Blocked. Imprisoned. Suffering.

Siddhārtha Gautama also made this point when he declared the first of four noble truths to be that life is suffering. But just like the Christ, the Buddha saw a way out of this condition. Both masters taught that living in harmony with the truth is how we attain liberation, inner peace and salvation.

It all sounds simple enough, but we immediately face another predicament. We must determine exactly whose version of truth about God and the essence of life, if any, is to be believed and followed.

While commonality exists between Buddhism, Christianity and the other major religions, they differ substantially on the details. In fact, their differences are often at the root of their origins.

For instance, Jesus conflicted with the teachings of his native Judaism, and the violent end to their debate spawned a new religion. Although Islam acknowledged the prophets of its Western predecessors, it claimed to be the last and fullest measure of divine truth.

On the Eastern side of the religious slate, Buddhism was born out of Siddhārtha's break from the tenets of Hinduism. And just as the Western religions have their divergent branches, so it is with Hinduism and Buddhism. For instance, when Buddhism crossed paths with the Confucianism and Taoism of ancient China, Zen Buddhism was born. In sum, humanity has a slew of renderings as to what is really going on in the universe.

1.2.b. A World of Philosophers

"Religion" typically refers to a system of beliefs involving the supernatural. Yet the juggernaut of science should also be considered a religion, for it steadfastly embraces a null belief about the supernatural. But to prevent a debate about semantics from sidetracking the issue, let us instead use the term "worldview paradigm."

A paradigm is the mental foundation from which we perceive information and think about problems. The deeply ingrained beliefs that comprise a paradigm are almost invariably assumptions and far removed from conscious attention. A worldview paradigm, then, is how we conceptualize life and the universe. A worldview paradigm is our map of reality, and its root assumptions are rarely scrutinized.

Scientists typically have a worldview paradigm that is built on the tenets of positivism and materialism. From the positivism lens, a map of reality can only include that which can be undeniably proven or objectively verified. From the materialism lens, the universe consists of only the stuff of matter and the void in between. As this worldview sees it, there is nothing beyond the four dimensions of space and time, and the experience of consciousness is the exclusive product of the electromagnetic and biochemical processes of the body and brain.

So what is really going on in the universe? Whether you want to be one or not, you are a philosopher. You cannot help but to have your own worldview paradigm. While countless people from ancient and modern times have proclaimed their experiences, insights and theories, only you can decide what you will believe. Like it or not, you must answer life's most perplexing questions for yourself.

Your choice is whether you do so consciously or unconsciously. Most people opt for the latter by sticking with what they were taught by their culture of origin. So do you choose to let where you were born dictate your answers to the most vital questions of our existence? Do you choose to mindlessly buy into somebody else's answers?

1.2.c. Avoiding Pain

This may seem like a meaningless intellectual exercise, but nothing could be more mistaken. When you are suffering or lost, a better map will help you navigate out of trouble and on to your desired destination. As psychiatrist M. Scott Peck, MD, explains, an essential element of mental health is a dedication to reality—to the truth—at all costs.[1]

On a collective level, our beliefs have fostered the choices that have created our dire situation. The maps that led us into this desolation are incapable of leading us out.

However, most people are afraid to challenge foundational beliefs and build a more accurate map of reality. After all, those beliefs were instilled with cultural traditions and are intertwined with daunting emotions that will get triggered by such change. As Peck notes, "The process of making revisions, particularly major revisions, is painful, sometimes excruciatingly painful. And herein lies the major source of many of the ills of mankind."[2]

Meanwhile, seeing God and life in a new light is to break out of an illusion. This means also enduring the pain of disillusionment, which is usually accompanied by the isolation of believing differently than one's family and the mainstream of society. Although the situation has been changing, it has meant embarking upon a road less traveled. It is not for the faint of heart.

1.2.d. Metaphors of the Metaphysical

Before continuing, some spiritual terms need to be clarified as we get a glimpse of where we are heading. In its broadest and truest sense, the spiritual realm includes unfathomable dimensions that transcend the physical universe. It is home to nonphysical (discarnate) entities that all have free will. On one end of the spectrum are demons whose choices are purely negative. On the other are angels and ascended masters who continually serve God's will.

For simplicity's sake, though, the book only uses "spiritual realm" to refer to God and the highest spiritual beings of light and love. As will be evident when the apocalyptic prophecies are revealed, the spiritual realm has infinite intelligence and the ability to foretell the future.

"Metaphysical" refers to a transcendent reality that is beyond our ability to perceive with our five senses. It is the mysterious essence and foundation of our physical universe.

"Metaphysical dynamics" are the laws and intangible structures that impact our lives, society and history. The most well-known metaphysical laws are the law of attraction (like attracts like) and the law of karma (you reap what you sow). A metaphysical structure is to the law of attraction what a heavy object is to the law of gravity. It is a habituated pattern of beliefs, thoughts, attitudes and emotions that shapes our choices, all of which are the input to the metaphysical laws that render our fate.

By the way, the most common metaphysical structure is the ego, which is a conglomeration of many intertwined patterns. It is not a tangible structure that can be registered by a scientific instrument, but it surely exists. Because the ego is such a powerful driver of our individual and collective choices, understanding these dynamics is important.

Communicating about metaphysical dynamics is greatly enhanced and simplified by using metaphors. As for the nature of the human condition and our spiritual evolution, there is no greater metaphor than that of light and darkness. As Jesus supposedly said, "I am the light of the world. Whoever follows me will never walk in darkness, but will have the light of life" (Jn 8:12). He was obviously not referring to a world without electricity and light bulbs. Rather, he used the metaphor to reflect our metaphysical situation.

On one end of the spectrum of good and evil is the metaphysical darkness, which refers to a world that lives in fear, deception and unawareness and is ignorant about greater spiritual truths. The metaphysical light (or "the Light") refers to the opposite polarities and the divine intention for humanity. It refers to a world that lives amid love, honesty and great awareness and knows the truth (has wisdom) about God, ourselves and life.

Although Jesus came to illuminate the way out of the metaphysical darkness, his teachings were distorted and convoluted by it. The world thus remained lost in it. That long-standing situation is rapidly changing, though, as a profound spiritual process is impacting an unprecedented number of people.

The metaphor used to depict the presence or absence of this inner growth is of being awake or asleep. It refers to human consciousness, but not in a physiological sense, such as being unconscious while you sleep at night or are under anesthesia. Rather, it refers to consciousness in a metaphysical sense and whether you truly see the Light or are still lost in the darkness.

If you are metaphysically asleep, you are still driven by unconscious fear, deceived by unenlightened teachings, unaware of your metaphysical situation and ignorant about greater spiritual truths. To wake up is to start seeing what you have been missing.

The nature of consciousness is mysterious. You will not know you were metaphysically sleepwalking until you awaken. You will not get it until you get it, and when you finally get it, you will wonder how you could have ever been so lost. It is like awakening from a hazy dream that you thought was real.

Coming to know the truth about God, ourselves and life is to see it all in a new light. When you awaken, the narrow gate will appear and the path of growth will become clear as the journey home begins in earnest.

In the apocalyptic prophecies, the spiritual realm communicated in metaphors about the metaphysical dynamics our world was and would be experiencing. It long ago depicted the bastions of the darkness that would be arresting our development while foretelling the era of the great awakening. Believe it or not, that time is now.

1.3. The Truth and Consequences of Free Will

To better understand where the Light is guiding us and why the prophecies convey what they do, we need to understand free will, responsibility and power.

1.3.a. Does Free Will Exist?

According to our experience of constantly making choices, we have an independent will. Yet some intellectuals argue that free will is an illusion. This doctrine is known as determinism and holds that our behavior is actually the product of genetics (nature) and past programming (nurture).

Psychologist B. F. Skinner (1904–1990) was a champion for the behavioral school of psychology. He studied how laboratory rats and pigeons would operate within their controlled environment of food, levers and buttons. He learned how to shape their behavior through certain patterns of positive and negative reinforcement.

He extrapolated his findings to conclude that our behavior is a similar result of positive or negative reinforcement. Hence, free will is illusory. Alongside the publication of a controversial book, he appeared on the cover of *TIME* magazine in September of 1971. His thesis was, according to *TIME*, "We can no longer afford freedom, and so it must be replaced with control over man, his conduct and his culture."[3]

The spiritual perspective concurs that we are encountering an illusion but differs substantially about its nature. That is, is our sense of having a free will really an illusion, or is the physical universe itself an illusion that has kept us from perceiving a greater reality?

1.3.b. The Character of Our Creator

If we believe the operative illusion is being tricked into the sense that we have independent choice but in fact do not, that leads to a depressing state of affairs. The trajectories of our lives have already been fated despite whatever fantasy has us believing we are actually navigating the journey. Like a child's ride at an amusement park, our hands are turning the steering wheel, but our cars will only follow the rail tracks underneath.

Devoid of independent choice, we would either be pawns in some bizarre game of otherworldly control or evolutionary victims of random happenstance. If there was a creative deity behind such an existence, such a god would have to have been sadistic, inept or some tragic mix thereof.

Indeed, many folks believe God is the direct author of everything that happens. If God was and is the only will (the only entity exercising creative choice), then is our world and its brutal history the best that God could do? The belief ignores the consequential effects of choices from billions of embodied souls and blames the horrific results on God. It is a blasphemy about the character and nature of God.

As awakening souls know so well, free will is a reality. They know this because they have tapped into their essence and can go against the grain of their genetic and environmental conditioning. They challenge their fears and defenses instead of being driven by them. Their transformative path through their suffering is yielding true freedom and power as conscious creators. Those who have not yet awakened, though, are usually slaves to their foundational programming.

This leads to an important insight. By observing that free will is a reality, we can deduce the essence of the deity who created and bestowed it.

Underlying every act of choice-limiting control upon mature adults is the fear of a possible outcome. For instance, a jealous husband limits his wife's social activities for fear she might meet another man and leave him.

Pure love, on the other hand, is the opposite of fear and has no fear of a possible outcome. Whereas fear tries to limit choice, love bestows freedom. Whereas fear arises from self-interest in controlling the outcome, love arises from a selflessness that accepts all outcomes. Whereas fear tries to set and bind conditions, love is boundless and unconditional. So when we accept the gift of free will, we can deduce with our minds and feel in our hearts that it was bestowed by a God of pure, unconditional love.

To fully experience free will with the gamut of options in a polarized universe, there can be no steel tracks underneath our cars. As a creator of pure, unconditional love, God does not infringe upon our choices and their consequential outcomes. If we steer ourselves off the edge of a mountain, down its slopes we will tumble.

The results we experience are because of our wills, not God's. But if we ever choose to consistently live God's will—to live like Jesus—the results will be heaven on earth. It is up to us, not God.

We are collectively creating among the interconnected world in which we live. Through our daily choices in relationship with ourselves and one another, we are either fostering reinforcing cycles of love, support, honesty, openness and connection, or hate, opposition, lies, defensiveness and isolation. War and peace are the most outwardly visible products of our choices and inseparable destinies. As for the earth, we either care for our collective home and make it a hospitable place for future generations to live, or we devastate it and leave behind a wasteland for the children we hypocritically say we love.

It is time to move beyond mistaken theologies about God's will being the direct cause of events. It is time to move beyond our questions as to why God would allow a particular event to happen. To truly grant us free will, our God must lovingly let it all happen.

[Note: Since nothing in the universe can truly damage an eternal soul, God lets us play the game of life however we wish. No matter how violently we might choose to play, we always walk away fully intact when the game is over from the illusory playground of the physical universe.]

It is time to realize we have been blessed with free will and a creative power that is far beyond our current imaginings. It is also time to realize the character of our Creator is of the purest and grandest love imaginable.

The essence of God's will is for our spiritual growth and the manifesting of heaven on earth. The nature of God's will is honoring our free will. As God's unconditional love wakes us up from our game of "let's fearfully isolate and create hell on earth," we will be guided toward our destined experience of playing "let's lovingly connect and create heaven on earth."

1.3.c. Free Will, Responsibility and Power

Without free will, we would be biological robots doomed to churn out the fateful product of the universal machine. Unable to alter the unalterable, there could be no responsibility for what was produced. In this universe, though, we are constantly creating and changing our selves, society and world with our never-ending choices. Free will and the responsibility for what we produce, then, are inseparable.

To truly own the gift of free will, we must fully own the responsibility that comes with it. Few people do. As Peck explains, we evade responsibility for our behavior when we assign it to another person or entity (such as a boss, corporation, government or even fate). When doing so, we also give away our power to that person or entity.[4]

Power is thus the third side of a triangle with free will and responsibility. To fully embrace one of them, we have to embrace the other two. Power is also at the heart of the apocalyptic prophecies, so understanding it is vital.

The creative engine of free will generates two types of power: spiritual and external. Most everybody is familiar with external power because the world has long been run by it. Very few people are aware of spiritual power, though, and even fewer have embarked on the arduous path of developing it.

Spiritual power is the ability to consistently live your highest choice and deepest truth. You surrender your spiritual power when you allow such choices to be hijacked by the fear of pain or death, an enticement (such as money, security, external power, prestige or sex), a concern about the opinions or emotions of others, or an aversion to challenging emotional states. To live with spiritual power is to live with true inner freedom where your choices are not swayed by reward, punishment, emotion, compulsion or addiction.

Spiritual power is developed by wading into the psychological pain that stands in the way of spiritual growth. It is an internal quality and independent of societal roles or positions, so it cannot be taken away. Most people, however, unconsciously give it away.

External power is the ability to coax or coerce the behavior of others. The person wielding it dangles the carrot (such as money, security, external power, prestige, sex or approval) or wields the stick (such as threats, punishment or disapproval) to get others to follow his will.

External power is primarily derived from a societal position that is backed by laws, rules or cultural norms. As most people's behavior can be bought if the price is right, money is also a tremendous source of external power. Unlike spiritual power, external power can be taken away or lost in a heartbeat. One way or another, it is always just a matter of time before life strips it away.

External power does not exist over those who have cultivated their spiritual power. In 1918, British scholar Gilbert Murray observed this truth as he referred to Mahatma Gandhi:

> Persons in power should be very careful of how they deal with a man who cares nothing for sensual pleasure, nothing for riches, nothing for comfort or praise or promotion, but is simply determined to do what he believes to be right. He is a dangerous and uncomfortable enemy, because his body, which you can always conquer, gives you so little purchase upon his soul.[5]

The critical insight is that external power aggregates from the unenlightened masses who have relinquished their spiritual power. In other words, power is a zero-sum game.

Indoctrinated by the norms of hierarchy and subservience, people have perpetually forsaken their highest choice and deepest truth to obey orders from above. They bestow great external power upon those in charge because the body can always be conquered and they are identified with anything but their immortal essence. Metaphysically speaking, they are plugged into and tendering their power to the ruling institutions. Historically speaking, their spiritual power has been dormant, so external power has run rampant.

People of high spiritual power do not blindly abdicate their choices to the will of another. Not identified with their bodies or egoic concerns, they cannot be bought or coerced. They naturally prefer cooperation, but a leader needs to justify a collective action to gain their participation.

A nation obviously needs men and women who will defend it when necessary, and it fights best when operating as one under a unified hierarchy. But if it is not fighting a just war, its citizens and soldiers are justified in being conscientious objectors. Since people of high spiritual power take full responsibility for the bullets and bombs they would otherwise be unleashing or helping to unleash, they would rather endure the wrath of their fellow citizens and punishment of their government than contribute to an immoral and murderous cause.

As awakening souls reclaim their spiritual power, the external power of various institutions and authorities will dissipate. When spiritual power is fully owned and developed by all, the mountains of external power will have been leveled and the valleys of the oppressed will no longer exist.

1.3.d. The Bonding of Partnerships

With that flat terrain still far off in the distance, tremendous external power is still wielded by the leaders of governments, corporations and other institutions. Since they direct behavior on such a large scale, it is tempting to blame them for the ills of the world. Yet now we are seeing another side of the story.

Partnerships are always sustained by a complementary bond. As a popular cliché explains, "It takes two to tango." Spiritual illness may be readily apparent in one of the partners, but it always has a complementary component nestled within the other. Otherwise, the healthier partner would not continue to dance.

For instance, an alcoholic husband may persist in a destructive lifestyle because of an enabling wife. But if she addresses her fear-based reasons for collusion, she will no longer partner with him as things are. He will have to either confront his illness as he spiritually grows to remain paired on a healthier plane or ride out the divorce and pair up with another who will allow his illness to remain.

Consider as well the atrocities of Nazi Germany. Adolf Hitler's illness is obvious, but the crimes of his regime would not have been motivated and could not have been committed without a spiritual illness on the other side of the pairing. The Holocaust was spawned and enabled by a roiling antisemitism[6] that had been deeply ingrained across Europe for centuries. Moreover, he could perpetrate it only because millions of Germans had surrendered their spiritual power to him and dutifully did his bidding.

Here is the wisdom from the complementary nature of partnerships. When a destructive spiritual illness becomes apparent in a partner (which could be a person, institution or nation), consider it a heaven-sent message to become aware of the enabling complement within, engage a path of inner healing and growth, and no longer allow the unhealthy dance to continue.

The worst manifestations of evil are not maliciously and deliberately chosen by millions but rather chosen by a few and fearfully and ignorantly enabled by millions. Condemning just the few who present as the face of evil is a failure to see the darkness within the many who constitute its empowering body.

1.3.e. Developing Awareness

We are best served, then, by not only searching for the truth about God and life but also shining the light into deeper layers of ourselves and our beloved institutions. Be forewarned, though, that developing a greater awareness will include some unsettling discoveries.

It will soon be evident our world is still dominated by a darkness whose tentacles are strangling us from the most unsuspected sources. Although the light is dawning as we awaken to a higher consciousness, we are still lost in the illusion of the physical universe, deceived by misguided paradigms, separated from a God of pure, unconditional love, and bound by deeply ingrained fears.

As the process unfolds, spiritual illness will be easier to observe in ourselves and others. This is not cause for condemnation but rather compassion.

Nobody was or is inherently bad or evil at his core (not even Hitler). To the contrary, we are all fundamentally good, for we are all beautiful souls of the Light and interconnected with God. Trouble is, we all got lost in the darkness, fell for its deceptions, and got disconnected from God and our own essence. We have all chosen bad or downright evil behavior at some point in our eternal existence.

Having free will and succumbing to the darkness is part of the grand game of life. It was by divine design that good souls would get so lost in the illusions and deceptions of a polarized universe that bad choices and behavior would routinely occur and life would get so ugly. So have compassion for yourself and others as the great awakening continues to unfold like a movie.

Take heart that a happy ending—heaven on earth—is a preordained part of the divine script. Be forewarned, though, that because of free will, the details and timing of our experiential movie have yet to be created. Will we spend a few more centuries watching the same old horror film unfold? Or will we awaken, step into our leading roles, and begin creating the kind of world our hearts so deeply desire?

1.4. The Stages of Spiritual Growth

We are spiritual beings who are immersed in a process of life that is driving and nurturing our spiritual growth. The ultimate goal of this purpose-driven universe is for us to manifest and experience our divine essence. This section explores the stages of the transformation, which is like having a map of the metaphysical terrain to help guide us through the wilderness.

1.4.a. Background and Structure

James Fowler, PhD, was the first to posit a theory of developmental stages pertaining to faith and our quest for meaning. His theory primarily differentiates its six stages upon the structure of a person's guiding beliefs. Building upon Fowler's work and drawing from his clinical experience, Peck formulated a more content-based model of four general stages of spiritual growth.[7]

The journey is far too mysterious and multidimensional for any theory to fully capture and explain. Yet a rough sketch of the terrain is all we are looking for, and Peck's theory will be used because it yields a more accurate and valuable reflection.

The stages of spiritual growth will be easier to understand with an analogy. The four stages are like the four levels of America's educational system. Stage 1 is like elementary school, stage 2 is like high school, stage 3 is like undergraduate college, and stage 4 is like graduate school.

Meanwhile, Peck's model will be enhanced with another dimension: the major lines of development that constitute spiritual growth. The four developmental lines are like subjects that can be studied at each level of school. Think of one developmental line as being like reading and writing, another would be like history, another like math and one more like science.

1.4.b. The Developmental Lines of Spiritual Growth

To prevent confusion with the numbering of stages, the developmental lines of spiritual growth will be identified with the letters A through D. They are presented in a spectrum format of one end of a continuum to the other. On one end is the spiritual-growth equivalent of starting elementary school with that subject. On the other is the equivalent of finishing graduate school with it.

<u>Developmental line "A" involves the state of one's ego</u> and its cravings for self-preservation, pleasure, external power and social acclaim. At one end of this spectrum, the ego dominates choice-making with the compulsion to

survive, thrive and dominate. Because of the ego's deeply buried shame, such a person regularly *deceives* others. The ego-driven person is *ignorant* of spiritual truths, *lacks awareness*, bristles with psychological defenses, and is emotionally disconnected. Choice is a sole function of "my will," and unconscious *fear* is its driving force.

Spiritual growth surfaces and heals the ego's roots. Having *wisdom* of spiritual truths, there is minimal concern for physical survival. No longer feeling there is anything to hide, such a person lives with *honesty* and authenticity. Having developed *deep awareness*, dissipated psychological defenses, and deflated the ego, the soul-guided person has reunited with the divine and feels connected with everything. Choice is a soul function of "thy will," and unconditional *love* is its driving force.

[Note: The signature qualities of the metaphysical darkness and light (§1.2.d.) are italicized to show how that polarity can also be viewed in terms of the ego's presence or absence.]

Developmental line "B" involves the state of one's spiritual empowerment. At one end of this spectrum, a person lives with minimal spiritual power and avoids responsibility whenever possible. Those who lack external power blame superiors and hide behind "just following orders." Those on top blame predecessors, subordinates or circumstances. All routinely avoid seeing and acknowledging their contributions to undesirable results.

Spiritual growth develops spiritual power (§1.3.c.). A person of high spiritual power cannot be coerced or enticed by the agents of external power to act in ways that contradict the soul. No longer piping spiritual power into society's vast reservoirs of external power, such a person takes full responsibility for the consequences of his/her choices. Having accepted co-creative responsibility for the state of the world, he/she does not check out from society but rather is an inspired force for its healing and transformation.

Developmental line "C" involves the state of one's consciousness in the realm of emotion. At one end of this spectrum, a person feels nothing and is disconnected from the inner world of emotions, desires, subtle sensations and intuition. Feelings are avoided, repressed or masked with a variety of psychological defenses and chemical or behavioral coping mechanisms. With an unawareness of and lack of empathy for other sentient beings, such a person can inflict emotional or physical pain upon them without any felt sense for what the recipients of their cruelty are experiencing.

Spiritual growth leads to being intimately connected with one's vast inner world. Such people are fully embodied, clearly present to inner realities and naturally empathic to the felt experiences of other sentient beings. They accept and experience uncomfortable feelings and delve into their deeper layers (e.g., the hurt, shame, emptiness and fear that underwrite anger) instead of unconsciously reacting from them. Masters of processing emotions, they keep their bodies free of emotional toxicity. Deeply connected with their intuition and passion, they are aware of and have the courage to live their divine callings.

<u>Developmental line "D" involves the state of one's consciousness in the realm of cognition (thinking)</u>. At one end of this spectrum, a person is out of touch with reality and refuses to accept new information to build a better map. Such a person clings to a mistaken worldview paradigm, has no curiosity to explore and learn, and allows contradictory beliefs to persist. Moreover, such a person is unable to detach from personal bias to think about a situation objectively or from the viewpoint of another. Critical-thinking skills are nonexistent, as is the ability to perceive problems systemically and to embrace uncertainty and complexity.

Spiritual growth eventually results in an accurate worldview paradigm. Having wrestled with and resolved the underlying roots of contradictory beliefs, the psyche is integrated and is constantly assimilating new information for an ever-improving conception of the universe. Such people think deeply, critically and systemically about problems. They are able to do so from multiple points of view and without being influenced by personal bias or the anxiety of uncertainty. They are also able to move beyond logic to embrace the universe's grand paradoxes.

1.4.c. Notes on the Developmental Lines

Just as proficiency in science is usually accompanied by proficiency in math, the developmental lines are highly correlated. Nevertheless, they reveal the fallacy of only focusing on some aspects of spiritual growth.

A classic example is when a seeker spends decades minimizing the ego (A), releasing emotions (C), and developing spiritual knowledge (D). But a failure to wield power and responsibility (B) is expressed in the wisdom "If you know but do not act, do you really know?" To be more explicit, the Eastern mystical teachings generally fail to inspire action to remove thorns of human suffering like oppressive governments and exploitative industries. Eastern gurus like Mahatma Gandhi who boldly work for political and societal transformation are the exception, not the norm.

Another classic example is when a religious zealot surrenders the self for a greater cause (A) and acts upon his convictions (B). The results are disastrous, though, when there has been no growth in the realms of emotion (C) and cognition (D). Lacking empathy and oblivious to the possibility his convictions are askew, the zealot is navigating with a grossly distorted map of reality. Although boldly living with selfless dedication, he is blind to the mental and emotional warning signs that he is charging in the wrong direction. This dynamic has driven the Crusades, Inquisition, colonialism and jihads of the

Western religions.

This leads to a critical nuance about spiritual growth in the realm of the ego (A). Although ego about one's life may be surrendered, ego about one's beliefs can be firmly locked in place and defended with pride that is beyond reproach. When the ego's unassailable beliefs are energized by a life dedicated to a greater cause, a fanatic is born.

To spiritually grow, we have to perpetually challenge our egos by embracing doubt and uncertainty in search of greater understanding. To create the space for doubt, we must first embrace the wisdom of the old folk saying "It ain't so much the things we don't know that get us into trouble. It's the things we know that just ain't so."[8]

Two more points need to be made about the developmental lines. First, progression in any one of them may be quite variable across different life areas. This is like saying one's proficiency in math may be excellent with solving algebra problems in a textbook but poor when applying math to real-life situations. For an example regarding spiritual power (B), a man may have admirable maturity in the working world if he is able to conflict with management or leave a job before selling out. Yet he could be concurrently crippled in the romantic realm if he is unable to tell the truth about himself for fear of the relationship falling apart.

Second, with multiple lines of development that are multifaceted across various areas of life, we can hardly expect people to neatly conform to a linear model of spiritual growth. Again, it is meant to provide orienting guidance for navigating the human predicament.

1.4.d. Stage 1

The stage 1 paradigm is that life is about survival and self-gratification. The law of the jungle reigns supreme, and the ultimate authority for such people is their ego. Choices are driven by selfish concerns and only align with society's laws because of the principles of risk and return. That is, the problem with committing a crime is not in the infringement upon the rights and welfare of others but rather the consequences of getting caught. A stage 1 person says whatever he needs to protect himself and achieve his aims and is thus prone to habitually lying.

The stage 1 psyche represses feelings and is epitomized by the saying "Ignorance is bliss." When painful feelings start rumbling, it does whatever it takes to quell or vent them, such as alcohol or other drugs, aggression, overwork or sex. There is little capacity to empathize with other people and animals, who are merely objects to be interacted with to maximize gratification.

Those in stage 1 who lack education and sophistication usually succumb to a life of drugs or crime. The far greater threat to society, though, comes from stage 1 people with intelligence and ambition. The stage 1 psyche uses all its tools to achieve its aims, the most valuable of which is maintaining a well-cultivated image. As such, talented stage 1 competitors often rise to prominent positions to serve the ego's quest for external power, wealth, sex and fame.

Despite the cool exterior of a dominant ego, the stage 1 psyche is immersed in an unconscious sea of chaos. If and when the egoic shell finally breaks, it can be a very painful process. The conversion to stage 2 is often clear and dramatic. It happens when the ego's command and control is surrendered to a higher authority.

1.4.e. Stage 2

People in stage 2 submit themselves to a higher authority and embrace rules, order and structure. An authority may be a nation, military or corporation, but the highest authority for most is the God of their religion. Just as stage 2 soldiers submit to military codes and commanding officers, stage 2 worshippers submit to their holy book and commanding God. The benefits of relinquishing their spiritual power are security, simplicity, collective belonging and abdicating responsibility.

The God of stage 2 religion is external, separate from humanity and atop a hierarchy of holy people. Underneath them is the common man, who has primacy over the woman, creatures of the earth and the rest of nature. The Almighty expects obedience to doing the right thing and is a great arbiter of justice who will punish the wicked.

The stage 2 psyche is often immersed in black-and-white thinking and a literal interpretation of religious texts. Even if it is razor sharp in other areas of life, it can be surprisingly devoid of critical-thinking skills with its religious beliefs. Its emotional state enables this aberration, for it is dreadfully afraid of uncovering truths that would rock its foundation.

Stage 2 people are taught to love others, but their loving behavior is often distorted by the compulsion of "have to" or "should" and a lack of deeper emotional healing. Where their holy book justifies hatred of others, such as Jews or homosexuals, their repressed darkness often floods out scathingly.

1.4.f. Stage 3

Whereas the transition to stage 2 hinges on the developmental line of the ego and will (A), the transition to stage 3 primarily comes from growth in the realms of emotion (C) and cognition (D). Sufficient courage enables a path of doubt and truth-seeking, which is the signature mindset of stage 3.

The stage 3 psyche does not blindly accept somebody else's version of the true nature of things, especially the stories and beliefs of the ancient religions. It thus takes responsibility for arriving at its own conclusions instead of surrendering its critical faculties to the cultural authorities.

The home of science, stage 3 is rational, empirical and committed to discovering universal laws through objective examination. It thus rejects the idea that God is directly responsible for earthly events. Those who have stepped up to stage 3 have also dismissed beliefs like the universe being created in six days and animal life surviving a global flood because of Noah's ark.

Stage 3 is home to agnostics and atheists whose worldview paradigm is the positivism and materialism of science. While stage 1 is also home to nonbelievers, the crucial difference between these stages is still the psyche's choice of its ultimate authority.

The stage 3 scientist surrenders her ego to the truth about the way things really are, not the way the ego would like them to be. Moreover, stage 3 people usually submit themselves to greater-than-self values, such as peace, justice and equality. Those in stage 3 often care deeply for the environment and doing what they can to make the world a better place. The typical stage 3 mind examines human positions and values in relative terms, considers the perspective of the enemy, and perceives life beyond the simplistic lens of black and white.

Stage 3 welcomes growth toward mind-body integration and dissolving shame and guilt about the body and sexuality (instead of the "spirit is good and flesh is evil" teachings of stage 2 religions). Many people in stage 3 are inspired to grow toward self-actualization by working on psychological defenses and their underlying issues.

If a growing stage 3 psyche avoids diversions, it will eventually run out of intellectual and emotional real estate. It will encounter an ultimate crisis of meaning as articulated by the existentialists, who answered that life is inherently meaningless except for the meaning each person gives it. The only way out is an ego-dissipating move into stage 4.

1.4.g. Stage 4

If a stage 3 person pays close attention to what is happening in life, she will eventually perceive the omnipresent force of divine love. Observing grace and how it fosters spiritual growth, though, is just one of many paths back to God. Somehow, someway, a uniquely personal and mysterious something awakens and hearkens the consciousness of a lost psyche back toward its divine roots.

Although tremendous progress occurred to arrive at the narrow gate, stage 4 is where the path of spiritual growth really begins. Now the journey home is conscious and intentional, for the psyche is aware of the grand purpose of life.

Despite its latent suffering, life now sparkles and dances with supreme meaning. The psyche has become aware of its soul and its foremost desire of manifesting and experiencing its divinity. As Jesus informed his disciples in numerous parables, the wise man will give all to have this treasure. But with this joy comes the awareness of the difficult path that lies ahead of walking the walk of Jesus and other spiritual masters.

Acquiring knowledge has been an integral part of the journey, but now the mind faces the universe's paradoxical truths. Logic crumbles in trying to comprehend realities such as light behaving as both waves and particles, time both existing and not existing, and the universe being both dual and nondual.

Most importantly, the stage 4 psyche begins embracing the paradox of individuality and unity. Every spiritual being has the same divine essence at its core. Commonly referred to as the soul, it is an individuation of God that is unified with God. All souls have a unique consciousness and free will, yet we are all extensions of God like individual waves are extensions of the ocean. We are all one.

Aware it is immortal and has journeyed through numerous lifetimes, the stage 4 psyche realizes its soul has been buried by a dense jungle of egoic patterning and energetic wounding that has previously dominated its consciousness. Unless it begins healing and releasing this pain-laden structure, it is still going deeper into the darkness and thickening its isolating cocoon with unenlightened and fear-based choices.

The original *Stars Wars* trilogy provides a superb analogy wherein the stage 4 psyche realizes its ego is like Darth Vader. Inherently dark in nature, autonomous, bristling with defenses and obsessed with control and dominance, this imposing black shell has commandeered its consciousness and buried its essence. Only by peeling back this layering of armoring is it seen how deeply and pervasively the ego's roots have been entrenched. The *Return of the Jedi* represents this with the ravaged face of Luke Skywalker's father, whose essence had been buried by his Darth Vader persona.

The stage 4 psyche also becomes aware that the rational mind has been the ego's servant as it fearfully tries to direct and control life. Spiritual growth uncovers and addresses the fears that substantiate the ego and spur an overactive mind. The psyche thus begins letting go and surrendering into the mysterious unknown and a divine union that lives in the eternal moment of Now. The exquisite joy of being is thus found on the other side of a paradox with spiritual growth.

In addition, the stage 4 psyche finds a world that is perfect as it is, right here and now, even though heaven is meant to manifest on earth (the paradox of being and growing at the global level). Regardless, taking action is not forsaken, for the fullest spirituality includes being an intentional and responsible creator. Until we wield our spiritual power to create a better world, it will forever remain in the future while God honors our free will.

Therein resides a vital part of the stage 4 existence: the surrender of "my will" to "thy will." The stage 4 psyche has free will to do whatever but freely chooses to do God's will, which is fostering spiritual growth in ourselves and one another so we experience our divine nature, triumph over the darkness, and create heaven on earth. By living our true nature, we joyfully align with God's bountiful design. It all comes around full circle.

If this all seems impossible to accomplish within a single lifetime, that is because it probably is. Heaven knows how many lifetimes we have spent going deeper into the darkness. Expecting to release all the egoic patterning and energetic wounding in a single lifetime is probably unrealistic. So worry not about how long the journey is going to take, and focus instead on consistently moving in the right direction while smelling the roses along the way.

What we can see on this horizon is probably just the beginning of the glories that await for those who accept the divine invitation. A caterpillar's life on the ground is all it has ever known, so how could it possibly fathom it might one day be flying? It would never experience that joy if it stopped growing in alignment with its hidden nature and divine blueprint.

A thousand-mile journey begins with a single step. No matter how daunting the fear or uncertainty, the stage 4 psyche has long since learned to trust the process and keep taking the next one.

1.4.h. Notes on the Stages

Since stage 3 lacks a belief in God, some folks may wonder why it is more advanced than stage 2. Consider a parable from Jesus about a father and his two sons. The father told his first son to work that day in his vineyard. The son said no but later went and worked. The second son got the same directive and said he would but never did (Mt 21:28–31). Which son fulfilled his father's will?

The first son obviously did. Jesus's point is to not judge the matter on words and beliefs but rather look to who actually serves God by working for results such as peace, freedom, justice and equality for all.

Stage 3 has a much better track record with such matters. As Martin Luther King Jr. observed, secular humanism was doing laps around Christianity as agencies like the Supreme Court were leading humanity to greater understandings while the church was meekly following.[9]

Meanwhile, stage 3 embraces truth-seeking instead of dogma. Those who were raised in a stage 2 religion must overcome the deeply ingrained fears of a punishing God and possible damnation, reject a culturally glorified holy book, and accept the isolation that comes with forsaking family traditions of countless generations. Folks who were raised in a nonreligious culture will be hard-pressed to fathom how deep these emotional hooks can be.

Again, the stages of spiritual growth are just a sketch of the actual territory. Whereas the spectrum shifts colors from stage 1 to stage 2 rather abruptly and definitively, the transition from stage 2 to stage 3 resembles an abstract work of art. The painting is red on the left and blue on the right, but it is tough to say where the transition occurs.

Nevertheless, the process is clear. The growth is driven by the desire to know the truth and requires the courage to dive off stage 2's popular cruise ship and swim in the lonely waters of stage 3's ocean of doubt.

Can a person go straight from stage 2 to stage 4 and skip the doubt of stage 3? Not really. Hopefully, millions of stage 2 believers will rapidly embrace the great spiritual truths of stage 4. To do so, though, they will have to face some serious disillusionment and fear as they reject the hierarchical and wrathful God of stage 2.

Those who rapidly shift from stage 2 to stage 4 had probably been subtly growing in that direction for some time anyway. Moreover, there is a part of everybody that is already at the end of stage 4. The soul is already perfected, for it is God. The daunting task is getting our consciousness that is fragmented off in the other three stages to grow and integrate into harmony with it.

1.5. Spiritual Evolution at the Collective Level

Having gained a bird's-eye view of spiritual growth at the individual level, let us now consider what it looks like at the collective level.

1.5.a. Life in the Metaphysical Light

In the metaphysical light, awakened souls are aware of their divine essence and interconnection. Their lives are driven by love, guided by awareness and wisdom, and marked by honest expression.

Society thus thrives upon cooperation, a win-win mindset and integrated thinking. The ability to empower others is highly esteemed, and feeling empathy for them is encouraged. As spiritual power is widely developed, there is minimal external power to be had in institutional positions or wealth. Personal responsibility is widely embraced.

Governing leaders are committed to the best interests of all, humbly serve with the utmost integrity, and cooperate to deliver mature and intelligent long-term solutions. Free speech and other civil liberties are guaranteed, and governing activities are completely open and accountable. All forms of prejudice are nonexistent, for the equality of all beings is deeply ingrained in laws and cultural norms.

Armies do not exist, for all nations have submitted themselves to the rule of international law and resolve their disagreements via peaceful and mutually respecting processes. Citizens never again need to unite for a military effort and live in the diversity of a divine unity where love is the bonding energy.

As for religious beliefs, awakened souls know a God of pure, unconditional love who has bestowed unequivocal free will. There is no divine favoritism or chosen people, for all people are chosen and equally loved.

There are no hierarchical religious organizations, for awakened souls engage their own search for truth and follow their unique paths. Spiritual leaders authentically share their lives and experiential lessons, perpetually develop their own understanding, and do their greatest teaching by how they are living.

In sum, the experience of life for a planet of awakened souls is like living in a heavenly world. This reinforces everything that makes it so.

1.5.b. Life in the Metaphysical Darkness

In the metaphysical darkness, lost souls believe they are rulers over everything in a godless universe or are evil sinners and separate from their creating deity or pantheon. Their lives are driven by fear, enabled by unawareness and ignorance, and marked by shameless deception.

Society thus thrives upon competition, a win-lose mindset and compartmentalized thinking. The ability to dominate others is rewarded, and feeling empathy for them is chastised as weak. As spiritual power is nonexistent, vast amounts of external power are wielded by those who are at the top of a hierarchy or have great wealth. Personal responsibility is routinely denied.

People are governed by a monarch or dictator who is driven by egotistical desires and crushes any attempt to critique him. Civil liberties are throttled, and the regime's activities are secretive and beyond reproach. Severe inequalities are deeply ingrained in laws and cultural norms, such as highly privileged royal blood, racial superiority and inferiority, slavery and social classes.

Nations are bent on conquest or protecting themselves from such enemies. War is an inevitable part of life and the primary means of conflict resolution. Rather than being overrun by an enemy that attacks, rapes and pillages, citizens dutifully live in the conformity of a false unity where fear is the bonding energy.

As for religious beliefs, many believe that God does not exist. Those who do believe are fearfully submissive to a deity or pantheon that rules over them and threatens eternal punishment to obtain strict obedience. Some people and races are favored and chosen while others are despised and cursed.

As for religious organizations, a ruling hierarchy claims to be a heavenly intermediary and enforces what God is (or the gods are) clearly not doing from above. Demanding strict obedience to the creed under the pretense of creating a unity that is pleasing to God (or the gods), it pursues the forceful conversion or killing of heretics. Its dogma is beyond reproach, and truth-seeking is thus condemned as a great affront to God (or the gods).

The holy people indoctrinate their scriptures as infallible, and beliefs barely change over the passage of centuries. While their preferred method of preserving authority is coercion, their organization's fallback defense is a carefully cultivated image that prevents its true colors from being seen.

In sum, the experience of life for a planet of lost souls is like living in a fallen world. This reinforces everything that makes it so.

1.5.c. The Spiritual Dawn Has Arrived

If you noticed the latter description was not that far from pegging our prior and current existence, it might have felt disheartening. Even though we have made some progress, our world is still dominated by the darkness.

If neither God nor divine love existed, we would be doomed to an ever-strengthening whirlpool of its black tar. Fear, hatred, violence and deception would generate even more and eventually implode society into a black hole. The metaphysical gravity would be impossible to overcome.

Fortunately, however, the game of life has been rigged in the most beautiful of ways. As we are all divine beings whose true nature is of the Light, we are all geared to recognize and live the truth. Since it is not a matter of learning something radically new but rather remembering something long forgotten, a planetary transformation is far more probable than what we have been led to believe.

Moreover, take heart that God designed the universe to foster our spiritual growth. Like a trade wind blowing over the tropical seas, the omnipresent force of divine love will eventually awaken and inspire every ocean-sailing being to tack with the spirit and journey toward the Light.

Despite the momentous gravity of the swirling darkness, God's inspiration and love has been overcoming it. We are spiritually evolving, albeit slowly, but our pace will soon be ramping up dramatically.

The spiritual dawn has arrived, and we have a golden opportunity to leave our collective nightmare behind. Yet the future of our dreams will arrive only if we live a higher truth. So shall we continue in our search for it?

1.6. Conclusion

The path of spiritual growth is blazed by a burning desire for the truth about God and the essence of life and the fortitude to go through a gauntlet of emotions. The truth is a spiritual treasure of incomparable value, so let us pursue it without personal bias, unchallenged assumptions or fear.

As the West has relied so heavily on science and religion to understand life and the universe, we will examine the efficacy of these mighty institutions. After Chapter 2 surfaces the limitations of science and its practitioners, Chapter 3 applies similar scrutiny to the traditional Western religions.

Chapter 2

The Trustworthy Horse of Science

2.1. Introduction

In its search for truth, humanity has been riding the trustworthy horse of science through the murky forest of life. The Church had previously confined such riders to an enclosed field, but they eventually bolted over the stone wall. In just a handful of centuries, their journey has extricated us from the haunting shadows and cobwebs of our prior existence. The steed that has carried us so far has thus become greatly revered, and many believe it is the only means by which we can ever arrive in the golden meadow of ultimate truth.

This chapter briefly covers the virtues and limitations of science before assessing the riders of this dutiful horse. Most of them have been unable to see certain features of the terrain because their mental map says these landmarks should not exist. By identifying the blinding power of a paradigm, surfacing mistaken assumptions, and presenting evidence of a greater spiritual reality, the chapter heralds the end of the religion of scientism.

2.2. The Nature of Pure Science

The truest version of science will be referred to as "pure science." The term will help illuminate the flaws in how human beings practice the discipline.

2.2.a. The Spiritual Virtues of Pure Science

As the essence of pure science is seeking the truth without bias or prejudice, it is a natural part of a true spirituality. Just like spirituality, the trustworthy horse of science welcomes all riders. God does not play favorites, and neither does pure science. If you wish to ride, the mount will serve you as faithfully as it does all others.

Just like spirituality, pure science pays no heed to the powers that be or popular opinion. Truth is not what people want or need it to be, and pure science eventually advances despite what people currently believe.

Giordano Bruno was a brilliant truth-seeker and mystic who encountered a mighty Church that needed to preserve its power and dogma. Refusing to recant despite the Church's torture and lethal threat, he was executed in 1600 for heresy. He had participated in a debate a dozen years prior and proclaimed (in a biographer's paraphrasing words), "It was proof of a base and low mind for one to wish to think with the masses or majority, merely because the majority were the majority. Truth does not change because it is or is not believed by a majority of people."[1]

Just like spirituality, pure science abhors dogma and shines the light of consciousness upon all matters. Skepticism and questioning are the reins that guide the horse into realms that might otherwise remain in the dark. While many religious and scientific folks fear what may be revealed, spirituality and pure science do not. If a belief is actually aligned with universal truth, it will continue to shine despite endless challenges.

Old beliefs and frameworks are dropped by those who embrace what the process reveals. Those who do not are ignored as they stagnate in their outdated knowledge. While humanity advances, those who succumb to a defending ego will be left behind.

Just like spirituality, pure science fosters collective growth as each generation builds upon the gains of its predecessors while discarding their misconceptions. As Isaac Newton wrote to a colleague with a saying whose origins trace back at least five centuries earlier, "If I have seen further, it is by standing on the shoulders of giants."[2]

2.2.b. Science's Achilles' Heel

The tenets of science arose because our ability to perceive reality is easily distorted by entrenched beliefs and vested interests. To counter this insidious problem, only objective data would be acceptable. Experiments and studies would also have to be verified by independent replication. To be objective and repeatable, data would have to be measurable and quantifiable.

This has been fine and well, but a price has been paid for gaining protection from the ego. Pure science had to forsake inner subjectivity as a means for learning about reality. This limitation will be referred to as science's Achilles' heel. It is inextricably bound to the mystery of consciousness and has resulted in a trio of problems.

Pure science's smallest problem involves its exploration of the human experience. For instance, how do you measure the taste of chocolate, the feel of a baby's touch or the nature of an emotion?

Its medium-sized problem involves its study of the human psyche. Barring inner subjectivity is not an issue when it comes to understanding the world "out there." With the possible exception of quantum physics, the hard sciences can remain oblivious to the inner world of the scientist. The soft science of psychology, though, is a horse of a different color. The psychologist is not trying to learn about things "out there" but rather something much closer to home. He is confronted by all manners of subjective distortions within himself and those being studied.

This problem can be avoided by studying the human being as a black box, which is what the behavioral branch of psychology does with its focus on environmental inputs and behavioral outputs. But despite its valuable contributions, this framework only suckered B. F. Skinner and his kin into a logically flawed and dreadfully mistaken conclusion about free will (§1.3.a.).

Meanwhile, psychology has been dipping its toes in the waters of inner subjectivity and reaping the rewards. For instance, wise therapists know that carefully monitoring their internal reactions can yield diagnostic insight into their clients' disturbances. Because countless therapists have witnessed this dynamic, it is being taught to students.

Pure science's biggest problem, though, is its inability to unravel the biggest mysteries of life. It deals with carefully defined aspects of the universe that can be studied with existing methods and technologies. As the process uncovers and polishes one natural law after another, it is a bottoms-up approach to understanding the universe.

Developing a top-down understanding of the big picture of life is well beyond its competency. For instance, practically all scientists agree their discipline will never be able to conclusively prove or disprove the existence of God. Moreover, they are apparently running into a spectacular dead end. Quantum physicists have tunneled into a mind-blowing realm of paradoxes where the infinitesimal amounts of matter that comprise the physical universe have essentially vanished into a bizarre playground of energy and probabilities.

Therefore, we need to embrace another means for reliably seeing the big picture. If consciousness can exist without a brain and there are other dimensions to the universe beyond the four of space and time (which many physicists believe there are because of string theory), incorporating subjective data may be the only means by which grander universal truths can be methodically attained.

This is no small task, for the human impact on the scientific process has presented a far greater problem than anything yet discussed. Our attention now turns in that direction.

2.3. The Egoic Trouble With Scientism

As defined by a scientific encyclopedia, "Scientism is a philosophical position that exalts the methods of the natural sciences above all other modes of human inquiry. Scientism embraces only empiricism and reason to explain phenomena of any dimension." Furthermore, "such a doctrinaire stance associated with science leads to an abuse of reason that transforms a rational philosophy of science into an irrational dogma."[3]

In other words, scientism is the marriage of pure science to the worldview paradigm of positivism and materialism (§1.2.b.), and it has devolved into ideological imperialism. As the marriage has shackled pure science to a dominant and abusive husband who is set in his ways, we should demand a divorce.

Science is being practiced by far too many men and women who are entrenched in a theoretical view of reality that is mistakenly embraced as an undeniable fact. They are thus blinded by their discipline's assumptions, and it has kept us from attaining a far better comprehension of the universe. To better understand this pervasive problem, we need to take a few steps back and refresh our memory as to what we really know.

2.3.a. The Arbitrary Starting Point

Should a suspected criminal be deemed innocent until proven guilty, guilty until proven innocent or somewhere in between? Trials begin from the starting point of presumed innocence, thereby placing the burden of proof upon the prosecution. The point is the truth-seeking process has to start from somewhere, and that place is an arbitrary choice that reflects the values of those who established the system.

As for the ultimate question about God and a spiritual realm, science began with presumed nonexistence. Until enough evidence convinces the skeptics otherwise, God and a spiritual realm do not exist. Yet science could have begun from the opposite starting point until enough evidence could convince the believers otherwise.

In starting where it did, science deemed the lesser of two evils was being oblivious to God and a spiritual realm than falling for a mass delusion. Given the brutal history of religion, the value choice is completely understandable.

Scientism has been constructing its map of reality upon an arbitrary assumption. Far too many scientists, however, are oblivious to the situation. Especially when it comes to medicine and psychology, they have been building theories as if they are founded upon the bedrock of undeniable fact. Their construction, though, is actually occurring over the landfill of a long-forgotten presumption.

Atheists will often claim their core belief (God does not exist) is very scientific. Their assertion is patently false, as atheism is a religious dogma of the opposite kind. The only acceptable answers from science are either agnostic (the jury is still undecided) or in favor of a spiritual realm as attested by the evidence (summarized later).

If a pure scientist was asked about a patient who had reported seeing ghosts, her opinion would include the caveat that science is uncertain about their existence. But far too many psychiatrists and other clinicians have been indoctrinated by the priests of scientism and are confident that all such visions are hallucinations. This hubris is toxic when mixed with external power, which is clearly the case with the medical establishment.

The issue of an arbitrary starting point would not matter much if scientific minds were receptive to all empirical data and able to revise their maps of reality. No matter where they started, they would align with the most coherent integration of the data and thus arrive on the correct side of the great divide. Trouble is, scientists are just as prone to being blinded by their paradigm as everybody else.

2.3.b. The Blinding Power of a Paradigm

William James (1842–1910) was a highly regarded philosopher and psychologist. He was a founding member of the American Society for Psychical Research, which was formed in 1885 to mirror its predecessor in England. Its mission was to apply unbiased, exact and unimpassioned inquiry into topics such as telepathy, hypnotism and spirit mediums.

By rigorously testing the amazing spirit medium Leonore Piper (summarized later), the Harvard professor and numerous colleagues gathered undeniable evidence supporting the supernatural. But James encountered a stubborn problem amid the broader scientific community. Although "paradigm" was decades away from gaining its popular significance, he explained its power in an 1890 essay:

> If there is anything which human history demonstrates, it is the extreme slowness with which the ordinary academic and critical mind acknowledges facts to exist which present themselves as *wild* facts with no stall or pigeon-hole, or as facts which threaten to break up the accepted system.[4]

In a landmark book published in 1962, physicist and scholar Thomas Kuhn imbued "paradigm" with its now widely accepted meaning and explained its formative role in the history of science. He delivered numerous examples of how quantum leaps were made because of a paradigm shift—the ability to see the same things but in a radically new way. These revolutions were usually sparked by "men so young or so new" to their field that their practice had "committed them less deeply than most of their contemporaries to the world view and rules determined by the old paradigm."[5]

These scientific breakthroughs were not accepted in the short term, for paradigms are notorious for preventing experts from accepting a different understanding. In each instance, the old vanguard vehemently opposed the new theoretical framework. As physicist Max Planck (1858–1947) reflected, "A new scientific truth does not triumph by convincing its opponents and making them see the light, but rather because its opponents eventually die, and a new generation grows up that is familiar with it."[6]

The blinding power of a paradigm is especially active when contradictory data is first surfacing and beckoning for the prevailing mindset to be reworked. As James observed, avoidance and denial are the predominant responses.

Kuhn also noted the rigorous defense of prevailing beliefs. Most scientists, he pointed out, are almost exclusively dedicated to the practice of "normal science" that assumes their "community knows what the world is like." A significant part of their institution's success depends on the active defense of this assumption, even if it exacts a heavy price. Normal science regularly suppresses anomalous findings because such data threatens its core assumptions and commitments.[7]

A modern example will enrich the point. The University of Virginia's Ian Stevenson, MD, gathered extensive empirical data for four decades about reincarnation. He asked a skeptical journalist who was scrutinizing his work, "Why do mainstream scientists refuse to accept the evidence we have for reincarnation?"[8]

The answer, of course, is his evidence contradicts their paradigm. As one of his critics admits, "The problem lies less in the quality of data Stevenson adduces to prove his point, than in the body of knowledge and theory which must be abandoned or radically modified in order to accept it."[9]

Most scientists have been unable to integrate such evidence because they are unwilling to consider a paradigm shift. They are far more comfortable staying within a framework of arbitrary assumptions that has led them to arrogantly believe, as Kuhn wrote, they know "what the world is like." That is where, in the words of Stevenson's critic, "the problem lies."

2.3.c. Case Study: The Deleterious Ego

The blinding power of a paradigm is usually fueled by emotional pipelines that emanate from personal investments in the outcome. In other words, the truth is being sought by people with identities, careers and paychecks at stake. A case study shows how the ego can derail the scientific process.

Perhaps no other man's theories have impacted as many lives in Western society as those of Sigmund Freud (1856–1939). Shocking the genteel culture of the European elite, he posited the human psyche is structured around a tortured attempt to navigate societal life while satiating strong drives for sex and aggression.

Carl Jung (1875–1961) was a Swiss psychiatrist who first met Freud in 1907, and the men formed an immediate professional and personal bond. Jung was two decades younger and realized he had much to learn from Freud, while Freud recognized Jung's potential and eventually acknowledged him to be the heir apparent of the psychoanalytic movement. Their friendship fractured in 1913, though, after Jung published theoretical ideas that strongly challenged Freud's.

During their first meeting, Jung observed something deeply troubling about Freud and his core theory. As Jung recalled in his memoirs, "There was no mistaking the fact that Freud was emotionally involved in his sexual theory to an extraordinary degree."[10] In a 1910 meeting, Jung received another startling insight into Freud's professional stance:

> I can still recall vividly how Freud said to me, "My dear Jung, promise me never to abandon the sexual theory. This is the most essential thing of all. You see, we must make a dogma out of it, an unshakable bulwark." He said that to me with great emotion, in the tone of a father saying, "And promise me this one thing, my dear son: that you will go to church every Sunday."[11]

Jung knew he could not maintain a professional relationship with a mentor and colleague who had such an attitude. As he saw it, "A scientific truth was a hypothesis which might be adequate for the moment but was not to be preserved as an article of faith for all time."[12]

He withheld his own theoretical ideas for a while as he continued to learn. Facing his deepest fears, he finally published them. As expected because of Freud's attitude, their once-vibrant friendship came to an acrimonious end.

Jung advocated that an understanding of libido (life force energy) should not be limited to just sexual desires. Instead, he saw this energetic drive in other channels such as artistic expression, intellectual achievement and individuation (personal growth). Although modern psychology has overwhelmingly sided with Jung, the point is not about who was more correct at the time. Rather, it is about openness to alternative theories and allowing empirical data to guide the process.

One would hope this case is atypical. It seems only logical the better theory will eventually prevail, so why fight the process? Yet who among us is not emotionally attached to an outcome when an identity, career or paycheck is on the line?

In modern times, the egoic and emotional impact is summarized by a scientist who has written about thousands of psi experiments, which explore psychological phenomena that cannot be explained by ordinary biological mechanisms. Dean Radin, PhD, describes how the scientific community has responded to them:

> The difficulty of getting scientists to attempt to replicate, or even pay attention to, psi experiments is related to what Thomas Gold of Cornell University has called the "herd effect." This is the tendency for scientists (or any people, for that matter) to cluster together in groups where only certain ideas or techniques are acceptable. A scientific herd forms for essentially the same reason that sheep form a herd—to protect individuals. It is very risky for one's career to stand apart from the herd, given the rapidly diminishing likelihood that one can continue to practice science outside the herd.[13]

Alex Tsakiris has interviewed hundreds of scientific experts for his podcasts and encountered a more insidious pathology in their community. He has witnessed denial, illogical conclusions and sometimes shameless deception from many of the well-credentialed defenders of scientism who have appeared on his show. As he noted after one such encounter, "I came away with a new understanding of how far some otherwise rational people will go to protect their worldview."[14]

Referring to the "careless disregard for the facts" and "misrepresentation" or "lying" he had experienced, he reflects, "It's stunning but it would be more stunning if it hasn't happened over and over and over again on this show. We have countless examples." He adds, "It has to do with the bias, the worldview. It clouds their vision and they—just like the fanatical fundamentalist religious folks they so despise—can't get past the obvious problems in their logic. It's the same situation repeated over and over again."[15]

2.4. Prelude to the Great Paradigm Shift

To set the stage for the great paradigm shift, this section looks at what it takes to transcend a prevailing mindset and overviews the two paradigm shifts of the 20th century.

2.4.a. The Two Essential Ingredients of a Paradigm Shift

An instructive example of a paradigm shift was written by Frank Koch and published in the US Naval Institute's journal *Proceedings* in 1987:

> Two battleships assigned to the training squadron had been at sea on maneuvers in heavy weather for several days. I was serving on the lead battleship and was on watch on the bridge as night fell. The visibility was poor with patchy fog, so the captain remained on the bridge keeping an eye on all activities.
> Shortly after dark, the lookout on the wing of the bridge

reported, "Light, bearing on the starboard bow."

"Is it steady or moving astern?" the captain called out.

Lookout replied, "Steady, captain," which meant we were on a dangerous collision course with that ship.

The captain then called to the signalman, "Signal that ship: We are on a collision course, advise you change course 20 degrees."

Back came a signal, "Advisable for you to change course 20 degrees."

In reply, the captain said, "Send: I'm a captain, change course 20 degrees!"

"I'm a seaman second class," came the reply, "You had better change course 20 degrees."

By that time, the captain was furious. He spit out, "Send: I'm a battleship, change course 20 degrees."

Back came the flashing light, "I'm a lighthouse!"

We changed course.[16]

This story is apparently a yarn, for variations on it have been cropping up for the last seven decades and American lighthouses were automated by the time Koch wrote his version.[17] Nevertheless, the tale is still a vessel of wisdom that flashes its light upon the two essential ingredients of making a paradigm shift.

First, you have to be willing and able to challenge your core assumptions. Second, you have to be willing and able to be wrong. The greatest block to both is self-righteous pride.

2.4.b. The Grand Illusion

All is not what it appears to be in this grand illusion of life. For instance, our minds tell us that objects like steel beams are made of solid material, but they are almost entirely a void.

To get a feel for the vast nothingness that comprises the building blocks of our universe, imagine expanding a uranium atom up to the size of the United States. If it occupied the space from Los Angeles to New York, its nucleus would be hard to find in Kansas with a diameter of just 594 feet.

Meanwhile, the subatomic particles that comprise an atom are not even solid. Rather, they are packets of vibrating energy with some extremely bizarre properties. We are thus paralleling Dorothy's experience in *The Wizard of Oz*: "I've a feeling we're not in Kansas anymore."

2.4.c. The Paradigm Shifts of the 20th Century

If science has taught us anything about reality, it is that common sense does not make sense. To follow the paradigm shifts of the early 20th century, we have to embrace paradoxical mysteries.

With the theories of special and general relativity, Albert Einstein showed that space and time are not independent and rigid domains. Instead, the three dimensions of space are flexibly intertwined with the dimension of time, so much so that time would come to a standstill if we could travel at the speed of light. Yet even Einstein had a hard time accepting the next paradigm shift.

Quantum physics deals with the subatomic world. Its theories of quantum mechanics were first proposed in the 1920s and experimentally verified in subsequent decades.

At the heart of the quantum world is light's paradoxical behavior as both a wave and a particle. In other words, light does things that only an oscillating wave should be able to do as it concurrently does things that only a stream of particles tracking straight as an arrow should be able to do. Moreover, electrons and all other quantum material were also found to be just like light in having both wave and particle properties.

Even stranger is that the location and movement of electrons were found to be indeterminate and completely at odds with a mechanistic model of the universe. Rather, an electron's location and movement are a cold case of probabilities whose mysteries can only be described by paradoxical explanations that defy logic.

Perhaps the most fascinating phenomenon is that a scientist's expectations are a principal factor in the results of many quantum experiments. So try as the prince of scientism did to banish the lowly maid of consciousness from his truth-seeking dance, he has lifted up a veil to see that she is the most beautiful lady present.

In sum, what is happening at the quantum level is beyond bizarre and is best summarized in a quote by one of its pioneers, Niels Bohr: "Anyone who is not shocked by quantum theory has not understood it."[18] To be shocked is to come across information that is radically different from what your paradigm was expecting.

Today's physicists are wrestling with a unifying theory that offers explanations and equations to many of their discipline's biggest mysteries. String theory posits seven additional dimensions to the universe beyond the four we know so well, and its adherents routinely discuss the possibility of parallel universes. If they are eventually proven right (although no experiment has yet been devised that might prove or disprove the theory), the truth may be stranger than science fiction.

All in all, science is slowly bridging the chasm between its originating assumption and ultimate truth, but it need not be so difficult. Scientists need only renounce the dogma of scientism, expand their horizons to other areas of exploration, and follow the evidence. When they do, the greatest paradigm shift of all will transpire.

2.5. Empirical Data Supporting a Spiritual Paradigm

Ever since science escaped the oppression of religion, the two realms kept their distance. Times have changed, though, and scientific forays onto the supernatural turf of religion are now common. This section summarizes the most prominent findings.

2.5.a. The Proven Power of Prayer

Numerous studies have demonstrated prayer has healing power. For instance, a landmark study published in 1988 by cardiologist Randolph Byrd, MD, put prayer on the scientific map. In a randomized, controlled and double-blind study of 393 patients in a coronary care unit, the group receiving remote intercessory prayer fared far better in numerous measures of recovery.[19]

In 1998, another randomized, controlled and double-blind study of remote intercessory prayer also achieved statistically significant healing results but for subjects with advanced AIDS.[20] In 1999, a third study of this type showed statistically significant healing results for coronary care patients.[21]

The power of prayer has been validated by numerous studies that have demonstrated its healing or life-empowering effects on animals and lower life forms such as bacteria, fungi, microbes and enzymes.[22] That said, other studies have failed to generate such results. The mixed bag is demonstrating that prayer can indeed produce healing results but is not so powerful that it will always deliver for all conditions and measurement criteria.[23]

By the way, the research shows no correlation between the effectiveness of prayer and the religious affiliation of the people doing the praying. As Larry Dossey, MD, explains, "The prayer experiments showed clearly that no religion has a monopoly on prayer and that prayer is a universal phenomenon belonging to all of humankind and not to any specific religion."[24]

2.5.b. The Psi Experiments of Paranormal Psychology

Science is realizing we also have other supernatural potentials. Psi phenomena include telepathy (exchanging information between minds), clairvoyance (gathering information from a distance), psychokinesis (mentally altering physical objects or systems) and precognition (having information about future events).

In his 1997 book, Radin reviews a century of experiments that have proven their reality. As he summarizes, "Psi has been shown to exist in thousands of experiments."[25] He adds, "The evidence for these basic phenomena is so well established that most psi researchers today no longer conduct 'proof-oriented' experiments."[26] Rather, they are typically trying to understand what influences it and how it works.

2.5.c. Scientism's Biochemical Faith

At the core of these phenomena is the mystery of human consciousness. Scientism believes it is produced by the biochemical and electrical activity of the brain. If the brain dies, so does the mind and consciousness.

Gary Schwartz, PhD, a professor and author of more than four hundred scientific papers in his career, used to accept this indoctrination. As he comments, "It is the prevailing model in contemporary science. It is assumed to be true and, for all practical purposes, it is taken on faith by modern Western science. Until a few years ago, I took it on faith, too."[27]

Scientism points to reams of data to support its case. Inject a brain with some drugs, probe it with an electrode, or damage some of its matter, and the mind's functionality and experience will be dramatically impacted.

However, the causality road is a two-way street, for the mind can sharply impact the body. As the bizarre cases of dissociative identity disorder (DID) have shown, a switch to differing personalities can instantaneously shift conditions such as allergies, diabetes, sobriety, cerebral activity, left- or right-handedness and handwriting style.[28]

Consider as well how the mind can heal the body if it believes a doctor has rendered a cure even though nothing was done. The placebo effect must be controlled out of experiments. In addition, cognitive-behavioral therapy has amply proven the mind's ability to heal the biochemical imbalances of depression with a rigorous change in thinking.

Moreover, laboratory research is demonstrating that our genes are not the absolute determinants of physical traits that they were long believed to be. Whether and how genes are expressed is influenced by the energy and environment of the developing fetus.[29] It should not surprise us, then, to learn that reincarnation research has implicated past-life trauma in the etiology of some birthmarks and birth defects (§A.5.c.).

Like a dog chasing its tail, scientism has only been circling around the mind/body problem that has dogged philosophers for thousands of years. Its data fails to prove the mind is created by and dependent upon a body and brain. Analogously speaking, a television breaks and the viewer erroneously concludes the incoming signals must no longer exist. Technically speaking, scientism cemented a conclusion upon data that only demonstrates correlation. Practically speaking, scientism deified its hallmark theory on faith.

The problem extends beyond this monstrous error in critical thinking. When it comes to explaining how life and consciousness ever evolved from so-called dead matter, scientism needs to insert a black-box event that might as well be labeled "Magic happens here." That is, how did a bunch of supposedly lifeless elements in the air, water, rocks and dirt ever give birth to the first forms of life? That would have been an exponentially greater miracle than the purported transformation of one lifeless liquid into another (water into wine).

In sum, scientism demands an amazing faith in the random creative power of electricity and chemicals. In a world supposedly devoid of the supernatural, it postulates the mother of all miracles.

[Note: There is truth to both sides of the debate between creationism and evolution. God/life/consciousness is infused within every band of energy that comprises the physical universe. In other words, the tree of life was dancing in the air, water, rocks and dirt all along (consult the book *Radical Nature* for a philosophical explanation). Meanwhile, evolution has indeed occurred over billions of years. It has been emanating, however, from a supernatural source that has been pulsing its desire for evolutionary growth through all physical matter. Although the eternal process and universal canvas were created by an infinitely intelligent designer, the stepwise nature of evolutionary growth amid low levels of consciousness often looks quite unintelligent to biologists.]

Granted, consciousness without a brain does not make common sense. Yet if we held firm to common sense and not the evidence, we would still believe the sun revolves around the earth. We would also still think a rock is pure solidity instead of the 99.9999 percent pure nothingness that unbiased inquiry found it to be.

Common sense is not geared to accept the theory of relativity, and it rejects the bizarre paradoxes of quantum mechanics. As physicist Brian Greene explains, "Beyond the fact that it is a mathematically coherent theory, the only reason we believe in quantum mechanics is because it yields predictions that have been verified to astounding accuracy."[30]

Surely, enough discoveries have demonstrated that a common-sense belief as to how the universe works is most likely erroneous. History has repeatedly affirmed the wisdom of trusting the evidence—not assumptions and unsubstantiated beliefs—and following where it leads. Speaking of empirical data, there is an impressive collection showing that personal consciousness is not produced by the brain.

2.5.d. Surviving Death, Part 1: The Near-Death Experience

Near-death experiences (NDEs) have been investigated for over four decades, and the data strongly suggests that personal consciousness continues after death. One of the foremost experts in the field, Kenneth Ring, PhD, describes the visual awareness aspect of a prototypical NDE:

> The first thing you'd notice is that while you—the real you— appear to be watching everything from above, your *body* is

"down there" surrounded by a knot of concerned individuals. Indeed, you have never felt better in your life—your perception is extremely vivid and clear, your mind seems to be functioning in a hyper-lucid fashion and you are feeling more fully alive than you can ever remember.[31]

Thousands of people have testified the experience was, as Ring summarizes, "compellingly real and absolutely objective: it was more real than life itself." The typical NDE is so authentic and vivid that it often transforms the subject's life, a statistically significant dynamic that researchers have repeatedly observed.[32] Ring notes, "This pattern of changes tends to be so highly positive and specific in its effects that it is possible to interpret it as indicative of *a generalized awakening of higher human potential*."[33] NDErs tend to release their fear of death, strive to be more compassionate, and live more altruistically.

From 1988 to 1992, researchers examined 344 consecutive patients who had clinically died from cardiac arrest but were resuscitated in ten different hospitals in the Netherlands. All were interviewed within a week of the event, and researchers did selected follow-ups at two and eight years later.

Only 18 percent reported some recollection of the time of clinical death, which subdivides into 6 percent overall having only a superficial NDE and the other 12 percent a core NDE. There was no correlation between having an NDE and the duration of unconsciousness, their medications or the fear of death before the cardiac arrest. Undercutting the false-memory theory that people who recall NDEs many years later are unintentionally concocting them, the researchers noted, "It is remarkable that people could recall their NDE almost exactly after 2 and 8 years."[34]

The researchers concluded, "Our results show that medical factors cannot account for occurrence of NDE; although all patients had been clinically dead, most did not have NDE."[35] Moreover, and in statistically significant contrast to the patients who survived cardiac arrest without an NDE, "Our longitudinal follow-up research into transformational processes after NDE confirms the transformation described by many others."[36]

Countless NDErs have testified to clearly witnessing physical events because their consciousness was well above their bodies and lucidly observing the crisis. Yet since these reports are hardly ever substantiated with independent verification, skeptics suggest NDEs might be dreamlike productions of the brain.

However, Ring and a colleague studied the NDEs and out-of-body experiences of 31 men and women who were blind, finding that 80 percent of them were able to clearly view scenes of both the physical world and realms beyond. As the congenitally blind do not experience visual images in their dreams, the dream hypothesis fails as a universal explanation.[37]

The situation, however, is not so simple. Doctors have found that the anesthetic drug ketamine can induce some of the characteristic features of an NDE.[38] Moreover, by stimulating a particular part of a woman's brain with an electrode, the out-of-body perception of hovering above could be induced for a few seconds.[39]

Nevertheless, the data suggests that consciousness is actually viewing physical events from a disembodied position. As for independent confirmation of such testimony, many so-called veridical cases are on the record.

One of the most prominent cases with independent verification of an NDEr's testimony was published in 1984, and Ring has published four more cases.[40] Cardiologist Michael Sabom, MD, documents another.[41] Physician Barbara Rommer, MD, reports one as well.[42] In the Dutch study, the researchers quote verbatim the testimony of a cardiac-unit nurse whose patient was in a deep coma and undergoing CPR yet was later able to accurately describe the nurse's unique actions.[43]

Psychiatrist Brian Weiss, MD, risked his scientific and medical credentials by publishing his clinical experience on the effectiveness of past-life regression therapy (§A.4.b.). He thereafter became a sanctuary for doctors to disclose events felt to be career ending if reported elsewhere. As for cases in which patients described events that were independently verified, he records abbreviated versions of four such accounts as told to him by medical colleagues.[44] He vouches for the credibility of the reporting doctors:

> I have heard these and other stories of clinical accounts of patients with near-death and out-of-body experiences from so many physicians that I cannot explain them away on medical or physiological grounds. These are highly educated, logical, and skeptical doctors, rigorously trained in medical schools. All were telling me that, beyond a doubt, their patients, although unconscious, had left their bodies and "heard" and "observed" events at a distance.[45]

Sam Parnia, MD, took a similar risk in launching a groundbreaking NDE study at his hospital, whereupon he was approached by a fellow cardiologist who had a secret to share. Testifying to the credibility of Dr. Richard Mansfield, Parnia explains, "If I'd heard this story from anybody else, I probably wouldn't have believed it."

Mansfield told Parnia of trying for half an hour to resuscitate a 32-year-old patient who had no pulse, was not breathing, and was in asystole (no electrical activity in the heart). He twice checked the equipment to verify the patient was truly flatlined, and his team reluctantly gave up after their abnormally long effort. Roughly 15 minutes later, the doctor reentered the room and noticed the patient had signs of life. The team was able to resuscitate the man, who later recounted everything that was said and done while he was flatlined. As Mansfield summarized:

> He got all the details right, which was impossible because not only had he been in asystole and had no pulse throughout the arrest, but he wasn't even being resuscitated for about 15 minutes afterward. What he told me really freaked me out, and to this day I haven't told anyone because I just can't explain it.[46]

Going far beyond the veridical cases just mentioned, Janice Holden, PhD, scoured the scientific record for them. For a study published in 2009 in which she excluded many accounts because they did not meet her criteria, she still tallied 107 published cases.[47]

The weakest of her three classifications were cases in which the NDEr subsequently investigated to determine if he or she had indeed accurately witnessed material events while being incapacitated. However, no validating testimony from an objective witness (such as a doctor or nurse) was provided in the NDEr's report. These cases comprise less than 16 percent of the 107.

The rest of the cases were just about evenly split between the other two classifications. The moderately strong cases were from NDErs who reported not only their subsequent investigation but also validating testimony from one or more witnesses. The strongest veridical NDE cases were either directly reported by an objective witness who validated the NDEr's account or a researcher who also gathered testimony from an objective witness.

Holden's weakest classification of cases has some corroboration from Jeffrey Long, MD, an oncologist who created an online survey in the late 1990s for people to report their NDEs. He analyzed 617 sequential reports from English-speaking individuals over a four-year period (2004–2008) to see how their out-of-body experiences (OBEs) squared with reality. He reported that 65 of these respondents "described personally investigating the accuracy of their own OBE observations following their NDE. None of these 65 OBErs described any inaccuracy in their OBE observations based on their later investigations."[48]

The perception mechanism of NDEs has been corroborated by Dr. Ian Stevenson's research into young children who produce verifiable information about past lives. He reports how some children added to their details about being a previous personality (the man or woman the young child had been in a past life) with "correct statements about events in the previous family that occurred after the previous personality's death and of which the subject could not have learned normally, so far as I could tell."[49] The children explained they obtained this information from a hovering-above position.

In two different cases investigated by Stevenson's successor, a young boy reported observing events in his parents' lives that happened before his birth. The parents were shocked because nobody had ever informed their son about them. The boy explained he had seen the events from the Other Side (§A.5.h.).

The veridical cases strongly suggest that consciousness can register information that did not come from the body's five senses or the brain's accumulated depths. Consciousness is apparently able to move beyond the body and perceive reality from a different vantage point.

But if consciousness is still entangled in a healthy body and ketamine or a doctor's electrode triggers an out-of-body experience, how does this happen? To answer the question, we must remember that no subject of an NDE has ever crossed the line of irreversible death. The debate thus needs to move beyond the assumption that consciousness is always either completely in or out of the body.

In a paradoxical universe, it is a wise bet to posit that consciousness can be both in and out of the body concurrently. Until irreversible death has arrived, there is always some aspect of the psyche that is still coupled to and in the body. Yet, as also evidenced by the remote viewing experiments of paranormal psychology, some aspect of the psyche seems capable of journeying out of the body. This malleability of consciousness not only resolves the NDE riddle and the mechanism of remote viewing but also the mystery of multiple personalities in legitimate cases of DID (explained in §B.2.j.).

As for the brain's role in NDEs, neurosurgeon Eben Alexander, MD, had always believed it was generating the experience. In 2008, though, he had an NDE himself at the age of 54. It proved to him beyond a shadow of a doubt that the medical theory he had embraced without question was badly mistaken. That is because his NDE occurred while his entire neocortex was completely shut down by an extremely rare form of bacterial meningitis that put him in a coma for seven days.

As the medical data for those days confirmed, the part of his brain that has to be functioning for just about every theory of a brain-created NDE was essentially dead. As he later wrote, "Mine was a technically near-impeccable near-death experience…What really mattered about my case was not what happened to me personally, but the sheer, flat-out impossibility of arguing, from a medical standpoint, that it was all fantasy."[50]

His case is even more impressive because he also experienced being lost in brain-generated fantasies. That is, he had a typical case of temporary psychosis while recovering from his coma: intense episodes of paranoia, hallucinations and delusions. "But once they passed," he wrote, "I quickly recognized those nightmares for the delusions they were: neurophantasmagoria stirred up by brain circuitry struggling to get running again."[51]

Dr. Alexander was thus able to compare his NDE with his brain's psychotic show. For a host of reasons, he knew for sure his NDE was not that at all. Like countless NDErs before him, he ran into the limitations of language in trying to convey the "ultra-real" nature of his NDE and other amazing facets of the spiritual realm: "What I'd experienced was more real than the house I sat in, more real than the logs burning in the fireplace."[52] Yet he did a superb job in his 2012 book, which should be required reading for those who still embrace an old medical theory.

2.5.e. Surviving Death, Part 2: The Spirit Medium Experiments

Perhaps you have seen a television show of a spirit medium communicating with a client and his/her deceased loved ones. Skeptics believe mediums are cold readers who are masters of testing for information and rapidly aligning their messages to resonate with their clients.

If you ever witness a legitimate spirit medium, your intuition will probably inform you the process is authentic. Yet testimony about inner experience is inadmissible in the scientific court of law, so the debate would remain deadlocked were it not for the unbiased truth-seekers of pure science.

In the late 1990s, the aforementioned Gary Schwartz examined this practice under laboratory conditions at the University of Arizona. He and his colleague Linda Russek, PhD, tested five different spirit mediums in a series of blind and double-blind experiments.

Schwartz and Russek went to extraordinary lengths to prevent deception or cheating. The experiments were videotaped, professional cold readers and magicians were brought in to review their procedures and videotapes, and a devil's advocate team of scientists was formed to detect any flaws in their increasingly robust designs.

Each spirit medium had to produce personal information for anonymous sitters (random people whom the medium had never met before and who were brought into the lab at the last minute). The medium was completely deprived of cues because the sitters were not allowed to be seen or make any statements. "Yes" and "no" feedback was permitted from the sitter to the medium in some testing phases while in others even this was eliminated. Yet the mediums regularly stunned the scientists with the information they apparently received from the sitter's deceased relatives and friends.

But tear-jerking moments counted for nothing. Each informational item produced during a reading was conservatively and quantitatively graded for accuracy and compared to how it applied to other people in a control group. In essence, it would only earn credibility points if it was true for the sitter but false for other people.

The spirit mediums repeatedly delivered overwhelmingly impressive and statistically significant results. This practically proves the information they delivered was not from random guessing. The results were first published in a series of articles in academic journals, whereupon Schwartz summarized them in a 2002 book.[53]

The most natural explanation is the spirit mediums had communicated with the deceased. However, scientific minds have to consider other explanations. Yet even acquiescing theories that the mediums somehow tapped into the sitter's mind or a universal energetic storehouse of past events do not square with the evidence. During testing phases when yes/no feedback was permitted, numerous exchanges occurred in which a discarnate relative stubbornly argued through the medium with the living sitter on certain matters of fact. Subsequent research proved the discarnate relative had been correct.

Although the experiments did not prove the mediums had communicated with discarnate spirits, no other explanation comes even remotely close to explaining the data. When we consider all the other evidence about spiritual matters, we have even greater reason to believe the mediums had communicated with the deceased.

In any case, the scientific process demands independent replication. What actually happened, though, is that Schwartz and Russek validated a similar effort that was conducted by the most reputable men of science of the late 19th century. The bottom line is the five spirit mediums who proved their mettle in the 1990s were not the first to garner scientific validation. That distinction belongs to Leonore Piper, who was first tested by William James for two years in the mid-1880s.

Dr. Richard Hodgson had previously exposed numerous frauds in London, so he came to America to take over the case. He hired a detective to secretly monitor the woman, but nothing illegitimate could be found about her. He responded by cutting off all possible forms of trickery with a change of scenery.

In 1889, Hodgson shipped the housewife to London for three months of study under round-the-clock observation, during which 88 readings were delivered under the scrutiny of numerous scholars. She delivered esoteric personal facts about anonymous sitters that, as another researcher published in 1890, in some instances could not have been uncovered even by a skilled detective. Hodgson published a conclusion in 1897 that beyond all doubt Mrs. Piper was communicating with discarnate personalities and not using telepathy with other people.[54]

In 1898, William James wrote how for nearly 15 years she had been scrutinized "by a large number of persons, eager, many of them, to pounce" on the slightest misstep. Yet "*not only has there not been one single suspicious circumstance remarked, but not one suggestion has ever been made from any quarter* which might tend positively to explain how the medium…could possibly collect information about so many sitters by natural means."[55]

As James famously reasoned, "To upset the conclusion that all crows are black, there is no need to seek demonstration that no crows are black; it is sufficient to produce one white crow; a single one is sufficient." Vouching for the legitimacy of his white crow (Mrs. Piper), he wrote, "I am quite satisfied to leave my reputation for wisdom or folly, so far as human nature is concerned, to stand or fall by this declaration."[56]

[Note: Descriptions and references to a few other successful spirit medium experiments in the 20th century can be found in a journal article by Montague Keen.[57]]

As for the 21st century, more such experiments have produced statistically significant results. This includes efforts by researchers in Scotland (published in 2004) and at the University of Virginia (published in 2011).[58] The foremost scientific researcher of spirit mediums, though, is Julie Beischel, PhD, of the Windbridge Institute in Tucson, Arizona. She and her associates have developed rigorous protocols that far exceed the toughest designs used by Schwartz and Russek.

In 2007, Beischel and Schwartz published a "triple-blind study" that delivered statistically significant results.[59] In 2015, she and three other colleagues published a replicated and extended version that also delivered "highly statistically significant results."[60] She summarizes the aggregate results of the studies:

> These statistically significant (that is, real and evidential) accurate data from a combined total of seventy-four mediumship readings performed under more-than-double-blind conditions that eliminated fraud, experimenter cueing, rater bias, and cold reading show that mediums report accurate and specific information about discarnates without prior knowledge about the discarnates or sitters and with no sensory feedback. In other words, certain mediums have unexplainable (by current materialistic science) abilities to say correct things they shouldn't otherwise know about dead people.[61]

2.5.f. Surviving Death, Part 3: Reincarnation and Possession

Two more areas of scientific inquiry are making an even stronger case for the spiritual paradigm. Because they substantially impact Western religious beliefs and there is so much scientific and clinical data about them, they are presented more thoroughly in the first two appendixes.

The first half of Appendix A ("Reincarnation") discusses the conflicting reports in the gospels about reincarnation. The second half presents the scientific evidence about it.

Since we have been learning that personal consciousness enters and leaves the human body, it should not come as much of a surprise that more than one such entity might be entangled within a living body. As presented in Appendix B ("Spirit Possession"), there is a tantalizing body of clinical data about this phenomenon. By the way, William James knew about an amazing case from one of his colleagues and thus wrote near the end of his life:

> The refusal of modern "enlightenment" to treat "possession" as an hypothesis to be spoken of as even possible, in spite of the massive human tradition based on concrete experience in its favor, has always seemed to me a curious example of the power of fashion in things scientific. That the demon-theory will have its innings again is to my mind absolutely certain. One has to be "scientific" indeed, to be blind and ignorant enough to suspect no such possibility.[62]

2.5.g. The Paradox of Time

Humanity has always been fascinated with the prospect of knowing the future. Believers study their prophets to learn what God has in store for us, and the masses consult psychics about their personal destinies.

Scientism dismisses it all as rubbish. This paradigm contends the future can be known only so far as someone can factor all the variables and underlying forces to make an accurate prediction. Meanwhile, life has far too many unknowns and surprising developments to be calculated all that far down the road.

Yet many people have had the uncanny experience of precognition. Information about a future event is received, usually in a dream, and sometime later the event actually transpires. The surreal experience delivers an unforgettable message that there is a lot more to the universe than meets the eye.

One such case made national news when the Chicago Cubs won the World Series in 2016 for the first time in 108 years. Back in 1993, a fan named Michael Lee wrote this caption for his high school yearbook photo: "Chicago Cubs. 2016 World Champions. You heard it here first."

Lee eventually forgot about it and discarded his yearbook. In 2009, though, a classmate reminded him of his bold prediction and sent him a picture of it. This was not a hoax, for *Inside Edition* captured video of the 1993 yearbook shortly before the World Series began. Lee reported his prediction came from a dream he had back in 1983 in which he saw "Cubs World Champions 2016" on the team's iconic sign at Wrigley Field.[63]

Meanwhile, psi experiments have shown that precognition is demonstrable in the laboratory, especially in the form of unconscious physiological reactions called presentment. For instance, scientists found that when test subjects were shown a random image on a computer that was either calming or emotionally stirring, physiological reactions that only accompanied the erotic or violent images had already started a few seconds before the image was displayed to the person being monitored.[64]

Dozens of similar studies have successfully demonstrated this dynamic. A meta-analysis of 26 of them showed the odds of getting these combined results from chance are at least 17 million to one.[65]

Just like quantum physics, this is all mind-blowing because of our deeply ingrained paradigm. When we embrace the truth of a spiritual paradigm, though, it all makes sense.

Indeed, those who have connected with otherworldly sources report that time only exists from our embodied perspective. On the Other Side, we are told, time does not exist. This dynamic has been confirmed by countless NDErs who are at a loss for words to describe how time was no longer operative. It is also being documented by clinicians who have dealt with spirit possession (§B.2.d.).

This might be too much for a skeptical mind if not for the theory of relativity and the interwoven dimensions of space and time. Yet the emphasis is not on current theory. Inquiring minds probably want to know if there is any evidence beyond the study of precognition, NDEs and spirit possession that demonstrates an aspect of the universe that is not ruled by linear time. Is there any empirical data that a person had detailed knowledge of the future centuries before it happened?

Many Christians point to the Old Testament prophecies that were supposedly fulfilled by Jesus. However, many of them were rendered in generalities that are far too open to fulfillment. For instance, imagine an American colonist had prophesied in 1740, "A great man will lead our forthcoming nation, but his enemies will gun him down in a public place." That such an event would one day come to pass is all too predictable. Moreover, was that Abraham Lincoln, James Garfield, William McKinley, John F. Kennedy or somebody yet to come?

Far more problematically, the validating reports cannot be trusted. As Chapter 4 presents, the only sources of detailed information about Jesus were written decades later by men who knew the prophecies, had serious agendas, and were prone to inventing material. Although the gospels may have truthfully testified to such events, they are nowhere near the level of reliability that a truth-seeker needs to substantiate a conclusion about the universe.

Nevertheless, the prophecies in the Book of Daniel deliver an amazing set of empirical data that the spiritual realm can foretell future events. As they rendered such an accurate and precise description of world history from the sixth to second centuries BCE, a vast majority of scholars have concluded they were fabricated in the 160s BCE. Yet *Illuminating the Narrow Gate* demonstrates they continued to be fulfilled with chilling accuracy and precision into the fourth century CE. These fulfillments are based on well-established facts from secular history. Moreover, the appendixes also prove that Daniel indeed penned his prophecies back in the sixth century BCE.

Although the prophecies' biggest treasures are some world-rocking messages from the spiritual realm, they deliver a profound reward for scientific readers. We now have undeniable empirical data that practically proves the paradox of time: it both exists and does not exist. Although a linear progression of past-present-future exists from our physical perspective, the nonexistence of time is also a reality from a spiritual perspective.

2.6. Conclusion

The riders of the trustworthy horse of science are staring at the edge of a cliff. As the existence or absence of God cannot be proven either way, there is an unbridgeable chasm in between. They arbitrarily started their journey on the side that presumed we are living in a godless universe of only four dimensions that somehow came into existence without meaning or purpose. Across the great divide is the presumption that we are living in a divinely created universe with additional spiritual dimensions, great meaning and purpose.

The horse is pawing at the ground and wants to jump, for it knows where its home is. Thanks to its maverick riders, it has produced all kinds of evidence indicating the truth is on the other side of the abyss.

The rest of the scientific cavalry, though, has dismounted. These professionals have been blinded by their paradigm and stopped following the empirical data. Putting their faith in their beliefs instead of the evidence, they are religionists, not scientists. Their paradigm served us well by freeing us from the Church's intellectual dungeon, but it is lost when it encounters the mystery of consciousness and the totality of life. As the empirical data portends, the writing is on the wall for scientism.

Having looked at one of the West's mighty institutions for understanding life and the universe, our attention now turns to the other. As the next chapters show, traditional religion is also facing an inevitable revolution.

Chapter 3

The Frozen Pillars of Religion

3.1. Introduction

After explaining the psychological underpinnings of the traditional Western religions, this chapter surfaces the foundational errors of Judaism and Christianity. It then presents a more enlightened version of Christianity and addresses those primal fears about the devil, deception and hell.

3.2. The Nature of Western Religious Truth

The traditional Western religions claim to be the ultimate source of truth. Determining if the favored one really knows best, though, is ultimately a matter of faith.

3.2.a. Blind Faith vs. Knowing the Truth

Faith implies the existence of some doubt, for otherwise it would be a case of full knowing. After all, we do not say, "I have faith the sun will rise tomorrow." We know it will.

By not examining the doubts that separate faith from full knowing, we make it a blind faith. Moreover, blind faith and fear are intertwined because if there was no fear about what an examination might reveal, we would never accept the resolution of such a vital matter on blind faith. To the contrary, we would carefully explore the doubt. Therefore, blind faith represses doubt and is cemented by fear.

To move beyond the stagnating triangle of blind faith, repressed doubt and fear, we must commit to knowing the truth at all costs. An unbridled search for truth eventually resolves all doubt and results in full knowing, which is a spiritual state far superior to faith.

Carl Jung exemplified this path. The son of a Protestant minister, he dismissed all such dogma to pursue the truth as an empiricist of objective and subjective evidence. Two years before he died, he was asked if he believed in

God. He replied, "Difficult to answer (*pause*); I don't need to believe, I know."[1]

However, this is not the path of the traditional Western religions. They deify and demand blind faith in the Tanakh (Jewish scriptures), Bible or Quran.

3.2.b. Frozen in Belief

Gross errors occur when premature conclusions are locked down as doubt is repressed and contradictory data is ignored. On the other hand, healthy minds are open and inquisitive. For example, a hiker in the mountains gets a glimpse of a black animal and warns her companions, "There's a black bear on the other side of the meadow." With further examination, though, she modifies her assessment. "Never mind. It's just another hiker's dog, a black Lab."

The traditional Western religions are the antithesis of open and inquisitive. Indoctrinated with the views of their trailblazing forefathers, they are convinced they still see a bear despite the green collar and shiny tags.

Since they generally fail to integrate scientific findings and personal experiences to improve their conceptions, they are similar to the fate of Lot's wife. As the tale goes, she looked back at the destruction of Sodom and Gomorrah behind her and was morphed into a pillar of salt (Gn 19:26). These religions are frozen in dogmatic belief because of their fixation on looking backward at their predecessors' understandings.

Freezing core beliefs coincides with a state of self-righteousness. After all, only those who fervently believe they have the complete truth about God and the essence of life will lock down their beliefs. The opposite of self-righteousness is the healthy doubt that one's worldview paradigm might not be entirely accurate.

Self-righteousness is essentially a state of pride. The darkness of self-righteous pride—what this book terms "egoic pride"—will be illuminated in Chapter 5. For now, observe that egoic pride represses doubt and thereby strangles truth-seeking and spiritual growth. Following doubt is the path to the Light (§1.4.).

To protect the shotgun marriage of frozen beliefs and self-righteousness, the traditional Western religions prey upon fear and do all in their power to repress doubt. The core beliefs are not to be questioned and must be accepted on blind faith. <u>The stage 2 religious psyche is thus swimming in frozen beliefs, self-righteousness and blind faith while unconsciously brimming with repressed fear and doubt.</u>

3.2.c. The Unseen Blind Spots of Consciousness

Most stage 2 religious psyches are thus lacking in consciousness. Indeed, many Christians deplore the ancient Jews for being lost in frozen beliefs and rejecting Jesus, but they are unaware of being anchored in a similar boat.

Such is the nature of consciousness, and the term "unseen blind spot" is not redundant. When you do not see life clearly, you are usually *not aware* you do not see it clearly. But when you later perceive it more clearly, you wonder how you could have ever been so lost. The metaphor of having awakened aptly describes such a shift (§1.2.d.).

The key is knowing that while we see all kinds of evil in the world, the mask through which we see is convoluted. A lack of awareness of this beguiling dynamic—this blindness of our inner darkness—keeps us enslaved as unconscious perpetrators of the darkness. Jesus purportedly advised us about this trap:

> Why do you look at the speck of sawdust in your brother's eye and pay no attention to the plank in your own eye? How can you say to your brother, "Let me take the speck out of your eye," when all the time there is a plank in your own eye? You hypocrite, first take the plank out of your own eye, and then you will see clearly to remove the speck from your brother's eye. (Mt 7:3–5)

Since the plank in our eyes is that which we are not currently aware of, awakening souls pay attention to subtle clues that lead them to their blind spots. They know this way of growing in consciousness is much easier than being woken up the hard way.

3.2.d. The Bonding Fears of the Darkness

Undergirding blind faith are deep-seated fears that are spurred by the anxieties of life. Many people assuage them by committing to a religion and receiving the sanction and comforting presence of confident teachers, hallowed traditions and older generations. The beliefs and customs may seem a little odd, but these followers have the approval of a world of fellow travelers.

Being responsible for finding and living the truth can be frightening, especially when it means doing so alone. It is so much easier to surrender the task to a religion and stand with a like-minded crowd.

The religious authorities are even more entrenched in such fears because of their careers. They feed upon the prestige and power of directing the beliefs of followers who affirm their theologies and pour money into their ministries. Why would they ever want to encourage spiritual growth that would propel folks away from their institution and livelihood?

The rampant fears bond everybody in collusion against a tough-minded examination that might crumble the pillars of their union. All in all, the religious authorities and their obedient masses are immersed in the pathology of a codependent relationship.

3.2.e. Unconscious Creation, Free Will and Divine Love

Humanity has long been creating a collective nightmare. We keep living from the same beliefs and have been suffering for far too many centuries.

Religion has been the great plank in our eyes that has blindfolded us in the darkness. Its teachers are ignorant of the grand picture of universal truth and have been unwittingly deceiving billions of followers. They are all unaware of the problem, and rampant fear has chained it together in blind faith and self-righteousness. As shown in Chapters 11 and 12 and Appendix L, the arrangement has repeatedly led to catastrophic consequences.

Fortunately, this will not continue forever. Although our free will is always honored, divine love is driving our spiritual growth. This force will eventually break through and awaken us to create anew. As Jesus was quoted in response to the Pharisees he had offended, "Every plant that my heavenly Father has not planted will be pulled up by the roots. Leave them; they are blind guides. If the blind lead the blind, both will fall into a pit" (Mt 15:13–14).

The spiritual gardening has become a necessity because unaware religious leaders have led billions of unaware followers into one hell of a hole. As it transpires, bear in mind it is not a simplistic case of black and white. There is plenty of wisdom in the traditional Western religions that will be preserved. Yet like a cancer patient who needs a malignant tumor removed, the Western religious body would be in peril if its physician ignored the disease and pronounced a clean bill of health. In any case, Jesus assured us that God would eventually unearth the noxious religious plants that have squelched our spiritual growth and produced horrific results.

3.3. The Foundational Errors of Judaism and Christianity

The book's primary emphasis is on Christianity while Judaism draws a secondary focus. Islam will be almost completely off the radar until suddenly reappearing in the unraveling of Revelation.

This section digs into the roots of the Judeo-Christian paradigm by examining its four foundational errors. These roots run through the Garden of Eden and will be surfaced to face the light of awareness and truth.

3.3.a. The Genesis of Western Beliefs About God

<u>*Foundational Error #1*</u>: Assuming the Tanakh or Bible is God's authoritative and flawless communication to man that supersedes all other messages. "Inerrancy" is used to describe this doctrine. A corollary is that God thereafter stopped communicating anything important to us about the big picture of truth.

A textbook on Christian theology explains, "The authority of Scripture means that all the words in Scripture are God's words in such a way that to disbelieve or disobey any word of Scripture is to disbelieve or disobey God."[2]

The textbook defends this assertion alongside inerrancy, which "means that Scripture in the original manuscripts does not affirm anything that is contrary to fact." More simply, inerrancy means the Bible "always tells the truth concerning everything it talks about."[3]

[Note: According to a Gallup poll of American adults in 2017, 24 percent believe the Bible is "the actual word of God and is to be taken literally, word for word." Another 47 percent believe it is the "inspired word of God but not everything in it should be taken literally." Only 26 percent view it as "an ancient book of fables, legends, history and moral precepts recorded by man."[4]]

The belief is an assumption that must be accepted on faith. Although some historical figures and stories have been corroborated by archaeology, all we can logically conclude is the Tanakh/Bible is not a complete fabrication. Even if some of its books were truly flawless messages from God, a few good apples would not guarantee an entire bushel.

Truth is, the core assumption is horribly mistaken. As will be seen later, at least a few of the apples have been munched on by worms (Genesis, Daniel and Ezra), and two are entirely soured (Job and John). In addition, scholars have identified at least four more rotten apples in the New Testament. Moreover, the gospels were written with, as scholar John Dominic Crossan summarizes, "a creative freedom we would never have dared postulate had such a conclusion not been forced upon us by the evidence."[5]

The opening chapters of Genesis posit a monumental question. Should we open our eyes to examine these literary apples in search of truth and greater awareness or keep them shut in blind faith?

Opting to open our eyes, we will look at the two different stories of creation and see how inerrancy never even made it out of the gate. Many believers have never noticed there are two of them while others apparently assume the second story is a detailed expansion of the first. A deeper examination, though, reveals an inescapable contradiction.

According to the first account, God created the heavens, earth, day, night, land and sky on the first two days. On the third day, he created the vegetation across the land with plants and trees that bore fruit (Gn 1:3–13). God then created the sun, moon and stars on the fourth day and the fish and birds on the fifth day. On the sixth day, he created all the animals. God then made man in his image and likeness to rule over every creature on the earth. The account reiterates, "So God created mankind in his own image, in the image of God he created them; <u>male and female he created them</u>" (Gn 1:27). God rested on the seventh day.

The second chapter of Genesis offers a much different rendition as to how and when men and women were first created:

Now <u>no shrub had yet appeared on the earth and no plant had yet sprung up</u>, for the Lord God had not sent rain on the earth and there was no one to work the ground, but streams came up from the earth and watered the whole surface of the ground. Then the Lord God formed a man from the dust of the ground and breathed into his nostrils the breath of life. (Gn 2:5–7)

Genesis thus has a contradiction about the relative timing of God's creation. Did he create men and women on the same day—the sixth day—and long after all the vegetation, plants and trees had been created on the third day (per chapter 1)? Or did he create Adam before any shrubs or plants had appeared on the earth outside the Garden of Eden and then Eve well after him (per chapter 2)? At least one of the stories is erroneous.

The second account continues with Eve being created from one of Adam's ribs and their adventure with the serpent in the Garden of Eden. Trouble is, the tale portrays our Creator as a bald-faced liar. With the possible exception of Adam, the serpent is the only one who spoke the truth.

God commanded Adam to "not eat from the tree of the knowledge of good and evil, for when you eat from it you will certainly die" (Gn 2:17). Eve stated God's command to the serpent, who replied that she would not "certainly die." Instead, the serpent explained, "God knows that when you eat from it your eyes will be opened, and you will be like God, knowing good and evil" (Gn 3:5).

According to Genesis, God lied because Adam and Eve ate from the tree and did not die. Rather, they grew in consciousness exactly as the serpent had said they would.

Arguing that God used "die" in a metaphorical way (to become self-conscious and experience separation) is a baseless defense. First, the serpent explicitly differentiated the intended meaning of "you will certainly die" by stating that contrary to God's warning, greater consciousness would result from eating the forbidden fruit. Thus, the tale was only using "die" as a reference to physical death.

Second, God thereafter made no reference whatsoever to any kind of manifestation of his previous warning. If he had really intended "die" to mean self-consciousness and separation, the result itself would have been viewed as a painful consequence. He probably would have delivered an "I told you so" lecture about why he had forbidden that fruit. To the contrary, the natural consequences were only the gain of divine attributes. God had lied with a falsified threat to prevent Adam and Eve from growing in consciousness and becoming more like him.

Having been disobeyed, God punished both of them. He then acknowledged that they had called his bluff while moving on to prevent them from gaining more divine attributes: "The man has now become like one of us, knowing good and evil. He must not be allowed to reach out his hand and take also from the tree of life and eat, and live forever" (Gn 3:22).

Going back to when God first noticed something was amiss, Eve lied when she said the serpent deceived her, so she ate (Gn 3:13). The serpent did not deceive anybody, for it spoke the truth. But God fell for Eve's deception and also punished the innocent serpent. The tale thus portrays God as lacking omniscience.

All in all, either God lies and is easily deceived, or the Tanakh/Bible lies and deceives. Along those lines, should we follow Genesis and remain ignorant and unconscious, or should we grow in knowledge and awareness by seeking and finding as encouraged by Jesus (Mt 7:7–8)? Should we follow Genesis and never again strive for divine attributes, or should we strive to be perfect like God as directed by Jesus (Mt 5:48)?

Is Genesis correct that we were banished by a lying and punishing God, or are we being welcomed home by a loving and forgiving God as revealed by Jesus in numerous parables (Lk 15:1–32)? Finally, did all the falsehoods in Genesis really come from a God who stopped communicating with us after Jesus, or is God perpetually calling like a voice in the wilderness to guide us home from the darkness? Are we finally ready to forsake an erroneous holy book to really listen and awaken?

3.3.b. The Intent Behind the Creation Stories

Science has proven the creation stories are not literally correct. The world and all life forms were not created in six days (144 hours), and the first woman was not formed from the rib of the first man. Nevertheless, the stories can be interpreted metaphorically for insight into the human condition.[6]

But just because we can derive mythical meaning does not mean the storytellers had such insight. Rather, they surely intended a literal meaning as evidenced by the millions of intelligent adults who read their words that way. Considering as well the contradictions between their stories and other displays of ignorance, they were not spokesmen for God. Instead, they were propagating their own cherished beliefs.

Most scholars believe Genesis was the merger of at least three source documents that came from different oral traditions. As for another example of the data for this conclusion, the first creation story uses a generic term for God (Elohim), but the second uses the personal name of Yahweh/Jehovah.

The first creation story follows a Mesopotamian tradition of beginning stories from the very beginning. It is almost identical to, and was in all likelihood derived from, the ancient Babylonian version of creation. The only essential difference between them is the one big difference. Whereas the Babylonian version involves numerous deities, the Hebrew version only has one. This story's originator was striving to shift the prevailing cosmology to monotheism.

The originator of the second creation story was targeting a more obstinate issue. To understand the situation faced by the Hebrews about 3,500 years ago, an overview of prior history is needed.

Extensive archaeological evidence demonstrates that before the fourth millennium BCE, numerous agricultural societies across Europe, Africa and Asia were immersed in goddess worship.[7] Since serpents shed their skin, they represented rebirth and were a predominant symbol in the goddess religions. Serpent goddesses were also widely regarded as possessing great wisdom.

Women were believed to be the preeminent sex because of their unique ability to give birth. Although the evidence does not suggest these societies were structured in a matriarchy, family lines were traced through mothers, not fathers. There are no signs of war from this era, nor is there evidence of distinguished rulers or slavery. These societies were built upon community partnership.

In a series of migratory waves beginning about 4300 BCE, however, nomadic tribes from northern lands in Eurasia began invading the agrarian, goddess-worshipping societies. The conquering Indo-Europeans were the predecessors of the Aryans (in Iran and India), Hittites and Mittani (in the Fertile Crescent), Luwians (in Turkey), Kurgans (in Eastern Europe) and Achaeans and Dorians (in Greece).

Because the goddess-worshipping societies had been using copper to fashion jewelry and agricultural tools, the Indo-Europeans learned how to forge weapons of war by 3500 BCE. Artistic renderings of weapons and warrior gods suddenly began, and slavery apparently originated then as well. Burial sites show large skeletons of male chieftains accompanied by sacrificed women. Indo-European societies were ruled by warriors and priests with religions based on gods of mountains, light and war.

The world's first great kingdoms began forming around 3000 BCE with the Sumerians of Mesopotamia and the Egyptians of northern Africa. All in all, humanity was becoming engulfed by unifying kingdoms of conquest and protection. Religions were reflecting and reinforcing this dark reality as goddesses succumbed to lesser roles in the pantheons of the third and second millennia BCE.

The Old Testament portrait of the Hebrews was being painted against this backdrop. While conquering Canaan to claim their promised land, they encountered a culture that worshipped multiple deities.

Scholar R. K. Harrison describes the Canaanite religion as a "sensuous fertility-cult worship of a particularly lewd and orgiastic kind."[8] Its pantheon was led by a god named El and his feminine consort, Asherat. Baal was the male god of fertility who controlled rain and storms, and his sister-spouse Anat (also known as Astarte) was a great fertility goddess. Harrison notes, "Cult objects such as lilies (representing sex appeal) and serpents (symbolic of fertility) were associated with the sensuous worship of Anat."[9] She was frequently depicted by and with serpents.

The Hebrews were given barbaric commands to eliminate this religion. As supposedly instructed by God, Moses ordered them to completely obliterate every structure and article associated with the worship of other gods (Ex 34:11–14; Dt 12:2–3). If God had given them a town to live in but some of its folks were advocating the worship of other gods, they were to slay every adult and child and all the livestock of that town (Dt 13:12–18).

The Hebrews were also ordered to execute family members if they even so much as suggested worshipping other gods. God commanded that whether it was a brother, son, daughter, wife or closest friend who had posited the worship of other gods, no pity should be shown. The hand of the God-abiding Hebrew should be the first in executing the offender, followed by the hands of the community (Dt 13:6–9).

How a Christian could ever believe this material came from God is not the point for now. Rather, it demonstrates the ancient Judaic authorities were willing to cross any moral line to win their cultural war.

In all likelihood, then, the tale of Adam and Eve was told to sabotage the fertility-goddess religions.[10] In a masterful piece of propaganda, its author portrayed the serpent (symbolic of the goddess) as claiming to have wisdom but actually rendering deception. Eve followed the serpent's advice, and look where it landed us. The goddess is wickedly cunning and dangerous.

The author also carefully condemned the goddess-based celebration of fertility and sexuality. Judaic leaders had no interest in renouncing sex but needed to quell its religious appeal. The tale therefore implied the seemingly innocuous fruit of the goddess path would lead to unforeseeable doom. Its instruction was to obey God and forsake the desirous but off-limit things like rapturous sex in a goddess temple.

Furthermore, the author flipped the ancient paradigm that women were superior because men are created from a woman's body. Now men were superior because the first woman was created from a man's body (Adam's rib).

Finally, he added a directive from God that women were to be ruled by men. With God also punishing women with the intense pain of childbearing and serpents with forever slithering in the dust, he had appealed to physical facts as proof of his invented truth.

3.3.c. Mistaken Projections Upon God

Foundational Error #2: Comprehending the character and nature of God by observing human characteristics and traits.

Genesis includes the great truth that God created us in his image (§3.3.a.). However, the ancient Hebrews made a critical error of interpretation. They assumed that what they knew a lot about (humans) should be used to understand what they knew precious little about (God). Rather than discovering the true nature of God and thus knowing ourselves as spiritual beings of unconditional love and eternal life, they attributed all kinds of human characteristics to God.

Psychologically speaking, this was a projection. Historically speaking, it was the mother of all projections.

The ancient Hebrews also mistakenly assumed that all life events are of God's direct intending. Naturally driven to explain such results (what psychology calls attribution theory) but not yet aware of natural laws and the consequences of free will, they heaped one explanative projection after another upon God.

The resulting perceptions were that God was a father who was generally loving but would harshly punish in fits of anger, a commander of great authority and a neurotic and jealous deity who demanded sacrifices to atone for sins and prove loyalty. This faulty character sketch began in the opening chapters of Genesis (§3.3.a.) and continued with the story of Cain and Abel.

Cain was a farmer and his younger brother was a shepherd, and both made offerings to God. God looked favorably upon Abel's offering but not Cain's. Enraged with jealousy, Cain murdered Abel (Gn 4:2–8). While most folks draw lessons about coping with anger and jealousy, at the heart of the story is a bold assertion: God plays favorites.

This falsehood contorted the truth in a lethal way. The ancient Hebrews correctly perceived that they are God's chosen people. Trouble is, they failed to see the other side of the coin and realize that everybody else is too.

The fallacy that God favors certain people is one of the greatest delusions plaguing our planet. After all, what side of any conflict has ever believed God was not on their side? For instance, Judaism pronounced divine blessing upon its extermination of Canaan, and Islam morphed into a religion that justified its empire's conquering expansion. As for now, fundamentalists of both sides have been driving the conflict over the land they believe was promised to them by God.

Christianity launched the Crusades, and its European nations had no qualms with colonizing the world. After Catholic Spain conquered the natives of Central and South America, Protestant America followed suit and conquered the Native Americans to claim their land too. Because this Christian nation believed God favored whites over blacks, it also sanctioned the abomination of slavery.

The ghastly error of projecting human qualities onto God has also empowered domination and injustice upon gender. For instance, Christianity teaches that the man is the spiritual leader of the house to whom the wife should submit (Eph 5:22–24; Col 3:18; 1 Tm 2:11–14; 1 Pt 3:1–7).

The traditional Western religions were clearly built upon a faulty foundation. In addition, Jesus later proclaimed a radically different understanding about God, ourselves and the nature of our relationship. There are only two options for explaining such a progression.

The first credits the ancient Hebrews with accurately depicting God's character and nature, but God subsequently matured. He learned to control his temper, worked through issues of insecurity, and offered redeeming love to his wayward creations. An old folk saying reflects the distortion of this perception: "When I was a boy of 14, my father was so ignorant I could barely stand to have the old man around. But when I got to be 21, I was astonished at how much the old man had learned in seven years."[11]

The obviously correct option is that the Old Testament's depiction of God is severely flawed. As the folk saying conveys, we are the ones who need to mature and improve our conception of God. To do so, we first have to renounce the deceptive book that proclaims its misconceptions as divine truth.

3.3.d. The Assumptive Rejection of Reincarnation

Foundational Error #3: Assuming we walk this earth for only a single lifetime.

The concept of reincarnation is unnatural because we were indoctrinated by the West's religious and scientific paradigms. But have we been taught an accurate view of reality?

The gospels say Jesus never directly discussed reincarnation. However, he purportedly twice made statements that strongly imply its reality, and he also derided Judaic beliefs about the afterlife as badly mistaken (§A.2.).

As for scientism, how does it know we only have one life on this planet? After all, the single-life belief is only a hypothesis without conclusive evidence. In fact, the empirical data is overwhelmingly testifying to the reality of reincarnation (§A.4., §A.5.).

3.3.e. Christianity's Savior Theology

Foundational Error #4: Believing whether or not we accept Jesus as our Lord and Savior will determine the divine judgment upon us and our eternal existence in heaven or hell.

With numerous quotes of Jesus about the reality of hell, Christians have been trying to determine who goes there. The Catholic Church has not definitively answered the question. For mainline Protestants, though, the New

Testament is clear. If you have accepted Jesus, you will enter heaven because he atoned for your sins. Everybody else is doomed to an eternity in hell.

This theology was built upon a matrix of faults. As the next chapter explains, Jesus had come to uproot the mistaken beliefs of Judaism. However, the apostle Paul had been a zealous Jew before his conversion, and he and his fellow travelers failed to make the paradigm shift. When they created a new religion with their misguided interpretations, it was a case of rearranging the deck chairs on the *Titanic* and painting it a new color. Underneath the waterline was a Judaic hull that was still gashed with fatal flaws.

These evangelists still believed in a God who was rendering judgment and wrathful punishment and had a need for all sin to be atoned for with a sacrifice. They therefore theorized that Jesus had come as a sacrificial savior for those who accepted the divine gift (Rom 3:25, 8:3; Heb 2:17, 9:28; 1 Jn 4:10).

However, Jesus had purportedly twice told Jewish leaders to learn what this prophecy meant: "I desire mercy, not sacrifice" (Mt 9:13, 12:7). He was quoting the prophet Hosea, who had quoted God: "For I desire mercy, not sacrifice, and acknowledgment of God rather than burnt offerings" (Hos 6:6).

Jesus rendered many of his teachings through parables, apparently so only those who got it would get it. As Paul and his fellow travelers never got the full extent of Jesus's revolutionary teachings, they failed to get God's request of "mercy, not sacrifice." They failed to realize that slaughtering and roasting animals to appease God was another erroneous tenet that needed to be discarded.

God did not send Jesus to be the mother of all sacrifices to appease his perfectionism and neuroticism. Rather, Jesus taught about a loving God who has no need to ever judge or punish. As Jesus was quoted, he could only do what he saw his Father doing, and "the Father judges no one" (Jn 5:19–22). Because God was not going to judge anybody, neither would he. As he also supposedly said, "I pass judgment on no one" (Jn 8:15).

Moreover, the gift of free will testifies to a God of boundless love who is well beyond the fearful need to control us with judgment and punishment (§1.3.b.). Consider as well the wisdom in 1 John: "There is no fear in love. But perfect love drives out fear, because fear has to do with punishment. The one who fears is not made perfect in love" (1 Jn 4:18).

We are here to flow and experience perfect love, which cannot happen if there is a fear of punishment. God's perfect love is helping us drive out all forms of fear, including our fear of punishment.

The purpose of punishment is getting people to fear it so they do not behave in ways that result in it. So if God had any interest in controlling our behavior, he would reinforce this fear by publicly wielding such punishment. But she has given us free will and has no interest in judgment or punishment.

Is God really so inept and neurotic that he created a world where our sins need the slaying of an innocent animal or person to atone for them? Is he really so sadistic that he condemns those who do not accept such a sacrifice to an eternity of agony? Was having his son brutally tortured and crucified the best solution he could find for protecting us from his pathology? Please observe the dark shadow cast by the savior theology, for it paints a wicked portrait of God that is an utter blasphemy.

Amazingly, most Christians believe their god is one of pure, unconditional love. Now if God arrived on the universal scene *after* an immutable law had been established that all people who were not perfect needed an atoning sacrifice to prevent damnation, he displayed exceptional love by sending his son to the cross for us. Trouble is, the Bible says God created the jacked-up system to begin with that made such a sacrifice necessary.

Imagine a principal at an elementary school informed his students on the first day of class in August that they had to get a perfect score on every test they took. Anyone who missed a question would be burned to death at the end of the school year.

One morning in April, though, he announced over the intercom: "Since you have all failed to be perfect, you are slated to be torched on May 25. However, I am a principal of love and will save you all by having my only son, Jose, butchered after school today to atone for your errors. All you have to do is accept him as your savior."

As promised, some vicious men inflicted horrible pain upon Jose until his blood was splattered everywhere and he was dead. After the kids got over their shock, they rejoiced and worshipped Jose for saving them from being burned alive by the principal.

Would you call this principal a loving man? Obviously not. This sadistic and neurotic sociopath would be arrested for abusing his students and murdering his son.

The problem is clearly in the system that was originally created. Just as the principal established a wicked system at his school before intervening to look like a loving guy, Christians believe our Creator established a wicked system on this planet before intervening to look like a loving god.

As the next chapter explains, the execution of Jesus had nothing to do with him being an atoning sacrifice. But Paul and his colleagues projected the story upon their Judaic theology, and the rest was history.

As logic dictates, the god of mainstream Christianity does not love us unconditionally. That is because loving people unconditionally means loving them without conditions (no matter what they have done or believed). But the Christian god only loves people *on the condition* that they accept Jesus as their personal savior, for otherwise this god inflicts eternal torture.

A god of infinite love does not need to save us from his/her neuroticism and sadism. A god of infinite love is far beyond the insecure need to judge or punish.

As for the question of how God decides who goes to heaven and hell, Christianity theorized an answer from its Judaic paradigm. Ultimately, though, it is a bogus question because God does not make those decisions.

The empirical evidence has essentially proven the reality of reincarnation, which means there is no need for God or any divine servant to judge how we lived and dispense us into heaven or hell. Instead, we decide through our perpetual choices as we create our energetic state and the corresponding experiences of heaven or hell.

Even though we have just begun our truth-seeking journey, we can already see the fallacy of mainstream Christianity. Its theology arose because one faulty idea was built upon another, and it has persisted for thousands of years because of the blinding power of a paradigm that is defended by pride and fear.

3.4. A "New" Christianity

Jesus only scratched the surface of universal truth. As he purportedly told his disciples, "I have much more to say to you, more than you can now bear. But when he, the Spirit of truth, comes, he will guide you into all the truth" (Jn 16:12–13).

That quote should send chills through the spine of any Christian with frozen beliefs. In any case, the time has come to hear more than what his closest followers could bear.

3.4.a. Just Like Jesus

We are all made in God's image and just like Jesus, for we are all sons and daughters of God. As he was quoted, "Very truly I tell you, whoever believes in me will do the works I have been doing, and they will do even greater things than these" (Jn 14:12).

Erroneous conclusions come from not having all the facts and building upon prior mistakes. Truth is, we have an eternity to grow to be like Jesus and experience perfect love, radiant spiritual power and divine union. Or we can believe ourselves to be far less and keep living a morbid existence in one life after another.

Jesus supposedly advised us to enter through the narrow gate that only a few could find (Mt 7:13–14). Unlike Christianity's "believe and you are in" doctrine that has billions of followers, a more challenging path needs to be found that only a few have been able to find. As he was quoted, "Can the blind lead the blind? Will they not both fall into a pit? The student is not above the teacher, but everyone who is fully trained will be like their teacher" (Lk 6:39–40).

Will you follow the blind preachers who deem you an evil sinner who needs a sacrificial savior, or will you follow a wise teacher who wants you to be just like him? Will you fearfully languish in a popular pit, or will you courageously engage the spiritual training and climb out of it?

Your masterful brother is calling you to grow to be just like him. The epic journey begins by finding and embracing the truth about God and the essence of life.

3.4.b. The Meaning of Every Moment in Life

At its core, mainstream Christianity believes your life has no meaning other than your choice to accept or reject Jesus as your savior. After all, everything else has minimal impact on your eternal destiny. You can also find meaning in saving others, but that is about all this paradigm can legitimize.

It also gives you little reason to be an environmentalist because you will never return and God is going to eventually torch this place anyway during the end times. So pay no heed as nations and corporations pillage and poison the earth, get what you can to appease your ego's miserable cravings, and say good riddance when you die.

Meanwhile, the so-called bride of Christ is a collection of folks who are far from living the ways of integrity, spiritual power and unconditional love. This theology is thus analogous to God proclaiming that all second-grade kids on the basketball court are world champions while those monkeying around with other playground activities go to the principal's office for an eternity.

Is that all there is to life? Could it be we all have a far greater destiny that is part of a far more amazing master plan? Life has infinitely more meaning when it is viewed as a process of perpetual creation and spiritual growth in which every moment has meaning and impact.

3.4.c. A Universal Understanding

This version of Christianity is not new. Rather, another group of early Christians knew they shared the spark of divinity that Jesus had manifested. Known as the Gnostics, they also knew the pursuit of truth was the key to the narrow gate. They embraced some pretty bizarre beliefs as well, but those errors are inconsequential because they were the antithesis of static dogma. Their pursuit of truth would have eventually ironed it all out. However, they were crushed in the fourth century by the great beast of ideological control—the marriage of church and state.

This version of Christianity has also been articulated for thousands of years by great minds from around the world. This broadly encompassing paradigm was thus termed the "perennial philosophy" by the philosopher Liebniz (1646–1716). Aldous Huxley (1894–1963) resurrected it with this definition:

> The metaphysic that recognizes a divine Reality substantial

to the world of things and lives and minds; the psychology that finds in the soul something similar to, or even identical with, divine Reality; the ethic that places man's final end in the knowledge of the immanent and transcendent Ground of all being.[12]

M. Scott Peck came to a similar conclusion. He wrote, "To explain the miracles of grace and evolution we hypothesize the existence of a God who wants us to grow—a God who loves us." However, "this simple notion of a loving God does not make for an easy philosophy." For then we have to ask, "Why does God want us to grow? What are we growing toward? Where is the end point, the goal of evolution?"

We eventually arrive at a terrifying and burdensome conclusion: "God wants us to become Himself (or Herself or Itself). We are growing toward godhood. God is the goal of evolution. It is God who is the source of the evolutionary force and God who is the destination."[13]

3.5. A Question of Deception: Not If, but How

Many fundamentalists will probably denounce this book as the work of the devil. Are they correct that you are being led into the same trap that ensnared your God-serving, truth-seeking author?

If you are a mainstream Christian, you are being deceived. The question at hand is how you are being deceived. Is Lucifer luring you away from the Bible, or has the inerrancy assumption about the Bible kept you and billions of others from learning greater truths and finding the narrow gate out of the darkness?

Figuring out which deception you are up against is vital. To assist in this discernment, we will direct our attention upon the devil.

3.5.a. The Origins of the Devil and an Underworld

The concept of the devil did not originate with Judaism or Christianity. Rather, Zoroastrianism preceded them in promoting the idea that God is locked in a rather evenly matched cosmic war with an archenemy from the underworld. Founded by the prophet Zarathustra (the Greeks later called him Zoroaster) somewhere between 1700 and 600 BCE, it was the primary religion of Persia until the rapid spread of Islam.

Although Zoroastrianism introduced the cosmic war theology, its ideas about post-life judgment and hell were preceded by the ancient Egyptians. A god named Anpu was depicted in tomb paintings as a black jackal-headed mix between a man and a beast. Possessing a tail and horns, Anpu drawings often showed him with scales for weighing the souls of the dead. The conception of an underworld and attending deity also traces back to ancient Mesopotamia.

That said, exactly how and when humanity arrived at these beliefs is immaterial. What matters is recognizing that the devil idea was a downstream addition to Judaism and came from another religion.

The devil is absent from the earliest books of the Old Testament, which declare that God was orchestrating all life events as he rewarded and punished the Hebrews for their behavior. Now if God was indeed locked in a cosmic war with an archenemy, surely he would have immediately apprised his chosen people that a rebellious angel was orchestrating some of life's most calamitous events.

Instead, the devil did not make its first biblical appearance until much later. As Chapter 5 shows, the Zoroastrian cosmology was fabricated into the story of Job to explain a sinless man's suffering. The Bible thus made one hell of a shift by incorporating the devil into its testimony, which later solidified into Christian theology.

3.5.b. The Satanic Encounter in the Desert

As for the most popular biblical story of Satan's existence, Matthew and Luke describe how Jesus went into the desert and fasted for 40 days and nights after he was baptized. At the end of his fast, the devil tempted him to turn stones into bread, test God by falling from the highest point on the temple, and bow down and worship the devil and receive power over the world's kingdoms (Mt 4:1–11; Lk 4:1–13).

Mark only summarizes the desert excursion in two sentences, but the gospel's chronology leaves no room for anything in between the baptism and desert excursion (Mk 1:12–13). It transitions between the two events with a Greek word that has been translated as "immediately," "at once," "quickly," and "just then."[14]

After the baptism and 40 days in the desert, the three synoptic gospels present this chronology. According to Matthew, Jesus returned to the region of Galilee (roughly 40 miles north of the traditionally recognized site of the baptism). He first went to Nazareth and then the lakeside town of Capernaum. Along the shores of the Sea of Galilee, he called his first four disciples: Simon (Peter) and Andrew, then James and John (Mt 4:12–22).

Luke follows suit in describing Jesus's journey to Nazareth and then Capernaum (Lk 4:14–5:11). The abbreviated account in Mark is essentially harmonious (Mk 1:14–21).

Now consider the detailed account in John, starting from the days before Jesus was baptized. Thrice quoting its source as John the Baptist (Jn 1:15–32), this gospel describes how John had to answer to various authorities and exactly where this interrogation occurred (Jn 1:19–28). John baptized Jesus the next day (Jn 1:29–34).

Remember that in the synoptic gospels, Jesus then went into the desert for 40 days before traveling north to Galilee and calling his first disciples along the lakeshore. But the fourth gospel delivers a radically different story and chronology.

On the next day (the first day after the baptism), John the Baptist returned with his disciple Andrew and another unnamed follower. Andrew and this anonymous disciple left John to follow Jesus. This gospel even details the time of day that Andrew fetched his brother Simon (Peter) to meet Jesus (Jn 1:35–42). On the next day (the second day after the baptism), Jesus left for Galilee and called Philip and Nathanael (Jn 1:43–51).

Locking down a no-gaps chronology of next days, the fourth gospel notes, "<u>On the third day</u> [after the baptism] a wedding took place at Cana in Galilee" (Jn 2:1). After Jesus turned water into wine at the event, he went to Capernaum (Jn 2:2–12).

So what happened to the lengthy desert excursion that the synoptic gospels say occurred right after Jesus was baptized but before his trip to Galilee and the calling of his first four disciples? The fourth gospel testifies that it did not occur.

All in all, the satanic encounter was surely a fictional story. But if something even remotely resembling it actually transpired (such as Jesus meditating in the desert for six weeks), the fourth gospel is blatantly erroneous.

3.5.c. The Fundamentalist Response to the Incongruent Passages

Fundamentalist scholars have long been aware of the many passages where the gospels conflict about the sequence of events in Jesus's life. They argue the authors sometimes arranged their material topically instead of chronologically, so the gospels should still be considered inerrant.

This is akin to somebody writing that Ronald Reagan served two terms as president and was succeeded by Bill Clinton, George W. Bush and Barack Obama. After these two-term presidents, Jimmy Carter only served one term, whereupon George H. W. Bush did the same. So is this topically arranged account free from error? Ask the student who memorized it and flunked her history exam.

As for the gospel discrepancies, why buy into such twisted apologies to defend them as perfect? Why not simply acknowledge that the authors cobbled together different versions of what really happened and thereby ensured an error in at least one of them? After all, if God really wanted the Bible to be an inerrant document, do you really think he would have allowed such warts to be in his holy message to mankind?

Although this book has more examples of where the Bible is corrupted by contradictions, it is not concerned with completing this line of inquiry. Should you wish to see more, scholar Bart Ehrman has already provided quite a rendition of them.[15] In any case, one more case should suffice for now. Did Judas buy a parcel of land before he died with the 30 pieces of silver he had been paid to betray Jesus (Acts 1:18–19)? Or did he return the payment to the chief priests before hanging himself while they used the blood money to buy the land (Mt 27:3–10)?

Logic has proven the Bible is not inerrant, but the paramount issue pertains to whether or not it includes errors about overall meaning. Fundamentalists contend it is infallible (it is not even somewhat mistaken about what it teaches about God and life). As will be seen in later chapters, however, it is dreadfully fallible in revealing universal truth and guiding its followers.

3.5.d. The Alpha Demon

The devil of Christian theology does not exist. Nevertheless, clinical evidence strongly suggests some domains of the universe are inhabited by demons that are ruled by an alpha demon that deceived and coerced its way to the top of a totalitarian hierarchy (§B.3.).

However, spirit-release clinicians have also learned this alpha demon is inherently no more powerful than any other spiritual being, including us. This entity is not God's archenemy. To the contrary, it is nothing more than just another individuation of God off exercising its free will in the most negative of ways. It is no more of a threat to God and any less loved by God than a two-year-old toddler who is breaking toys and defying his parents.

So based on the definition you use, the devil both exists and does not exist (§B.4.c.). Trouble is, Christianity has projected exponentially more power upon this wayward entity than it actually possesses, and its existence has been used as a supreme defense against all truth-seeking challenges to the Bible.

3.5.e. Deciphering the Nature of the Deception

It is theoretically possible this truth-seeking book and countless others are part of a gargantuan satanic deception. If this is indeed what we are experiencing, we must conclude that God's archenemy is far more powerful than anybody has yet conceptualized. Such a devil would have greater control over our destitute lives than God.

If this horrific scenario were so, how could we even trust the Bible? If the devil is able to spin such phenomenal deception, how could 40-some different authors have written the biblical books without this super-controller's influence? If you argue God shaped and protected the Bible every step of the way, is he that lame or mean that he only protected the Bible as he let the devil have its way with us with everything else?

In any case, life would have no meaning other than avoiding the conspiracy of all conspiracies and believing in Jesus to save you from a neurotic and sadistic

God. Nobody could be trusted, not even yourself.

This life path, of course, would be the ultimate expression of paranoia, isolation and disconnection. It would also be the epitome of a spiritual irony as you fully become the darkness you so fearfully seek to avoid.

Jesus advised us to avoid being deceived. As Chapter 9 discusses, he apparently knew what would happen to his teachings as they were interpreted, recorded and institutionalized. He thus sagely warned us to avoid religion's earth-blanketing deception.

So here we have another spiritual irony. Fearfully avoiding a satanic deception is actually part of the religious deception that has ensnared billions of people.

If you fear a satanic deception is trying to fool you into leaving your biblical cocoon, you are still entrapped by *the* deception. For if you already saw this well-cloaked deception, you would not be deceived by it. Instead, this deception has prevented you from searching for the truth and finding the narrow gate and path back home to God. Again, figuring out which deception you are up against is vital.

If your head is spinning, a little perspective might help. Scientists calculate that the sun is but one of 200 to 400 billion stars in our galaxy (the Milky Way). Now consider that our enormous galaxy is but one of an estimated 100 to 200 billion galaxies in the universe.

The universe's size is beyond comprehension, but the Bible was written by folks who thought the earth was the pinnacle of God's creation. No wonder some of its downstream authors followed the Zoroastrians in believing tragic life events were resulting from a cosmic war between God and an ultrapowerful adversary.

As evidenced by the incomprehensible enormity of the universe and the paradoxical mysteries of its quantum underpinnings, might you agree that God is exponentially greater than what our minds could ever possibly comprehend? Is it not time we expand our minds accordingly instead of trying to shrink God down to fit the simplistic and childish conceptions of our ancestors?

3.6. Souls Existing in Hell: Not If, but Why

The gospels have numerous verses that reference hell (Mt 5:22, 5:29–30, 8:12, 10:28, 11:23, 13:42, 13:50, 16:18, 18:9, 22:13, 23:15, 23:33, 24:51, 25:30, 25:41; Mk 9:43–47; Lk 10:15, 12:5, 13:28, 16:23; Jn 15:6). Given its apparent existence, mainstream Christians have to again confront spiritual irony and determine if their fear is creating what they seek to avoid. In other words, is their fear of a punishing God and eternal hell actually a part of their ongoing creation of a developing condition?

3.6.a. Stuck in a Pattern or an Eternal Punishment?

Let us consider what the first *Conversations with God* book has to say about hell. God says it exists, but it is not at all what we have been led to believe. It is not a location of eternal torture, such as a lake of fire. Rather, "it is the worst possible outcome of your choices, decisions, and creations. It is the natural consequence of any thought which denies Me, or says no to Who You Are in relationship to Me." It results from embracing unhealthy beliefs (which perpetuate unhealthy thoughts and actions).

Ultimately, "hell is the opposite of joy. It is unfulfillment." The soul can have the experience of being so unfulfilled, fractured, less than, unhappy and separated from God and nirvana that it experiences hell. "But I tell you I do not send you there, nor do I cause this experience to be visited upon you. You, yourself, create the experience, whenever and however you separate your Self from your own highest thought about you."[16]

God adds that the experience of hell is not eternal. Although we may deny the truth about ourselves (§1.4.g.), God will never deny the truth about us, and that truth will eventually prevail.

3.6.b. An Inescapable Choice

So what are you really facing here? Do you need to be afraid of God's eternal condemnation, or are you developing a fear-based hell of your own creation? Are you going to keep living in fear of a satanic deception, or will you start addressing the fears that have bonded you with the religious deception?

By the way, religious deceptions are easy to spot when you look underneath the polished teachings for the presence or absence of ego. They are perpetuated by a grandiose ego who sees himself as divinely special and superior to others. This leader inserts himself as a middleman between his followers and God, and he expects subservience to his dictates and conformance to his doctrines (all in the name of God).

Numerous inferior egos ignorantly align with the charlatan. They fail to see how and where their leader's egoic cravings for power, praise, pleasure and/or security are corrupting his teachings. When it is all said and done, the so-called holy teachings employed to justify the arrangement are an abomination to the truth.

The dark, encircling cloak is easy to see with leaders like Jim Jones and David Koresh. However, the Catholic Church is also wrapped in the same metaphysical garment. The papacy is the epitome of a grandiose ego, for Catholicism believes the man in this office is so special and superior that he is Christ's ruling deputy on earth. Moreover, Catholicism believes he is incapable of making an error. Meanwhile, the masses have long been indoctrinated with inferiority, subservience and conformity.

Jesus never considered himself to be superior to anybody else. He washed the feet of his disciples and taught people to be servants of one another, not rulers over one another.

The key idea is that a college graduate is not innately superior to a kid in the second grade. Rather, she is simply further along in her development, and it is only a matter of time before the younger one develops as well. The difference between Jesus and the rest of us, then, is nothing but choice and time, not innate essence.

As the next chapter reveals, a deliberate act of deception underwrote the idea that he is innately superior and fundamentally different. In conjunction with other fabrications and errors, an inferiority complex has been ingrained in Christianity when it was never an original teaching of Jesus.

This paradigm will bellow at you, "How dare you think yourself to be like God. How arrogant!" Those words will trigger the fears that have been deeply ingrained for so long. Yet in your denial of a God of pure, unconditional love and Who You Really Are, your fears of a punishing God and your less-than beliefs are creating an ongoing hell.

There is hardly any middle ground between the broad road of religion and the narrow path of spirituality, and you are always choosing which direction you are traveling. Since the experience of hell is riding on this choice, you would be wise to keep searching for the truth so you can make an informed decision.

3.6.c. Guidance From the Parable of the Talents

So which way to go? Jesus supposedly rendered another big clue in the Parable of the Talents. A talent represented a huge amount of money (something like 20 years of wages for a typical laborer).

Before a master went away on a long journey, he entrusted his three servants with varying amounts of money. The servant with five talents put the money to work and doubled it. The servant with two talents did the same and also doubled up, but the servant with one talent dug a hole in the ground to safeguard it.

The master returned and checked in with his servants. The first two reported their success, and he was thrilled and rewarded them greatly.

The servant with the one talent returned it while explaining that he knew his master was a hard man who harvested where seeds had not been sown, so he was afraid and had hid that talent in the ground. The master chastised him as a wicked and lazy servant who should have at least deposited the money with bankers to earn interest. The master gave the talent to the servant with ten of them and ordered the fearful servant to be cast out into the darkness of weeping and teeth-gnashing (Mt 25:14–30).

As the parable communicates, caving in to your fear of screwing up the life and eternal soul God gave you is what really lands you in hell. As the fearful servant observed, God is interested in abundant growth. Those who fail to comprehend and live that truth will consequently experience the darkness.

All in all, this can be a very scary process for the mainstream Christian, who will probably experience a profound fear of eternal damnation for discounting the Bible and discarding the ancient theology. Those very fears, though, are what stand in the way of your salvation and our collective growth toward heaven on earth.

The only way out is through it. We all have to face down the life-thwarting fears that have buried our souls in the darkness.

3.7. Conclusion

Since the core beliefs of the traditional Western religions are not based on absolute certainty, they must be accepted on faith. Trouble is, these religions have made it a blind faith by repressing their doubts and fears. Self-righteously defending their frozen beliefs as well, they have stonewalled the spiritual growth of their followers.

They believe they are the kings of the divine castle but are actually in one hell of a hole. Escaping this trap requires a no-holds-barred search for the truth about God and the essence of life. This means journeying into the center of the repressed doubt and fear to challenge all assumptions.

The chapter unearthed the fallacious roots of the Judeo-Christian paradigm, yet the process is just beginning. The next chapter delves more deeply into Judaism, the life and teachings of Jesus, and the version of Christianity that came to power and destroyed its competition.

Chapter 4

Judaism, the Messiah and the Hybrid Religion

4.1. Introduction

Paul believed God needs all sin to be atoned for with a blood sacrifice, so Jesus must have been a sacrificial savior (§3.3.e.). Most Christians also believe Jesus was an angelic teacher whose other primary purpose was getting people to love one another. However, the Romans would not have executed a peaceful man who was only teaching folks to be forgiving and kind.

This chapter delves into the most important story of history. It describes how Jesus had a revolutionary purpose that was diametrically opposed to his native religion and spurred its leaders to scheme his execution.

The chapter also shows how the gospel stories were gravely distorted amid intense religious debate, whereupon the Pauline version of Christianity used deliberate deception to cover up its flaws and sell its theology. The chapter then explains why it was a hybrid religion instead of a pure one and how it devolved into a monolithic institution that destroyed its competition.

4.2. The Prophesied Messiah

The Jewish scriptures foretold a special prophet who was described therein as an "Anointed One" (Dn 9:25–26). The Hebrew word for anointed is *mashiah*, so the Hebrew-based term "the Messiah" and the Greek-based term "the Christ" (*Christos*) both mean "the Anointed One." The terms have nothing to do with being a sacrificial savior, which was a later Christian projection upon them.

In any case, the Messianic prophecies set the stage for the drama that unfolded with Jesus of Nazareth. Although Christians would later identify a host of ambiguous passages that they believe had foretold him, only a few of them explicitly informed the ancient Jews of their forthcoming Messiah.

Moses supposedly declared to his people that God would raise up a prophet like him from among them and speak through this prophet. However, any prophet who presumed to speak in God's name anything God had not commanded was to be executed (Dt 18:15–20; see also Acts 3:22–23, 7:37).

Future Jewish leaders would have to ascertain whether a contemporary prophet was indeed representing God and kill him if he was not. Trouble was, if these leaders thought they already knew God through their ancient scriptures, what would happen when a divine spokesman delivered a radically different message?

The other explicit predictions are in the Book of Daniel and will be presented in Chapter 7, which shows how a trio of prophecies from the sixth century BCE foretold the Messiah's arrival with increasing levels of precision. They present an undeniable case that Jesus was the fulfillment of the Messianic promise.

4.3. The Revolutionary Messiah

Although the gospels diverge about the details of Jesus's trial and execution, the heart of their stories is accurate about Judaism's leaders being the initiators and drivers of his elimination. This section explains why they so desperately wanted him dead.

4.3.a. Beware the Alterations and Probable Omissions

We need to bear in mind a forthcoming conclusion. As the earliest stories about Jesus were passed along, they were spun to portray him as an observant Jew.

This means there was jet-washing incongruence between the agenda of presenting him as an observant Jew and the testimony that Judaism's leaders schemed his crucifixion. In other words, if he was really an upstanding adherent of Judaism, why did its leaders get the Romans to drive nails into his flesh?

It also means that if Jesus ever went beyond denouncing the religious authorities to clearly rebuke Judaism, this agenda would have been very prone to not passing along that data. After all, the earliest accounts were propagated by Jews to fellow Jews, and these storytellers would have abruptly lost their audiences with anything that portrayed their attested Messiah as anything less than a champion of their beloved religion.

Nevertheless, this agenda's reconciling apologetics could not fully cleanse the stories of what really happened. Despite the alterations and probable omissions, a clear-enough picture is still discernible because far too much data made it through this jet-washing distortion.

4.3.b. The Messiah's Revolutionary Purpose

Most Jews of the first century CE were expecting their Messiah to be a warrior-king, a Jewish version of Julius Caesar. After all, they had been ruled by a succession of foreign powers for over six centuries. Case in point: They revolted in the early second century CE with the belief their zealous leader, Simon ben Kosiba, was the Messiah.

As reported in John, the masses believed Jesus had come to lead a resurgent kingdom in Jerusalem. He knew they intended to use force to make him a king, so he withdrew to a mountain in solitude (Jn 6:14–15).

He had indeed come to save them, but they were not aware of what they needed saving from. They were making a spiritual error that humanity has made ever since. They believed salvation is to be found in an external change in worldly conditions, not in an internal change of personal conditions.

Jesus's purpose was to awaken them to a higher understanding. To do so, though, he had to unseat their beliefs and was thus essentially pronouncing:

> Friends, Jews, Gentiles, lend me your ears.
> I come to bury Judaism, not to praise it.
> The evil that men do lives after them.
> The good is oft interred with their bones.
> So let it be with Judaism.

Jesus supposedly disclosed his mission to uproot the Judaic paradigm: "Every plant that my heavenly Father has not planted will be pulled up by the roots" (Mt 15:13; §3.2.e.). The Gospel of Thomas—a collection of Jesus's sayings whose original version will later be demonstrated to be earlier and more credible than the Gospel of John—corroborates the statement. As it quotes him, "A grapevine has been planted outside of the father, but being unsound, it will be pulled up by its roots and destroyed" (GTh 40).[1]

Jesus was stirring up a hornets' nest. That is because nothing is more important to religious families than the ancestral identity, culture and tradition of their religion.

He supposedly counseled against thinking that he had come to bring peace to the world. Instead, he had come with a sword to turn men against their fathers, daughters against their mothers, daughters-in-law against their mothers-in-law; a man's enemies would be members of his own family. Anyone who loved a father, mother, son or daughter more than him would not be worthy of him, nor would anyone who did not bear a cross to follow him (Mt 10:34–38; Lk 12:51–53, 14:26; GTh 55, 101).

Jesus thus announced he was here to do battle but not with a physical sword. Rather, he was wielding a metaphysical sword of truth to cut through religious dogma, for the path to salvation entailed breaking from one's culture and religion. Although doing so would mean being ostracized by one's family and community, it would open the door to spiritual truth and unity with God and humanity.

Jesus's message was so objectionable that Judaic leaders were driven to eliminate this threat to their religion. Their problem was how to silence him without violating their law against murder. According to Mark, the Pharisees plotted with the Herodians to kill him early in his ministry (Mk 3:6; see also Mk 11:18; Mt 12:14; Lk 6:11; Jn 11:53).

According to John, the Jewish leaders and crowds wanted to kill him long before the Passion Week (Jn 5:18, 7:1, 7:19, 8:37, 8:40, 8:59). This gospel says Jesus addressed them in a heated exchange. Arguing they were not the children of Abraham or God because they were determined to kill him, he said they were the progeny of a different family: "You belong to your father, the devil, and you want to carry out your father's desires. He was a murderer from the beginning" (Jn 8:44).

4.3.c. Teaching and Living a Greater Spirituality

According to the synoptic gospels, Jesus did not directly confront Judaism until he entered Jerusalem for his final days. Until then, he primarily did so with parables and suggestive challenges. After all, he was addressing folks who were deeply ingrained in a Judaic paradigm and needed to be brought along gradually.

Nevertheless, he taught and lived a greater spirituality that conflicted with the core of Judaism. One of his themes was that the rigors of Jewish law had led people astray from living from their hearts and with an all-encompassing love for humanity. He routinely flouted the law where its indoctrinated version had gotten in the way of more divine behavior.

For instance, Jesus healed a man with a shriveled hand on the Sabbath, which the witnessing Pharisees held to be illegal because it was doing work on that mandated day of rest. He supposedly rebuked their interpretation: "If any of you has a sheep and it falls into a pit on the Sabbath, will you not take hold of it and lift it out? How much more valuable is a person than a sheep! Therefore it is lawful to do good on the Sabbath" (Mt 12:11–12).

[Note: According to the gospels, Jesus rarely violated the scriptural version of the law. As scholar Bart Ehrman points out, "What he violated was the understanding and interpretation of the law by other Jewish leaders of his day, especially the Pharisees, who had developed complex rules to be adopted in order to be sure the law was kept."[2]]

The contemporary version of the law prohibited "a Jew to associate with or visit a Gentile" (Acts 10:28), but Jesus healed a Roman centurion's servant (Mt 8:5–13). He also violated it by associating with the unclean prostitutes and tax collectors, befriending the despised Samaritans, sharing a drink with a Samaritan woman, and picking grain on the Sabbath. As will be seen later, he violated the scriptural law by touching a leper.

More importantly and dangerously, though, he refuted the law's foundation as he promoted a greater spirituality. He did this in four signature areas.

The first had to do with the core belief of God requiring sacrifices to atone for sins. When the Pharisees supposedly confronted him on two different occasions for having broken the law, he did not atone for his sins with a sacrifice. Instead, he twice rebuked the law's foundation by telling them to learn what this prophecy meant: "I desire mercy, not sacrifice" (Mt 9:13, 12:7; §3.3.e.).

Secondly, Jesus rebuked the regulations about clean and unclean foods from the Torah (the first five books of the Jewish scriptures). According to Mark, he preached that nothing from the outside could make a man unclean by entering him. Instead, what came out of a man's heart—such as evil thoughts, adultery, murder, theft and greed—was what made him unclean (Mk 7:14–23). This gospel thus declares, "In saying this, Jesus declared all foods clean" (Mk 7:19).

The third principle of the law that Jesus denounced was its eye-for-an-eye and tooth-for-a-tooth essence. Instead, he supposedly preached nonresistance. If slapped on the right cheek, offer up the left cheek as well. If sued for your shirt, offer your coat too (Mt 5:38–40). Forgive others of their sins, and God would forgive you too (Mt 6:14–15).

The fourth and final staple of Judaism that Jesus renounced was its conception of a vengeful God. As Paul declared, "Do not take revenge, my dear friends, but leave room for God's wrath, for it is written: 'It is mine to avenge; I will repay,' says the Lord" (Rom 12:19, citing Dt 32:35). However, Jesus taught his followers to emulate God by loving everybody. Countering the popular conception of loving your neighbor and hating your enemy, he preached instead to love your enemies and pray for your persecutors (Mt 5:43–45).

One of the over 600 commandments in the Torah was to forsake revenges and grudges against other Jews and instead love those neighbors as yourself (Lv 19:18). Although it did not make God's top ten list for Moses, Jesus made it the second greatest commandment (Mt 22:34–39).

More importantly, he expanded its coverage by expecting the Jews to also love despised folks like the Romans and Samaritans. In doing so, he also invalidated the prohibition against such associations. In a mirror image of his uprooting of the kosher food laws, he inherently taught that it was not the outside-in that made a man unclean (camaraderie with a Gentile) but rather the inside-out (love or hate in a man's heart).

Jesus's teachings and actions that conflicted with Jewish law was the paramount issue. As scholar John Dominic Crossan explains:

> Very often Christians will think what happened between Christianity and Judaism—in so far as those two religions eventually split—was that some Jews believed Jesus was the Messiah, other Jews would not, and so the big split was over the Messiahship of Jesus. That is almost totally wrong. What the split is over is the attitude towards God's law. Can we begin

to decide there are parts of God's law that can be left aside?[3]

Despite the reconciling apologetics in the transmission of the Jesus stories, his revolutionary agenda could not be whitewashed. Further proof can be derived from the reaction of the Pharisees. As historian Max Dimont explains, "They were exceedingly tolerant in their religious views, totally different from the New Testament picture of them as narrow-minded bigots...Whenever two interpretations of the Torah—the Law—were possible, they always chose the more lenient view."[4]

If Jesus's preaching could have fit within the Judaic framework, the New Testament's characterization of the Pharisees was devious propaganda. But if he had been challenging the pillars of Judaism, the gospel reports of close-minded and emotional reactions from otherwise tolerant men are par for the psychological course.

4.3.d. The Paradox of Abolishing and Fulfilling the Law

Jesus had clearly been undercutting Judaism, yet even more evidence attests to this mission. As he was quoted in a gospel that was written for a Jewish audience, "Do not think that I have come to abolish the Law or the Prophets; I have not come to abolish them but to fulfill them" (Mt 5:17). Because the gospel stories were altered to portray him as an observant Jew and the quote does not appear in the other synoptic gospels, it was probably fabricated so that Jewish audience would not categorically reject him.

Yet even if he actually said something to that effect, it still shows he had been carving up the law. For if he had been promoting Judaism and its law instead, such a verse would be bizarre, illogical and never would have been written. But because he was challenging Judaism so severely, he may have felt the need to answer his critics. If he actually made such a statement, he would have been acknowledging the other side of the paradox of abolishing and fulfilling the law. That is, he was unseating all the religious rules so a greater spiritual system could arise.

The difference parallels stages 2 and 4 of spiritual growth (§1.4.). An existence in stage 2 is built upon rules and structure. You discipline yourself to do right because you *have* to, or else you will be punished. It is outside-in living as you strive to meet behavioral standards. Because such behavior is attained by compulsion, it does not feel free and gets tinged with frustration.

In stage 4, you choose the highest path because you *love* to, for it is an expression of your essence. It emanates from a deep transformation that has you living from divine interconnection. It is inside-out living as righteous behavior naturally arises without any contrived effort. It feels joyous and free.

Although Jesus preached against and subverted the law, he may have wanted to prevent his message from being misinterpreted as a license to wreak havoc. After all, he was raising the spiritual bar to not only behave in an upstanding way on the outside but also cleanse the impure thoughts and energies on the inside. In any case, what he supposedly said next is extremely problematic:

> For truly I tell you, until heaven and earth disappear, not the smallest letter, not the least stroke of a pen, will by any means disappear from the Law until everything is accomplished. Therefore anyone who sets aside one of the least of these commands and teaches others accordingly will be called least in the kingdom of heaven, but whoever practices and teaches these commands will be called great in the kingdom of heaven. For I tell you that unless your righteousness surpasses that of the Pharisees and the teachers of the law, you will certainly not enter the kingdom of heaven. (Mt 5:18–20)

This passage creates a flaming contradiction, for Jesus declared radical changes to the Torah and taught others they could break its food restrictions. He even broke it himself by touching a leper. He also routinely broke its derivative laws that were meant to ensure it would not be broken. Therefore, either the passage is grossly erroneous, or Jesus was the world's greatest hypocrite.

4.3.e. Shining the Light on the Judaic Darkness

After Jesus had entered Jerusalem and knew he was living his last days, he spoke more directly against the existing order. In the Parable of the Tenants, the owner of a vineyard (God) sent one servant (prophet) after another to the vineyard for some of his fruit. But the tenants (the Jews) kept beating up the owner's servants and sending them away empty-handed. So the owner sent his son (Jesus), whom the tenants killed with the mistaken belief they would get the son's inheritance. The owner would respond, Jesus ominously warned in the parable's climax, by killing those tenants and giving his vineyard to others (Mk 12:1–12).

He also supposedly unleashed a stinging rebuke of the Pharisees and other teachers of the law. Repeatedly calling them hypocrites and blind guides, his point was that their arrogance, ignorance and obsessive legalism were shutting their followers out from the kingdom of heaven (Mt 23:1–39).

As is now abundantly clear, Jesus was uprooting the misguided tenets of Judaism. The signature event of his revolutionary ministry was the confrontation at the temple. Having already challenged the theological basis of the animal sacrifices, he signed his death warrant by acting out his detestation with this part of the religion.

Because of the gospels' reconciling apologetics, they portray him as an observant Jew who was trying to purify the temple and its holy ritual of slaughtering animals. They imply he was only offended by the marketplace activity around the temple (Mk 11:15–18).

Nothing could be further from the truth. In fact, the animal sellers and money changers were a necessary and legally valid part of temple operations to assist thousands of visiting Jews who had to offer sacrifices and pay the temple tax in acceptable coinage.

When we scrub off the apologetic distortions, a congruent picture of Jesus's ministry remains crystal clear. He was not trying to purify the temple cult as a pious Jew. Rather, he rejected its bloody practice as a paradigm-breaking spiritual warrior. As Crossan explains, "Jesus does not cleanse or purify the Temple. He symbolically destroys the Temple by attacking its fiscal, sacrificial, and cultic necessities."[5]

Because Jesus rocked the Judaic apple cart so violently, its leaders did all they could to eliminate the threat. He entered Jerusalem on a Sunday and was dead by that Friday.

Jesus did not go to the cross because it was God's plan to slaughter an innocent lamb to atone for our sins. If that was really the case, he would have done two things. First, he would have lived as an innocent lamb that was pure as the driven snow. By never once violating or speaking against any aspect of the law, he would have remained sinless so the sacrifice would be effective. Second, he would have preached that to enter heaven, we had to prayerfully accept his atoning sacrifice.

According to the synoptic gospels, however, neither of these things ever happened. Rather, Jesus went to the cross because he had challenged the dogma of a mighty institution and threatened its existence. Instead of considering the possibility it might be wrong about the whole God thing, the institution destroyed the man who had been shining the light upon its darkness.

4.3.f. The Corroboration of Stephen

As further proof of Jesus's revolutionary mission, consider the story of a disciple named Stephen and his trial before the Sanhedrin (Judaism's highest judicial council). Witnesses accused him of perpetually speaking against the law and the temple and saying that Jesus would destroy it and change their customs (Acts 6:8–14).

The Book of Acts calls them false witnesses, but their testimony was true. Jesus had preached against the Torah, repeatedly broken the prevailing laws, and tried to change their customs. According to Matthew, two witnesses testified that Jesus had said he could destroy the temple yet rebuild it in just three days (Mt 26:61). He did not deny the charge. Per the Gospel of Thomas, he

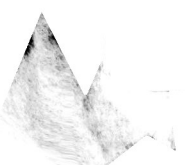

said, "I shall [destroy this] house, and no one will be able to build it" (GTh 71).⁶ Stephen had simply quoted his master.

As for Stephen's trial, the high priest asked him if the charges were true. He replied by delivering an extensive speech about Jewish history that concluded with the building of the temple as a place for God to live. He then abruptly shifted gears into a stinging rebuke of those beliefs. Stephen said that God does not live in any kind of house made by men and then quoted God via an ancient prophet that his throne is heaven, and the earth is but his footstool. After insulting the Sanhedrin for having killed yet another messenger of God (the Messiah), Stephen was immediately stoned to death (Acts 7:1–8:1, citing Is 66:1–2).

Jesus must have taught about a spiritual life without a temple. Otherwise, why in the world would Stephen have ever made such a proclamation that would surely result in his execution?

4.4. Recording the Life and Teachings of Jesus

Fundamentalists imagine the Holy Spirit ensured the gospels were recorded without any errors. That obviously did not happen, so we will now look at the dynamics that impacted their development.

4.4.a. The Canonical Gospels

The synoptic gospels of Matthew, Mark and Luke have extensive similarities in language, content and chronological order. According to Crossan, "a massive scholarly consensus" has agreed that Mark was written first and was leveraged as a source by Matthew and Luke.⁷ About 90 percent of Mark was included in Matthew, and about two-thirds of Mark was included in Luke.

Most scholars believe the authors of Matthew and Luke also sourced from a long-lost document of Jesus's sayings. Referred to as "*Q*" (*Quelle*, German for "source"), this hypothesized document was comprised of roughly 200 verses that explain the commonality of Matthew and Luke that did not come from Mark.

Mark was believed to have been written somewhere between 50 and 70 CE, although the majority of scholars now peg it to c. 70 CE. Matthew had been dated from the 50s to the 70s CE, but now the preferred date is c. 85 CE. Luke had been pegged from 59 to 63 CE or in the 70s or 80s CE, although now the scholastic majority puts it at c. 90 CE. Most scholars believe John was composed at about that time as well.⁸

John is substantially different from the synoptic gospels. For instance, it refutes the story of Jesus being tempted in the desert after his baptism (§3.5.b.) and dates the crucifixion to Nisan 14 versus the synoptic gospels' Nisan 15 (§K.3.f.). It also says Jesus's first public act was confronting the temple marketplace a few years before his death whereas the synoptic gospels make it his last public act just days before his death. Meanwhile, its signature story of Jesus raising Lazarus from the dead goes unmentioned in the synoptic gospels.

Yet the most important difference is how they explain who Jesus was. The synoptic gospels describe him as a divinely blessed man but still fundamentally human, but John portrays him as an incarnation of God. As noted by the ancient scholar Origen, "For none of these [synoptic gospels] plainly declared His Godhead, as John does."[9]

According to the synoptic gospels, Jesus talked very little about himself. Per Mark, he asked his disciples who they thought he was, and Peter replied that he was the Messiah (Mk 8:29). Jesus never proclaimed he was divine, and Mark's only statement about him being the Messiah is in that verse. According to John, however, Jesus declared he was our savior and one and the same as God. Scholar Marcus Borg explains the ramifications:

> When once this fundamental contrast between John and Mark was seen, a great historical "either/or" presented itself to scholars. Either the historical Jesus openly proclaimed his divine identity and saving purpose (John), or he did not (Mark). To put the issue most directly, Jesus could not *consistently* proclaim his identity and at the same time *not* do so. Thus the question became, "Which image of Jesus is more likely to be like the historical Jesus, John's or Mark's?"[10]

4.4.b. Authorship of the Canonical Gospels

Nobody knows who wrote any of the canonical gospels. When Justin Martyr quoted from them in the 150s, he called them the "Memoirs of the Apostles." The earliest testament to them being written by Matthew, Mark, Luke and John was from a bishop named Irenaeus in the 180s.[11]

As will be seen later, the second-century Catholics had a dire need to show their gospels were written by reputable authors. Mark was thus named after John Mark, an acquaintance of Peter (Acts 12:12). Since the author of Luke and Acts disclosed being a traveling companion of Paul, Luke's name was picked from Paul's many friends (Acts 16–28; Col 4:14). Scholars doubt these attributions for a host of reasons.[12]

Matthew was named after the disciple who had previously been a tax collector. This attribution is highly improbable because the author of Matthew sourced so heavily from Mark and Q. If the author really was that disciple, surely we would see some unique personal testimony from his many experiences with Jesus. Moreover, the gospel is like Mark and Luke in having not a single internal reference that it was written by an eyewitness.

John is the only canonical gospel with text that might lead us to believe it was penned by a disciple of Jesus. However, scholars almost universally reject the idea that the disciple John penned it. It will soon be evident that the gospel is an integration of various sources and outright fabrications.

All in all, not a single gospel was written by a man who had interacted with Jesus. Instead, these authors were dependent upon their oral and written sources.

4.4.c. The Distortions of Assimilating Information

Jesus did not publish his sermons, so people who listened to him had to remember what he said. Since 95 to 97 percent of Jews of that era were illiterate, human memory was critical while stories were retold and passed along to others until the composition of source documents like Q and eventually the gospels.

Trouble is, psychologists have learned that our memory is not as reliable as we think.[13] Meanwhile, our consideration of new information is also prone to confirmation bias. This means we tend to embrace information that confirms our cherished conceptions and ignore or rationalize away that which does not.

These are not the only kinds of distortions that occur when assimilating new information, but they are enough to make the point. We obviously hope they had a minimal effect on the collection and transmission of Jesus's teachings, but ignoring their impact is naive and foolish.

4.4.d. The Distortions of Translations and Redactions

Jesus's native language was Aramaic, but the New Testament was written in Greek. So unless your Bible is in Greek, you are reading words that have been through two translations.

Far more troublesome, though, is that the New Testament's oldest surviving manuscript only dates back to the middle of the fourth century. The oldest fragment only goes back to the second century. For most of the New Testament, there is a multiple-century gap from each text's original composition to the manuscripts that are translated into Bibles.

Scholar Bart Ehrman began his career by learning the ancient languages and analyzing this process. He believed the Bible was inerrant when he began his collegiate studies but soon realized he was mistaken. As he summarizes, the manuscripts were significantly distorted amid this roughly three-century gap: "The scribes who produced them inadvertently and/or intentionally changed them in places. All scribes did this. So rather than actually having the inspired words of the autographs (i.e., the originals) of the Bible, what we have are the error-ridden copies of the autographs."[14]

Of greatest concern is the deliberate modification, insertion or deletion of material. For instance, the earliest manuscripts do not include Mark 16:9–20 and John 7:53–8:11, and scholars have proven they were later additions.[15]

Consider the warning at the end of Revelation. Its author wrote that if anybody added any words to or deleted any words from it, God would harshly punish the offender (Rv 22:18–19). The practice of inserting and deleting text must have been prevalent, or else the author would not have felt the need to render his warning.

4.4.e. The Agenda Factor, Part 1: Intense Religious Contention

Jesus's ministry produced an emotionally charged atmosphere of religious contention. There was not only passionate debate among the Jews about the law and his identity but also major ideological divisions within the new world of Christianity. The earliest Christian storytellers and writers were acting within this milieu and trying to advance their camp's agenda. That was, after all, the reason for their stories and reports.

People with agendas naturally remember and subtly spin things in their favor to advance their ideologies. Moreover, personal agendas usually dictate whether or not certain pieces of information are passed along. Quotes or stories that run counter to an ideology will most likely be excluded.

With the gospels, though, the evidence shows the agenda factor went a lot further than just subtle spins and omissions. It sometimes produced deliberate fabrications that scarred the gospels with willful deception.

4.4.f. The Agenda Factor, Part 2: Deliberate Alterations

The gospel authors wanted to prove that Jesus was the fulfillment of the Messianic prophecies. The author of Matthew was especially driven to do so as he primarily addressed a Jewish audience and included many additional instances of such fulfillments.

Did these events actually happen? Unfortunately, we cannot trust the gospel reports about them because we were lied to in at least a few cases. Therefore, what happened with the other alleged fulfillments has to remain in doubt in the absence of corroboration from a reliable source.

Consider Zechariah's prophecy to the Jews: "See, your king comes to you, righteous and victorious, lowly and riding on a donkey, on a colt, the foal of a donkey" (Zec 9:9). In what is called a parallelism in Hebrew poetry, Zechariah had reiterated "donkey" with greater specificity.

Mark and Luke both describe Jesus asking for and then riding into Jerusalem on a colt (a young male donkey). In Matthew, though, Jesus instructed his disciples to return with two animals: "Go to the village ahead of you, and at once you will find a donkey tied there, with her colt by her. Untie them and bring them to me" (Mt 21:2). After quoting the prophecy, the author alluded to Jesus somehow riding into town on both: "They [the disciples] brought the donkey and the colt and placed their cloaks on them for Jesus to sit on" (Mt 21:7).

The author of Matthew (or his source) thus jury-rigged a story to align it with a misunderstood prophecy. A major contradiction thus resulted as to how many animals Jesus was riding on as he entered Jerusalem.

In another case, Matthew quotes the prophet Isaiah: "The virgin will conceive and give birth to a son, and they will call him Immanuel" (Mt 1:23, citing Is 7:14). Trouble is, Isaiah was prophesying about events in the eighth century BCE regarding Ahaz (the king of Judah), who was being attacked by Aram (Syria) and Israel. Isaiah prophesied that while Immanuel was still a boy, both Aram and Israel would be rendered a wasteland (Is 7:16). It was fulfilled as promised in 732 BCE when Assyria sacked both Aram and Israel.

Isaiah neither forecasted the Messiah's birth nor made any kind of reference to a virginal conception. Rather, he simply used the Hebrew word *almah*, which means a virgin who had just been married but had not yet become pregnant, in a matter-of-fact way amid his warning to Ahaz.

Many people argue the story of Jesus's virginal conception was fabricated to compete with preexisting pagan myths. It probably was, but conclusive evidence is lacking. What is obvious, though, is somebody deviously quoted Isaiah to legitimize the story and tally a fulfilled prophecy.

What is also obvious is the Messiah was called Yeshua (Jesus), not Immanuel. In fact, "Immanuel" does not appear anywhere else in the New Testament. Matthew thus makes Isaiah look like a prophetic hack for predicting the name of the Messiah and striking out. Isaiah gets a bum rap for this, for he was not even playing in the Messiah ballpark in that passage, much less swinging at a pitch about his name.

With two blatant cases of this author (or his source) having tweaked or invented material to proclaim a Messianic fulfillment, we know his agenda significantly impacted his work. Ultimately, Matthew cannot be trusted.

As for Mark, its author emphasized more of what Jesus did than what he said. The agenda factor seems to be comparatively reduced with the original version of this gospel. A subsequent addition to it, however, was clearly a product of the agenda factor and will be presented later.

The author of Luke severely manipulated some quotes to defend the Judaic belief about the resurrection of the dead from Jesus's teachings against it (§A.2.a., §A.2.b.). Another case of him defending Judaism from Jesus's ministry will be seen in the next subsection.

Furthermore, consider how he and the author of Matthew tried to explain how Jesus was raised in Nazareth (about 60 miles north of Jerusalem) yet had been born in Bethlehem (about five miles south of Jerusalem) as prophesied by Micah (Mi 5:2). Their accounts are hopelessly incongruent, which proves at least one is pure fiction.

Per Luke, Joseph and Mary were living in Nazareth but had to travel to Bethlehem because of an imperial decree for a global census. Jesus was then born in a manger. After waiting out a purification period of 40 days to satisfy the law, Joseph and Mary went to Jerusalem to consecrate their baby before returning home to Nazareth to raise him (Lk 2:1–40). According to this gospel, Jesus spent no more than a few months in Bethlehem and never journeyed to Egypt.

Per Matthew, Joseph and Mary were living in Bethlehem when Jesus was born. The better part of two years passed before they fled to Egypt to avoid Herod's slaughter of male infants. Upon returning after Herod's death, they were warned in a dream not to return to Bethlehem and instead settled in Nazareth (Mt 2:1–23). According to this gospel, Joseph and Mary were not living in Nazareth before Jesus was born, there was no global census that forced them into traveling to Bethlehem and lodging in a barn outside of an inn, and they only settled in Nazareth upon returning from Egypt.

As Crossan explains, the tale in Matthew was intended to parallel the tale of Moses, who was also the target of a king's decree to massacre newborns but survived and became the Israelites' great leader. The irony of the tale is Jesus had to flee *to* Egypt, not from it.[16]

Doing whatever it took to rack up fulfilled prophecies, the author of Matthew tallied another one with "Out of Egypt I called my son" (Mt 2:15). Yet, like his misappropriation of Isaiah, he failed to recognize or admit that Hosea was not prophesying about the Messiah. Rather, Hosea was quoting God in talking about his chosen people: "When Israel was a child, I loved him, and out of Egypt I called my son" (Hos 11:1).

All in all, the agenda factor produced significant distortions and inventions in Matthew and Luke. The author of John, though, took this dynamic to a stratospheric level. Because his agenda's impact was so profound and pervasive, it will be more thoroughly explained later.

4.4.g. The Agenda Factor, Part 3: Was Jesus an Observant Jew?

Remember the passage in Matthew that branded Jesus as a hypocrite with his denunciation of anyone who breaks even the least of the commandments or teaches others to do the same (§4.3.d.)? It most likely came from the agenda of portraying him as an observant Jew.

Such manipulations apparently occurred as the earliest oral traditions about him were propagated among his fellow Jews. After all, a pro-Jesus storyteller would have lost his audience at hello if he characterized the Nazarene rabbi as an enemy of Judaism.

Since this dynamic impacted the transmission of the Jesus stories from the outset, it also appears in the other synoptic gospels. Crossan untangles such literary knots by discerning three different levels in the gospel stories: what actually happened (the original level), what got told about it (the transmissional level), and what was finally written about it (the redactional level). A good example is in Mark's story of Jesus healing a leper:

> A man with leprosy came to him and begged him on his knees, "If you are willing, you can make me clean."
>
> Jesus was indignant. He reached out his hand and touched the man. "I am willing," he said. "Be clean!" Immediately the leprosy left him and he was cleansed.
>
> Jesus sent him away at once with a strong warning: "See that you don't tell this to anyone. But go, show yourself to the priest and offer the sacrifices that Moses commanded for your cleansing, as a testimony to them." (Mk 1:40–44)

At the heart of the story (what actually happened), Jesus violated the scriptural law by touching the leper (Lv 5:3). Since he also demanded legal conformity from the leper, he was either an arrogant hypocrite who felt he was above the law, or the story was corrupted. In all likelihood, Jesus had directly challenged the religious authorities, but the storytellers had tried to gloss it over.

As Crossan explains, "What we see at the *transmissional* level is intense apologetics seeking to bring Jesus into line with traditional biblical and legal practice—to show him, in terms of purity regulations, as an observant Jew."[17] This effect is particularly evident in the passage's final paragraph, wherein the storyteller depicted Jesus as obedient to priestly authority by sending the leper away to satisfy the law with sacrifices.

It is also evident in the original words of the second paragraph, as the older (more original) manuscripts of Mark say Jesus was "filled with anger." Most Bibles, though, go with the downstream manuscripts and report that Jesus was "filled with compassion" (including the previous version of the NIV). However, a strong scholarly case exists that scribes changed the text from anger to compassion (which is why the NIV switched to "Jesus was indignant").[18] The transmitting storyteller made Jesus out to be upset because an observant Jew would have been offended at the leper's disregard for the law.

Trouble is, being offended and upset is incongruent with Jesus's loving character, his track record of preaching against the law and breaking its prevailing codes (for which he seemed to derive satisfaction in agitating the legal authorities, not being agitated himself as an upholder of the law), and most importantly, his healing action that broke the law to begin with. In all likelihood, then, the anger with the leper never actually happened but rather was introduced at the transmissional level.

When downstream scribes changed the manuscripts from anger to compassion, they did so for the wrong reason of trying to make Jesus look more divine. Yet they ultimately got it right, for the anger had been spun into the story many decades prior by the agenda factor.

As for the early storytellers, they wanted to believe Jesus had been a pious Jew and thereby engendered some major contradictions. As Crossan reiterates, "At the second or transmissional level, the story was adapted to make Jesus legally observant, something that creates a war of interpretation within the narrative itself."[19]

The third and final level occurred when Mark was written after decades of religious strife and by an author who had more affinity with a defiant Jesus. After Jesus told the leper to make his sacrifices, the author added "as a testimony to them." The underlying message was the temple authorities should take heed of the real divine authority. Crossan comments about the author's intention, "Jesus is enjoining the visit to the Temple not as legal observance but as confrontational witness."[20]

In sum, the story's transmitters glossed and apologized for the original event, but the truth about Jesus's radical challenge to Judaism could not be hidden. As Crossan notes, "No amount of theological apologetics at the second level…can ever obliterate the first or original level in which Jesus heals by refusing to accept traditional and official sanctions against the diseased person."[21]

By the way, the author of Luke delivered a much different version of the story so Jesus could be an observant Jew throughout. Ten men with leprosy called out from a distance for Jesus to heal them, he told them to show themselves to the priests, and they were healed as they went (Lk 17:11–19).

It is doubtful the earliest storytellers deliberately modified the Jesus stories to smooth over his conflict with Judaism. Instead, they most likely did so unconsciously without really noticing the contradictions they were creating.

Their deeply entrenched worldview kept them from seeing the forest for the trees. They were unable to comprehend that Jesus had been uprooting their religion, which was the last thing on earth any Jew could have imagined their Messiah had been sent to do. Challenging religious leaders who were doing wrong in the eyes of God? No problem there. Going after the law and Judaism itself? Utterly unthinkable.

Blinded by their paradigm, these folks were unable to see beyond the events and teachings to read the writing on the wall. So they naturally and unconsciously tweaked their transmission of the Jesus material to harmonize it with their sacred worldview.

That said, the *why* is speculative and unimportant. What really matters is observing *what* those processes did to the gospels and *how* we should therefore read them, which is with the awareness that their stories about Jesus's life and teachings were compromised by an array of omissions, distortions and inventions.

4.4.h. The Agenda Factor, Part 4: Blame for the Crucifixion

The agenda factor disfigured the gospels, but some scholars have overcompensated for it when discerning the historical truth. Consider the question of who was to blame for the crucifixion. The Romans executed Jesus, but who really wanted him dead and pressed for this result?

Until 1965, the Catholic Church had blamed the Jews and deemed them all guilty. Because antisemitism was the root cause of the Holocaust, the question still hits a very sensitive nerve.

Scholars are thus naturally inclined to devalue the gospels on this matter to help heal the cultural wound. Some have argued the Romans were the primary movers behind the prosecution of Jesus, but the gospel authors had an ax to grind with the Jews who were not converting and falsely depicted Pontius Pilate (the Roman governor who presided over Judaea from 26 to 36 CE) so their stories could blame the Jews.[22]

This hypothesis draws heavily from a report by Philo of Alexandria that Pilate was a man of "inflexible, stubborn, and cruel disposition."[23] Philo's assessment was later supported by Josephus.

The first problem is that those ancient Jewish writers also had big agendas. As scholar Helen Bond describes, Philo's work was "highly polemical in nature," and he used "all the drama and rhetoric at his disposal to cast Pilate in a particularly brutal light."[24] According to historian Jona Lendering, Josephus's "portrait of Pilate is little short of a character assassination" to support his thesis.[25]

Even if Pilate was stubborn and cruel, the second problem is assuming his character always dictated his behavior. As a collegiate textbook on psychology reports, "People exhibit far less consistency across situations than had been widely assumed...*both* the person and the situation are important determinants of behavior."[26]

As for Pilate's situation, the third problem pertains to the political climate of the Roman Empire. For the first five years or so that he presided over Judaea, his stern posture was both possible and enabled because the second most powerful man in the empire, L. Aelius Sejanus, was staunchly antisemitic. Sejanus appointed Pilate to his position in 26 CE but was executed for a conspiracy in October of 31 CE. The emperor Tiberius subsequently ordered more hospitable treatment of the Jews throughout the empire.

Pilate thereafter locked horns with the Jews over a contentious religious issue and refused to back down. The regional Jewish kings (tetrarchs) appealed to Tiberius in Rome, who rebuked Pilate and ordered him to surrender his position. The date of the event is unknown, but scholars are confident it came after Sejanus's execution and was probably in the spring of 32 CE.[27]

As scholars have confidently dated the crucifixion to 33 CE (§K.3.), Pilate was skating on thin political ice when the Jesus dilemma arose. By the way, his precarious position is further demonstrated by Rome ending his rule over Palestine in 36 CE for attacking a Samaritan religious procession he felt was a political rally.

So even if Pilate was stubborn and cruel, he most likely behaved as the gospels reported. Having lost his powerful ally in Rome, he needed to appease the Jewish authorities with the Jesus controversy, or else they would have surely gone over his head again to a sympathetic emperor. Moreover, Jesus's amazing presence may have touched the heart of a man who was politically vulnerable and feeling the heat of a combustible situation.

Jesus had shown no interest in a violent uprising and never condemned the Roman Empire. The only rationale Pilate possibly had for prosecuting him was for the disturbance at the temple. Yet if the Romans had felt it crossed their line of public order, surely they would have immediately arrested him instead of letting over three days pass.

All four gospels testify that Jewish authorities wanted to kill Jesus long before he entered Jerusalem (§4.3.b.). His symbolic attack against the temple was a public slap in the face to the Sadducees and Sanhedrin, and their desire to kill him surely went through the roof. Pilate had a serious problem, then, because his collaborating religious rulers were hopping mad. Their authority was being undermined, and Jesus was drawing widespread support.

Pilate surely feared that if he did not side with the Jewish authorities, he would jeopardize their working relationship and might lose his job if they went over his head again to the emperor. He would also spur political instability that might devolve into a revolt. Caught in a no-win situation, no wonder he did not want to antagonize either the Jewish authorities or the masses.

The details of the gospel accounts are wide open for critical debate. Yet the heart of their stories is congruent with the political calculus of the day. The Sanhedrin pressured Pilate to eliminate Jesus, and Pilate tried to avoid getting in the middle of the Judaic squabble.

The gospels also align with the nature of dark institutions. It makes complete sense that the Jewish institution pressed for the execution of a man who was threatening its existence. After all, the Christian institution did the very same thing a thousand years later but on exponentially more occasions and for so much less. That is, the Church got the secular authorities to execute thousands of docile people who simply held nonconforming beliefs.

Consider as well the psychology of the Sadducees. Though small in numbers, they were the primary wielders of Jewish power. Theirs was the sect of the aristocrats, the wealthy and the priests, and they ruled the Sanhedrin. These ultraconservatives fought to preserve the status quo and their beloved temple cult. As Dimont explains, "Their ritual was rigid and fixed, permitting little change, hewing to the letter of the law, not its spirit."[28] No wonder they wielded their power with Pilate to eliminate the thorn of change that was twisting around in their side.

All in all, the hypothesis that the Romans were the primary drivers of Jesus's prosecution requires the rejection of not only a lot of scriptural material but also a chain of motivations and events that are politically and metaphysically congruent. Lacking supportive evidence as well, it should therefore be dismissed.

We can confidently accept the core of the trial and crucifixion accounts as historical truth, but they are far from inerrant. As scholar Paul Winter observes, "Seldom is there in the Gospels such a variety of diverging and repeatedly conflicting accounts of the same events as in the narratives describing the arrest, trial, crucifixion and resurrection of Jesus."[29] Something is surely amiss when Mark and Matthew describe two trials, Luke describes three, and John describes but one and a half.

Moreover, consider how the fourth gospel tries to explain why Jesus had been executed by the Romans when Jewish leaders were the ones who really wanted him dead. Per John, Pilate told the Jewish leaders to judge Jesus by their own law, but they objected that they were not allowed to execute anybody (Jn 18:31). This occurred to fulfill a previous Jesus quote that foretold a crucifixion (Jn 12:32–33, 18:32).

Trouble is, the gospel's claim that the Jewish authorities could not execute somebody at the time of Jesus is false. Case in point: They had no issues with prosecuting and stoning Stephen (§4.3.f.). As scholar Alan Watson notes, "A large proportion of scholars believe on balance that the Sanhedrin had the power to put Jews to death."[30] The evidence contradicting this verse in John is "overwhelming."[31] Furthermore, the Jesus prediction about crucifixion implies the existence of a more probable alternative, which was being stoned to death by the Sanhedrin.

In sum, this gospel was mistaken because it was written over two decades after the revolt of 66–73 CE. Its author was clearly ignorant of the ruling realities of 33 CE that preceded the Roman crackdown of his era.

So why did the Sanhedrin not execute Jesus? Some of the judges may have been troubled by flaws in their proceedings, for the first trial in the middle of the night was illegal. This would have prevented a conviction at the mandatory second meeting on the next day. The Sanhedrin may have also feared the repercussions from the masses.[32]

Whether or not some judges declined to convict because of the illegal process, the fear of public repercussions was surely the main driver of the Sanhedrin's behavior. It is why they first arrested and tried Jesus in the middle of the night. As reported in Mark, the Jewish authorities were looking for a way to arrest and kill Jesus but feared doing so during the Passover because the people might riot (Mk 14:1–2).

These considerations produced a political game of hot potato. The Sanhedrin desperately wanted the execution but did not want to pay the price for stoning Jesus to death, so they fired it over to Pilate with all the pressuring heat they could put on it.

Pilate was backed into a corner but escaped his political bind with a cunning stratagem. Letting the crowd choose the pardoning of Jesus or Barabbas would either get himself off the hook with the Sanhedrin (if the crowd chose Jesus) or deflect a potential backlash (if the crowd chose Barabbas).

[Note: As Watson argues, it is very unlikely Pilate's offer to pardon a dangerous man was a regular custom as the gospels state.[33] Moreover, the synoptic gospels make it Pilate's custom while John makes it a Jewish custom. Yet given Pilate's precarious situation, it makes sense that he created the custom to win favor with the masses and extricate himself from the quagmire.]

When the masses chose the release of Barabbas, they relieved Pilate of the blame for the crucifixion as they shouldered the load. He wisely symbolized this reality to them by washing his hands of the mess even though he was the one who condemned Jesus to the cross, and he came out of the dilemma smelling like a rose.

Political insiders know the game they play is blood sport, and the bottom line is this particular match ended with an ironic contradiction. A nonviolent man who was, as Winter concedes, "devoid of revolutionary ambitions" was executed under the Roman charge of insurrection (Mk 15:26).[34]

Our concern at this point, though, is how it got reported in the Christian papers. As decades passed amid heated religious conflict, the gospel authors came down more heavily on the Jews. As Winter observes, "The stern Pilate grows more mellow from Gospel to Gospel…The more removed from history, the more sympathetic a character he becomes."[35]

Consider as well Pilate's stratagem of pardoning either Jesus or Barabbas. Mark reports "the crowd" (stirred up by the chief priests) turned against Jesus when Pilate attempted to release him instead of Barabbas (Mk 15:6–15). Matthew concurs but includes this historically lethal statement: "All the people answered, 'His blood is on us and on our children!'" (Mt 27:15–26). Finally, John pinned the blame on an entire race by reporting that "the Jews" repeatedly called for the execution of Jesus (Jn 18:28–19:16).

In conclusion, the essence of the trial and crucifixion accounts are true, but their details are unreliable. These reports were rendered many decades after the fact, and the agenda factor warped them against "the Jews."

Trouble was, these caustic words were extremely combustible in Christian psyches. Instead of faulting the Sanhedrin of 33 CE for behaving as a dark institution and Pilate for selling out one man's justice to protect his power, Christian leaders believed their Bibles and blamed an entire race for killing Jesus. This was the primary source of almost two thousand years of antisemitism, and this destructive undercurrent eventually crested and crashed down upon humanity in the 20th century.

4.5. The Heated Debate Among the Christians

The agenda factor had its biggest impact in John. This section explains how the battle for Christian supremacy was the driving force behind that gospel and how it also marred a downstream version of Mark.

4.5.a. Paul Conflicts With the Nazarene Jews

Three major branches of Christianity developed after Jesus was crucified. The first recognized him as the Messiah but maintained strong adherence to Judaic laws and customs. These Christians were known as the Nazarene Jews and were led by James (the brother of Jesus) and Peter. They resonated most strongly with indigenous Jews who only spoke Aramaic.

Meanwhile, there were other Jews in this community who had lived abroad and were either Greek-speaking or bilingual. They were allowed to form a squad of seven apostles, the most prominent of them being Stephen (Acts 6:1–7). Not as entrenched in the law, their more radical understanding of Jesus's teachings got them into serious trouble (§4.3.f.). After Stephen's stoning, the Jewish authorities led a "great persecution" against the Grecian Jews of the Messianic community and drove them out of Jerusalem (Acts 8:1–3). James, Peter and the Nazarene Jews, however, were allowed to remain.

A zealous Jew named Saul was journeying to Damascus to advance the persecution when he had a supernatural conversion. Thereafter known as Paul, he reconciled with the Nazarene Jews and preached to Jewish communities throughout the eastern Mediterranean. Having been rejected on a regular basis, he and Peter started preaching to the Gentiles. The issue quickly arose as to whether the converting Gentiles needed to follow the law by undertaking circumcision and eating kosher foods. A tenuous compromise was reached in Jerusalem in about 49 or 50 CE (Acts 15:1–29).

Paul eventually became convinced that Jesus had been a divine sacrifice to cleanse all believers of their sins. Therefore, adherence to Jewish laws and customs was ultimately irrelevant. Whether or not he was the first to posit the human-sacrifice theology, he became the champion of this branch of Christianity.

His ideology created an irreconcilable conflict with James and the Nazarene Jews while Peter was caught in the middle. Although Peter previously had a supernatural experience wherein God renounced the law's requirement of eating only kosher foods and its prohibition against associating with Gentiles (Acts 10:9–29), he maintained his Jewish tradition instead of embracing his revelation and was no longer eating with the Gentiles.

This did not sit well with Paul. As he explained, he confronted Peter because Peter was clearly wrong (Gal 2:11). Paul called him out on his hypocrisy and explained the new ideology: "We who are Jews by birth and not sinful Gentiles know that a person is not justified by the works of the law, but by faith in Jesus Christ" (Gal 2:15–16; see also Rom 3:28).

Paul disclosed his spat with Peter to the churches in Galatia because this issue was creating dissension therein. He also expressed astonishment that these folks were deserting him and embracing a different gospel. He wanted them to have nothing to do with it or anything else (Gal 1:6–7). As he wrote, "Even if we or an angel from heaven should preach a gospel other than the one we preached to you, let them be under God's curse!" (Gal 1:8).

[Note: Be aware of Paul's religious pride. Even if "an angel from heaven" were to reveal that his sermons had not represented divine truth, he would reject the path of growing to better understand God. Rather, he would want the Galatians to condemn God's angel so he would be right in what he had previously preached.]

Paul's "faith alone saves" theology was opposed by James. Faith without any accompanying deeds, Jesus's brother supposedly wrote, is dead (Jas 2:14–17). A person was justified by both his faith and his deeds (Jas 2:24).

Another New Testament letter also disagrees with Paul. The author of 1 John—long presumed to be the disciple John—wrote that to truly know Jesus, we have to do what he had commanded and walk as he did (1 Jn 2:3–6).

Paul's theology is even contradicted by a gospel. As Jesus is quoted in Matthew, observing every aspect of the law is required for entering the kingdom of heaven (§4.3.d.).

After James was martyred in 62 CE, the Nazarene Jews began receding. The Romans drove them out of Jerusalem after the Jewish revolt of 66–73 CE, but they persisted into the third century in various locations throughout the Middle East with Matthew as their gospel. Scholar Norbert Brox explains, "They observed the Law (at least in part), revered Moses as a prophet, and hated and repudiated Paul as a 'traitor' who wanted to 'abolish' the Law."[36]

4.5.b. Doctrine vs. Gnosis

The third major Christian movement of the first century was Gnosticism. The Greek language differentiates between intellectual and experiential knowledge, and gnosis means the latter. The Gnostics perceived Jesus's primary teaching to be that experiential knowledge of the mysteries of life was the key to salvation (Jn 8:31–32; §1.2.a.).

Gnosticism fused elements of various religious and philosophical traditions. Scholars favor the view that it was a subset of broader movements that predated Christianity. Moreover, it may have been most prevalent amid the

Pauline churches as inner circles of the spiritually elite (people who felt they had more enlightened and secret insights into the scriptures and sacraments).

Whereas the Pauline churches glorified the teachings of their gospels and letters, Gnostics prioritized their personal experiences of truth-seeking. Whereas the Pauline churches were gravitating toward common doctrine and institutional authority, Gnostics had varying systems of belief, numerous sects and no organizing authority. Whereas the clergy of the Pauline churches eventually inserted themselves as a mediating hierarchy between the masses and God, Gnostics typically believed all were equal and had the same avenue to God.

The beliefs of the widely varying Gnostic sects are not important. What matters is observing that Jesus's teachings were originally grasped and promulgated in radically different ways.

4.5.c. The Hypocrisy of Denouncing Gnosticism

In a letter to the church in Corinth, Paul addressed a congregation that had been listening to other teachers of Christianity. Having heard they were better orators than him and concerned the Corinthians would be led astray, he felt the need to defend his status as the true teacher of Christianity (2 Cor 11:1–15). He thus alluded to how he had gained his knowledge. Fourteen years prior, he wrote, he had journeyed into the spiritual realm. He did not know if he was in or out of his body, but he learned "surpassingly great revelations" (2 Cor 12:2–7).

Trouble was, Paul's movement was hypocritically denouncing the Gnostics for coming to such knowledge via the same method of profound personal experience. Was his knowledge more divinely authoritative than what the Gnostics had learned from their own experiences? Than what anybody else has reported in modern times from a supernatural encounter or interaction with an otherworldly source?

By the way, Paul and his contemporaries were wrong about the resurrection of the dead and Christ's second coming happening within their era (§9.3.c.). Therefore, his theology is definitely not omniscient and should be scrutinized all the more by any diligent truth-seeker.

4.5.d. Opposing and Crushing the Heretics

Paul and his colleagues successfully established their churches across the Roman Empire. Those churches soon claimed to represent the orthodox (right/correct) version of Christianity, but theirs was just one of many claiming to be the best. Ehrman therefore calls it the "proto-orthodox" movement ("proto" means the first or earliest form of something), for it was just a popular version of Christianity until the Roman Empire decreed it to be the only acceptable one, whereupon it had the legal status of orthodox.[37]

The proto-orthodox (Pauline) churches were flourishing as well as variants of the movement that branched off in the second century. Gnosticism was also thriving. These diverse groups all felt they were the truest version of Christianity and fervently argued their cases about having a superior ideology. As the proto-orthodox movement fought these battles, it labeled the other Christians who did not embrace its ideology as heretics.

In the second century, the proto-orthodox churches gravitated to authoritative hierarchies that were headed by bishops. Some bishops began referring to these like-minded churches as the "Catholic" Church. From a Greek word meaning "universal" or "whole," the term was used to convey the monolithic and all-encompassing nature of this loose federation of churches and to claim it was the correct version of Christianity.

Meanwhile, a host of second- and early-third-century Catholic authors like Justin Martyr, Irenaeus, Tertullian and Hippolytus wrote stinging polemics against the Gnostics, Marcionites, Valentinians and other Christian sects. All the while all Christians were subject to waves of local persecution. It ramped up dramatically in the latter half of the third century when the state formally enacted laws against Christianity.

Everything changed, though, when Constantine (312–337) emerged victorious from a devastating civil war to become the ruler of the Roman Empire. To help gain legitimacy and unify the empire, he sanctioned the Catholic version of Christianity. The new emperor was a brilliant politician who had the pagans thinking his supreme god was Apollo and the Christians thinking it was their holy trinity (§G.3.e.).

It was a match made in authoritative heaven. The emperor catapulted the Catholic Church from the empire's outhouse to its penthouse. In return, the bishops overlooked his pagan sympathies and murderous behavior, praised him like a saint, and gave him the allegiance of a well-organized and obedient constituency.

The emperor's only condition was another dream come true for the bishops. Constantine wanted to quell the violent debates that had been transpiring within Catholicism, which was the impetus for the Council of Nicaea in 325. Desiring an immediate end to theological dissension so peace and conformity would help unite a beleaguered empire, he allowed the bishops to create edicts and laws to achieve these aims. The bishops were all too happy to wield the awesome power of the Roman Empire against their Christian counterparts. They had Constantine enact decrees that obliterated all other variants of Christianity (§G.3.b.).

Catholicism thus won the battle for Christian orthodoxy, not by having proven that it was better aligned with truth but because it had absolute power at its disposal. Its first marriage to a totalitarian government also came with a special gift that would keep on giving: the power to cement its version of

Christian history and repress or destroy all dissenting works.

4.5.e. Archaeology Sheds New Light on the Ancient Debate

It used to be the only information scholars could gather about Gnosticism was from what its Catholic opponents had written about it. However, archaeologists found a few pieces of Gnostic literature in the 19th century and then struck gold in 1945 with a collection of Gnostic texts near the Egyptian town of Nag Hammadi.

Rendered in Coptic (an Egyptian language), 52 texts were buried in a jar between 350 and 400, apparently to prevent destruction by the Roman Catholic Church. Scholars believe the material was originally written in Greek. The texts are widely divergent in their origins and viewpoints. Written in different times and places by different authors, they did not come from the same Gnostic movement.

These texts should not be imbibed as newfound gospels. Just as the early Church fathers attributed a couple of their gospels to Jesus's disciples, so it was with Gnosticism. Far more importantly, almost all the texts were composed no earlier than the second century.

When it comes to ascertaining facts about the historical Jesus, most of them should be severely discounted or ignored. Yet the collection does contain one extremely valuable exception: the Gospel of Thomas. Written in the first century, it articulates the heart of Gnosticism (§4.5.b.) while differing substantially from the theology of the Nag Hammadi library.

4.5.f. The Gospel of Thomas Sheds New Light on John

The Gospel of Thomas presents 114 sayings attributed to Jesus. Although it claims to have been authored by the disciple Thomas, scholars view it as the work of one or more compilers who collected and documented traditional sayings.

In contrast with the canonical gospels and their abundance of narrative accounts, Thomas does not have even a trace of one. Hence, it is rather improbable that Thomas was sourced from a canonical gospel. Meanwhile, scholar Helmut Koester notes that "a large number" of the sayings in Thomas have parallels with the synoptic gospels and some "especially striking" parallels with John. He states:

> If one considers the form and wording of the individual sayings in comparison with the form in which they are preserved in the New Testament, *The Gospel of Thomas* almost always appears to have preserved a more original form of the traditional saying (in a few instances, where this is not the case, the Coptic translation seems to have been influenced by the translator's

knowledge of the New Testament gospels), or presents versions which are independently based on more original forms. More original and shorter forms are especially evident in the parables of Thomas.[38]

Scholars who have scrutinized the Gospel of Thomas now perceive John much differently. As scholar Elaine Pagels explains, "Many scholars are now convinced" that John was written amid "an intense debate over who Jesus was—or is."[39]

John and Thomas agree about many teachings that break sharply from the synoptic gospels, and scholars who first compared them were surprised by their similarities. For instance, while the synoptic gospels identify Jesus as God's human servant, both John and Thomas say he was God's own light in human form. In contrast with the synoptic idea that the kingdom of God would come in the future, both John and Thomas convey it was already present as a contiguous spiritual reality.

However, John and Thomas have crucial differences that have shed new light on the genesis of John. According to Thomas's Jesus, the light of God was not just in him but deep within us all, and we should seek for and know God experientially as we grow to be like him. The author of John, though, was vehemently opposed. Only Jesus was innately divine, and only a belief in him could deliver eternal life and save us from God's wrath.

Pagels thus comments, "I have now come to see that John's gospel was written in the heat of controversy, to defend certain views of Jesus and to oppose others." The outcome would have massive ramifications for the future of Christianity, as John "helped provide a foundation for a unified church, which Thomas, with its emphasis on each person's search for God, did not."[40]

Perhaps the most revealing evidence that John was written amid intense Christian debate are its peculiar defamations of the disciples Thomas and Peter. As the synoptic gospels say nothing of the sort, the chances of them being actual events are miniscule. Rather, the author of John apparently spun some yarns to accentuate his gospel's theology and discredit the gospels associated with Thomas and Peter.

4.5.g. "John" Disparages Thomas

Had the synoptic gospels not included Thomas in their lists of the disciples, he would have been completely anonymous. In other words, Thomas is not a character in any of the stories told in Matthew, Mark and Luke. In John, though, he was resurrected from obscurity to figure prominently in a trilogy of tales.

The author of John began his characterization of Thomas when Jesus announced plans to travel to Bethany and heal Lazarus. The disciples questioned their master's decision because of previous threats on his life while in the area. Jesus indicated he would be fine and twice stated he was going forward with his plan (Jn 11:1–15). Yet Thomas said to the other disciples, "Let us also go, that we may die with him" (Jn 11:16).

Some interpreters find devotion and courage in Thomas, but the author implied sarcastic pessimism and a negative attitude. The author's intent is clear from the placement of the Thomas quote immediately after Jesus had said that all would be well. The quote portrayed this disciple as having no trust in Jesus.

The author then showed in his second Thomas tale that the disciple had no knowledge of the Lord either. This effort began with Jesus telling his disciples that they knew the way to where he was going, which implied he had already imparted that knowledge (Jn 14:4). Thomas declared his ignorance, though, by saying they did not know where Jesus was going or the way there (Jn 14:5). The author thus mocked Gnosticism by having its figurehead say he knew nothing about such an important matter.

The author then had Jesus say, "I am the way and the truth and the life. No one comes to the Father except through me" (Jn 14:6). The author thus trumpeted the proto-orthodox theology, which saw Jesus as superior, of a vastly different essence and a required intermediary between us and God. It also rebuked the Gnostic theology that we have the same divine essence and can reunite with God through our own experiential paths. The author capped his snippet with Jesus chiding Thomas that if Thomas really knew him, Thomas would also know his Father (Jn 14:7).

The author was clearly undercutting the Gospel of Thomas and Gnosticism, and he saved his best for last. The final tale of his Thomas-bashing trilogy was also the final story in his gospel (because the 21st chapter of John was a later addition).[41] He once again denounced the path of gnosis and reiterated his gospel's thesis.

To deliver his grand finale, which was built upon the disciples' purported encounter with the risen Jesus, he deviated again from the synoptic gospels (§K.3.f.). His defamation made a lasting impression with the popular phrase "doubting Thomas." Before looking at it, though, let us consider how the synoptic gospels tell the story.

In Luke, the resurrected Jesus appeared to two of his followers. The two told the eleven remaining disciples, and they all believed the duo's report. As the disciples were hashing over the story, Jesus again appeared and offered them all the chance to touch his body to see he was not a ghost (Lk 24:13–43). So according to Luke, the story of doubting Thomas was a fabrication because none of the disciples doubted the duo's report.

Mark's version appears in text that is not in the earliest manuscripts and has been proven to be a later addition (§4.4.d.). It also says two followers met the risen Jesus, but none of the eleven disciples believed the duo's report. Jesus then appeared and rebuked them for refusing to believe that he had been seen (Mk 16:14). So according to this enhanced gospel, the story of Thomas being the only doubter was a fabrication because they all doubted.

In Matthew, Jesus appeared to all eleven disciples. This gospel splits the difference, though, by saying that they worshiped him, but some doubted (Mt 28:17). So according to Matthew, the story of Thomas being the only doubter was a fabrication because there were other doubters.

In John, the resurrected Jesus appeared to a gathering of every disciple except Thomas. Jesus gifted the ten disciples with the Holy Spirit and the power to forgive or not forgive sins (Jn 20:19–24). Thomas was thus left behind as an impotent and inferior evangelist.

The author of John then delivered his crowning blow. When Thomas was told what he had missed, he garnered his famous nickname by saying that unless he could put his finger in the nail holes in Jesus's hand and his hand into Jesus's side (where it had been gouged by a spear), he would not believe the report (Jn 20:25). Jesus appeared a week later to convince this gospel's lone skeptic to believe.

As scholar Gregory Riley explains, there was an intense debate within early Christianity as to whether Jesus was physically resurrected (body and all) or not.[42] The proto-orthodox Christians believed so while the Gnostics did not.

The author of Luke "proved" the proto-orthodox belief with Jesus granting his disciples the opportunity to touch his risen body to show them he was not just a ghost. But Luke is the only synoptic gospel with this tactile option, and it further embodied the point by having Jesus eat some broiled fish (Lk 24:39–43).

The author of John reinforced the belief by introducing the disgusting graphic of Jesus inviting Thomas to probe his mortal wounds (Jn 20:27). The author used Thomas to make his point of a full-body resurrection while defaming the Gnostic figurehead. Moreover, the author once again put Jesus on a divine pedestal above humanity by having Thomas exclaim to Jesus, "My Lord and my God!" (Jn 20:28).

Most importantly, the author reiterated his thesis while denouncing the heart of Gnosticism. He had Jesus belittle Thomas's acceptance by telling him, "Because you have seen me, you have believed; blessed are those who have not seen and yet have believed" (Jn 20:29).

In conclusion, the Gospel of Thomas already existed when John was penned during a time of intense debate between Christian movements. Otherwise, there is no way to explain why the author of John disparaged the disciple so severely despite no such reports in the earlier gospels. Indeed, this author exercised more creative liberties than the typical Christian could have ever possibly imagined.

[Note: In 1993, an organization of over 200 renowned scholars known as the Jesus Seminar published their conclusions from six years of analysis and debate about the gospels. They believe the Gospel of Thomas was written about 50–60 CE, and the Gospel of John was written about 90 CE.[43] This subsection's insights, which Riley first introduced in 1995, corroborate the Jesus Seminar that Thomas was written well before John.]

4.5.h. "John" Undercuts Peter

The author of John also threw a few jabs at Peter. The "disciple whom Jesus loved" was reclining next to Jesus during the Last Supper when Jesus announced that one of his disciples would betray him. Peter asked this unnamed disciple to ask Jesus who it would be. The unnamed disciple then asked Jesus, who identified Judas with a piece of bread (Jn 13:21–27).

The double disparagement was that the unnamed disciple had the privileged seat next to Jesus, and then Peter was unable to ask Jesus directly and needed an intermediary. Trouble is, Matthew and Mark have the same story of Jesus announcing his betrayal but do not report Peter's query.

Strangely enough, the author of John had no problem with Peter directly asking Jesus a question just minutes later. Just like his tale about Thomas, the author had Peter announce his ignorance by asking, "Lord, where are you going?" (Jn 13:36).

The next slight occurs in the crucifixion story. Per the synoptic gospels, none of the disciples witnessed it. In John, though, the unnamed disciple was there as well as Jesus's mother. Jesus declared them to be mother and son to each other, and the disciple thereafter took Mary into his home (Jn 19:26–27). The unnamed disciple was thus a greater man than Peter.

The Peter-denigrating party concludes with the resurrection story. In Luke, all eleven disciples heard the report of an empty tomb, but only Peter believed it and ran to the tomb to see for himself (Lk 24:12). In John, though, both Peter and the unnamed disciple ran for the tomb upon hearing the news, and the latter outran Peter to arrive first. But the unnamed disciple was once again the greater man by waiting for Peter to arrive and then graciously allowing the slower disciple to enter first (Jn 20:4–6).

In sum, the author of John repeatedly contradicted the synoptic gospels to disparage Thomas and Peter. We should thus expect to find a gospel that had Peter's name on it, was written before John, and was conflicting with the proto-orthodoxy. Sure enough, the Gospel of Peter existed and apparently did just that.

The church historian Eusebius reported that Serapion, the bishop of Antioch from 190 to 203, wrote to the church in Rhossus about a controversy that had arisen involving that church's use of the Gospel of Peter. Serapion had tracked down a copy and read it, wherein he found "many things in accordance with the true doctrine of the Saviour, but some things added to that doctrine."[44] Eusebius classified it as a forged and heretical gospel.

In 1886, a fragment of the Gospel of Peter was found in Egypt. The fragment is a narrative about the crucifixion and resurrection. Crossan differs from many scholars by arguing this passion narrative predated the canonical gospels.[45]

In any case, this gospel was making an impression. As Ehrman notes, "There are indications that the Gospel of Peter was widely popular in the early church, arguably at least as popular as one of the Gospels that did make it into the New Testament, the Gospel of Mark."[46]

The Thomas and Peter gospels were apparently guiding some early Christian communities when the author of John tried to discredit them with his creative writing. There was a big difference in the ferocity of his attacks, though, as he threw the kitchen sink at Thomas while only chipping at Peter. That is to be expected, for the Gospel of Peter does not appear to have strayed very far from the proto-orthodox line.

The author of John threw these literary punches because the proto-orthodox movement was in an ideological fight and he obviously had no qualms with inventing material. We will soon see how he told far greater lies so his side could more easily win its battle for followers.

4.5.i. The Author's Modus Operandi

That John was written to undercut competing traditions is corroborated by the insights of Alan Watson. Like most scholars of John, he believes the author drew from multiple sources. He makes the case that one of them was an anti-Christian writing that he calls "S."

Most Jews did not believe Jesus had been the Messiah. They also told stories about him but with a countervailing effect. The much-maligned Pharisees surely told theirs, too, and Watson sees them in *S*. This narrative depicted Jesus as a hostile and sometimes raging opponent of Judaism who routinely spoke and acted in offensive ways. A primary intention of *S* was defending the Sanhedrin's role in having Jesus executed.

As Watson sees it, the author of John was facing a popular tradition in *S* that had to be addressed. So he "incorporated parts of it into his writing, making small but significant changes to defang it and adding his theological message. But, as is standard with composite works, important traces of the sources shine through."[47]

Consider the confrontation at the temple. *S* surely depicted Jesus as having been on a rampage, and the author of John broke from his synoptic predecessors to concede that Jesus had used a whip. The author also used a different Old Testament quote that admitted and explained Jesus's rage: "Zeal for your house will consume me" (Jn 2:17, citing Ps 69:9). In his biggest deviation, the author of John apparently moved the event to the beginning of Jesus's ministry to deflate its value as a Jewish justification for the execution.

Another example occurs with Jesus's scorching assault on his Jewish audience—"You belong to your father, the devil, and you want to carry out your father's desires"—that has no parallel in the synoptic gospels (§4.3.b.). It makes sense that Jesus challenged his religion about its prideful inability to hear his message. If so, *S* portrayed him as arrogant and inflammatory in doing so.

Did Jesus actually cast the devil word on his brethren, or was it invented to depict him as excessively caustic? Either way, the author of John most likely sourced this passage from *S* and found its essence to be congruent with his message. Whatever reframing he did notwithstanding, he happily conceded that Jesus was guilty as charged.

All in all, the author's modus operandi is obvious. Whether it was the mystical view of the Thomas tradition, the atypical view of the Peter tradition or the oppositional view of the Pharisaic tradition, he assimilated it while "making small but significant changes to defang it and adding his theological message."

This explains, of course, the similarities between John and Thomas that run afoul of the synoptic gospels. As Thomas was probably resonating with many communities, the author of John incorporated its mystical teachings to capture its allure while sharply bending its theology in the direction of the proto-orthodoxy.

By the way, he was a talented writer but failed to notice a telltale gaffe in his account of the Last Supper. Peter asked Jesus where he was going (Jn 13:36), and Thomas said shortly thereafter that the disciples did not know where he was going or the way there (Jn 14:5). Yet during the very same meal, the author allowed this quote of Jesus to remain: "Now I am going to him who sent me. None of you asks me, 'Where are you going?'" (Jn 16:5).[48]

Unless Jesus was the first recorded case of attention deficit disorder or short-term memory loss, this blunder is further evidence of the author's identity. John was not composed by an eyewitness but rather a much later ghostwriter who wanted us to assume he was the "disciple whom Jesus loved." His flair for bending preexisting sources and blending in his fabrications was a few steps short of undetectable perfection.

4.5.j. The Gaping Hole in the Proto-Orthodox Theology

The first-century debate between Christian movements was surely exposing a gaping hole in the proto-orthodox theology. Nowhere in the original versions of Matthew, Mark or Luke had Jesus directly expressed its core tenet that we had to believe in him and his atoning sacrifice to gain salvation.

In the original version of Mark, the closest statement was this quote of Jesus as he settled a dispute among his disciples: "For even the Son of Man did not come to be served, but to serve, and to give his life as a ransom for many" (Mk 10:45; see also Mt 20:28).

In Matthew, the strongest testimony is when Jesus passed around a cup of wine at the Last Supper and supposedly said, "Drink from it, all of you. This is my blood of the covenant, which is poured out for many for the forgiveness of sins" (Mt 26:27–28). Trouble is, Mark's version of the quote does not include "for the forgiveness of sins" (Mk 14:24). The author of Matthew (or a subsequent scribe) apparently added the phrase to strengthen the proto-orthodox position.

Anyway, notice how Jesus only made those statements to his disciples and how they only support the human-sacrifice theology when you favorably interpret them that way. Moreover, those two gospels lack corroborating verses and clearer expressions of the theology.

This begs a slew of questions. If accepting his sacrificial gift was required to enter heaven and failing to do so would condemn us to eternal hell, why did he not repeatedly preach about it in his sermons to the masses? Why did he not include it in the Lord's Prayer when he taught the masses how to pray (Mt 6:9–13)?

Why did Jesus contradict the theology by teaching that not everyone who called upon his name would enter the kingdom but only those who did the will of his Father (Mt 7:21–23)? Why did he contradict the theology with his quotes about God desiring "mercy, not sacrifice" (Mt 9:13, 12:7; §3.3.e.)? Why did he contradict the theology in his parable of the sheep and goats where dispensation into heaven or hell was based on what folks had done for the least of his brethren (Mt 25:31–46)?

Meanwhile, consider the glaring absence of the savior theology in Luke and its sequel, Acts. Even though the author of these books sourced from Mark, he did not pass along that gospel's strongest verse in favor of the proto-orthodoxy.

Understanding how this author viewed Jesus's death is easily seen in Acts. He recounts a host of missionary sermons therein, but none of them say anything about Jesus atoning for our sins. Rather, people had rejected Jesus and had him executed, so they should repent before God to receive forgiveness. As Ehrman summarizes, "Luke's view is that salvation comes not through an atoning sacrifice but by forgiveness that comes from repentance."[49]

[Note: Luke 22:19–20 suggests the savior theology, but this text is not in some of the ancient manuscripts, and scholarly analysis has practically proven it to be a later addition. Acts 20:28 can be favorably interpreted for the savior theology, but it lacks corroboration from elsewhere in Luke and Acts and has other issues.[50]]

All in all, the original versions of the synoptic gospels were practically worthless for evangelizing the proto-orthodoxy's core tenet. Moreover, the source document Q had no such statements either.

Before John was written, the proto-orthodoxy was relying on Paul's letters as a testimony to its creed. But Paul's words probably carried as much weight with outsiders as a television evangelist's do today. If Hollywood made a movie about the situation, its signature line would be "Jerusalem, we have a problem." But the proto-orthodoxy did not crash and burn because necessity was the mother of one hell of an invention.

4.5.k. Bridging the Chasm

In addition to everything else the unscrupulous author of John was accomplishing, he was committed to bridging the chasm between Jesus's teachings and the proto-orthodoxy's preaching. He began by having John the Baptist declare Jesus to be "the Lamb of God, who takes away the sin of the world!" (Jn 1:29).

The synoptic gospels all tell the story of John baptizing Jesus, but none of them say John ever referred to Jesus as God's lamb or that Jesus had come to take away the sin of the world. However, we have repeatedly seen how the author of John deviated from his predecessors at will.

The author then had Jesus deliver the core tenet of the faith. The foundation was laid with the questions of a Pharisee, and Jesus answered with a litany of the proto-orthodoxy:

> For God so loved the world that he gave his one and only Son, that whoever believes in him shall not perish but have eternal life. For God did not send his Son into the world to condemn the world, but to save the world through him. Whoever believes in him is not condemned, but whoever does not believe stands condemned already because they have not believed in the name of God's one and only Son. (Jn 3:16–18)

Proto-orthodox evangelists would finally have Jesus on the record to win converts. No longer would they have to build credibility about Paul's words. The author also had John the Baptist speak a juicy quote for them as well: "Whoever believes in the Son has eternal life, but whoever rejects the Son will not see life, for God's wrath remains on them" (Jn 3:36).

In addition, the author changed the date of Jesus's crucifixion. It occurred the day after the Passover Feast (Nisan 15) according to the synoptic gospels, but the author changed it to the daylight hours before the Passover Feast (Nisan 14). This was most likely done to portray Jesus as a Passover lamb himself who was slaughtered on the same day as the Passover lambs and whose sacrifice was also atoning for sins (§K.3.f.).

Meanwhile, our propagandist also invented a Jesus quote to oppose and contradict the Jesus teachings in Mark and Matthew that Elijah had returned as John the Baptist (§A.2.a.). He invented yet another Jesus quote to defend the dogma about the resurrection of the dead (§A.2.b.).

It may be shocking to think the sacrificial-lamb material was fabricated many decades after the fact. But if we embrace the fourth gospel as honest and infallible, we had better examine the shadow its casts. If Jesus really preached it as proclaimed in John, we have to explain how the earlier gospels missed it. Either somebody invented the quotes in John, or the earlier gospels are untrustworthy and erroneous (for they lack the most important message of all and present far too many quotes that sharply contradict it).

By the way, Ehrman had an epiphany that corroborates our conclusion. Despite Jesus and the author of John coming from different times, places, cultures, educational backgrounds and languages, the narrator of John sounds identical to Jesus in many passages. Ehrman wondered how that could be until the answer hit him with "breathtaking suddenness." There were never two voices (of Jesus and the narrating author of John). Instead, "We are hearing one voice. The author is speaking for himself *and* he is speaking for Jesus. These are not Jesus's words; they are [the author of] John's words placed on Jesus's lips."[51]

4.5.1. More Deception for a Solid Foundation

We now know why John was written roughly six decades after the crucifixion. The proto-orthodoxy had serious competition, and the synoptic gospels were not proclaiming its sacrificial-lamb theology. The author of John responded with his flagrantly dishonest gospel, but the earlier ones were still an inexplicable void.

Somebody felt the urge to fix this flaw. Again, the closing verses of Mark were a later addition (§4.4.d.). As the *NIV Study Bible* explains, "They are absent from important early manuscripts and display certain peculiarities of vocabulary, style and theological content that are unlike the rest of Mark."[52]

The difference in theological content is at the heart of the matter. Although no other part of Mark directly conveys the savior theology, the spurious text has the resurrected Jesus stating it to his disciples: "Go into all the world and preach the gospel to all creation. Whoever believes and is baptized will be saved, but whoever does not believe will be condemned" (Mk 16:15–16).

A similar markup was made to Luke (§4.5.j.). Thanks to the author of John and his fellow ghostwriters, the proto-orthodoxy was finally preaching from a solid foundation. Jesus and John the Baptist had clearly proclaimed its theology.

These gospel lies should not come as a surprise as if they happened like a lightning bolt out of the blue. Rather, a thunderstorm of religious contention was pelting the first-century world and generating numerous strikes of deliberate deception. According to an almost unanimous conclusion of critical scholars, four New Testament letters (1 Timothy, 2 Timothy, Titus and 2 Peter) were penned by anonymous writers but deviously portrayed as the work of Paul and Peter.[53] A majority of critical scholars believe another four letters (2 Thessalonians, Ephesians, Colossians and 1 Peter) were also forgeries.[54]

In any case, the proto-orthodox theology eventually triumphed and is now believed by over a billion people. The Nazis would have been proud, for the big lie was boldly expressed, endlessly repeated and eventually embraced as the truth.

4.6. Cementing the Power of the Holy People

This section describes how the proto-orthodoxy could not sustain the Messiah's counterculture of equality and collegiality and instead developed into a religious monarchy.

4.6.a. Building on a Faulty Foundation

According to the Christian doctrine of election, those who believe in Jesus for their salvation had already been chosen by God to make that decision. That God has been playing favorites since Cain and Abel is another Judaic principle that should have been discarded (§3.3.c.). The doctrine casts a dark shadow that God is not fair and just, but Paul tried to hide this affliction in his letter to the Romans while discussing Rebekah's twin children:

> Before the twins were born or had done anything good or bad—in order that God's purpose in election might stand: not by works but by him who calls—she was told, "The older will serve the younger." Just as it is written: "Jacob I loved, but Esau I hated."
>
> What then shall we say? Is God unjust? Not at all! For he says to Moses, "I will have mercy on whom I have mercy, and I will have compassion on whom I have compassion."
>
> It does not, therefore, depend on human desire or effort, but on God's mercy. (Rom 9:11–16)

Paul's logic is badly flawed, for a god who arbitrarily bestows mercy and compassion on some but not others is not fair and just. Paul's absurdity is akin to this argument: "What then shall we say? Is that animal a duck? Not at all! For it walks like a duck, swims like a duck, and quacks like a duck."

The passage is another example of the proto-orthodoxy's fusion of Jesus's teachings with its Judaic foundation. Because Paul and his colleagues jammed a square peg into a round hole, the New Testament has plenty of splinters.

Another Judaic principle is the patriarchy of its male deity. Here the Old Testament errors flowed smoothly into the New, and pretzel logic was not required to merge them. Paul perpetuated the deception about the Garden of Eden (§3.3.b.) to justify the man's authority over the woman. As he wrote, the woman came from the man and was created for the man (1 Cor 11:8–9).

Paul's greatest error, though, was failing to grasp the essence of the conflict between Jesus and Judaism. He made sense of the crucifixion through his Judaic paradigm of a God who required animal sacrifices to atone for sins (§3.3.e.).

All in all, the proto-orthodox movement failed to establish a pure religion because it built its theology upon a faulty foundation. The result was a hybrid religion that is dreadfully askew from universal truth.

4.6.b. The Character of the Proto-Orthodox Movement

From the traditional view of authorship, Paul was one book shy of publishing half of the New Testament (13 of 27). Even though some of the biblical letters attributed to him were written by impostors (§4.5.l.), those forgeries were intended to look like they were written by him.

In any case, mainstream Christianity has bet the farm on his beliefs. It would be understandable if he had traveled with Jesus for years, but he never once heard Jesus speak in person. So who was this man?

Before his conversion, Saul supported the stoning of Stephen and the persecution of Christians (Acts 8:1–3). He was a zealous Jew whose actions were rooted in the first stage of spiritual growth (§1.4.). After being blasted out of stage 1 while traveling to Damascus, he became Paul and lived a legitimate stage 2 existence.

His transformation did not catapult him to the higher spirituality of stage 4. Rather, he was still entrenched in his lifelong paradigm and was a few breakthroughs away from understanding what Jesus had done and taught.

4.6.c. The Pillars of Ecclesiastical Authority

The proto-orthodox movement was not originally planning for the long haul, for these folks believed the end of the world would happen before their generation had passed away (§9.3.c.). Paul and his fellow missionaries were preaching far and wide with little attention to long-term considerations.

Church communities in the first century were governed by a collegial group of equals. These leaders were known as presbyters (from a Greek word that means "elder") in some churches and bishops (from a Greek word that means "overseer") in others. The words were used interchangeably in the earliest decades. There were also deacons (from a Greek word meaning "to serve") who performed material duties as assistants to the elders/overseers.

Variations between the churches abounded in just about every aspect of church life, such as scriptures used, theology, liturgy, discipline, customs and rituals. Nevertheless, these communities felt bonded by their common faith in Christ.

The elders/overseers and deacons had some authority but held it in the context of Jesus's teachings. The Messiah had embodied a counterculture whose themes were freedom instead of ruling domination, serving people instead of exerting power over them, inclusiveness instead of culturally mandated exclusion, and equality and fellowship among brothers and sisters instead of the social caste and patriarchy. The churches were thus very attractive to women, peasants and slaves who had no political or economic power.

Unfortunately, the collegial spirit of the early church communities did not survive. Near the end of the first century, they began morphing into the hierarchical institution of the Church. For the men who desired it, the first step was regressing their communities to the prevailing Roman culture of submission to authority.

In about 96 CE, a letter was sent from the church in Rome to the church in Corinth that began justifying this dynamic. The unsigned letter was later attributed to a presbyter named Clement. The author made no claim to be a bishop, and his letter made no distinction between presbyters and bishops and always referred to them in the plural (which suggests the church in Rome was organized collegially at the time).

He sought to resolve strife and schism in the Corinthian church, and his solution was strengthening the hierarchical chain of command. He wrote, "Let us consider those who serve under our generals, with what order, obedience, and submissiveness they perform the things which are commanded them." From the officers down to the soldiers, "each one in his own rank performs the things commanded by the king and the generals."[55]

After making his case for the divine appointments of church leaders, he called on the Corinthians who were stirring dissension to "submit yourselves to the presbyters, and receive correction so as to repent, bending the knees of your hearts. Learn to be subject, laying aside the proud and arrogant self-confidence of your tongue."[56]

The letter was not included in the New Testament but was still very impactful. As Eusebius wrote over two centuries later, it "has been publicly used in a great many churches both in former times and in our own."[57]

Early in the second century, the bishop of Antioch wrote a series of letters to other churches that justified the emerging trend of the monarchical bishop (a man with full teaching and administrative authority over a church community). Ignatius advocated submission to the three ranks of bishop, elder/priest and deacon, and he began granting divine authority to the bishop. As he extolled, "Your bishop presides in the place of God."[58]

In another letter, Ignatius stated the authority in an introductory phrase, "Since ye are subject to the bishop as to Jesus Christ..."[59] He implored in another letter, "We should regard the bishop as the Lord himself."[60]

To the masses who had known nothing but the rule of the Roman Empire, it all made sense. Hierarchical authorities were a fact of life, so why would it be any different with Almighty God and his officers in the local church? So it was for those who were attracted to this version of Christianity as its bishops were erecting the pillars of ecclesiastical authority.

4.6.d. A Wise Observation About the Proto-Orthodox Canon

In about 140, a wealthy business owner and philosopher named Marcion moved to Rome and gave generously to its church. From his study of the scriptures, he was aware of some major contradictions. The God of the Old Testament demanded strict conformance to the law, but the God of Paul's letters expected only a belief in Jesus to attain salvation and thus rendered the law obsolete.

The Old Testament's God had instructed the ancient Hebrews to kill everything that breathed in the cities of their Promised Land (Dt 20:16), which led them to slaughter every man, woman, child and animal in Jericho (Jsh 6:21). In stark contrast, the New Testament's peaceful and merciful God wanted us to love our enemies.

Acclimated to Roman polytheism, Marcion concluded that he was witnessing the words and actions of two different gods. He reasoned the transcendent and benevolent god of Jesus and Paul had intervened to save us from the oppressive laws and wrath of the Jewish creator god.

He was excommunicated in 144 and responded with his own Christian movement. He specified a canon that only included Luke and the ten letters from Paul that he knew about. He was the first Christian in history to specify a canon of scripture.

Marcion had not solved the theological riddle, for he needed to challenge the veracity of the Jewish scriptures instead of adding a deity. Nevertheless, he was closer to the truth than anybody else in the proto-orthodoxy.

By the closing decades of the second century, the proto-orthodox churches had widely embraced the four gospels and the letters believed to have been penned by Paul. Differences and doubt, though, still surrounded many other Christian writings. All the while Marcion's insight had escaped the proto-orthodoxy, for it was wholeheartedly embracing the Old Testament as God's holy words.

4.6.e. The Curious Case of Roman Catholicism

In the 180s, a young bishop named Irenaeus wrote an indictment of Marcion and the proto-orthodoxy's other Christian competitors, most notably the Gnostics, in a five-volume polemic. He argued the Catholic Church was the only valid form of Christianity and began empowering Rome with a dubious rationale that is still used today.

He believed Peter and Paul "founded and organized" the church in Rome and "every Church should agree with this Church, on account of its preeminent authority." He then listed the first twelve bishops of Rome who had succeeded those founders until his present time.[61] Later Catholic writers bolstered the case with this Jesus quote: "You are Peter, and on this rock I will build my church" (Mt 16:18).

The claim that divine authority resides with the bishop in Rome was built on four assumptions. First, Jesus wanted a centralized church with the power to dictate the correctness of beliefs and behavior. Second, he had given Peter the authority to establish and rule such an institution. Third, the city of Peter and Paul's later ministries and executions made it the seat of such authority. Finally, this special commission would magically transfer from one bishop in Rome to another for all time.

According to three of the gospels, Jesus never uttered the word "church." Only Matthew reports that Jesus talked about such an organization and only on two occasions. The first is in the aforementioned verse, and the other is in a command for adjudicating a conflict (Mt 18:17). Not surprisingly, then, biblical scholars concur that Jesus had not been advocating a centralized church but rather the kingdom of God. As Catholic theologian Hans Küng notes, "According to all the evidence Jesus did not found a church in his lifetime."[62]

Moreover, the churches that sprouted like weeds across the eastern Mediterranean had collegial leadership and egalitarian membership. Paul did not attempt to establish them as legal institutions, nor did he promote having a single ruling leader or priestly caste. To the contrary, he viewed each of them as complete unto themselves as Christian communities and able to handle their needs and functions organically.

The second assumption about Peter being the exclusive authority of the Messiah's church is also refuted by the evidence. Regarding the Catholic Church's capstone verse, which can only be found in Matthew, Küng explains: "Today even Catholic exegetes accept that the famous saying about Peter as the rock on which Jesus will build his church…is not a saying of the earthly Jesus but was composed after Easter by the Palestinian community, or later by Matthew's community."[63]

[Note: Such justification is also derived from the final chapter of John, wherein Jesus supposedly told Peter to "Feed my sheep" (Jn 21:17). Scholars have concluded that the chapter was a later addition.[64]]

If Jesus intended for Peter to have monarchical authority over a centralized church, why did this disciple neither enact nor indoctrinate it? To the contrary, Peter never acted like Jesus had given him such a commission. James was the leader of the Nazarene Jews, not Peter. Furthermore, Paul and James were the ideological heavyweights who battled about faith versus observing the law while Peter bounced between both sides. When Paul opposed Peter to his face (§4.5.a.), it proves Paul did not view Peter as Jesus's duly appointed authority.

Peter did not see himself that way either. He admonished Christians to submit themselves to every societal authority but never declared himself to be one (1 Pt 2:13). When he addressed his fellow elders, he did not direct them with divine authority but rather appealed to them as an equal among them (1 Pt 5:1).

The final two assumptions—Peter's divine authority was deposited in Rome and thereafter transferred down the line to its bishops like a baton in a relay race—are fanciful ideas that are dependent upon the prior assumptions that have been disproven. Nevertheless, historical facts continue to dismantle the theory.

The church in Rome was not "founded and organized" by Peter and Paul. The New Testament says nothing about Peter having ever gone to Rome, and only the possibility of what may be a coded message can suggest he was ever there (1 Pt 5:13). In any case, the church in Rome already existed before Paul arrived (Rom 1:10–15).

More importantly, the church in Rome was not being ruled by a single bishop at the end of the first century (§4.6.c.). This was still the case at least a generation later. *The Shepherd of Hermas*, which was written in Rome early in the second century, refers to the "officials of the church" and the "elders who preside over the church."[65] The document also identifies Clement not as a monarchical bishop (he was third on Irenaeus's list) but rather as the elder who was responsible for corresponding with churches in other cities. We do not know if *Hermas*'s Clement was the same Clement who wrote the letter of 96 CE, but it seems likely.[66]

These facts are not challenged by any refuting evidence. As Küng points out, "Catholic theologians concede that there is no reliable evidence that Peter was ever in charge of the church in Rome as supreme head or bishop."[67] Moreover, a monarchical bishop in Rome is backed by historical facts only from about the middle of the second century.

As for Irenaeus's rendition of how the authoritative baton got magically passed down the line, numerous attempts have been made to verify his claim but are sorely lacking. As Church scholars of the late 19th century had to acknowledge, "The lists of early Roman bishops are in hopeless confusion, some making Clement the immediate successor of St. Peter, others placing Linus, and others still Linus and Anacletus, between him and the apostle."[68]

The young bishop was probably trying to mirror his list of the first 12 bishops of Rome to the 12 apostles. To do so, Irenaeus has the sixth bishop after Peter as being "Sixtus." As Catholic scholar Eamon Duffy notes, "It all seems suspiciously tidy."[69]

In sum, the justification for centralized power in Rome was a sham. The proto-orthodox churches, though, were moving forward without this knowledge and in an authoritative empire where all roads led to Rome. It was thus only a matter of time before the bishop of Rome commandeered power over his peers.

4.6.f. Mirroring the Empire and Empowering the Papacy

By the end of the second century, the three-tier hierarchy of a monarchical bishop, priests and deacons had been established in the proto-orthodox churches. Yet the Catholic Church was just a federation of bishops who were developing a pecking order among themselves based on the cities and traditions they represented.

The first documented instance where the bishop of Rome claimed primacy over his peers was with Stephen I (254–257), who quoted Matthew in making his case amid a quarrel with an African bishop. Strong objections were made from various churches, though, and nobody accepted Stephen's claim.

Meanwhile, the tradition of the metropolitan began developing with the church in Alexandria and its sister churches in Egypt. A metropolitan was the bishop of a major city who was considered to have authoritative precedence over other bishops in his province. This mirrored the Roman political structure of a capital city's authorities holding sway over the whole province.

All the while the proto-orthodox bishops did not have any power beyond the realm of Catholicism. It was still just a war of words between them and their Christian competitors in which no higher authority was declaring a winner. That changed in the fourth century when Constantine sanctioned Catholic Christianity and availed the empire's laws so the Church could crush the "heretics" (§4.5.d.).

The Council of Nicaea affirmed the power of the metropolitans, of which Rome, Alexandria and Antioch were named as the preeminent principalities. With Constantine building his new capital city of Constantinople (now Istanbul) and reinvigorating Jerusalem with pilgrimages and a dazzling new church, those two cities quickly joined them in Christian prominence. Rome was the only one of the big five in the Latin-speaking western half of the empire. The other four were in the Greek-speaking eastern half.

After Constantine's death in 337, the empire was often split between co-Augusti ruling out of Rome and Constantinople. In 379 and 382, the Augusti surrendered their title of Pontifex Maximus (head of state religion), which opened the door for somebody to claim the role of the empire's top religious leader.

Siricius, who had become the bishop of Rome in 384, took a step in that direction when he became the first man to issue a decretal (a papal letter to authoritatively resolve an issue). He was also the first man to use the title of "pope" in a monarchical way—the term had long been used as an honorific for any bishop. By the time Innocent I (402–417) was continuing the drive for Roman primacy, the western half of the empire had pretty much accepted Rome's claim for apostolic supremacy. However, this privilege only meant Rome was acting as the highest court of appeals at the time; it had not yet been granted executive control.

In 451, Constantinople and Jerusalem were formally recognized with metropolitan power and thus rounded out the five chief sees (seats of religious authority) of Christendom. The bishop of Rome held patriarchal privilege over the European churches in Greece and everything westward and over the African churches in what is now western Libya and everything westward.

The drive for Roman primacy was further aided by the collapse of Rome in 476 and the rise of the European kingdoms that embraced Catholicism. In the seventh century, the Islamic Empire engulfed the patriarchates of Antioch, Alexandria and Jerusalem, which left only Rome and Constantinople as the chief sees of Christendom.

All the while the papal movement had been citing a slew of forged documents to bolster its case for divine authority. In the eighth century, the movement took another huge step through the crowning of Pepin as king of the Franks and Pepin's gift of land in central Italy, which was combined with estates the Church already owned to become the Papal States.

The bishops of the East never submitted to the bishop of Rome, which was a major reason for the schism that split the Church in 1054. Yet papal power was firmly established in the West and reached its zenith under Innocent III (1198–1216) with the launching of more crusades and the dawning of the Inquisition.

Though it took many centuries, the Roman Catholic Church modeled itself in the totalitarian image of its beloved groom. Roman citizens had long deemed their emperors to be demigods, and the Church duplicated this as well with the deified monarchy of the papacy.

4.6.g. Nailing Down the Canon and Eliminating the Competition

Our historical recap needs to go back to the fourth century and include the last two pieces of the authoritative puzzle. The first was the canon of the Bible. Athanasius, the bishop of Alexandria, rendered the earliest document of our familiar list of books in 367, yet debates about inclusion and exclusion continued for many decades thereafter.

The other authoritative development was the Church's war against its religious competitors. The bishops had crushed the non-Catholic versions of Christianity during the reign of Constantine, but they still had to deal with the Arian faction of Catholicism. Arianism had arisen from the ashes of defeat at Nicaea to become dominant in the eastern half of the empire because it was championed by Constantine's son and successor, Constantius II. The

Catholic bishops were also facing Roman paganism and new religions coming in from afar.

This is when the marriage of church and state finished its transformation into a totalitarian beast. The eastern Augustus Theodosius, in collaboration with his western co-Augusti, made Catholic Christianity the empire's official and exclusive religion in 380. The power couple defeated the Arians at the Second Ecumenical Council of 381 and thereafter began eliminating paganism and all other religions.

From 381 until his death in 395, Theodosius enforced the Nicene version of Catholicism with 15 different edicts that were backed by legal penalties. Anybody who openly dissented was deprived of serving in public offices, of inheriting or bequeathing property, and of making legal contracts. Heretics were also subject to fines, banishment and corporal punishment.

Execution was also a possible consequence, as a law passed in 382 declared heresy to be a capital offense. The law claimed its first Christian victims three years later when a devout mystic named Priscillian and six of his followers were executed for heresy (§G.4.c.).

In sum, Christianity was indoctrinated as the empire's exclusive religion with breathtaking speed. The drive for religious conformity was also accompanied by widespread violence against the pagans.

The marriage of church and state—this wicked template of stifling dogma enforced with terrifying power—would crush the religious freedom and truth-seeking spirit of Christendom for over a thousand years. It would become history's greatest hypocrisy, for it would all be done in the name of Christ.

4.7. Conclusion

As the Old and New Testaments are seriously flawed, so is the religion that was built upon them. Christianity's original sin was failing to comprehend Jesus's purpose of overcoming Judaism's grave misunderstandings.

Despite the reconciling apologetics in the gospel stories, the historical truth could not be glossed over. He was a revolutionary threat to his religion, so it eliminated him. But the proto-orthodox Christians failed to make the paradigm shift, and their savior theology was built upon the mistaken tenets of Judaism. Moreover, they blindly incorporated the Old Testament into their Bible when this material should have been retained only as a side reference to provide context for his contrasting messages.

Furthermore, their gospels were significantly distorted by human processes. The most impactful dynamic was the agenda factor.

As John Dominic Crossan summarizes, the evidence gave scholars no choice but to conclude that the transmitters of the gospel material had exercised significant creative freedom (§3.3.a.). For instance, when the authors of Matthew and Luke sourced from Mark, they were "unnervingly free about omission and addition, about change, correction, or creation in their own individual accounts—but always, of course, subject to their own particular interpretation of Jesus."[70]

Crossan's summary was published a year before the landmark insights about John. Now we know how unnervingly free the author of that gospel felt to invent quotes to promote the proto-orthodoxy. It did not take long for those lies to become the truth.

Meanwhile, the proto-orthodox churches were devolving from the Messiah's counterculture toward being a hierarchical institution. The bishops later accepted Constantine's wedding proposal, Catholicism became the empire's exclusive religion, and the mighty beast of church and state began its tyrannical reign.

All things considered, we are awakening to see the ancient layers of unrenounced tenets and traditions from the Old Testament, the unacknowledged errors and fabrications in the New Testament, and the unchallenged theologies and authorities that resulted. The ultimate meaning of it all is a profound and painful irony: <u>the religion based upon the man who came to uproot Judaism must itself be uprooted</u>.

Even though the Eastern Orthodox Church split off in the 11th century and the Protestants and Anglicans broke away in the 16th century, they are not exempt from the spiritual gardening. For even though their branches and leaves are different from the Catholic Church's, they share the same New Testament trunk and Old Testament roots where the foundational errors are deeply embedded.

This shocking conclusion will soon get supernatural corroboration from the apocalyptic prophecies. To fully understand their meaning, though, we must first develop wisdom about the metaphysical darkness.

Chapter 5

Egoic Pride and the Book of Job

5.1. Introduction

At the heart of M. Scott Peck's *The Road Less Traveled* is his definition of love: "The will to extend one's self for the purpose of nurturing one's own or another's spiritual growth."[1] He made a greater contribution to our spiritual evolution, though, with a less popular book about the other side of the polarity. In *People of the Lie*, he illuminated the dynamic that opposes love and spiritual growth.

This chapter begins with wisdom about the nature of evil, for it is the key to more deeply understanding the Book of Job and unlocking the secrets of the apocalyptic prophecies. After reviewing the prevailing interpretations of Job and a modern case study that parallels the ancient story, the chapter leverages this wisdom to see the Old Testament book in a whole new light.

5.2. The Nature of Evil

At the most fundamental level of reality, only love exists and all beings are divine, interconnected and one. Yet we immortal souls of the Light are immersed in a polarized physical universe of everything and its opposite. Clothed with flesh and blood in this multifaceted spectrum of the purest light to the darkest dark, we have free will to create and experience what we will.

So the paradoxical truth is that evil both exists and does not exist. We are in the world but not of it, and living amid this polarized realm requires us to become aware of the evil in our midst.

The Eastern mystical teachings fail to comprehend this reality when they say evil does not exist. By only embracing one side of the paradox, they are unintentionally enabling the darkness. As God is quoted by Walsch, "The biggest evil would therefore be to declare nothing evil at all."[2]

Failing to be aware of evil is by definition a lack of consciousness. You are in the dark about what is going on, and your lack of awareness is fostered by denial and/or ignorance as one aspect of your darkness begets another. By being blind to evil, you are helping it do what it does best: remain out of conscious awareness and deviously operate from its well-hidden quarters. So even if you have the best of intentions, you will be blindly enabling and perhaps even actively supporting the darkness.

Simply witnessing the dynamics of the darkness, though, is an expansion of consciousness, for you have become more aware of what is really going on. Observing the presence and nature of the darkness reduces its power to deceive as you no longer enable or support its well-cloaked ways.

Indeed, the greatest antidote to evil is consciousness. Evil cannot flourish in its presence because we are all fundamentally moral and good. When evil is exposed and seen by the light of consciousness, it is just a matter of time before more open and loving choices are made that put an end to the dark behavior.

Because evil cannot survive in the midst of higher consciousness, it depends on deception to keep people unaware and in the dark so they keep empowering its agenda. So it is that wicked intentions are cloaked in deception—what those who study evil call its "pretense"—to either hide them or make them appear to be good.

By shining the light of awareness on the ways of the darkness, we weaken it by waking up those who are participating with it so they can withdraw their empowerment of it. To serve this vitally important part of our evolution, this section illuminates the dynamic.

5.2.a. Egoic Pride

The term "egoic pride" will be used to reflect a psychological stance that steadfastly maintains, "I am free from error; I am perfect as I am; I have nothing to change." It is all about maintaining self-esteem and projecting an image of a perfected self to the world.

Egoic pride is highly correlated with narcissism, which is a character structure of self-absorption that is preoccupied with maintaining self-esteem by obtaining affirmation from others. Narcissists satisfy this need by striving to perfect the self and being identified with the best people and organizations.

[Note: As "pride" and "proud" describe a variety of feelings and attitudes, "egoic pride" is used to differentiate it from phrases like "a proud parent." Defending your self-esteem and image (egoic pride) is substantially different from having a deep sense of dignity from making healthy choices (being proud of yourself). For instance, your egoic pride may be stung heavily by confessing to regrettable behavior, but you can feel proud of yourself for speaking the truth, accepting responsibility, and growing from the experience.]

Because egoic pride rigidly defends the self as free from error and beyond reproach, it actively opposes spiritual growth. Rather than accept the truth of life events that beckon for healing and development, it denies the truth and rejects such personal change.

The problem stems not from the existence of issues and wounds, for we all have them. Instead, it arises from the avoiding and/or hiding of them. As an Ethiopian proverb explains, "He who conceals his disease cannot be cured."[3]

Here are some other signature behaviors. Egoic pride presents a squeaky-clean exterior image to appear blameless and above reproach to the world. As Jesus purportedly observed it in the Pharisees, "You are like whitewashed tombs, which look beautiful on the outside but on the inside are full of the bones of the dead and everything unclean. In the same way, on the outside you appear to people as righteous but on the inside you are full of hypocrisy and wickedness" (Mt 23:27–28).

Egoic pride compartmentalizes. Peck explains, "To compartmentalize is to take things that are properly related and stick them in separate, airtight compartments in our minds where they don't have to rub up against each other and cause us any stress or pain."[4] For example, a business executive worships God's creation on Sunday but has no problem with his company dumping toxic waste into a river on Monday. Egoic pride drowns the awareness of contradictions that would otherwise spur spiritual growth toward integrity and wholeness.

Egoic pride deceives and lies to avoid scrutiny and protect self-esteem. Whereas the truth shines light upon all aspects of a situation, egoic pride creates the illusion that it has done so. In reality, however, its slick deception is a smoke bomb of darkness that prevents the truth from being seen.

Egoic pride blames someone or something else rather than accepting responsibility and the inherent admission the self is in need of healing and growth. The classic Christian example is "The devil made me do it." With egoic pride, fault is always found somewhere in the world outside, never within.

Egoic pride projects unconscious material upon others that it cannot acknowledge and accept about itself. Unable to own its deep fear and deceptive nature, it attributes such aspects to and condemns them in others. Projection serves egoic pride like a weapon serves a murderer.

Egoic pride refuses to bear the pain of personal growth and transformation. Rather than experience what Jung termed "legitimate suffering" by facing and transforming through the roots of one's issues, egoic pride projects its darkness onto others and thereby suffers those around it.

At its most extreme, egoic pride destroys whatever evidence and source thereof that threatens to cast light upon its darkness. For example, Jesus illuminated the spiritual flaws of Judaism, but its leaders could not tolerate his teachings and eliminated the threat to their institution's self-esteem and well-being (§4.4.h.).

In sum, egoic pride is the core dynamic perpetuating the darkness that shrouds our planet. As Martin Luther King Jr. observed, "The Darwinian concept of the survival of the fittest has been substituted by a philosophy of the survival of the slickest."[5]

5.2.b. Perspectives on Evil

Egoic pride is built upon fear and is protected internally by ignorance and unawareness and externally by deception. These traits are the fabric of evil (§1.2.d.) and produce choices that oppose love and spiritual growth.

Jung identified the root of evil as "the refusal to meet the Shadow."[6] "Shadow" refers to the aspects of our psyches that we judged a long time ago to be "not me" and banished into the unconscious. But try as we might to run away from it, our Shadow remains. The best means for learning about our Shadow is the presence of hatred, for we feel hatred toward those who manifest what we despise and cannot acknowledge about ourselves.

But shadow material is not what creates evil, for we all have it. The critical difference is how we relate to the shadow material in our unconscious depths. The "refusal to meet the Shadow" occurs when egoic pride has gained a stranglehold on the psyche and repudiates the deeper thoughts and feelings that might otherwise lead to integration and healing. As Peck explains, "The briefest definition of evil I know is that it is 'militant ignorance.' But evil is not general ignorance; more specifically, it is militant ignorance of the Shadow. Those who are evil refuse to bear the pain of guilt or to allow the Shadow into consciousness and 'meet' it."[7]

That said, egoic pride's refusal to meet the Shadow is not the only factor behind the worst manifestations of evil. After all, millions of ordinary people do all they can to avoid their Shadow yet are still caring and productive members of society.

Rather, the most destructive results are produced when the Teflon armor of egoic pride colludes with an ambitious will of unilateral selfishness. Psychologist Erich Fromm termed the condition "malignant narcissism," which is a powerful will that is solely driven to serve itself no matter what kind of damage is done to others.

Malignant narcissism is the other central piece in the puzzle of evil. As Peck explains, mentally healthy adults submit themselves to something greater than themselves. Whether it is God, truth, morality or another such ideal, they prioritize it above their selfish desires. He concludes, "In summary, to a greater or lesser degree, all mentally healthy individuals submit themselves to the demands of their own conscience. Not so the evil, however. In the conflict between their guilt and their will, it is the guilt that must go and the will that must win."[8]

5.2.c. Examples of Evil

Nazi Germany exemplified the dynamics of evil. Upon gaining power in 1933, the Nazis imprisoned their outspoken opponents and a year later assassinated other German leaders who might be threats to their policies and power. Hitler subsequently decreed that anyone who dared challenge the state would meet with certain death. The Nazis thus prohibited the criticism that is an essential part of national self-examination.

The Nazis characterized the Jews as deceptive, greedy, selfish, power-hungry, bent on global domination, heartless, treasonous, the primary cause of Germany's problems and ultimately evil. The Nazis were refusing to see these traits in themselves and projecting their Shadow upon the Jews. In a flagrant case of malignant narcissism, they later tried to annihilate the target of their projection.

So guess how life works? The Nazis blindly manifested their denied and projected traits in spades. They regularly deceived their own people and the world. They greedily and selfishly invaded other countries to gain more living space and resources as their power-hungry appetite grew for global domination. Their heartless triggering of World War II and the Holocaust betrayed the soul of Germany, which eventually realized the Nazis were the primary cause of its suffering and unequivocally evil.

For an example of evil at the individual level, the movie *American Beauty* offers a chilling depiction in the character of Frank Fitz, a retired Marine Corps colonel who appeared to be a responsible and upstanding citizen. But driven by a need for power, control and institutional order, he inherently opposed life and individuality in his wife and teenage son. His overbearing egoic pride had psychologically destroyed his wife, who was a disassociated shell of a woman bent on keeping an ultraclean house even cleaner.

Fitz also refused to observe clues that his son, Ricky, was selling marijuana and living beyond his tyrannical control, thereby avoiding the truth that his militant approach to life and parenting was a failure. As Ricky commented to their neighbor Lester, "Never underestimate the power of denial."

Fitz expressed an intense hatred for homosexuals but later came to a surprising epiphany that he had homosexual desires within. But when his advance upon the heterosexual Lester was rebuffed, he returned with a gun to murder in his neighbor what he despised and could not love and accept in himself.

5.2.d. Dealing With Evil

Wisdom is needed to deal effectively with evil. The space and possibility for it arises from the paradox of unity and individuality (§1.4.g.). It can be generated because all eternal beings have been granted the freedom to choose as they wish in a polarized universe of opposites. Be encouraged, though, that evil is not a cosmic or eternal force. Instead, it is only a pattern of choice-making that manifests a dark force.

Because embodied souls or discarnate spirits that oppose love and spiritual growth can never be destroyed, evil cannot be defeated with force. As the universal law is communicated in spiritual circles, "What you resist, persists."[9] As Jesus purportedly taught, "Do not resist an evil person" (Mt 5:39).

As it is impossible to destroy evil, the only way to eradicate it is to heal it in those who perpetuate it, and to heal an illness, we must first understand it. Evil choices come from lost souls who are caught in the stranglehold of egoic pride and are not aware of and in touch with who they truly are.

So far, so good, right? That is because the darkness is comparatively easy to recognize in others. Trouble is, the dynamic can be very difficult to recognize in ourselves and our beloved institutions. As Jesus supposedly admonished, "Why do you look at the speck of sawdust in your brother's eye and pay no attention to the plank in your own eye?" (Mt 7:3; §3.2.c.).

So if the darkness is so beguiling and insidious, how do we know if we are being unwittingly driven by it? A couple of heuristics will help.

Trying to eliminate evil with condemnation or force is a ghastly failure to witness the darkness in oneself. As Peck observes, "It is characteristic of those who are evil to judge others as evil."[10] If so, look within and lovingly address the arrogance, repressed fear and spiritual ignorance.

Secondly, if you are partnered with a person, institution or nation that is manifesting the darkness, you have a complementary version of a spiritual illness (§1.3.d.). If so, look within and lovingly address the bonding agent of fear and the protective covers of unawareness, ignorance and compartmentalized thinking.

All in all, the only way out of this universal predicament is love that fosters spiritual growth from individual to national levels. Granting acceptance and forgiveness is easier by realizing that we are all beautiful beings of the Light who got lost in the darkness. We have all chosen inhumane or downright evil behavior at some point in our eternal existence.

Love does not attack those who are enacting evil. What love will do, however, is illuminate the dynamic and refuse to enable it in any way.

The foundation for extending love is deep awareness, and our primary focus should be on our inner darkness. Generally speaking, we should approach the problem of evil by first transforming ourselves. As the only way out is through it, we must surface and move through our deepest fears lest we continue to be run by them. By also growing in consciousness and wisdom, the darkness will be easy to see.

As for the evil around us, do not enable or collaborate with it, and neither attack it nor submit to it (these actions all come from fear). Courageously and lovingly speak the truth about the situation, though, to illuminate the dark dynamics so they can be seen by others. Help those who are inadvertently partnering with it to understand how they are doing so and encourage them to withdraw their empowerment of it. The dark playground of evil will empty only as lost souls awaken to their fear-based collaboration in its wicked games and decide not to play there anymore.

[Note: There are times when the highest choice calls for the use of force to end overbearing abuse that cannot be halted in any other way.[11] For instance, because the Vatican and German Christianity failed to undercut Hitler's power when he wielded it murderously, which would have been the ideal nonviolent solution (§L.2., §L.3.), the Allies fought a just and necessary war to halt the Nazi assault upon the world.]

5.3. Modern Interpretations of Job

Our attention now turns to Job, but the dark fabric that weaves the chapter together will reappear soon. This section summarizes the Old Testament story and its prevailing interpretations.

5.3.a. The Story of Job

Job was a God-fearing man who was blameless and righteous. He had a large family, great wealth and numerous servants.

Satan challenged God by saying that Job was loyal only because of God's bountiful blessings. God accepted that as a possibility and allowed Satan to wreck Job's life to determine the true nature of his fidelity. Job's thousands of sheep, camels, oxen and donkeys were stolen or killed along with many servants. His ten sons and daughters were all killed in a freak accident, and he contracted a painful skin disease.

Despite his undeserved suffering and criticism from his friends, Job persevered through his ordeal. God thereafter blessed him by bringing him ten new children, doubling the wealth he had before, and granting him a very long life.

5.3.b. Kushner Empathizes With Job and God

Rabbi Harold Kushner delved into the story in his book *When Bad Things Happen to Good People*. He points out that of the following three suppositions, only two can hold true: (1) God is omnipotent and in control of all events, (2) God is moral, fair and just, and (3) Job was blameless and righteous.

To believe God is omnipotent, moral, fair and just (1 and 2), we must admit Job deserved what came his way. In this scenario, Job was not blameless and righteous.

To believe God is omnipotent and Job was blameless and righteous (1 and 3), we must admit God has an amoral mean streak and is not always just. In this scenario, God condoned the infliction of great suffering that Job did not deserve, so God can be cruel and unfair.

To believe God is moral, fair and just and Job was blameless and righteous (2 and 3), we must admit God is not controlling all earthly events. In this scenario, God is kind and fair but often powerless to alter or prevent tragedies from striking innocent people.

Opting for the last scenario, Kushner accepts the Bible at its word that Job was "blameless and upright; he feared God and shunned evil" (Jb 1:1). Also believing in a moral God of love, Kushner challenges the idea that God is omnipotent and in control of earthly events.

He describes how free will and natural laws impose limitations on divine intervention. Free will would not really exist if we were choosing to love God and be good to avoid divine punishment or garner special rewards. Meanwhile, universal laws must treat everyone equally to deliver unfailing precision and order for us all.

Kushner argues that God is neither causing nor preventing tragedies but rather inspiring us to make a difference in the lives of others and a better world for future generations. We can turn to God for strength and support in persevering through our crises rather than being crushed by them. Neither God nor his creation is perfect, but we can still choose forgiveness, love and life despite whatever befalls us.

5.3.c. Defending Job, Jung Grills God

Carl Jung published the most controversial book in his distinguished career, *Answer to Job*, at the age of 77. Accepting God as omnipotent and Job as blameless and righteous, he diced up the supposition that God is always moral, fair and just.

Jung pointed out that a father is just as guilty if he knowingly allows a criminal to walk into the family's home to steal and murder. According to Jung, God violated at least three of his own commandments in his treatment of Job.[12]

Per the biblical story, Job held firm through numerous debates with his friends while pleading for a hearing with God to defend himself. Per Jung, Job's steadfastness "forced God to reveal his true nature." God did not direct his wrath upon the slanderer (Satan) or call the troublemaker to account, "nor does it even occur to him to give Job at least the moral satisfaction of explaining his behavior. Instead, he comes riding along on the tempest of his almightiness and thunders reproaches at the half-crushed human worm."[13]

Jung saw no fault in Job except for his "incurable optimism" that he could "appeal to divine justice."[14] However, God was not just as he instead responded with might over right.

God had been manipulated by Satan and was never fully aware of it (as evidenced by how he treated Satan with surprising tolerance and instead lashed out at Job). If God really trusted Job, he would have defended his faithful servant and held Satan to account for the sadistic scheme. But that never happened, and God's "readiness to deliver Job into Satan's murderous hands proves that he doubts Job precisely because he projects his own tendency to unfaithfulness upon a scapegoat."[15]

Kushner offered an optimistic view of God's role in life's tragedies but avoided the dark side of the book. Jung did not, though, and identified what the story reveals about the God of the Old Testament.

5.4. Shining the Light Upon Job

Both Kushner and Jung assumed the Bible is a trustworthy document for learning about God. By challenging that assumption, though, the Book of Job is easily unmasked.

The true colors of Job will become clearer by first observing the relevant dynamics elsewhere. To understand the difficult life of Job, we begin with a case study of the difficult life of Joe.

5.4.a. Case Study: The Difficult Life of Joe

"Joe" came from a tough family background. His alcoholic and hard-driving father divorced his undisciplined mother in his early teens. He had to grow up in a hurry to be the man of the house for his unreliable mom and younger brother.

He graduated from college and had a solid professional career, but his drive for success was mostly channeled into a higher endeavor. He had long been a churchgoing man who was intent on living a righteous Christian life of discipline. From an Old Testament standpoint, he was blameless and righteous.

Frustrated by an immoral and immature world, Joe routinely said, "I love humanity, but I hate humans." He praised our spiritual evolution but loathed how most people avoided self-discipline and personal growth. He was convinced he had it right and others only had to listen to him on how to get their lives in order. He was a strong and bullish debater who rarely agreed to disagree.

Joe had been married for over a decade. As he saw it, he had been lovingly helping his wife grow in the walk for all those years. "Jill" eventually went beyond her role as a housewife to their children and earned a collegiate degree. When she was invited to be an instructor because of her excellent grades, she wanted to purchase some new clothes and shoes to build her confidence and appear professional.

Joe, however, was oblivious to his own insecurities and fears and incapable of emotionally supporting her. He was making good money as a corporate professional and buying sporting goods and power tools, but he would not allow her to purchase even a new pair of comfortable shoes to lecture in because of his Christian beliefs that materialism and image were false gods.

The day inevitably came when Jill found her spiritual power and began bringing up issues with their relationship. After months of marital counseling to no avail, Joe began confiding to a few trusted friends that the model marriage he had preached about for years was in trouble.

Spurred to look deeper, he excitedly reported an epiphany that he had been bound in a pattern of narcissism that had been passed down through his paternal lineage. He acknowledged that although his wife had her issues, his was the "great cancer" in the relationship that first needed clearing so everything else could follow.

Within a few weeks, though, his perspective snapped back to normal, and he talked about having to "chop off a healthy and vital branch of my tree [personality] to save my marriage." He sided with the counsel of an unwise friend to just be himself, that there was nothing much wrong with him, and it was only a matter of Jill now desiring an apple and he was an orange. Since nothing was changing, Jill demanded a divorce.

Joe was devastated and lamented about the harshness of God's will, especially since he had been such a righteous man with God and Christ at the center of his life. He repeatedly wondered how this could possibly be God's will. He withdrew from the world and was extremely close to taking his own life during that dark time of anguish. Meanwhile, Jill was advised to read *People of the Lie*, but she found it too traumatic to read because of how insightful it was about her ex-husband's core issue.

Over a year later and in a moment Joe described as similar to Saul's "saw the light" experience, he came face to face with his dominating pride and embraced the vital imperative to confront it. He sought therapy and thereafter began openly praising God for what had transpired. He was able to appreciate the divine love behind his life-shattering breaking point, for he had become a much healthier and more genuinely loving man.

5.4.b. Examining Job With a Spiritual Paradigm

Ancient Judaism taught that God is omnipotent, moral, fair and just. Meanwhile, the standards of righteous living were all about behavior. It hardly mattered what went on inside a man's psyche as long as he spoke and acted appropriately. Being blameless and righteous meant being a master of outside-in living and never breaking any part of the law. By those standards and just like Joe, Job was blameless and righteous.

A theological clash ensued when a lot of bad things happened to a good man. Job complained and argued that God had wronged him. His friends suggested instead that he must have sinned and thus needed to repent. This exquisitely written book allowed both sides to express themselves as it danced around the mystery of God's ways.

The Judeo-Christian world has been baffled by Job because it examines the book with the same old worldview. Therefore, it has not yet recognized Job's darkness, the book's deceptions and how horribly misleading the book is about God and life.

An enlightened spirituality goes far beyond meeting behavioral standards. This path is about inside-out living from deep inner transformation in which righteous behavior naturally results without any contrived effort (§4.3.d.). Addressing the darkness of the ego is an essential part of the development.

Meanwhile, life was designed to foster our spiritual growth. When we believe instead that life should be gratifying and mollifying our egos, we resist the divine process and suffer exponentially.

We can empathize with what Job went through, but we should not ignore his spiritual afflictions. Rather, we should learn from him as we find the narrow gate out of the darkness.

5.4.c. Job's Response to Tragedy

We are now ready to see how the life of Job was cut from the same cloth of egoic pride and narcissism as Joe's. The first two chapters describe how Job suffered great loss. He and his friends thus spent seven days and nights weeping and mourning together. The rest of the book tells how he thereafter dealt with his situation. Laced within these 40 chapters are the telltale symptoms of his spiritual illness.

If Job was spiritually healthy, he would have followed his grieving by embracing an attitude along the lines of, "Damn that hurt, but I still have a loving wife, my land and good friends. Life pulled the rug out from under me, but I'll get back up. God will help me heal and grow from this." Remaining emotions would have been released over time so he could have continued to live and love.

If Job was spiritually healthy, there would not be a book in the Bible with his name on it. Instead of engaging in a great debate with his friends, he would have accepted their empathy and continued along his journey. What else would there have been to report other than another person who had experienced great tragedy?

Instead, Job lamented about the day he was born and wished it would perish, that darkness would envelop it and blackness crush its light (Jb 3:3–5). In fact, his disdainful diatribe fills the entire third chapter. For instance, he asked why he did not perish when he was born. Why had there been knees to catch him and breasts to nurse him? If not, he would be resting in peace with the kings and wise men of yesteryear (Jb 3:11–15).

Job was suffering from narcissism and its core belief that one is greater and more important than others. He felt he was royalty who should be with the kings and wise men of the earth. Peck notes how the roots of depression often grow in the dark soil of narcissism:

> What can lie at the base of the cognitive difficulty of depressives is this core fantasy that bad things shouldn't happen to them. Of course they selectively perceive the negative when they believe they should be exempted from it—and fail to perceive the positive which they feel should be their royal right.[16]

Job's friend Eliphaz advised him to remember the advice he gave others and how he helped them when they were down. Yet when trouble came his way, Eliphaz observed, he was discouraged and dismayed (Jb 4:5).

Eliphaz also shared a revelation he had received from a heavenly spirit in the middle of the night. Eliphaz said it glided by his face as his bones shook with fear. This form stood before him and asked, "Can a mortal be more righteous than God? Can even a strong man be more pure than his Maker?" (Jb 4:12–17).

Eliphaz encouraged Job to submit to God and trust in his ways and plans. After praising God's goodness and justice, Eliphaz spoke what would be a theme of the forthcoming discourse from Job's friends. A man is blessed when God corrects him, so do not despise his discipline. The Almighty injures, but he also heals (Jb 5:17–18).

Eliphaz wanted Job to quit rebelling against God because he thought he knew better and to get back to trusting God and his ways. Job, though, would have none of it.

Another trait of narcissism is the attitude, "It's my way or no way at all." Surely Job still had a better situation than most everybody else in his country, yet he whined like a spoiled child. He asked if tasteless food is consumed without salt or if egg whites have any flavor. He refused to touch such food, for it made him ill (Jb 6:6–7). He also expressed his prideful self-pity: "My eyes will never see happiness again" (Jb 7:7).

5.4.d. Job's Prideful Protest

Instead of sinking into a deep depression, Job got angry: "I will not keep silent; I will speak out in the anguish of my spirit, I will complain in the bitterness of my soul" (Jb 7:11). Because such a reaction is so common for narcissists when life does not go their way, therapists long ago termed it "narcissistic rage."

Those suffering from narcissism may even forsake their own lives to prove themselves right as victims of a perceived injustice. As Job preached, "Although I am blameless, I have no concern for myself; I despise my own life" (Jb 9:21). He also spoke his fear about standing up to the Almighty, but the righteous-victim dynamic soon overrode it: "I loathe my very life; therefore I will give free rein to my complaint and speak out in the bitterness of my soul. I say to God: Do not declare me guilty, but tell me what charges you have against me" (Jb 10:1–2).

His friend Zophar was appalled. After quoting Job saying to God that his beliefs were flawless and he was pure in God's sight, Zophar wished the Almighty would speak up and enlighten Job with wisdom (Jb 11:4–6). Zophar implored him to stop thinking he could possibly know all the divine mysteries. If he would only return to God while putting away his sin, he would be standing tall without shame and fear and life would be bright (Jb 11:13–17).

But Job's friends were not affirming his royal ego, so he lashed out at them: "I desire to speak to the Almighty and to argue my case with God. You, however, smear me with lies; you are worthless physicians, all of you! If only you would be altogether silent!" (Jb 13:3–5). He also delivered another classic line of egoic pride: "I will surely defend my ways to his face" (Jb 13:15).

Job's friends sensed the root issue but were unable to name it. Eliphaz saw sin driving his words of craftiness and asked him why his eyes flashed as he vented his rage at God (Jb 15:5–13).

Job expressed his distress but maintained his unyielding pride: "My face is red with weeping, dark shadows ring my eyes; yet my hands have been free of violence and my prayer is pure" (Jb 16:16–17). However, his prayers were like a toddler's demands in the midst of a temper tantrum: give me what I want, or I will keep pitching this outrageous fit.

Another friend, Bildad, wondered when Job would finally end his speeches and why he was regarding his friends as cattle and viewing them as stupid (Jb 18:2–3). Bildad reflected, "You who tear yourself to pieces in your anger, is the earth to be abandoned for your sake?" (Jb 18:4).

Job was oblivious to the rampant darkness within as his royal ego screamed bloody murder. He exclaimed to his friends:

> If indeed you would exalt yourselves above me and use my humiliation against me, then know that God has wronged me and drawn his net around me. Though I cry, "Violence!" I get no response; though I call for help, there is no justice. He has blocked my way so I cannot pass; he has shrouded my paths in darkness. He has stripped me of my honor and removed the crown from my head. (Jb 19:5–9)

Job had no idea his ego was the reason his path was shrouded in darkness. Entrenched in egoic pride, he was spewing his darkness around like a firefighter's hose on the loose at full blast. He projected even more of it with more accusations against God: "He tears me down on every side till I am gone; he uproots my hope like a tree. His anger burns against me; he counts me among his enemies" (Jb 19:10–11). Job needed a revelation that it was his ego and its mistaken beliefs that were tearing him down, uprooting his hope, burning him up in anger, and waging war against his soul.

Eliphaz wisely counseled Job to submit himself to and be at peace with God. He would be restored if he simply returned to God (Jb 22:21–3).

But Job still proclaimed he was a righteous victim. God had denied him justice, he stated, and made him taste bitterness in his soul. He said he would not speak wickedly or deceitfully yet also declared, "I will never admit you are in the right; till I die, I will not deny my integrity. I will maintain my innocence and never let go of it; my conscience will not reproach me as long as I live" (Jb 27:5–6).

Job thus announced he was the epitome of egoic pride. He claimed unassailable self-righteousness, denied any possibility of a personal shortcoming, and was refusing to allow his will to be challenged by his conscience. A young man named Elihu testified in agreement that he had heard Job say these very words: "I am pure, I have done no wrong; I am clean and free from sin" (Jb 33:9).

5.4.e. God Intervenes

Elihu counseled humbly and wisely for six chapters but had no better luck than his elders (Jb 32–37). God finally had enough and spoke directly to Job: "Who is this that obscures my plans with words without knowledge?" (Jb 38:2). God then fired a multitude of rhetorical questions at Job about what it takes to be the creator of life and God over it all (Jb 38–39).

Job answered, "I am unworthy—how can I reply to you? I put my hand over my mouth. I spoke once, but I have no answer—twice, but I will say no more" (Jb 40:4–5). Amazingly, Job had only conceded to no longer speaking in his angry and accusatory self-righteousness. He was still refusing to own any semblance of a shortcoming.

God continued to sternly lecture through the next two chapters about the vast difference between himself and Job, thus giving Job another chance to understand and break through (Jb 40–41). The light bulb in Job's head finally brightened a bit. He replied that he had spoken of things he did not comprehend and that were too wonderful for him to know. He concluded, "My ears had heard of you but now my eyes have seen you. Therefore I despise myself and repent in dust and ashes" (Jb 42:5–6).

With that single sentence of repentance after chapter upon chapter of accusatory blustering, Job's ordeal finally came to an end. It was that simple. Acknowledge a personal shortcoming, and spiritually grow.

Granted, Job had not become aware of and surrendered his pride. Rather, his face-saving way of backing down from his conflict with God was admitting he was lacking in knowledge. But it was a growth step nonetheless, and it allowed him to accept God back into his heart.

The book concludes by stating that God blessed the latter part of Job's life more than the first. Job had twice as many sheep, camels, oxen and donkeys. He also had seven sons and three beautiful daughters. Moreover, he lived to be 140 years old and witnessed his family blossom through four generations.

5.5. The Wisdom and Deceptive Covering of Job

Job is clearly an open-and-shut case of egoic pride and narcissism. This section extracts the book's wisdom and exposes its deceptions.

5.5.a. The Real Wisdom of Job

To be human is to experience loss, for it is only a matter of time before life strips away everything from us but our essence. What ultimately matters is how we relate to these aspects of life. We can align with our souls as we embrace and spiritually grow with the process, or we can align with our egos as we despise and oppose it. Seen in these terms, Job's illness is obvious.

What happens in life is simply what happens. How we perceive it and the attitude we have about it determine how we experience it. Because Job was imprisoned by his ego, his mind went hard negative as he angrily fought God, resisted the process of his life, and suffered exponentially.

"Bad" things happen in life. They have nothing to do with divine punishment and everything to do with our previous choices and a universe that is fostering our spiritual growth. For just as Joe needed his life-shaking experience to heal and grow, so did Job.

Moreover, both cases demonstrate how the ego's resistance to God and life generates unnecessary pain. The ego is a structure of separation from God, who will always honor our free will but whose love will eventually break through our egoic shells and produce our reunification. Fighting the process creates additional and unnecessary suffering.

Spiritual teacher Eckhart Tolle explains, "The paradox is that suffering is caused by identification with form [being attached to things of the physical world] and erodes identification with form. A lot of it is caused by the ego, although eventually suffering destroys the ego—but not until you suffer consciously."[17]

We are meant to transcend suffering, but it will not happen on the ego's terms. Higher spiritual levels require the ego's dissolution, and a loving universe will not let us stay stuck in its darkness. The ego's way has to fail.

When we suffer consciously, we allow it to deepen our consciousness and burn up ego. Deeply letting go and merging with a deeper essence of life is how the transmutation occurs. As Tolle describes it, "The fire of suffering becomes the light of consciousness."[18]

Job believed he should be free from suffering. Such a belief is a common delusion that actually generates more suffering. As Tolle summarizes, "The ego says, 'I shouldn't have to suffer,' and that thought makes you suffer so much more...The truth is that you need to say yes to suffering before you can transcend it."[19]

Our growth shifts into high gear when we embrace the process of life and know that all events are serving our long-term best interests. The greatest obstacle to our development is egoic pride, which was Job's enormous stumbling block.

5.5.b. An Ancient Fish Story

Let us now look at how the story was framed. It begins, "In the land of Uz there lived a man whose name was Job. This man was blameless and upright; he feared God and shunned evil" (Jb 1:1). After mentioning his ten sons and daughters, 11,000 animals and numerous servants, it calls him the greatest man in the East.

One day Satan joined a staff meeting of angels for their periodic check-in with God: "The Lord said to Satan, 'Have you considered my servant Job? There is no one on earth like him; he is blameless and upright, a man who fears God and shuns evil'" (Jb 1:8). Satan countered that it was only because Job was blessed beyond measure and proposed that he would crack with a strong dose of misfortune. God approved the test and stipulated all was fair game except for Job's health.

Raiding parties then slayed Job's servants and stole his livestock, and his sons and daughters were killed when a house collapsed on them. He mourned but did not turn from God.

In a subsequent staff meeting, God once again brought up Job to Satan. God said, "There is no one on earth like him...And he still maintains his integrity, though you incited me against him to ruin him without any reason" (Jb 2:3). Satan argued it was only because Job still had his health, so God gave Satan permission to do all but take his life. Satan then afflicted him with painful sores, and the debate between Job and his friends thus unfolded.

Observe how Satan was not the one who brought up Job's name in either dialogue with God. With everything else we know about Job, the stench of an ancient literary herring is drifting into our presence. Yes, the glorification of Job apparently drove the story's claim that God had twice boasted about his greatness to the devil.

Yet even if we did not see the shiny scales of pride on this fish story, its ugliness and odor would still be shocking our senses. That is because the story has the same cohesiveness as a black oil spill trying to mix with turquoise ocean water, and truth-seekers cannot ignore the nauseating sight and smell.

If it was cohesive, its body and conclusion would have aligned with the crux of the story. According to the introduction, Job's tragedies were caused by a contest between God and Satan about the purity of Job's loyalty.

We thus expect God to have praised Job at the end of the story for stepping up to the plate for the home team and sticking one to the devil despite not having been forewarned of the dirty play that was on the way. In other words, a cohesive conclusion would have included or at least been harmonious with one or more of these elements: a celebration of God and Job having triumphed over Satan, God's explanation to Job about why he had experienced such unjust calamities, and God's glorification of Job for his dutiful perseverance.

Trouble is, none of these elements are even remotely present. Instead, the body and conclusion are completely incongruent with the introduction's quarrel between God and Satan. The primary conflict in the body and conclusion is between Job and God. The secondary conflict is between Job and his friends because they were siding with God, not him.

From the third chapter on, Job's ordeal was just a series of lengthy debates—the secondary conflict—before God finally confronted his angry accuser and resolved the primary conflict. Except for its first two chapters, the story has absolutely nothing to do with Satan at either the surface level of details or deeper levels of theme.

In the four chapters of God's discourse to Job at the end of the book, not once did the Almighty mention anything even vaguely alluding to a challenge from Satan or Job dutifully persevering so they could triumph over Satan. To the contrary, Job had been rebelliously complaining so violently that God had to make a thunderous appearance to snap him out of it.

Although the first two chapters tell us that Satan ruined Job's life with God's permission, the concluding chapter renders a different explanation. When Job's friends paid homage to Job, "They comforted and consoled him over all the trouble the Lord had brought on him" (Jb 42:11). According to the conclusion, God was responsible for Job's calamities.

In sum, the gross dissonance puts the lie to the introductory tale. Flopping around like a fish out of water, it appears to be a deviant fiction. Somebody opened up a can of theological worms by baiting the devil onto the story, and now it is far too late for the book to wriggle off the hook of the problems it ingested.

5.5.c. The Devil Rescues the Patriarch's Reputation

Because the book lacks historical markers and cross-biblical references, scholars are far from resolving its authorship and dating. Many believe the historical Job lived during the second millennium BCE and the author was an Israelite who penned it from oral and/or written sources somewhere between the tenth and sixth centuries BCE.

Most scholars think the book fuses two different stories and that its prologue (Jb 1:1–3:1) and epilogue (Jb 42:7–17) came from an independent, preexisting story. After all, the prologue (introduction) has a severe contradiction with the voluminous dialogue (§5.5.b.). Trouble is, a discrepancy also exists between the prologue and epilogue (conclusion) that were supposedly derived from the same older story, which undercuts that theory.

We can confidently conclude, though, that the creator of the biblical book was not the sharpest tool in the shed. Had he been more attuned to literary harmony, those problems would have been ironed out before it was published. In any case, the foremost question is what this author created versus what he built upon or adapted. So how about a speculative journey to see if we can develop a reasonable theory?

To begin, the devil is at the heart of the book's literary and theological contradictions. Since the author was unable to notice and reconcile those issues, he was probably the one who created them by adding the devil to the story. As for the opposite hypothesis of a preexisting devil story being the basis for the epic dialogue, surely such a dialogue would have made at least one reference to the devil. Hence, the dialogue probably predated the devil tale.

The historical Job probably contributed to the dialogue's composition, for he had spoken his need to someday be recognized and vindicated for his stand. He wished his words could be recorded on a scroll, inscribed on lead, or engraved on a rock so they could exist forever (Jb 19:23–24).

As the arguments of both sides are presented so fairly and poetically, it feels like Job sat down with his friends afterward to rehash who had said what and to polish everybody's words to their satisfaction. It feels like each side did so with the conviction that future generations would side with their position. Yet the driving intention behind the original story seems like it came from the narcissistic Job.

Let us presume the historical Job really existed in the East. Three different poems from ancient Babylon are about the suffering of a pious man. After them, a poem known as "The Babylonian Theodicy" has a stronger correlation with the Book of Job. Written about 1000 BCE, it presents a dialogue between a suffering man and his friend that involves the gods.

If the historical Job had heard it, perhaps it motivated him to take it to another level. Whether coming from personal experience or just an imaginative role play, a plethora of scenarios abound.

In any case, our theory goes with the historical Job and his friends composing the dialogue and including a brief introduction about an instigating tragedy to set the stage for it. Whether Job had really experienced such loss or had only developed an epic poem with his friends to wrestle with the thorn in their theology, it was surely a prized possession among his descendants and eventually embraced as historical truth.

Time would not have been kind to Job's position because his tragedy only had negative explanations. Was it pure randomness? If so, he was just another person whose ball on the roulette wheel of life had bounced into a slot of catastrophe. However, the prevailing theology did not allow for it. Instead, his tragedy had to have been the doing of a just and mighty God because he had indeed sinned badly but had not owned up to it.

Either way, Job's sinful allegations against God were completely unwarranted and would have been an ugly personal reflection. After all, he had confessed in the end that he did not know what he had been talking about. All in all, his reputation was surely taking a beating.

Fortunately for him, the devil cosmology was arising in the Middle East because of Zoroastrianism (§3.5.a.) and crossed paths with one of Job's descendants. An explanation had finally arrived for the blameless and righteous patriarch's tragedy. The descendant's epiphany inspired him to overhaul the original introduction and make the devil the impetus for Job's calamities.

Doing so rescued the patriarch from a theological trap and reinforced his greatness. After all, how special are you when a universal battle between good and evil is centered on you? In all likelihood, then, Satan was written into the story to rescue the patriarch's reputation and glorify his legacy.

5.5.d. The Deceptive Covering of Job's Arguing

This downstream author also added more misdirection to the prologue and epilogue. Desperately wanting us to believe Job was supremely righteous and God's greatest servant, his image-restoring work on the front and back ends of the book created another layer of contradiction.

We first need to observe how radically Job changed when given his spiritual test. He was not dutifully consistent but rather an ancient version of the good Dr. Jekyll and his dark opposite, Mr. Hyde.

After the first round of calamities, he made a spiritually healthy statement: "Naked I came from my mother's womb, and naked I will depart. The Lord gave and the Lord has taken away; may the name of the Lord be praised" (Jb 1:21). After the second round, Job's wife tried to get him to curse God. He replied, "You are talking like a foolish woman. Shall we accept good from God, and not trouble?" (Jb 2:10). The prologue comments, "In all this, Job did not sin in what he said" (Jb 2:10).

These statements reinforce the prologue's other verses that Job was blameless and righteous. For instance, Job routinely sacrificed burnt offerings on behalf of his sons and daughters in case they had sinned (Jb 1:5). He did not need to offer any sacrifices for himself, of course, because he was without sin.

Trouble is, the Job of the first two chapters (prologue) is a completely different person from the Job of the next 35 chapters (dialogue with his friends). The latter Job cursed God in his heart and angrily sought to argue his case before God that he was pure and without sin yet God had found fault in him. The heart of the book is about how Job pitched a fit of biblical proportions and demanded a hearing with God to accuse him to his face.

The prologue says, "Job did not sin by charging God with wrongdoing" (Jb 1:22). But charging God with wrongdoing was exactly what Job did throughout the book. It was the essence of his complaint, and he even stated it for the record with "Know that God has wronged me" and "Though I cry, 'Violence!' I get no response; though I call for help, there is no justice" (Jb 19:6–7).

The Job of those 35 chapters never would have said what the prologue says he said: "The Lord gave and the Lord has taken away; may the name of the Lord be praised" (Jb 1:21). It would have been the antithesis of his self-righteous anger, hatred of life and contempt for God. If his wife would have reflected his quote from the second chapter back around on him—"You are talking like a foolish man. Shall we accept good from God, and not trouble?"—he may have killed her in a fit of rage.

One might argue that Job had remained loyal to God despite his nuclear meltdown. After all, it is a natural emotional response for many people when their worlds get ripped apart.

However, the argument fails for a couple of reasons. First, the story is about God's greatest man on the planet, and the whole point of the calamities was to see if this super servant's affinity for God would change when trouble came his way. Arguing that Job had a natural reaction when trouble struck is an admission the devil really won.

Second, the epilogue claims that Job never broke down and was blameless and righteous throughout the ordeal. That is because the downstream author of the prologue and epilogue was intent on restoring Job's reputation and establishing his legacy as one of the greatest men to have ever lived.

After Job had finally backed down in the dialogue's closing statement, the epilogue begins with God chastising Job's friends and ordering them to take seven bulls and rams to Job to sacrifice. As God is quoted, "My servant Job will pray for you, and I will accept his prayer and not deal with you according to your folly. You have not spoken the truth about me, as my servant Job has" (Jb 42:8).

This covering lie is in flagrant contradiction with three interrelated facts from the dialogue. First, the devious quote says Job had been speaking right about God, yet the truth of his disdainful blustering and subsequent about-face surrender was that he had not been speaking right about God. Indeed, Job admitted to God that he had been inexcusably ignorant while popping off for all that time (Jb 42:3).

Second, the devious quote of God is the polar opposite of God's view about Job and the words he spoke to Job in the preceding four chapters. In addition to calling Job out for obscuring his counsel without knowledge (§5.4.e.), God also took Job to task for Job's scathing accusations: "Will the one who contends with the Almighty correct him? Let him who accuses God answer him!" (Jb 40:2) and "Would you discredit my justice? Would you condemn me to justify yourself?" (Jb 40:8). God thus took issue with Job because Job had not spoken of him what is right.

Third, the epilogue says that while Job had rightfully spoken about God, Job's friends had not. This is patently false, for a careful read of the dialogue shows that Job's friends had been saying essentially the same thing that God finally said to Job, which is to remain faithful to him, trust his justice is sound, and know that he knows how to be God far better than you. Job was the only one who had been speaking folly about God, and he was the only one who God had bellowed at to change his tune.

Yet the deceptive epilogue would have us believe the opposite. Despite God upbraiding Job for his ignorance and pride, the downstream author tried to make it look like Job had been right all along and his friends were the ones who had been foolishly running off at the mouth against God. The author wanted it declared that even though the patriarch had been called out by God, he was still more righteous than his friends and the greatest man in the East.

The prologue and epilogue were written by a hack who had no interest or ability in ensuring his work would seamlessly integrate with the voluminous dialogue. That said, he at least kept his devil story straight with the exact words he used for Satan's challenge. Satan supposedly said to God that with some calamity in his life, Job would "curse you to your face" (Jb 1:11, 2:5).

Satan won the essence of the bet, for Job's highly touted loyalty to God went up in flames. Job sinfully accused God of wrongdoing, and even God admitted that Job had condemned him to justify himself. But with a carefully worded clause that would make a lawyer proud, God won the bet on a technicality. Despite Job's blasphemous words that prove he had cursed God in his heart and among his friends, Job never cursed God to his face.

This epic piece of literature eventually crossed paths with the ancient Hebrews, who could surely relate to the theological problem of suffering and included it in their scriptures. Despite being a horribly conflicted book because of its downstream deceptions, it would later become a part of what many Christians believe is the inerrant Bible.

5.5.e. The Subsequent Spiritual Lessons

Job and his devious defender never understood the spiritual lesson of his ordeal.

They believed he was blameless and righteous and the epitome of greatness.

They never could have known that the Jewish Messiah would later preach a dramatically different paradigm. Jesus taught that we are all equal in God's eyes and that living with healthy energies and attitudes is just as important as adhering to behavioral codes. At the heart of his ministry, though, was a message of love and spiritual growth, and he welcomed the sinners who embraced a path of repentance. A balloon moving upward, even though it has just left the ground, will quickly pass a law-abiding balloon at 50 feet that is pridefully stuck where it is.

Job was an ancient version of a self-righteous Pharisee, but the world could not see through his whitewashed exterior to perceive his inner darkness. A new day has dawned, though, and we can finally see the essence of this book and its corresponding deceptions.

Observe how simple it is to see the truth in hindsight, yet the awareness had previously evaded us. The tricky nature of consciousness is demonstrated yet again. We thought we saw this book so clearly, only to realize just how lost we had actually been.

All the while God's sense of humor abounds. Job wanted to go down in history for his greatness, and God let him, but the joke is actually on Job despite it taking us a few thousand years to get the punch line.

Is the Bible the inerrant word of God? God has obviously honored our free will to write whatever we want about her, even when somebody wrote a story that he was a willing accomplice to theft and murder. The Bible can be insightful and illuminating, but Job is more evidence that it is not an infallible communication from our Creator.

5.6. The Devil and the Old Testament

The Book of Job was the Trojan Horse that slipped Satan into the scriptures. Nevertheless, the Old Testament is surprisingly devoid of corroboration for this infamous conception.

5.6.a. The Devil's First Appearance in the Scriptures

Prior to Job, the devil was completely absent from the scriptures. That is because the ancient Hebrews believed God was responsible for all earthly events. These folks believed bad times were divine punishment because "the Israelites did evil in the eyes of the Lord" (Jgs 3:12). As they saw it, no other supernatural power was involved in human affairs.

When the downstream author of Job adopted the devil from Zoroastrianism while trying to rehabilitate Job's reputation, his inventions produced a trio of dastardly consequences. First, his prologue and epilogue rendered a grossly incongruent book that eventually found its way into Judaism's sacred scrolls.

It marred the Old Testament with another obvious case of deception.

Second, the book rendered another defamatory story about God. It reinforced the idea that the Almighty was ruling with terrifying authority while showing he condoned acts of cruelty. In this case, it was over a petty issue about his ego, which the devil played like a fiddle by suggesting that Job's fidelity was not pure.

Third, Judaism recorded its first conception of God having an evil archenemy who could create earthly mayhem. Because of this imaginative book, the devil became a part of Judaic cosmology.

5.6.b. Satan's Encore Was Brief

The next Old Testament devil reference came in 520 BCE when the prophet Zechariah reported seeing Satan standing at the side of a high priest to accuse him. According to Zechariah, Satan did nothing but stand and receive a rebuke from God (Zec 3:1–2).

5.6.c. The Devil Takes the Blame

Satan's only other Old Testament appearance was in Chronicles, which was most likely written in the vicinity of 350 BCE (§E.2.). How the Chronicler reported an ancient event is another case of an author fabricating the devil into the scriptures.

Samuel was written many centuries earlier, and it tells how God burned with anger at Israel and incited David to take a census of Israel and Judah. Doing so was a grave sin, and David was given three options for God's punishment. David opted for a plague of three days that killed 70,000 people until God called back his angel that was executing the calamity (2 Sm 24:1–17).

The Chronicler reported the same event but with one dramatic difference. Instead of God doing the instigating, "Satan rose up against Israel and incited David to take a census of Israel" (1 Chr 21:1).

In the centuries that passed from the writing of Samuel to the writing of Chronicles, the devil had taken root in the Judaic worldview. The excuse of "the devil made me do it" was thereafter alive and kicking in the Western ego.

5.6.d. That's All, Folks

With the exception of Job and the aforementioned verses, the Old Testament is devoid of support for the theology that God has an evil archenemy. The closest remaining verse comes from Isaiah: "How you have fallen from heaven, morning star, son of the dawn! You have been cast down to the earth, you who once laid low the nations!" (Is 14:12). Yet even the *NIV Study Bible*, which supports the idea of a forthcoming antichrist, acknowledges that "the passage clearly applies to the king of Babylon."[20]

As for the Garden of Eden, no Old Testament author wrote anything about the serpent representing Satan. Again, the devil was a late arriver to ancient Judaic theology. Christians who think the serpent represents the devil are projecting their cosmology upon the Genesis story.

5.7. Conclusion

The chapter illuminated the dynamics of evil and its core enabler, egoic pride. Our growth in consciousness let us witness Job's darkness and unmask the book's deceptions.

Meanwhile, the case continues to build that God does not have a grand archenemy in the devil. However, many Christians will be loath to concede the point because they believe the apocalyptic prophecies have foretold how this adversary will eventually take to human form in the antichrist and march us into the battle of Armageddon. As they see it, the Book of Daniel foretells the coming of this evil ruler.

Because the book also prophesies about the time of the end and its metaphors are strongly interwoven with Revelation, our search for truth now turns to the most fascinating and spiritually important book of the Old Testament. Before Daniel's prophecies are unraveled in Chapter 7, though, we first need to look at the literary document that preserved them.

Chapter 6

The Book of Daniel

6.1. Introduction

Daniel's prophecies render an undeniable case of the future being foretold hundreds of years before it happened, so knowing when they were on the historical record is critical. This chapter introduces the debate about the dating of Daniel and the appendix that conclusively resolves it. Since the prophecies are so easy to unravel in hindsight, the rest of the chapter explains why they remained unsolved until now.

6.2. The Great Debate About Daniel

Given the prophecies' astounding knowledge of history from the sixth to second centuries BCE, a vast majority of scholars believe they were fabricated in the 160s BCE. To be referred to as the "hoax theory," it is based on the assumption that knowing the distant future is impossible. Per this theory, the prophecies were written during the Maccabean revolt of 168–164 BCE.

Meanwhile, others argue the book is flawless and was composed as advertised in the sixth century BCE. To be referred to as the "fundamentalist" position, it is based on the assumption the Bible is infallible.

6.2.a. The Stakes Are High

If it was ever proven the prophecies were penned in the sixth century BCE, scientism would be shattered. After all, this worldview would have no explanation whatsoever for how a person could so accurately and precisely foretell so many empires, rulers and events in the distant future.

Meanwhile, fundamentalists have just as much to lose. For if the prophecies were ever proven to be a wager made after the fact, their core belief in an infallible Bible would be shattered. After all, how would you explain the Almighty including a deliberate forgery in his holy book for humanity? Moreover, the Bible says Jesus quoted a Daniel prophecy as a trustworthy testament about the end times (Mt 24:15). How would you explain the purported Son of God quoting a forgery as divine truth?

6.2.b. The Source Documents

A cursory answer to the dating of Daniel is unacceptable. For instance, some fundamentalists believe the Septuagint translation of the Hebrew scriptures is sufficient proof that Daniel existed in the third century BCE. We begin with that claim.

The Greeks under Alexander the Great conquered the ancient world in the latter half of the fourth century BCE, and they began instilling their culture and language in a process known as Hellenization. After he suddenly died in 323 BCE, his massive empire fragmented in a series of wars among his successors. One of the Greek-speaking kingdoms that resulted was the Ptolemaic Kingdom, which ruled over Egypt and Judaea.

The scriptures were thereafter translated from Hebrew to Greek and became known as the Septuagint. Scholars widely agree that the Torah (the first five books of the Old Testament) was translated c. 250 BCE.[1] However, they diverge as to when the other books were translated. In any case, the Septuagint continued to expand as more scriptural books were written, translated and included.

Daniel is part of the Septuagint, but whether it was part of the original translation cannot be proven either way. Scholars have analyzed translating styles and word choices to estimate the era of a book's translation, but it is far from an exact science. The bottom line is Daniel's presence in later versions of the Septuagint does not prove it existed in the third century BCE, and when it was translated cannot be conclusively determined.

Snapshots in time of an expanding Septuagint are needed, but none exist. Unfortunately, its oldest surviving copies only date back to the fourth century CE (*Codex Vaticanus* and *Codex Sinaiticus*). Its oldest fragments date back just two centuries prior.

Conclusive proof cannot be found in the original Hebrew either. The Masoretic text, which is the master source of the Old Testament in modern Bibles, is the only existing record of the entire Old Testament in Hebrew. The oldest complete version is comparatively new, as it only dates back to 1008 CE (*Codex Leningradensis*). Its oldest fragments date to the ninth century CE.

The translation issue has an interesting wrinkle. The Septuagint version of Daniel includes a substantial amount of additional material that is not present in its Masoretic version. More information on the Septuagint and the additions to Daniel is presented in Appendix C ("The Septuagint and Daniel").

6.2.c. Referential Evidence of Daniel's Existence

As revealed in the next chapter, the same accuracy and precision of Daniel's prophecies from the sixth to second centuries BCE actually continued into the fifth century CE. For reasons that will be explained later, humanity failed to see the post-Maccabean fulfillments until now. Nevertheless, the prophecies did not skip a beat in foretelling the future with spine-tingling exactitude whether it was the fourth century BCE, the first century CE or the fourth century CE.

So is there even a remote possibility that Daniel was written after the later fulfillments? Absolutely not. Although no scholar claims a later date of composition than the Maccabean era (160s BCE), you might like some evidence that Daniel was on the historical record by the end of the first century CE:

- Two different stories from Daniel were referenced in 1 Maccabees, which was written in the late second century or early first century BCE (1 Mc 2:59–60).

- In Matthew, Daniel is named with the quoting of a segment of his prophecy (Mt 24:15). In Mark, the same segment is quoted (Mk 13:14). These gospels were composed in the first century CE.

- Daniel was retold in great detail by the Jewish historian Josephus (c. 37–100 CE).[2]

- In c. 96 CE, Clement of Rome mentioned Daniel by name alongside the story about the lion's den in his letter to the Corinthians.[3]

- Writing about the suppression of the Jewish revolt of 66–73 CE, the Roman historian Tacitus (c. 55–117 CE) said the Jews ignorantly acted on prophecy that was in all likelihood drawn from Daniel.[4]

Ironically, the attack against Daniel's authenticity began long before its prophecies about rulers and events in the fourth and fifth centuries CE had been fulfilled. In the third century CE, the philosopher Porphyry published *Against the Christians*, which included the contention that Daniel had to have been written in the second century BCE. Knowledge of Porphyry's work and accusations survived in a commentary on Daniel by Jerome (340–420 CE).[5]

6.2.d. Archaeological Evidence of Daniel's Existence

In 1947, a remarkable discovery occurred near the Dead Sea at a site known as Qumran. Over a thousand scroll fragments were found in 11 different caves. The scrolls were mostly of the Hebrew scriptures, and portions of every Old Testament book but two were part of the cache. Based on archaeological, historical and paleographic evidence that was corroborated for many items with carbon-14 dating, the scrolls and other Qumran artifacts were dated from the third century BCE to 70 CE.

[Note: With the Dead Sea Scrolls being roughly a thousand years older than the Masoretic text, scholars could see how well Jewish scribes preserved the material. The scribes did a remarkably good job, but there were some noteworthy differences. For instance, the Masoretic text says Goliath stood "six cubits and a span," or "over nine feet tall" (1 Sm 17:4). But a Dead Sea Scroll reads "four cubits and a span," which is a believable six-and-a-half feet for David's enemy (although still a giant back then), and is corroborated by the Septuagint. This strongly suggests "six cubits and a span" came from a scribal error in the transmission of the Masoretic text sometime after the Dead Sea Scrolls and Septuagint had been sourced from it.]

Eight manuscripts containing text from Daniel were found in Qumran caves 1, 4 and 6. Paleographic analysis determined that four of them (1QDan^b, 4QDan^a, 4QDan^c and 4QDan^e) were copied during the Hasmonean period of 167–30 BCE. The other four (1QDan^a, 4QDan^b, 4QDan^d and pap6QDan) were copied during the Herodian period of 30 BCE to 70 CE.[6]

The Qumran artifacts have thus proven that Daniel existed by 30 BCE. Taking other evidence into consideration, <u>all scholars agree that Daniel was on the record no later than the 160s BCE</u>.

6.2.e. The Flaws on Both Sides of the Debate

For critical scholars, none of Daniel's prophecies were fulfilled after the Maccabean era. Many Christians beg to differ, though, for they believe one of them foretold the exact day Jesus made his entrance into Jerusalem. Trouble is, this popular reconciliation uses an accounting trick and cuts a lot of corners to achieve the fit (§K.4.b.).

This state of affairs, however, is no longer the case. The pinpoint accuracy of Daniel's prophecies long after the 160s BCE makes a powerful case that they are all legitimate and were written as advertised in the sixth century BCE.

Yet a new conclusion about the prophecies does not carry over to the entire book in which they are contained. The narrative stories in Daniel are riddled with numerous flaws that have been the primary evidence for the hoax theory. These flaws are so blatant that even *The Catholic Study Bible* admits the book is fraudulent. As Daniel is introduced therein by Catholic scholars, "This work was composed during the bitter persecution carried on by Antiochus IV Epiphanes (167–164) and was written to strengthen and comfort the Jewish people in their ordeal."[7]

That a deliberate hoax is residing in God's unerring Word is one hell of a contradiction—not to mention Jesus having swallowed its bogus prophecies hook, line and sinker (Mt 24:15)—but the phenomenon of denial is not the point at hand. Rather, the emphasis is on the glaring flaws that led scholars to this conclusion.

6.2.f. Redirecting the Debate

So how can the prophecies be legitimate yet the narrative stories they were packaged with be so fraught with errors? This complex problem is answered in Appendix D ("Redirecting the Debate About Daniel"). The old saying of there being three sides to a story—one side, the other side and the truth—is eminently applicable. The appendix demonstrates that the hoax theory and fundamentalist position are both mistaken.

Although the veracity of the prophecies should be enough to sink the hoax theory, the appendix nevertheless proves the original version of Daniel was composed in the sixth century BCE. To do so, it debunks each and every argument behind the hoax theory's contention that it was composed four centuries later, albeit with one big exception.

An analogy will help depict the situation. The stories are like a document that was supposedly written by an aide to Abraham Lincoln in the 1860s. Although displaying impressive knowledge suggesting it was indeed written during the Civil War, it is betrayed by howlers such as Lincoln enjoying a musical performance that included electric guitars, appealing to the 50 states to remain united, demanding his generals conduct more kamikaze missions, and being succeeded by Theodore Roosevelt.

Each type of error occurs in Daniel. A musical instrument appears long before it was invented, a governing structure is referenced that did not exist until the next century, a word from a foreign culture is used even though it was not in the local lexicon at the time, and a famous leader is moved up a few decades before his time.

Since neither side has cornered the truth, the appendix dives in to find it. It explores what happens when we scrub each of the stories of their attached barnacles. The stories in four of the six chapters quickly rise to the surface of being based on historical truth while the other two sink like stones to the depths of baseless fiction. These two tales are the big exception. Showing no contemporary knowledge and riddled with historical and linguistic anachronisms, they are obvious fabrications that were written about two centuries later.

Appendix D also presents a reconciling theory to explain the carnage in Daniel. Appendix E ("The Egregious Error in Ezra") corroborates the theory by illuminating an outlandish error that was made during the compilation of Ezra, for the error appears to be intimately linked to the anomalies in Daniel.

The reconciling theory, though, is tangential to what these appendixes prove. First, the original version of Daniel was indeed penned in the sixth century BCE. Second, Daniel and Ezra are marred by a pack of howlers, which further cements the case that the Bible is not inerrant.

6.3. Why Daniel's Prophecies Remained a Mystery

As Daniel's prophecies are so easily unraveled in hindsight, you may wonder why they remained a mystery for all these centuries. There are at least five reasons why they were not solved until now.

6.3.a. The Printing Press and the Reformation

In the Middle Ages, very few people were able to read the Bible. Handwritten in Latin (in the West) or Greek (in the East), Bibles were exceptionally laborious to produce and rarely found outside of churches, monasteries and universities. Meanwhile, the Church and its partnering monarchs believed that translating the Bible into common language would desecrate God's holy words and foster heresies and rebellion.[8]

A 14th-century Oxford theologian named John Wycliffe begged to differ. The "Morning Star of the Reformation" challenged the Church's doctrines and practices in his extensive writings. In addition to denouncing its hierarchy and massive wealth, he accepted only the Bible as truly authoritative. Believing everybody should have access to its truth, he and his associates translated the Bible from Latin into English. He was banished from Oxford and condemned by papal bulls (formal decrees from the pope) before dying in 1384.

In 1408, the archbishop of Canterbury prohibited public and private reading of Wycliffe's translation until the Church had formally sanctioned it. In 1415, the Council of Constance examined his other writings, declared him a heretic, and ordered the burning of his books and bones.

In 1455, Johannes Gutenberg developed the movable-type printing press and produced the Gutenberg Bible (in Latin). His machinery had its greatest initial impact, however, by turning the equivalent of an interoffice memo into a global manifesto of protest and revolution.

Martin Luther did not plan on becoming a world-changing leader. Targeted for a law degree by his father, he was a 22-year-old university student when he was caught in a life-threatening thunderstorm in July of 1505. Praying to Saint Anne, he vowed to become a monk if his life was spared. He thus joined a strict monastic order and engaged his vigils, fasting, prayers, confessions and reading with extreme intensity. Stricken with fear of God's judgment, he later reflected that if ever a monk got to heaven by his monkery, he would be the one.

Luther was ordained as a priest and dispatched to the outlying town of Wittenberg (near modern-day Berlin) to attain a doctorate of theology, which he received in 1512. He was made a professor of the Bible the following year. All the while he realized that his guilt and fear could not be alleviated by more obsessive religious activity. Through his study of Paul's letters, he concluded that he was justified by faith and felt reborn in divine love.

Meanwhile, a monk representing the pope was selling indulgences, which the Church claimed would alleviate punishment that was due in purgatory for nonmortal sins. The sales were to finance the construction of Saint Peter's Cathedral in Rome. Offended at this biblical perversion but believing he could reform the Church, Luther wrote to his archbishop and enclosed his 95 theses.

Luther also posted them on the doors of the Wittenberg city church on October 31, 1517, which was common practice for enticing other scholars to a debate. Written in Latin, they were only intended for and could only be read by other scholars. Nobody showed up, which was also common. Contrary to his wishes, though, his document was fed to the printing presses, and copies were distributed and sold to thousands across Europe.

The furor quickly reached Rome. Luther was fortunate to have the protection of Frederick II of Saxony, so the pope could not summon him to Rome for a heresy trial and execution. In 1518, a cardinal met with him in Augsburg (near modern-day Munich) and demanded that he recant, but he refused.

In 1520, the pope issued a papal bull that denounced Luther's teachings and ordered the destruction of his works and his capture and deportation to Rome. The pope's legate was unable to carry out the order, though, and reported to Rome that 90 percent of the people in territories near Luther were firmly behind the rebel.

In 1521, the Church excommunicated Luther. Emperor Charles V signed the Edict of Worms shortly thereafter, which made Luther an outlaw. Anybody could thus kill him without punishment. He was "kidnapped" for his safety by supportive forces and hidden away at the Wartburg castle. There he began translating the New Testament from Greek into German, which was published in 1522. He moved back to Wittenberg, got married in 1525, and finished his translation of the Old Testament from its original Hebrew in 1530.

Meanwhile, an Oxford and Cambridge scholar named William Tyndale was pursuing a similar agenda in England. Fluent in many languages, he asked permission from the bishop of London to translate the Bible into English. Tyndale was denied. In 1524, he traveled to the Continent to do his work. He completed the first English translation of the New Testament from its original Greek in 1525. His work was printed from various cities as he eluded the authorities and began translating the Old Testament.

Back in England, numerous smugglers of his Bible were executed. Tyndale's run ended in 1535 when he was betrayed and captured in Antwerp. After being convicted of heresy, he was strangled and burned in 1536. His final words were spoken in prayer for all in attendance to hear: "Lord, open the King of England's eyes."[9]

Speaking of, Henry VIII (1509–1547) defied the pope to break his long-standing marriage to Catherine of Aragon and marry Anne Boleyn in 1533. He then teamed with Parliament to renounce England from the Catholic Church and make himself the ruler of the Church of England (also known as the Anglican Church). After he died, England vacillated between Protestantism and Catholicism as newer Bible translations proliferated.

When King James I (1603–1625) took the throne, England was polarized by Protestant and Catholic factions that were passionate about their extremist Bibles (the Geneva and Rheims versions) and strongly opposed to the Church of England's latest offering (the Bishops' Bible). The king thus commissioned yet another translation of the Bible. England's 50 best scholars were drawn from all theological camps and tasked with producing text they could all commend. The King James Version was completed in 1611.

In sum, the printing press and courageous reformers made the Bible available to commoners in their native language. As for the point of this history, most people did not have the opportunity to unravel Daniel's prophecies until the last five centuries.

6.3.b. Extensive Historical Knowledge Required

Unlocking the prophecies also requires historical knowledge over numerous centuries, and it was very hard to come by until the printing press made books more widely available. A significant fulfillment occurred in the fourth century CE, and those events may have triggered some bright minds who knew the scriptures. However, global history from three to six centuries prior was also needed to fully unravel the prophecies.

Yet who knew such history? The men of the fourth century CE who were well versed in the scriptures probably knew little to nothing about people and events from three to six centuries prior. After the fourth century CE, that history quickly disappeared from view, too, for the few who had access to the scriptures.

6.3.c. Daunting Fears and an Ingrained Paradigm

Even if an enlightened soul had the biblical and historical knowledge to unravel the prophecies, it would not have done anything for humanity. That is because the Church would have executed the rebel and obliterated his writings. Challenging the Church or its ideology was the equivalent of signing your own death warrant.

For instance, the story of Giordano Bruno (1548–1600) deserves enhancing (§2.2.a.). A Dominican monk at the outset of his career, this brilliant astronomer and mathematician embraced the insights of Copernicus and taught that the sun is at the center of our solar system. He was also a philosopher who essentially advocated that God is infused in all matter amid an infinite universe. Put on trial by the Roman Inquisition, he explained how his scientific and philosophical views were compatible with Christian doctrine.

The pope would have none of it and gave him eight days to recant. Bruno declined and said before being burned at the stake, "Perchance you who pronounce my sentence are in greater fear than I who receive it."[10]

The fear of torture and death was an incredibly potent means of control for the Church, but democratic governments eventually arose and divorced themselves from the colluding tyranny. Despite this religious freedom, two other forms of fear persisted and kept those with sufficient biblical and historical knowledge from unraveling Daniel. Because one must perceive the history of Christianity with an enlightened paradigm to unlock the prophecies, those fears kept the solution well hidden.

The first fear is of being damned to an eternity in hell. Even today most Christians have been indoctrinated with the idea that such a fate awaits those who forsake the Bible. Challenging the Church used to require tremendous courage because one's body hung in the balance. Challenging the religion would require tremendous courage because one's soul hung in the balance.

The second fear involves one's well-being in the physical world, wherein Jewish and Christian professionals have been deeply invested in perpetuating their beloved religions. In addition to the trauma from undercutting one's cherished beliefs, there would also be severe consequences for the upstart's career, finances and social life.

All in all, religious professionals have had as much incentive to challenge their core beliefs as they would to enter a cave filled with venomous snakes. Why go there?

6.3.d. Leaving the Darkness Behind

So what about people who were not bound by those fears or blinded by a religious paradigm? What kept one such person from solving the mysteries of Daniel?

Critical scholars would have been great candidates for doing so. However, they had embraced the hoax theory and were immersed in the scientific paradigm that long-range prophecy was impossible, so they did not bother trying to decode a fabrication. Meanwhile, spiritualists and followers of other religions had no reason to study the Jewish prophets. The pool of candidates was thus reduced to only those who had studied Daniel before departing their religion for a spiritual worldview.

However, these awakening souls hardly ever look back and routinely describe themselves as "recovering" Christians in reference to their healing journey out of fear, guilt and shame. Those who knew a lot about the apocalyptic prophecies probably felt the greatest need to make a clean break from their prior indoctrination. Such people discarded the Bible like a high school textbook and moved on.

6.3.e. A Supernatural Plan

Daniel's prophecies remained a mystery for a host of historical and psychological reasons. The greatest reason they remained unsolved, though, is because the spiritual realm designed them to be that way.

The timing of their unraveling was meant to coincide with our collective awakening. The spiritual realm did not override our free will and dictate this momentous breakthrough. Rather, it long ago saw when we would finally achieve it and decided to support our spiritual evolution with a supernatural revelation.

In other words, the spiritual realm intended for the prophecies to remain a mystery until the moment was right. When we finally began awakening, they would be easily solved as we unwrapped a gift of heavenly affirmation.

6.4. Conclusion

The chapter introduced the debate about dating Daniel and the book's assured existence by the 160s BCE. Nevertheless, Appendix D proves its prophecies were legitimately penned back in the sixth century BCE. That the hoax theory is incorrect should not come as much of a surprise, as the prophecies were just as accurate after the Maccabean era as they were before it. Yet as Appendix D also demonstrates, the fundamentalist position is not all that much closer to being correct either.

The chapter then reviewed some history that helps explain the shocking messages that are laced within the prophecies. The Church was concerned that putting the Bible into common language would instigate heresy and rebellion. That is exactly what was meant to happen, and the Reformation was just a prelude to our spiritual revolution.

The stage is set, and by now it should be clear as to how the divine play will unfold. It is time to see how Daniel was shown the script over 2,500 years before our historic performance of it.

Chapter 7

Daniel's Prophecies

7.1. Introduction

Daniel's prophecies were laced with ambiguities and mysteries that made them impossible for mainstream Christians to interpret. However, this chapter and its corresponding appendixes unravel them so easily that it is hard to believe they remained unsolved until now. Their foretelling of the future is truly astonishing, and their divine messages will be validating our awakening.

7.2. The Grouping and Purpose of Daniel's Prophecies

Daniel contains six long-range prophecies. They have been organized to simplify the forthcoming explanations.

7.2.a. Historical Prediction: The Four About the Four

What will be termed the "Four Prophecies About the Four Kingdoms"—or the "Four About the Four"—constitute the vast majority of the text and pertain to global history, and we need to properly interpret them to unlock the treasures of the other two. They are:

- <u>The Statue</u>. The first of the "Four About the Four" uses the imagery of a statue and was interpreted by Daniel (Dn 2:31–45).

- <u>The Four Beasts</u>. The second uses the imagery of four different beasts and was interpreted by an unidentified angel (Dn 7:1–28).

- <u>The Ram and the Goat</u>. The third uses the imagery of a ram and a goat and was interpreted by the angel Gabriel (Dn 8:1–27).

- <u>The Omniscient Angel's Lecture</u>. The fourth was a lecture about forthcoming history by an omniscient angel (Dn 10:1–11:45). An abstract description of the future, it did not need to be interpreted.

7.2.b. Spiritual Revelation: The Crown Jewel Prophecies

What will be termed the crown jewel prophecies are the real treasures of Daniel. Even though the "Four About the Four" deliver a spine-tingling experience of the spiritual fabric of the universe, they are comparative warm-up acts. The two crown jewel prophecies deliver a set of world-rocking messages to humanity. They are:

- <u>The 70 "Sevens."</u> Delivered by Gabriel, this prophecy was not interpreted (Dn 9:24–27).

- <u>The Great Awakening</u>. A continuation of the omniscient angel's lecture, this prophecy was not interpreted (Dn 12:1–13).

7.2.c. The Spiritual Realm's Agenda

The spiritual realm did not foretell history to be some kind of supernatural party trick in the 21st century. Rather, it had an epic agenda regarding Judaism, Christianity and our spiritual evolution.

The first aspect of that purpose involves Judaism, which still believes its Messiah has yet to arrive. The "Four About the Four" were given to nail down a timeline so there could be no doubt about his identity. A reinforcing trio of prophecies informed the Jews back in the sixth century BCE that their Anointed One would arrive during the reign of the Roman Empire, during the first century CE and between 27 and 34 CE.

The second aspect involves the version of Christianity that arose to dominate Western history. The prophecies were given to help expose the dark elephant in the Western religious sanctuary.

The spiritual realm designed them with ambiguities and mysteries so those who were metaphysically asleep could not decipher them. This let folks project onto the mysterious words what they were expecting to find.

For instance, many Christians believe Daniel has four different passages that are about an antichrist. However, those passages foretold the Roman Empire and its two emperors who had the most famous impact upon Christianity. This renders the Old Testament null and void of any veritable support for either the existence of Satan or a forthcoming antichrist (§5.6.).

As for the final aspect, the spiritual realm hid a special key for unlocking the final mystery. Only an enlightened paradigm could find it, but having it would allow us to calculate the era of the great awakening and have heavenly confirmation that we are on the right track with our spiritual evolution.

7.3. The Four Prophecies About the Four Kingdoms

Four different prophecies foretold the four dominant kingdoms from Daniel's life in the sixth century BCE to the arrival of Jesus in the first century CE. Those kingdoms were Babylon, Media-Persia, Greece and Rome.

By perceiving the "Four About the Four" with the framework of a four-by-four matrix, they unfold easily and perfectly. In other words, the four prophecies parallel one another in foretelling the same four kingdoms in different ways. They share a series of critical links that lock them in to those four kingdoms.

The first and second prophecies are coupled by identifying the Roman Empire with the themes of iron, numerous kings and ferocious power. The second, third and fourth prophecies are coupled through their identification of Alexander the Great (336–323 BCE) and his Greek Empire fragmenting into four different kingdoms. The third and fourth prophecies are coupled through the Persian kings, Alexander the Great and a king from one of the Greek offshoots, Antiochus IV (175–164 BCE), who tried to crush Judaism. Moreover, Gabriel identified the third prophecy's ram as Media-Persia and its goat as Greece.

Nevertheless, critical scholars compact the prophecies to fit their hoax theory and identify the four kingdoms as Babylon, Media, Persia and Greece (§D.2.a.). Christian fundamentalists commit the more prevalent error, though, by adding a fifth kingdom to the mix with a future kingdom of the antichrist.

7.3.a. Prophecy of the Statue (#1 of 4)

Within the story of the second chapter is a brief prophecy that is portrayed as a dream of Nebuchadnezzar (605–562 BCE). Daniel interpreted it for the Babylonian king during his second year, c. 603 BCE (Dn 2:1). Appendix D advances the theory that the tale was originally written about Nabonidus (556–539 BCE), who was the last official king of Babylon. If so, the prophecy was received c. 554 BCE (§D.2.c., §D.3.).

In any case, a legitimate prophecy was most likely woven into a fabricated tale (§D.7.). It has Daniel describe the king's dream:

> Your Majesty looked, and there before you stood a large statue—an enormous, dazzling statue, awesome in appearance. The head of the statue was made of pure gold, its chest and arms of silver, its belly and thighs of bronze, its legs of iron, its feet partly of iron and partly of baked clay. While you were watching, a rock was cut out, but not by human hands. It struck the statue on its feet of iron and clay and smashed them. Then the iron, the clay, the bronze, the silver and the gold were all broken to pieces and became like chaff on a threshing floor in the summer. The wind swept them away without leaving

a trace. But the rock that struck the statue became a huge mountain and filled the whole earth. (Dn 2:31–35)

After informing the king that he was the head of gold, Daniel interpreted the rest of the dream:

> After you, another kingdom will arise, inferior to yours. Next, a third kingdom, one of bronze, will rule over the whole earth. Finally, there will be a fourth kingdom, strong as iron—for iron breaks and smashes everything—and as iron breaks things to pieces, so it will crush and break all the others. Just as you saw that the feet and toes were partly of baked clay and partly of iron, so this will be a divided kingdom; yet it will have some of the strength of iron in it, even as you saw iron mixed with clay. As the toes were partly iron and partly clay, so this kingdom will be partly strong and partly brittle. And just as you saw the iron mixed with baked clay, so the people will be a mixture and will not remain united, any more than iron mixes with clay.
>
> In the time of those kings, the God of heaven will set up a kingdom that will never be destroyed, nor will it be left to another people. It will crush all those kingdoms and bring them to an end, but it will itself endure forever. (Dn 2:39–44)

The empire symbolized by the silver chest and arms was a blend between the Medes and Persians that was originally ruled by the Medes. A young prodigy named Cyrus was fathered by the vassal king of Persia, and his mother was the daughter of the Median king of Media-Persia. Cyrus claimed the throne from his Median grandfather in 550 BCE (§D.4.). The Persians were thereafter so dominant that historians simply call it the Persian Empire, which conquered Babylon in 539 BCE.

The belly and thighs of bronze refer to the Greek kingdom of Alexander the Great, who finished his conquest of the Persians in 330 BCE. When Alexander died, it fragmented into civil war and multiple kingdoms, two of which (the Ptolemies and Seleucids) alternated control of Judaea for the next two centuries.

The divided kingdom of iron and clay signifies the Roman Empire. It became the dominant world power in 201 BCE but did not commandeer Jerusalem until 63 BCE.

The symbols for the Roman Empire are vital. The prophecy indicated it would be a kingdom associated with iron. Indeed, its battlefield success was enabled by its state-of-the-art weapons and protective gear. For instance, a

Roman soldier was furnished with a rectangular shield that allowed him to block the lumbering swings of an opponent's longer sword or force the opponent backward with a thrust. He would then stab an off-balanced opponent's torso with his daggerlike sword.

The two legs foretold a divided kingdom. In 286 CE, Diocletian (284–305) made an organizational split of the empire. The West was thereafter ruled by an Augustus (emperor) in Rome and the East by an Augustus in Byzantium (later renamed Constantinople).

The prophecy also gave an iron/clay symbol and described a heterogeneous kingdom. Unlike the Greek process of Hellenization, the Romans did not try to unify their conquered lands into a cohesive culture or language. Moreover, the empire's brittleness was demonstrated by its numerous civil wars. Finally, the ten toes are of the same signature number at the heart of Roman counting.

In and of itself, this brief prophecy is rather pedestrian. It simply pours the foundation for the other prophecies that describe the four kingdoms far more impressively. Nevertheless, it serves another important role. It is the first of three prophecies that explicitly point Judaism to its Messiah.

By far the weakest of the three, it only alludes to the Anointed One's arrival sometime during the reign of the Roman Empire: "In the time of those kings, the God of heaven will set up a kingdom…" (Dn 2:44). Yet it sets the stage for more precise timing by the other two.

The prophecy declared this new and completely different type of kingdom would crush the existing kingdoms, grow to fill the whole earth, and endure forever. It conveyed the truth that all authoritative hierarchies that dominate humanity and perpetuate inequality will eventually collapse.

The prophecy foretold that the divine kingdom would begin its spiritual assault upon this form of government during the reign of the Roman Empire. Sure enough, Jesus embodied a counterculture whose themes were freedom instead of ruling domination, service to instead of power over, inclusiveness instead of culturally mandated exclusion, and equality and fellowship among brothers and sisters instead of the social caste and patriarchy (§4.6.c.).

Notice how the prophet Isaiah (late eighth century BCE) also channeled this theme: "Every valley shall be raised up, every mountain and hill made low; the rough ground shall become level, the rugged places a plain. And the glory of the Lord will be revealed, and all people will see it together" (Is 40:4–5; see also Lk 3:5–6).

7.3.b. Prophecy of the Four Beasts (#2 of 4)

Daniel received his second prophecy about the four kingdoms in the first year of Belshazzar's de facto reign over Babylon (c. 552 BCE). He described the "four great beasts" he saw:

The first was like a lion, and it had the wings of an eagle. I watched until its wings were torn off and it was lifted from the ground so that it stood on two feet like a human being, and the mind of a human was given to it.

And there before me was a second beast, which looked like a bear. It was raised up on one of its sides, and it had three ribs in its mouth between its teeth. It was told, "Get up and eat your fill of flesh!"

After that, I looked, and there before me was another beast, one that looked like a leopard. And on its back it had four wings like those of a bird. This beast had four heads, and it was given authority to rule.

After that, in my vision at night I looked, and there before me was a fourth beast—terrifying and frightening and very powerful. It had large iron teeth; it crushed and devoured its victims and trampled underfoot whatever was left. It was different from all the former beasts, and it had ten horns.

While I was thinking about the horns, there before me was another horn, a little one, which came up among them; and three of the first horns were uprooted before it. This horn had eyes like the eyes of a human being and a mouth that spoke boastfully.

As I looked, thrones were set in place, and the Ancient of Days took his seat. His clothing was as white as snow; the hair of his head was white like wool. His throne was flaming with fire, and its wheels were all ablaze. A river of fire was flowing, coming out from before him. Thousands upon thousands attended him; ten thousand times ten thousand stood before him. The court was seated, and the books were opened.

Then I continued to watch because of the boastful words the horn was speaking. I kept looking until the beast was slain and its body destroyed and thrown into the blazing fire. (The other beasts had been stripped of their authority, but were allowed to live for a period of time.)

In my vision at night I looked, and there before me was one like a son of man, coming with the clouds of heaven. He approached the Ancient of Days and was led into his presence. He was given authority, glory and sovereign power; all nations and peoples of every language worshiped him. His dominion is an everlasting dominion that will not pass away, and his kingdom is one that will never be destroyed. (Dn 7:3–14)

Daniel approached a being (presumably an angel) who was standing nearby, asked what they meant, and was told, "The four great beasts are four kings that will rise from the earth. But the holy people of the Most High will receive the kingdom and will possess it forever—yes, for ever and ever" (Dn 7:17–18). Daniel continued:

> Then I wanted to know the meaning of the fourth beast, which was different from all the others and most terrifying, with its iron teeth and bronze claws—the beast that crushed and devoured its victims and trampled underfoot whatever was left. I also wanted to know about the ten horns on its head and about the other horn that came up, before which three of them fell—the horn that looked more imposing than the others and that had eyes and a mouth that spoke boastfully. As I watched, this horn was waging war against the holy people and defeating them, until the Ancient of Days came and pronounced judgment in favor of the holy people of the Most High, and the time came when they possessed the kingdom.
>
> He gave me this explanation: "The fourth beast is a fourth kingdom that will appear on earth. It will be different from all the other kingdoms and will devour the whole earth, trampling it down and crushing it. The ten horns are ten kings who will come from this kingdom. After them another king will arise, different from the earlier ones; he will subdue three kings. He will speak against the Most High and oppress his holy people and try to change the set times and the laws. The holy people will be delivered into his hands for a time, times and half a time.
>
> "But the court will sit, and his power will be taken away and completely destroyed forever. Then the sovereignty, power and greatness of all the kingdoms under heaven will be handed over to the holy people of the Most High. His kingdom will be an everlasting kingdom, and all rulers will worship and obey him." (Dn 7:19–27)

The lion signifies Babylon, and chapter 4 of Daniel describes the humbling of this beast. The story was in all likelihood originally written about Nabonidus, who had a profound religious transformation that paralleled his bizarre ten-year exile in a distant Arabian city while his son Belshazzar ruled the empire (§D.2.c., §D.3.).

The bear symbolizes Media-Persia, and one side being higher depicts the

Persians' superiority. The three ribs portray its primary conquests of Lydia in 546 BCE, Babylon in 539 BCE and Egypt in 525 BCE.

The leopard with four wings represents Greece and Alexander the Great's campaigns that quickly conquered the ancient world. After he died in 323 BCE, his kingdom fell into a series of conflicts known as the Wars of the Diadochi. The four heads symbolize the fractured kingdom at the turn of the century with Macedon and Greece under Cassander, Thrace and Asia Minor under Lysimachus, Mesopotamia and Syria under Seleucus I, and Egypt and Judaea under Ptolemy I. The prophecy apparently presented the snapshot of four kingdoms at 300 BCE because Judaea changed hands six times from 323 to 301 BCE.

The first prophecy represents the fourth kingdom with iron, and the symbols and chronology are a spot-on match with the Roman Empire (§7.3.a.). The metallic theme threads in with this second prophecy and the terrifying fourth beast with iron teeth, and the chronology once again concurs. The Roman Empire came right after the Greek Empire and its offshoots, and it was the dominant empire when the Anointed One arrived.

So who was the little horn that spoke boastfully and waged war against the saints? According to mainstream Christianity, this is our first look at the antichrist. For instance, the *NIV Study Bible* declares the little horn is "The antichrist, or a world power sharing in the characteristics of the antichrist."[1]

There are five problems with this idea. First, we cannot have our cake and eat it, too, as to when the terrifying kingdom of iron existed and sprouted the little horn. Since it ruled the world when the Anointed One came, we have to identify it with the Roman Empire to have our Jesus-was-the-Messiah cake. Hence, we cannot also eat the idea that this kingdom will not exist until the 21st century or beyond so an antichrist can arise from it. It can only be one or the other. Moreover, the rest of Daniel's prophecies also point to the fourth kingdom being the Roman Empire as the Messiah arrived in the first century CE.

Second, pay close attention to how the angel answered Daniel's question about the little horn. The angel said absolutely nothing about it amid an explanation of more important matters. If the little horn really was the antichrist, surely the angel would have provided one hell of a warning on how to recognize and deal with Doctor Evil. Yet the angel said nothing about Tiny and instead stated, "The ten horns are ten kings who will come from this kingdom" (the Roman Empire). The little horn was one of those ten kings and simply got the prophetic spotlight for his metaphysical stature, boastful nature and war against the saints.

The third problem with the antichrist idea is that Tiny's moment of infamy would later be upstaged by "another king" who was "different from the earlier ones." As will be seen later, this different king arrived in the fourth century CE. The little horn long preceded this different king in the Roman Empire's long list of emperors.

The fourth problem is that nowhere else in Daniel is an antichrist represented. The other three passages in Daniel that are believed to be referring to an antichrist will be debunked later.

The final problem is that the antichrist idea for the little horn gets obliterated by the following interpretation. Taking a step back to the entire imagery of the terrifying beast, Appendix F ("The Beast With Ten Horns") explains why it symbolizes the Roman Empire and how the prophetic details nail it down with chilling precision.

Here is an executive summary. The ten horns refer to the first ten emperors of the Roman Empire, all of whom ruled in the first century CE. The imagery depicts ten horns because a crown jewel prophecy is deeply involved with the Roman Empire, Jesus and the Jewish revolt of 66–73 CE. Moreover, and as will be seen later, the "time of wrath" and "time of the end" that get discussed in other prophecies culminated in the crushing of that revolt.

The ninth emperor Vespasian was on the throne when forces commanded by his son Titus destroyed the temple in 70 CE. As the obvious heir, Titus was already being treated like an emperor at the time, and he later became the tenth emperor. The ten horns are also a numeric link with the ten toes of the first prophecy, and counting by ten was a very Roman thing.

Nero (54–68 CE) was the fifth emperor and the prophecy's little horn. He was embarrassingly boastful and depicted as a little horn because he had no desire to be a great conqueror like his fellow horns. Instead, his passion was for the arts.

Nevertheless, he was the first emperor to wage war against the Christians with the notorious persecutions he wrought after the great fire of Rome in 64 CE. He also waged war against the Jews by initiating the suppression of the revolt in 66 CE. Because of his ruthless assault upon both Jews and Christians, he earned prophetic prediction for our later recognition.

The most stunning historical fact, though, is that the three emperors who immediately preceded him were all assassinated. Nero's mother did the last deed herself by poisoning her third husband, Claudius (41–54 CE), after first ensuring her son would become the next emperor over Claudius's son Britannicus. That Nero's path to the throne was cleared by the uprooting of three of the first four emperors was long ago foretold when Daniel saw that the little horn arose as "three of the first horns were uprooted before it."

This is the second of three prophecies that foretold the Messiah's coming. This time his arrival was shown to be synchronous with the rule of the Roman Empire in the first century CE. Whereas the gospel reports of fulfilled prophecy about him are not trustworthy (§4.4.f.), the Daniel prophecies are immune to such criticism because they are being validated by reliable facts of secular history.

7.3.c. Waxing Philosophically

As for the prophecy's heavenly material, a trio of points should be made. To begin, it associates God with fire because his first communication with Moses was purportedly through a burning bush (Ex 3:1–6). God is also the All and the Everything, and fire beautifully represents the fabric of everything and the process of life that is perpetual change. That is, the universe is fundamentally comprised of energy that conglomerates to form physical matter. Energy is neither created nor destroyed, and fire is a visible process of energy changing forms.

The imagery of being cast into the fire is about returning to this energy and the crucible of spiritual growth in a new form, not eternal damnation. The law of consequences known by many as karma—returning to sleep in a bed that you made—is a vital reason to explore the scientific evidence for reincarnation (§A.4., §A.5.).

The next point pertains to the Anointed One being worshipped by everybody (Dn 7:14). This worship will not be in the manner hoped for by mainstream Christians. Rather, humanity will eventually celebrate a God of pure, unconditional love and our innate divinity. Even though many will not consciously praise Jesus, he will be followed and inherently worshipped nonetheless because of our divine unity and his ancient trailblazing of this path.

The final point is a refrain to the first prophecy about the demise of authoritative hierarchies (§7.3.a.). Jesus being given authority and sovereign power does not mean he is going to someday return as a benevolent king.

To the contrary, he already lived his calling and launched the divine kingdom. He was all about empowering humanity so the meek would someday inherit the earth (Mt 5:5), and he washed the feet of his disciples to demonstrate equality and humble service to one another (Jn 13:1–17). He also disapproved of ruling hierarchies. Although Gentile rulers lorded over their people, it would not be that way with his followers. Whoever wanted to be great would have to be a servant (Mk 10:42–44).

The human spirit is divinely driven to topple oppressive hierarchies. The unconscious lust for external power over others will eventually give way to a conscious quest for spiritual power with others.

We will still have leaders and organizational structures, but there will be an ever-growing consciousness that hierarchical positions are but roles certain people fill. This will manifest not only because it is spiritually sound and true but also because it works better. For instance, the realm of business management is starting to recognize the effectiveness of servant leadership. Robert Greenleaf reported the theory emerged in his mind during the turbulence of the late 1960s. In an essay composed in 1969, the corporate executive wrote:

> A new moral principle is emerging which holds that the only

authority deserving one's allegiance is that which is freely and knowingly granted by the led to the leader in response to, and in proportion to, the clearly evident servant stature of the leader. Those who choose to follow this principle will not casually accept the authority of the existing institutions. *Rather, they will freely respond only to individuals who are chosen as leaders because they are proven and trusted as servants.*[2]

7.3.d. Recovering the Key to a Crown Jewel Prophecy

Even if you doubt that Daniel wrote the prophecies in the sixth century BCE and thus deny what they foretold for everything before the second century BCE, they are still crushing baseballs out of the park without skipping a beat. As they just ripped the cover off a few fastballs from the first century CE, it is already clear there was no fraud involved.

Although it is breathtaking to watch this display of supernatural power (and there is much more to come), the spiritual realm stepped up to the plate for a far more important reason. It knew what would block the divine kingdom of freedom, truth-seeking, equality and love from manifesting after Jesus had suffered horrifically for proclaiming the truth to earthly power. It was not going to sit by idly and watch him pay the ultimate price for naught.

The spiritual realm observed how this adversary would build an impervious wall of holy dogma to block the masses from considering spiritual communication from other sources. The spiritual realm thus laced its revolutionary messages within the Bible. The beauty of the strategy is that modern Christians would not be able to denounce Daniel as an act of satanic deception because doing so would invalidate their infallible holy book.

As mentioned before, an enlightened paradigm is needed to unlock the prophecies (§6.3.c., §7.2.c.). We are now at that point as we return to the question about the fourth beast. After the angel said the ten horns were ten of its kings, he continued: "After them another king will arise, different from the earlier ones; he will subdue three kings. He will speak against the Most High and oppress his holy people and try to change the set times and the laws. The holy people will be delivered into his hands for a time, times and half a time" (Dn 7:24–25).

The *Jeopardy!* category is the Roman Empire. The answer is, "A king who came after the first century CE, subdued three kings, and was unlike his predecessors." The question the heavenly host has been expecting is, "Who was Constantine the Great?"

Eusebius (c. 260–c. 340) was a bishop and church historian who wrote glowingly about Constantine (312–337) as though he were an angel. The first Christian emperor has been greatly revered by Christianity, and the Eastern

Orthodox Church even deems him a saint who is equal in status with the apostles.

Therefore, this passage is a knee-buckling curveball that has been striking out just about every Christian who has ever taken a swing at biblical prophecy. Most of these hitters have bailed out of the batter's box because they judged the pitch to be a fastball about the antichrist bearing down on their skulls. The others were caught looking elsewhere, for the last place they ever expected the pitch to cross the historical plate was with the first Roman emperor to promote Christianity.

The second of four supposed antichrist references is instead another towering home run by the spiritual realm that is detailed in Appendix G ("Constantine the Great"). In brief, seven years after Diocletian split the Roman Empire so it was ruled by two Augusti, he added two Caesars (deputy emperors) to the mix. Constantine was just a Caesar when a massive civil war erupted in 310. He defeated three kings who were either official or de facto Augusti: Maximian in 310, Maxentius in 312 and Licinius in 324.

Constantine publicly supported Christianity, which made him very different from his persecutory predecessors. Trouble was, he wanted a uniform version of it that was free from internal turmoil and schism. He thus partnered with the hierarchical, popular and unified Catholic Church, and together they crushed all other variants of Christianity. Since the path to God is blazed by freedom of thought and truth-seeking (which is spurred by doubt, dissension and debate), this king began the oppression of the true saints who wished to travel it.

By stonewalling truth-seeking for over a thousand years, the dark marriage of church and state delayed whatever era we would have otherwise achieved a certain level of spiritual growth. Meanwhile, changes to the religious laws came fast and furious after Constantine supplied the means to enforce them. The first ecclesiastical canons were rendered in 325, which served as controlling and disciplinary measures for the Church. Christianity thus became a monolithic and dogmatic institution of Catholic theology.

The most prominent aspect of changing a set time and law, however, was much more blatant. The Ten Commandments declared the Sabbath as a mandatory day of rest on the seventh day of the week, Saturday (Ex 20:8–11). Constantine, however, enacted a law in 321 that changed the mandated day of rest to the first day of the week, Sunday.

Having identified this different king, we can now unravel the mystery of "a time, times and half a time." The Senate made Constantine an Augustus after his victory over Maxentius in 312, and his counterpart in the East, Licinius, deferred to him as the senior Augustus. He died in 337. Therefore, his reign over the Roman Empire was 25 years.

This is now an algebra problem with a twist. A "time, times and half a time" = 25. We need to solve for "a time" and "times." The twist is in the indefinite nature of "times." How many times is it? If this was purely a mathematical problem, it could not be solved because it has two variables and only one equation.

Because it is also a spiritual problem, though, our answer comes by accounting for the mystery. In the case of the saints being handed over to Constantine, the variable "a time" is ten years. Yes, this prophecy about the Roman Empire again comes back to the number ten. So the answer to the spiritual realm's mystery is that the same value applies again in the place of "times." A ten, another ten and half a ten equals 25.

In the case of Constantine, solving the value of "a time" was not important. What was critical to learn, though, was the secret to the mystery. With this key in hand, we are now able to unlock the second crown jewel prophecy.

Granted, the phrase "a time, another time and half a time" would have been preferable, but the spiritual realm did not want us to uncover the key until we started awakening (§7.2.c.). The mystery was created so it would be impossible to solve without first hitting the knee-buckling curveball about Constantine.

In the meantime, the ambiguous slack created a lot of intellectual rope, and the Christian world got tangled up in it by projecting onto the mystery what it expected to find. As will be seen later, ambiguity was also introduced with the multiple uses of "the abomination that causes desolation," and another theological trap caught the Christian world for believing it had the end times all figured out.

7.3.e. Prophecy of the Ram and the Goat (#3 of 4)

Roughly two years after the previous prophecy, Daniel received his third prophecy about the progression of the four kingdoms. In his vision, he saw himself next to the Ulai Canal in a citadel in Elam:

> There before me was a ram with two horns, standing beside the canal, and the horns were long. One of the horns was longer than the other but grew up later. I watched the ram as it charged toward the west and the north and the south. No animal could stand against it, and none could rescue from its power. It did as it pleased and became great.
>
> As I was thinking about this, suddenly a goat with a prominent horn between its eyes came from the west, crossing the whole earth without touching the ground. It came toward the two-horned ram I had seen standing beside the canal and charged at it in great rage. I saw it attack the ram furiously, striking the ram and shattering its two horns. The

ram was powerless to stand against it; the goat knocked it to the ground and trampled on it, and none could rescue the ram from its power. The goat became very great, but at the height of its power the large horn was broken off, and in its place four prominent horns grew up toward the four winds of heaven.

Out of one of them came another horn, which started small but grew in power to the south and to the east and toward the Beautiful Land. It grew until it reached the host of the heavens, and it threw some of the starry host down to the earth and trampled on them. It set itself up to be as great as the commander of the army of the Lord; it took away the daily sacrifice from the Lord, and his sanctuary was thrown down. Because of rebellion, the Lord's people and the daily sacrifice were given over to it. It prospered in everything it did, and truth was thrown to the ground.

Then I heard a holy one speaking, and another holy one said to him, "How long will it take for the vision to be fulfilled—the vision concerning the daily sacrifice, the rebellion that causes desolation, the surrender of the sanctuary and the trampling underfoot of the Lord's people?"

He said to me, "It will take 2,300 evenings and mornings; then the sanctuary will be reconsecrated."

While I, Daniel, was watching the vision and trying to understand it, there before me stood one who looked like a man. And I heard a man's voice from the Ulai calling, "Gabriel, tell this man the meaning of the vision."

As he came near the place where I was standing, I was terrified and fell prostrate. "Son of man," he said to me, "understand that the vision concerns the time of the end."

While he was speaking to me, I was in a deep sleep, with my face to the ground. Then he touched me and raised me to my feet.

He said: "I am going to tell you what will happen later in the time of wrath, because the vision concerns the appointed time of the end. The two-horned ram that you saw represents the kings of Media and Persia. The shaggy goat is the king of Greece, and the large horn between its eyes is the first king. The four horns that replaced the one that was broken off represent four kingdoms that will emerge from his nation but will not have the same power.

"In the latter part of their reign, when rebels have become

completely wicked, a fierce-looking king, a master of intrigue, will arise. He will become very strong, but not by his own power. He will cause astounding devastation and will succeed in whatever he does. He will destroy those who are mighty, the holy people. He will cause deceit to prosper, and he will consider himself superior. When they feel secure, he will destroy many and take his stand against the Prince of princes. Yet he will be destroyed, but not by human power." (Dn 8:3–25)

The foreknowledge about Greece, Alexander the Great, his early death and his empire's fragmentation is once again amazing. Such passages are the primary reason why scholars think Daniel was a hoax.

Because of the strong coupling between the second and third prophecies of the "Four About the Four," Media-Persia and Greece are undoubtedly the middle two kingdoms in the second prophecy. Media-Persia was represented by the bear with one side greater than the other in the second prophecy and the ram with one horn greater than the other in the third prophecy. Greece was represented by the flying leopard with four heads in the second prophecy and the flying goat that eventually sprouted four horns in the third prophecy.

With iron linking the Roman Empire in the first two prophecies and the incredible details about its emperors, the fourth and final kingdom is also a lock. All in all, the four-by-four matrix is proving to be a perfect reflection of the spiritual realm's intentions.

The four Greek kingdoms were reduced to three by 285 BCE, and only the Seleucids and Ptolemies remained just four years later. A third Hellenistic kingdom, the Antigonids, arose in 277 BCE when Antigonus Gonatas defeated foreign conquerors and reclaimed Macedonia (Greece). The three kingdoms ruled until the Roman Empire conquered the Antigonids in 168 BCE. The Seleucids (based in Syria) lost significant territory to the Romans in 141 BCE and were eventually conquered in 64 BCE. The Ptolemies (based in Egypt), however, wisely formed an alliance with Rome early in the second century BCE.

Our current prophecy, though, does not attend to the fourth kingdom (the Roman Empire). Rather, it zeroes in on the clash between the Hellenistic kingdoms and Judaism.

The Ptolemies ruled Jerusalem until 198 BCE, whereupon the Seleucids were in charge. Antiochus IV came to power by intrigue and deceit, for he was not the rightful successor to the Seleucid throne. In 168 BCE, he tried to eliminate Judaism. He decreed that all in his kingdom should forsake their customs and religions to unify around a common culture. He halted the Jews' daily sacrifices, and his soldiers desecrated the temple and erected an altar to Zeus on top of the Jewish altar.

These events sparked the Maccabean revolt. Judas Maccabeus's army eventually recaptured Jerusalem, and the temple was reconsecrated in 165 BCE. In 164 BCE, Antiochus IV died of an illness while in Persia. He was indeed "destroyed, but not by human power."

7.3.f. Differentiating Between the Abominations

An angel said there would be "2,300 evenings and mornings" before the sanctuary was reconsecrated (Dn 8:14). As explained in Appendix H ("The Numbering of Days"), the angel was referring to the evening and morning sacrifices being missed for 1,150 days.

Those years of persecution are correlated with a phrase that appears three different times in Daniel. Fully understanding the prophecies requires the insight that there are two different instances of an "abomination that causes desolation."

Antiochus IV's sacking of the temple and establishing an altar to Zeus will be termed the first abomination that causes desolation, or ACD-1. This king and ACD-1 were also foretold in the next (fourth) prophecy: "His armed forces will rise up to desecrate the temple fortress and will abolish the daily sacrifice. Then they will set up the abomination that causes desolation" (Dn 11:31).

The other instance (ACD-2) will be seen later in the crown jewel prophecies. Whereas ACD-1 is comparatively worthless to modernity, ACD-2 is the priceless gem that Jesus referred to when he was quoted, "So when you see standing in the holy place 'the abomination that causes desolation,' spoken of through the prophet Daniel—let the reader understand—then let those who are in Judea flee to the mountains" (Mt 24:15–16).

7.3.g. The Omniscient Angel's Lecture (#4 of 4)

In October of 539 BCE, the Persian Empire conquered Babylon. In 536 BCE, an omniscient angel gave Daniel a lecture about the future.

Although the discourse is contiguous, it is most easily presented by dividing it into three parts. The first two parts constitute the final prophecy of the "Four About the Four." The text is an abstract description of empires, kings and events through the demise of the Roman Empire. After this sweeping view of forthcoming history, the omniscient angel delivered the second crown jewel prophecy (the third and final part of his lecture).

The first part foretold history from 536 to 168 BCE (Dn 11:2–35). It outlines the Persian kings, Alexander the Great and the machinations and battles between the Seleucids and Ptolemies down through the reign of Antiochus IV. This section of prophecy and its fulfillments are provided in Appendix I ("The Angel's Prophecy of Ancient History").

There is no contention about the material's accuracy. It is such an impressive match that the only issue is the big issue. Either it was deviously written during the Maccabean revolt with the aid of a history book, or the omniscient angel observed and disclosed the course of future events to Daniel.

As for the second part of this straightforward prophecy (Dn 11:36–45), critical scholars think it is imaginative gibberish, and mainstream Christianity believes it predicts the antichrist. The *NIV Study Bible* comments, "From here to the end of ch. 11 the antichrist is in view. The details of this section do not fit what is known of Antiochus Epiphanes."[3]

However, the interwoven nature of the "Four About the Four" leads us to suspect these verses are really about the dominant kingdom that came after the Persians and Greeks. As it turns out, this is exactly what the omniscient angel long ago foretold. As revealed in Appendix J ("The King of the End Times"), Daniel 11:36–45 delivers a phenomenal depiction of the characteristics and military exploits of the Roman Empire. The prophecy's command of so many historical subtleties and nuances has to be read to be appreciated.

The first part of the omniscient angel's lecture is not astonishing because of the pall of doubt cast by the hoax theory. The second part, though, is breathtaking because it is mostly about the Roman Empire long after the second century BCE had come and gone. Comparing the prophecy with ancient history is like watching a highlight reel of the spiritual realm crushing tape-measure home runs into the upper decks.

Appendix J also evokes another level of astonishment in wondering how anybody could have ever thought the prophecy was about anything other than the Roman Empire. Whereas the Constantine reference was a big-league curveball, this material was mostly a sequence of batting-practice fastballs. All a Christian needed to do to hit them was leave the sold-out stadium of the apocalyptic future and take a few swings of research at the empty ballpark of the historical past.

That said, there is a reason why the Christian world has struck out on this part of the omniscient angel's lecture. The military exploits of the Roman Empire were introduced, "At the time of the end..." (Dn 11:40). Assuming this era was in the future and that an antichrist would be there, the Christian world had once again projected onto the mysterious words what it was expecting to find.

In any case, three of four passages in Daniel that are believed to be forewarning an antichrist have been debunked, and the fourth will be later. Billions of fans are thus anticipating an antichrist showdown that will never occur. They all bought tickets at World Series prices to nothing but a game of fantasy baseball.

7.3.h. The Time of the End

We now know the "time of the end" was concurrent with the Roman Empire.

To be sure, though, let us go a little deeper into this phrase.

The omniscient angel introduced the Roman Empire's military exploits: "At the time of the end the king of the South will engage him in battle, and the king of the North will storm out against him with chariots and cavalry and a great fleet of ships" (Dn 11:40). The king of the South was Carthage, and the king of the North was the Republic of Rome (§J.3.a.). Carthage initiated their first war (264–241 BCE). They fought two more wars that ended in 201 BCE and 146 BCE, with Rome winning all three and emerging as the dominant global power after its victory in 201 BCE.

So according to the omniscient angel, the "time of the end" is correlated with the late third and early second centuries BCE. But if you still think it is in the future, good luck waiting for the United States and other global powers to retool their armies with chariots and cavalry and then charge into battle with them.

Moving back to the third prophecy about the ram and the goat, we find that Gabriel concurs. Before interpreting it, he said, "I am going to tell you what will happen later in the time of wrath, because the vision concerns the appointed time of the end" (Dn 8:19). Gabriel thus said Antiochus IV's persecution would happen during the "time of wrath" and identified that era as the "appointed time of the end" (§7.3.e.).

So regarding the "time of wrath" and "time of the end," the prophecies indicate this era began as Rome was becoming the dominant global power. Interestingly enough, the Seleucid Kingdom that would be such a thorn in Judaism's side gained control over Judaea in 198 BCE. This era was highlighted on its originating side by Antiochus IV's assault upon Judaism in the 160s BCE.

The "time of wrath" was completed when the Roman Empire crushed the Jewish revolt of 66–73 CE, which was highlighted by the temple's destruction in 70 CE. Another passage from the omniscient angel about the Roman Empire corroborates this view: "He will be successful until the time of wrath is completed" (Dn 11:36). From the beginning of the time of wrath, the Roman Empire steamrolled the ancient world. After crushing the revolt, though, its conquering success only lasted for a few more decades, as the reign of Trajan (98–117 CE) marked the high tide of the Roman Empire.

In sum, when the spiritual realm spoke in the sixth century BCE about the "time of wrath" and "time of the end," it was referring to an era from the second century BCE to the first century CE. The "time of wrath" is easy to understand. The two most traumatic events for Daniel's people on the not-so-distant horizon would be the cultural assault and revolt of the 160s BCE and the revolt and destruction of the temple a few centuries later.

What is not as easy to understand is the "time of the end." Something must have ended during that era, at least according to the spiritual realm. So what was it?

The answer was disclosed in the first two prophecies and pertains to the overarching purpose of them all. The onset of the divine kingdom during the reign of the Roman Empire marked the end of a monopoly on power that the beastly empires had over humanity. The "time of the end" inscribed the writing on the wall for the beasts.

From then on, it was game on between the divine kingdom of freedom, truth-seeking, equality and love and the beastly empires of hierarchical dominance, conquering invasions, royalty, inequality, coercive submission and slavery. Yet the beastly empires were the ones doing the crushing for almost two thousand years after the divine kingdom was born.

From the big-picture standpoint of the spiritual realm, though, this was but a minor setback that would be overcome in due time. The end result was preordained and brought to earth in the first century CE. The divine kingdom was destined to rule the world, which meant the eventual end of the beastly empires. Hence, the spiritual realm considered it to be the "time of the end."

Granted, the spiritual realm could have been more forthcoming by using the phrase "the time of the beginning of the end." To do so, though, would have betrayed the purpose of the prophecies, which were designed to remain a mystery until we had begun awakening.

7.3.i. The Religious Kingdom That Opposed the Divine Kingdom

Despite being crushed for so long, the divine kingdom was never destroyed. The beastly empires eventually started cracking a few hundred years ago and are not far away from being eradicated on our planet.

So why did it take so long for the divine kingdom to start taking care of business? The spiritual realm is glad we finally asked. The answer is one of the most important dynamics of history. A religious kingdom arose and partnered with a parade of monarchical empires to maintain each other's power and suppress the divine kingdom.

As explained in Chapter 4, this began when an unenlightened version of Christianity was built upon Old Testament doctrines that the Messiah had come to uproot. It then counteracted his counterculture with its ecclesiastical hierarchy and drive for submissive conformity. Upon marrying the Roman Empire in the fourth century, it crushed its Christian competitors and indoctrinated its deceptions and dogma upon the Western world.

Although the Roman Catholic Church was widowed when its first beastly husband collapsed and died in the fifth century, it consistently found new ones. These marriages of church and state perpetuated into the 19th century.

Like most marriages, there were plenty of power struggles. After Pope Gregory VII (1073–1085) stood down the emperor of the Holy Roman Empire, the popes regularly claimed moral authority over all temporal governments. For instance, Pope Boniface VIII issued what might be the most famous bull in Church history in 1302. *Unam Sanctam* claimed papal superiority over all monarchs and people. Outside of the Church, it declared, there was neither salvation nor the dissolution of sins.

At the heart of the religious kingdom was a prideful hierarchy with a bloodlust for power. Lost in a dark paradigm and a litany of delusions, it applied every tool in its terrifying arsenal to maintain and expand its power.

The religious kingdom began to crack with the Reformation, but it fought back with everything it could muster. Religious wars raged across Europe during the 16th and 17th centuries as Catholic and Protestant partisans fought for political and religious control.

No small wonder the American colonists traveled across the ocean to gain their freedom from religious persecution. According to the Library of Congress, some came because of secular motives, but "the great majority left Europe to worship God in the way they believed to be correct."[4] A hallmark of democracy is freedom of and protection from religion. Our founding fathers established these rights for a painful historical reason.

Inspired by the American and French revolutions, humanity began deflating monarchies in favor of democracies. We did it not with the help of the Church but rather in spite of it. In the Church's eyes, totalitarian governments were not ugly beasts to be abandoned but rather beautiful grooms to be revered and empowered.

For instance, Pope Leo XII wrote to the king of France in 1824 and tried to impress upon him the wickedness of the French Constitution. The pope pressed the king to strike from it all articles that defended the rights and freedoms of liberalism.

In 1848, the Vatican still governed the Papal States of central Italy. Meanwhile, the Austrian Empire, a heavily Catholic nation whose monarchy was deeply in league with the Vatican, ruled or held sway over the northern Italian states. Amid uprisings that were embroiling Italian states in both of their domains, the Vatican candidly explained its unyielding position to its ally: "Our absolutist system, supported by the Inquisition, the strictest censorship, the suppression of all literature, the privileged exemption of the clergy, and arbitrary power of bishops, cannot endure any other than absolutist governments in Italy."[5]

In 1867, Austria finished its six-year transformation from an absolute monarchy to a constitutional monarchy that granted fundamental human rights and the separation of powers. This mirrored the kingdom of Bavaria to its north, which had done so back in 1818.

In 1870, Catholic scholars summarized their Church's reactionary opposition: "That the Bavarian Constitution, with its equality of religious confessions, and of all citizens before the law, is looked on with an evil eye at Rome, is sufficiently shown by the constant reproaches of the Curia [Vatican bureaucracy] since 1818."[6] They also quoted the Vatican's declaration in 1868 about the new Austrian Constitution, "By our apostolic authority…we declare these laws and their consequences to have been, and to be for the future, null and void."[7]

Meanwhile, Pope Pius IX (1846–1878) cursed the Austrian Constitution as an "unspeakable abomination."[8] A textbook case of projection, the pope was not aware of the unspeakable abomination of his own institution. He thus cast this dark charge upon Austria's spiritual evolution.

Although the Church lost a tremendous amount of external power during the Enlightenment of that century, it was not finished with its marriages to totalitarian governments. It went to the altar twice more with Fascist Italy in 1929 and Nazi Germany in 1933 (§L.2.). Despite its best efforts to keep those dictatorships afloat, they went down in flames from the war they started.

Obviously, then, there is one more monolithic beast that needs to come to an end, and its day of reckoning has finally arrived. So now that the big picture is coming so clearly into view, the crown jewel prophecies will not be as much of a surprise.

7.4. Crown Jewel #1: The 70 "Sevens" and ACD-2

In c. 538 BCE, Gabriel visited Daniel again and delivered the first crown jewel prophecy:

> Seventy "sevens" are decreed for your people and your holy city to finish transgression, to put an end to sin, to atone for wickedness, to bring in everlasting righteousness, to seal up vision and prophecy and to anoint the Most Holy Place.
>
> Know and understand this: From the time the word goes out to restore and rebuild Jerusalem until the Anointed One, the ruler, comes, there will be seven "sevens," and sixty-two "sevens." It will be rebuilt with streets and a trench, but in times of trouble. After the sixty-two "sevens," the Anointed One will be put to death and will have nothing. The people of the ruler who will come will destroy the city and the sanctuary. The end will come like a flood: War will continue until the end, and desolations have been decreed. He will confirm a covenant with many for one "seven." In the middle of the "seven" he will put an end to sacrifice and offering. And at the temple he will set up an abomination that causes desolation, until

the end that is decreed is poured out on him. (Dn 9:24–27)

7.4.a. Wisdom for Daniel's People

The angel spoke to Daniel about the Jews being "your people" and Jerusalem as "your holy city." As he did not say something like "God's chosen people" or "the holiest city," his words connote equality with the rest of humanity and that no city is more divinely favored than any other.

By also calling for spiritual growth, Gabriel issued an ominous clue that Daniel's kinsmen would be in for a rude awakening when their Messiah finally arrived. He suggested that if they got it together, they might be able to accept the Anointed One's revolutionary teachings. He already knew, though, they would not.

7.4.b. The Arrival of the Anointed One

Daniel had already received a prophecy that foretold the Messiah's coming to the first century CE (§7.3.b.). Gabriel took it to another level by measuring how long it would be until the Anointed One came.

The Persian king Artaxerxes I (465–424 BCE) issued two different rebuilding decrees to the Jews. Presuming the 69 "sevens" are in years, their tally of 483 is in the ballpark of connecting his reign to the ministry of Jesus, but does the prophecy deliver a precise fit?

Appendix K ("Understanding the 69 'Sevens'") presents the details of how the prophecy indeed delivered with incredible precision. Here is an executive summary.

The originating milestone is without question Artaxerxes's decree in the spring of 458 BCE, which authorized Ezra to implement Judaic law and appoint judges in restoring Jerusalem. The king also granted freedom of action, tendered a staggering amount of wealth, and allowed a contingent of over 1,500 Israelites to return with Ezra (Ezr 7:11–26). Upon arriving in Jerusalem, Ezra's brigade began rebuilding its wall.

The concluding milestone is surely Jesus's baptism, as this event marked the beginning of his public ministry. Its dating depends on the dating of his crucifixion, which had previously split scholars between either 30 CE or 33 CE. However, the weight of recent evidence and analysis has tilted the scale so heavily in favor of a death in 33 CE that the foremost expert in biblical chronology considers the case to be closed.[9] Since most scholars believe Jesus's ministry spanned a little over three years, he was probably baptized in late 29 or early 30 CE.

Meanwhile, the prophecy unfolds beautifully after making a couple of inquiries. First, why did Gabriel describe his passage of time in blocks of seven? Second, why did he divide it into seven "sevens" and 62 "sevens"?

He was referring to the seven-year sabbatical cycles, which was the Judaic practice of giving the fields a year of rest every seventh year (§K.4.c.). At the completion of every seven sabbatical cycles was a special Jubilee year. He spoke of seven "sevens" to signify his prophecy was based on the sabbatical cycles that were also used to calculate Jubilee years.

After the king's decree in the spring of 458 BCE, the first new sabbatical cycle began in the autumn of 457 BCE. Counting from there, the 69th sabbatical cycle completed in the autumn of 27 CE (§K.4.). Gabriel thus foretold that the Messiah would appear on the global stage in between 27 and 34 CE (after 69 cycles had transpired but not 70).

Gabriel also foretold that the Anointed One would not be a long-standing Jewish king whose army would defeat its oppressor. Rather, he would be "put to death and will have nothing." Indeed, Jesus was the furthest thing from a warrior-king and was crucified.

Gabriel thus disclosed an error-free means by which the ancient Jews could track a period of almost five centuries and have heaven-sent verification of their Messiah's identity. His use of the sabbatical cycles as a unit of measure was brilliant, and his forecast was stunningly accurate.

This concludes the trio of prophecies that specified the Messiah's arrival. Having already learned he would come during the reign of the Roman Empire (§7.3.a.) and then amid its first ten emperors in the first century CE (§7.3.b.), this prophecy pinpointed his arrival in between 27 and 34 CE. Jesus was clearly the Anointed One.

The prophecy is profoundly authentic. With another amazing fulfillment after the second century BCE, the hoax theory has surely been blown away like a feather in the path of a tornado.

7.4.c. The 70th "Seven"

Gabriel then explained what would later happen to Jerusalem and the temple. Since the final kingdom of the "Four About the Four" is the Roman Empire, it should come as no surprise this beast was the ruler who would "destroy the city and the sanctuary." Indeed, the final seven portended the most famous seven-year block of ancient Jewish history: the revolt of 66–73 CE.

"The end" (of the "time of wrath"; §7.3.h.) did in fact "come like a flood." In the spring of 66 CE, a complex revolt involving multiple and often quarreling Jewish factions erupted against the Romans. The first rebel victory came with the surprise capture of the mountaintop fortress of Masada. Jerusalem was immersed in violence, and the Romans were soon driven out.

In the autumn of 66 CE, the Romans attempted to retake the city but were forced to retreat while suffering heavy casualties. In 67 CE, Nero appointed Vespasian to quash the revolt. Vespasian promptly defeated a Jewish army led by Josephus, who subsequently sympathized with Rome, earned the favor of Vespasian, and later wrote his histories.

Nero's death in June of 68 CE halted the Roman campaign for almost a year. By the summer of 69 CE, however, Vespasian had recaptured Judaea except for Jerusalem and the fortresses of Herodium, Machaerus and Masada. Meanwhile, the Roman Empire was again immersed in a civil war, and legions loyal to Vespasian completed their victory over the reigning emperor in December of 69 CE. Vespasian put his son Titus in command and left the Middle East to claim the throne.

In March of 70 CE, Titus laid siege to Jerusalem and broke through its walls within a few months. He laid siege to the temple itself in June, whereupon the daily sacrifices ceased. In August of 70 CE, the Romans burned and obliterated the temple. They destroyed most of Jerusalem as well.

In 72 CE, the Romans captured Herodium and Machaerus. Fearing the rebels in Masada might make contact with and gain the support of the Parthians (Rome's archenemy in the East), Titus ordered the governor of Judaea to conquer the last remaining stronghold. After laying siege to Masada for approximately two months, the Romans conquered the final outpost of Jewish resistance in April of 73 CE. The revolt thus ended where it began.

So there we have yet another prophecy fulfilled after the second century BCE with astounding accuracy. The final seven occurred from the spring of 66 CE until the spring of 73 CE.

The Romans ended the sacrifice and offering just a handful of weeks after four of the seven years had passed, but Gabriel did not say it would happen exactly halfway through the period. Rather, his phrase was "in the middle of the 'seven.'" Most people would break up a block of seven into a beginning of one and two, a middle of three, four and five, and an ending of six and seven.

Given the symmetry of a seven-year revolt and how it made the 70th seven, Gabriel obviously rolled with the theme. Since it did not snap seamlessly into place on the sabbatical grid, he had to inform us that he was shifting gears. He did so with "He will confirm a covenant with many for one 'seven.'" While the Mosaic covenant and its sabbatical cycles were the basis of the 69 sevens, a different type of covenant defined the final seven.

It took two sides to create the bloody dance of revolt and suppression, and the Roman Empire fulfilled its end of the metaphysical deal with the "many" Jewish factions and people who triggered the final seven. We should also consider soul contracts, which are agreements made before birth concerning upcoming life events. This means a prior agreement for the war was probably made in the spiritual realm.

In any case, the final seven was a bookend on the Messiah timeline. Even though Gabriel had just provided a reliable method for knowing exactly when the Messiah would arrive, he also rendered a safeguard. If there was any doubt as to whether the Anointed One had yet arrived, the destruction of the temple would be an unmistakable sign that he had already come and gone.

Meanwhile, the "he" who would confirm the covenant is not the antichrist as many Christian interpreters believe. "He" was obviously the Roman Empire, and all four supposed antichrist references have been debunked.

7.4.d. The Abomination That Causes Desolation

After that prophetic jolt to Judaism, Gabriel concluded with another lightning bolt: "And at the temple he will set up an abomination that causes desolation, until the end that is decreed is poured out on him" (Dn 9:27).

The translation of this passage is not definitive. The previous version of the NIV states, "And on a wing of the temple he will set up…" The New Revised Standard Version states with a footnote, "And in their place [meaning of Hebrew uncertain] shall be an abomination that desolates…"[10] Fortunately, we will not need to know Gabriel's exact words, for his message is still crystal clear.

The first abomination that causes desolation (ACD-1) was installed by Antiochus IV in the 160s BCE (§7.3.f.). Yet Gabriel indicated this prophecy's abomination (ACD-2) would occur after the destruction of the city and temple in 70 CE. So what is this more recent abomination that would be set up at, on a wing of, or in the place of the temple and its sacrificial rituals that no longer existed?

It will not be a physical thing that will be erected by an antichrist. Whether or not the temple in Jerusalem is ever rebuilt, the good people of the world will not be returning home from work one day to watch an on-location report from CNN that a cult leader had just set up a revolting abomination in the old temple area. Whether a giant creature restrained by an iron leash and chain, an orgy of sexual activity or the golden arches of McDonald's, humanity will never see a television camera zoom in on such a spectacle.

Looking to the future for a fulfillment is a gross violation of the prophecies. The "he" that would "put an end to sacrifice and offering" refers to the Roman Empire. Since this beast did so in 70 CE and no longer exists, we must look to its closing centuries for a valid interpretation.

The only possibility the abomination was a physical thing is when Hadrian (117–138) built a temple to Jupiter on the site where the Jewish temple once stood. An equestrian statue of Hadrian was also erected in front of the pagan temple.

Trouble is, Hadrian's project did not cause any significant desolation. Moreover, it is devoid of the profound meaning that surely accompanies an epic prophecy involving a broad sweep of history. With the ability to see everything in the future after the Messiah's execution and the temple's destruction, why in the world would Gabriel foretell that meaningless pagan temple and statue? All in all, a physical fulfillment during the final centuries of the Roman Empire does not make any sense.

Instead, Gabriel spoke symbolically. If you have understood the spiritual realm's agenda of exposing the beasts that opposed the divine kingdom, his meaning is obvious.

With "at the temple" (or in the place of the temple and terminated sacrifices), the angel was identifying Judaism as the foundation of the abomination. If his language was more precise with "on a wing of the temple," he was referring to the Tanakh (Old Testament), which was an essential extension (a wing) of the temple and Judaism.

So what did the Roman Empire establish on Judaism or replace it with? Residing on top of the misguided Old Testament was Catholicism's agenda-distorted synoptic gospels, the flagrant deceptions in John and letters from evangelists who were still immersed in the Judaic paradigm. The world's most dominant empire institutionalized this version of Christianity as its only valid religion and eradicated all other options.

The "abomination that causes desolation" is the Roman Catholic Church and the Bible. The desolation occurred as the Church indoctrinated the fear of eternal damnation and other misconceptions while tyrannically crushing truth-seeking and alternative Christian paths. Many people are familiar with Lord Acton's observation from the 19th century, "Power tends to corrupt, and absolute power corrupts absolutely." What is not as well known is that the Catholic historian's statement was inspired by and refers to papal absolutism.[11]

The Roman Catholic Church was a wolf in sheep's clothing that was never close to being an adequate embodiment of the teachings of Jesus. When contrasted with the spiritual truths he taught, it truly was an abomination that caused desolation.

Gabriel impressively identified this beast by its Judaic foundation and Roman domination. Like the Constantine passage (§7.3.d.), his prophecy was designed to be a mystery until the paradigm shift had been made.

To better understand why the spiritual realm called out the Church almost a thousand years before it came to power, let us shine some more light on it. We will do so by examining the metaphysical underpinnings of four hallmarks of the second millennium Church: its authoritative hierarchy, doctrine of papal infallibility, persecution of heretics and censorship of books.

7.4.e. A Dark Institution, Part 1: A False Chain of Command

The Church began developing an authoritative hierarchy in the late first century CE and eventually completed its mirroring of the Roman Empire with the bishop of Rome gaining primacy as a religious king (see §4.6.). Trouble is, Jesus had initiated a counterculture that embraced everybody as equals. He had also dismissed the norm of external power that rules over and dominates people and instead taught spiritual power that lifts up and serves people (§7.3.c). Moreover, he neither founded nor advocated for a centralized church, and even Paul did not strive to inculcate a ruling leader or priestly caste (§4.6.e.).

Catholic priests are addressed as "father," which is also what "pope" means (from the Latin and Greek words for father, *papa* and *pappas*). The pope is thus known as the Holy Father. Yet consider what Jesus purportedly said after noting how the teachers of Judaism loved their positions of honor and being called "Rabbi": "But you are not to be called 'Rabbi,' for you have one Teacher, and you are all brothers. And do not call anyone on earth 'father,' for you have one Father, and he is in heaven" (Mt 23:8–9).

We are all equal, and any religion with a hierarchy of men above other men as special intermediaries with God is a separating abomination. The result is yet another layer of disconnection from God and more desolation. By the way, any religion that suggests a man is spiritually superior to a woman is still lost in the darkness.

Consider as well the nature of free will, which could only be gifted by a God of unconditional love (§1.3.b.). The choice to reconnect with such a God and to experience the wholeness (salvation) of divine unity can only be freely chosen from love, not coerced by a religious authority that preys upon fear.

As history sadly testifies, the Church exerted its terrifying power to coerce the masses into obedience. It justified its behavior as an acceptable means for combating heresy and fostering unity. Trouble is, its coercion did not create a divine unity but rather a militant (false) unity. The nature of its structure and unifying processes was no different than the fascism of Nazi Germany.

7.4.f. A Dark Institution, Part 2: The Pope Is Infallible

The formal doctrine of papal infallibility began emerging around 1300 as the Church began embracing the popular idea that the pope was so divinely blessed he could not possibly make an error. In 1870 and by a final vote of 433 bishops in favor versus only two dissenting, the First Vatican Council reaffirmed the doctrine:

> We teach and define as a divinely revealed dogma that when the Roman pontiff speaks *ex cathedra*, that is, when, in the exercise of his office as shepherd and teacher of all Christians, in virtue of his supreme apostolic authority, he defines a doctrine concerning faith or morals to be held by the whole church, he possesses, by the divine assistance promised to him in blessed Peter, that infallibility which the divine Redeemer

willed his church to enjoy in defining doctrine concerning faith or morals. Therefore, such definitions of the Roman pontiff are of themselves, and not by the consent of the church, irreformable.[12]

The pope was thus decreed to be completely free from error in his official duties, and subsequent popes or councils were banned from reforming any such declarations. This prohibited a pope from owning up to his errors or acknowledging and correcting those of his predecessors.

By deifying their religious monarch as infallible, the robed men in Rome cemented their ill-begotten hierarchy in the darkness. Such a position is a classic case of egoic pride—the unrepentant attitude of always being without error and immune from the call to spiritually grow (§5.2.a.).

Egoic pride is highly correlated with narcissism and its fixation on the unassailable greatness and perfection of the self. For instance, consider one of the assertions of the *Dictatus Papae* attributed to Pope Gregory VII: "That he himself [the pope] may be judged by no one."[13] Pope Innocent III (1198–1216) later proclaimed that his place was "between God and man, lower than God but higher than man, who judges all and is judged by no one."[14] That one man could judge millions of peers and not be judged himself is, of course, at the grandiose height of arrogance.

Dictatus Papae also decreed the same dark stance for the pope's institution: "That the Roman church has never erred; nor will it err to all eternity, the Scripture bearing witness."[15] The gospels actually bear witness in the other direction by teaching us to first remove the plank from our own eyes before trying to remove specks of sawdust from another's (§3.2.c.).

7.4.g. A Dark Institution, Part 3: The Inquisition

In the *Catholic Encyclopedia* published in 1910, Catholic scholars responded to criticism that the Inquisition was intolerant and cruel. Not yet privy to the lessons about fascism that would arise a few decades later, they wrote, "Intolerant it is; in fact its *raison d'être* is intolerance of doctrines subversive of the Faith. But such intolerance is essential to all that is, or moves, or lives, for tolerance of destructive elements within the organism amounts to suicide."

As for the charge of cruelty, "All repressive measures cause suffering or inconvenience of some sort: it is their nature. But they are not therefore cruel… Cruelty only comes in where the punishment exceeds the requirements of the case." To critics who claimed the Inquisition "violated all humane feelings," the scholars replied that the repressive measures offended "the feelings of later ages in which there is less regard for the purity of faith; but they did not antagonize the feelings of their own time, when heresy was looked on as more malignant than treason."

If you are guessing the horrors of the Inquisition ended because the Church became more humane, guess again: "Toleration came in only when faith went out; lenient measures were resorted to only where the power to apply more severe measures was wanting."[16] In other words, national governments had taken the progressive lead by withdrawing their complicity from the Church's wicked ways.

The Catholic scholars explained the official reason for the Inquisition: "The guilt of heresy is measured not so much by its subject-matter as by its formal principle, which is the same in all heresies: revolt against a Divinely constituted authority."[17] As the teachings of Jesus and the prophecies of Isaiah and Daniel have made abundantly clear, however, there was and is no such thing as a divinely constituted authority. Truth is, the Church long ago revolted against the divine kingdom of freedom, truth-seeking, equality and love.

All in all, the darkness was at the heart of the Church, which displayed a pristine image and deceived the world into believing the darkness was arising from the so-called heretics. It also tried to annihilate the evil it had projected onto the people who dared to think and live differently as it justified its murderous behavior as divine.

In addition, the implicit belief of the Inquisition was that God could not stick up for himself or would not properly punish the offending heretic. Either way, the Church's punitive stance against heresy was yet another example of grandiose arrogance. It commandeered God's role because God was not acting in a way that satisfied it.

Finally, the Church perpetually condemned the Jews for killing Jesus while being horribly unaware it was repeating the same dynamic thousands of times over. That is, a religious institution was threatened by what an upstart was saying or believing, so it condemned him to death and had the government execute him.

7.4.h. A Dark Institution, Part 4: Censorship of Books

The Catholic Church began banning and burning books with the Council of Ephesus in 150, but the problem of threatening ideas grew exponentially with the onset of the printing press in 1455 and Reformation in 1517. In 1529, Church authorities in various cities began producing lists of censored books. In 1557, authorities in Rome consolidated and published them as the *Index Librorum Prohibitorum* (List of Prohibited Books). The *Index* continued for four centuries. Its last edition was published in 1948 with a supplement added in 1959.

The *Index* listed over four thousand titles. It included scientific treatises like Copernicus's *On the Revolutions of the Heavenly Spheres*, historical classics like Edward Gibbons's *The History of the Decline and Fall of the Roman Empire*, and the works of acclaimed philosophers such as Immanuel Kant. Its authority in canon law was not abolished until 1966.

Cardinal Rafael Merry del Val wrote a preface to the 1930 edition that reveals the Church's darkness behind it. Having already described the Church as being engaged in a "terrible battle" against "the wicked printing press" and "constituted by God as infallible master and sure guide of the faithful and for this reason provided with all necessary powers," he justified the censorship: "It [the Church] has the duty and consequently the sacrosanct right to prevent error and corruption—however disguised—from contaminating the flock of Jesus Christ."[18]

We are meant to grow in consciousness and knowledge. If the Church was of the Light, it would have welcomed skepticism and allowed the crucible of debate to burn through the chaff. Again, if beliefs actually align with the truth, they will continue to shine through despite endless challenges (§2.2.a.). The Church would have also honored free will and allowed folks to believe what they wished and leave as they pleased.

However, the "error and corruption" is primarily at the heart of the Church, which is militantly ignorant of its flaws, arrogantly believes it is an "infallible master," and disguises its darkness exceptionally well. Refusing to bear the pain of growth from truth-seeking and constructive criticism, it tried to throttle the process with its *Index*.

The Church also projected its darkness upon the masses by deeming them to be prone to evil. As the cardinal also wrote in the preface, the Holy See was forbidding certain books because God "does not tolerate the loss of souls" and "man, fallen from the original justice, is strongly inclined towards evil and is consequently in great need of protection and defence."[19]

Actually, humanity was "in great need of protection and defence" from the Church, which was doing all it could to keep us in the dark. Clearly, this institution has been "strongly inclined towards evil."

7.4.i. Stepping Into the Light

All in all, the Catholic Church has been a bastion of darkness. Integrating the above points with the insights about evil (§5.2.), its affliction is reflected by these symptoms:

- ♦ It promulgated a beautiful image while hiding and denying its darkness.

- ♦ It proclaimed itself to be free from error and refused to acknowledge any sin in itself.

- ♦ It self-righteously judged evil in others.

- Rather than suffer the process of spiritual growth, it suffered those around it.

- It militantly destroyed any threat to its self-esteem.

- It placed itself above God instead of submitting itself to God and living his loving and accepting ways.

- The epitome of malignant narcissism, it cemented its will over its conscience as it prosecuted, tortured or murdered hundreds of thousands of innocent souls because of what they believed.

The spiritual realm foretold the darkness that would blanket the world after the Roman Empire married the Catholic Church. We are finally awakening to see it too.

Much has changed over the last few centuries, and the modern Church barely resembles the terrifying beast that dominated Western civilization throughout the Dark and Middle Ages. That is because it lost a tremendous amount of external power from the Reformation in the 16th century, the scientific revolution that fired up in the 17th century, the onset of the secular democracies in the 18th century, and the Vatican losing sovereignty over a major part of Italy in the 19th century.

Yet just because external power was taken away does not mean an inner transformation has taken place. Tragically, this has been the case with the Church. Appendix L ("The Catholic Church in the 20th Century") shows how even recently it has been an abomination causing desolation.

By the way, the above discourse is not a condemnation. It is simply a process of revealing the truth about a situation and making it conscious so we are empowered to make more enlightened choices from here on out.

If Catholicism is your religion, be aware that your beliefs and affiliations are not who you really are. They are only choices and always subject to change. It matters not where you are, only in which direction you are going. So let us each move toward a greater God and a greater awareness. Only egoic pride can thwart the process.

If you are a non-Catholic Christian, do not think your denomination is free from the shock waves of these revelations. Like Catholicism, your denomination has failed to renounce the wayward tenets and traditions from the Old Testament and to acknowledge the errors and fabrications in the New Testament (Chapter 4). Moreover, your theology is also based on beliefs in an antichrist and apocalypse that are dissolving before your eyes.

If this interpretation seems to be a lucky coincidence or is triggering fear and uncertainty, do not worry. It will be corroborated in the other crown jewel prophecy and yet again in the unraveling of Revelation.

7.5. Crown Jewel #2: The Great Awakening

After the omniscient angel rendered the final prophecy of the "Four About the Four" (§7.3.g.), he concluded his lecture and fielded a couple of questions. His statements comprise the second crown jewel prophecy.

7.5.a. The Time of Distress, Deliverance and Awakening

After summarizing the Roman Empire from its rise in the third century BCE (§J.3.a.) to its demise in 476 CE (§J.3.e., §J.3.f.), the omniscient angel shifted gears and capped his stunningly accurate prophecy:

> At that time Michael, the great prince who protects your people, will arise. There will be a time of distress such as has not happened from the beginning of nations until then. But at that time your people—everyone whose name is found written in the book—will be delivered. Multitudes who sleep in the dust of the earth will awake: some to everlasting life, others to shame and everlasting contempt. Those who are wise will shine like the brightness of the heavens, and those who lead many to righteousness, like the stars for ever and ever. But you, Daniel, roll up and seal the words of the scroll until the time of the end. (Dn 12:1–4)

The context of Michael arising "at that time" is in the vicinity of the fifth century CE. What it meant for the archangel to arise then is anybody's guess, but it probably had a lot to do with the Jews being under the boot of a powerful Church that would fan the fire of demonizing hatred until it had engulfed them in the Holocaust.

Speaking of, the omniscient angel then hearkened much further into the future with a mystical transition—"There will be a time"—to his four-sentence conclusion. Having already canvassed the sixth century BCE to the fifth century CE, he was alerting us to a radical shift in era and emphasis.

Humanity would once again project onto the words what it was expecting to find. We would once again need an enlightened paradigm to fully understand.

The "time of distress" refers to both the Jews and all nations. The omniscient angel talked to Daniel about "your people" in the sentences before and after the one about the "time of distress." With prophecies having already foretold the Jewish traumas in the second century BCE and first century CE, there was only one more monumental trauma to be experienced before their deliverance: the Holocaust.

Daniel's prophecies also pertain to the big picture of Western history, and the heart of the passage is about the multitudes awakening. Although World War II was the most destructive war in history, another form of great distress would subsequently occur with the great awakening. Those birth pains will be discussed in Chapter 9.

In all likelihood, then, the omniscient angel was referring to both the acute distress of World War II and the Holocaust and the general distress of the great awakening. In the grand sweep of history, it would all happen in the same era of our modern era.

Yes, there is a big leap in time from the Roman Empire's demise to the present. Yet this fast-forward is entirely congruent with the big picture of the prophecies. The spiritual realm had already specified the arrival of the divine kingdom vis-à-vis the four kingdoms and identified what would keep it from eliminating the monarchical beasts. Only one historical fact mattered for the fifteen centuries that got skipped: the religious beast ran amok and opposed the divine kingdom. Only one thing, then, was left to be foretold: the demise of the religious beast.

Hence, the omniscient angel simply moved on to what was truly relevant. He began by foretelling that when the era of unprecedented distress arrived, Daniel's people would be delivered. What would the Jews be delivered from? The same old dark beast, of course.

As will be seen in Chapter 11, the Jews suffered tremendously under the reign of the Church and its dogma that they were all guilty of deicide (murder of a god). Although they were finally granted political freedom in the 19th century, they had not been delivered from the religious beast. For the Church fought back with a cultural and political crusade against them that drove the politics of antisemitism, and it later partnered with Fascist Italy and Nazi Germany (§L.2.).

It all culminated in the Holocaust, which the Vatican did nothing to stop (§L.3.). Amazingly enough, the Church needed another two decades before it renounced the dogma of the Jews being guilty of deicide, which it finally did at the Second Vatican Council in the 1960s.

So it was the Jews would not be delivered until the latter half of the 20th century, which just so happens to coincide with the reemergence of Israel. Only then, Daniel was told, would "your people" finally be safe from the Church's demonization and its consequences. As the omniscient angel long ago foretold, the era of the trauma would also be the era of the deliverance.

Although Israel won its war of independence in 1948, it was far from secure until it demolished its enemies in 1967. With that victory, it gained critical buffers in the Sinai Peninsula, the West Bank and the Golan Heights.

As the Arab invasion of 1973 showed, Israel's life depended on those buffers. Moreover, the United States greatly escalated its military aid after 1967 as Israel became a strategic ally who could procure advanced weaponry (France had been Israel's chief military supplier for its first two decades). So here we are again in the 1960s.

The omniscient angel then described this era as a time when "multitudes who sleep in the dust of the earth will awake." This is not a physical reference meaning billions of corpses will suddenly be resurrected.

When you think about it, the ancient belief is preposterous. What about the people who were vaporized by a bomb, eaten by a wild animal, decomposed to just a skeleton or cremated into a pile of ash? Where are their bodies? When these folks are resurrected, do all those missing molecules suddenly depart from their current whereabouts to coalesce again into undamaged bodies? Or will there be zombies trolling around looking for missing body parts and other helpful organic matter?

Interpreting this passage in a physical manner is to be ignorant of not only how the universe works but also what Jesus taught. According to Mark, Jesus denounced the Judaic belief about the resurrection of the dead as "badly mistaken," for God is the God of the living, not of the dead (§A.2.b.). Jesus thus agreed with the scientifically validated fact that personal consciousness continues seamlessly after death.

The passage is a metaphorical reference to those whose consciousness is still buried by the illusion of the physical universe and the deceptions of the darkness (§1.2.d.). The "dust of the earth" symbolizes how the physical illusion covers up and hides the spiritual fabric of our existence. To be buried in the physical illusion is for consciousness to be owned by the ego's fears and cravings. It is living from physiology, and it always ends the same: ashes to ashes and dust to dust.

As for life in the darkness, being asleep is to have not yet found the narrow gate. Jesus supposedly explained why he spoke to the crowds in parables: "Though seeing, they do not see; though hearing, they do not hear or understand" (Mt 13:13). He could very well have added, "Though not sleeping, they are asleep." Although the multitudes may be devoutly religious, they are spiritually asleep. Their consciousness has not yet risen, for they are still ensnared by the deceptions and fears of the darkness.

Having foretold a great awakening, the omniscient angel concluded his amazing prophecy by praising those who awaken, shine and lead many to the truth. It was the end of his lecture.

What he did not say is just as important as what he said. There was no rapture of only those who believed in the Anointed One. There was no spectacular return of a warrior-Christ to fight the antichrist and his massive army.

There was no supernatural assault upon the heathens. To the contrary, the omniscient angel simply foretold a great spiritual awakening that would cap his epic sweep of history.

7.5.b. The Power of the Holy People

Daniel's prophecies foretold the demise of the beastly empires and the ascendancy of the divine kingdom. In a word, they are all about power. The divine intention is for it to be distributed to everybody (§7.3.c.). We are meant to reclaim our spiritual power, which by definition means the collapse of all towers of external power (§1.3.c.).

This will not happen, though, until we awaken. Although monarchical and dictatorial governments have finally been relegated to our rearview mirror, the Church and its many offshoots are still opposing our awakening.

The spiritual realm knew all about it. After the omniscient angel's lecture, another angel asked, "How long will it be before these astonishing things are fulfilled?" (Dn 12:6). He answered, "It will be for a time, times and half a time. When the power of the holy people has been finally broken, all these things will be completed" (Dn 12:7).

So how about that for some heavenly validation of our spiritual comprehension? We are obviously right on track. But God will not strip away power from the Church or any other institution, for its members have willingly tendered their power to it. Withdrawing power is a choice for its leaders and members to make, not God.

Should the Church ever teach the masses to search for the truth and spiritually grow instead of obeying the pope and learning the catechisms, its tower of power would collapse. So it keeps living its delusion and preaching its deceptions. Therefore, the power of the holy people will only be broken as the masses awaken and leave for greener spiritual pastures. This is why the great awakening is a prerequisite for this monumental occurrence.

The omniscient angel thus confirmed the nature of his intangible process—the great awakening—by identifying its visible impact. It is like a prophecy that we would know global warming had occurred when Greenland's covering ice was gone. We would know the great awakening had occurred "when the power of the holy people has been finally broken," which will be visible in membership counts of applicable institutions.

While this signature line refers most prominently to the Catholic Church, it extends far beyond. After all, the truths that portend the Church's doom apply to any institution that aggregates religious power from the Bible. Whether it has a deified ruler over a billion people or just an authoritative pastor over a few hundred, the principles are the same.

The holy people's power in any religion comes from the assumption that it teaches the highest truth about God and life. The darkness really sets in when the institution prioritizes its power and survival over the spiritual growth of its members. Because uniformity of belief is the bond between them, legitimate truth-seeking is shunned because it would undermine the institution.

Because we are here to spiritually grow, submitting to any religious institution is toxic to the soul. No religion has a monopoly on the truth about God and life, so we have to own the responsibility for finding and living it.

Yes, religious hierarchies and the holy books they were built upon are destined to collapse. The prophecies were couched in mystery and could not be solved by a traditional paradigm. But when we finally began seeing through the errors and deceptions of the Bible to embrace a far more spectacular God, they would all unravel like a child's riddle.

The spiritual realm was not playing around. Even though it always honors our choices, its kingdom of freedom, truth-seeking, equality and love would not be denied.

So here we are on the bleeding edge of the greatest paradigm shift the world will ever experience. The spiritual realm long ago confirmed that we are destined to drop all the ancient nonsense about religious intermediaries and hierarchies of any kind (including the patriarchy of male superiority). The same applies for beliefs in such absurdities as an unfair God who plays favorites, a neurotic God who requires blood sacrifices to atone for sins, and a sadistic God who would torture souls for an eternity.

All in all, the writing is on the wall for the mainstream Western religions as our spiritual evolution shifts into high gear. Despite the birth pains we will be going through, it is a time to rejoice, for our planet has been stuck in an unenlightened pattern for far too long. The time has finally come for us to awaken from our nightmare.

Lost souls will be reclaiming their spiritual power as they enter through the narrow gate and step up to stage 4 (§1.4.g.). As this happens, the holy people of the stage 2 religions will watch their external power over others dissolve from its base like a stick of butter on a hot skillet.

7.5.c. The Time, Times and Half a Time

Many prophecy interpreters believe "a time, times and half a time" is 3.5 years, which they derive from correlating the phrase with the termination of the daily sacrifices in the middle of the 70th seven (§7.4.). They believe this final seven-year period, which they call the tribulation, will be happening in the future and the antichrist is the "he" who will be terminating the sacrifices and setting up the abomination.

We now know how mistaken they are. Not a single passage in Daniel foretells an antichrist, and the Roman Empire was the "ruler who will come" who did these things. As for the "middle of the 'seven,'" the Romans terminated the sacrifices in the middle of the 70th seven in 70 CE (§7.4.c.).

By the way, these interpreters also turn to Revelation to support their theory about the 3.5 years. It is circular logic, though, for as will be seen in Chapter 10, the author of Revelation made the same mistake and included his misleading commentary about Daniel.

Then there are the two different instances of a "time, times and half a time." The first refers to Constantine and the second to the grand sweep of history. Most importantly, though, is the answer to this mystery. By hitting the knee-buckling curveball about Constantine, we learned the phrase means one unit of time, another such unit and then half a unit (§7.3.d.).

The omniscient angel was asked how long it would be before the astonishing things he had spoken about had transpired. Again, his lecture began by foretelling the next Persian kings and was capped by the time of unparalleled distress, the deliverance of the Jews and the great awakening.

In the case of Constantine and "a time, times and half a time," the variable "a time" is ten years. As for the omniscient angel's use of this equation, the variable is one thousand years. His coded answer was, "It will be 2,500 years. When the power of the holy people has been finally broken, all these things will be completed."

Daniel received this prophecy in the first month of the third year of Cyrus's rule over Babylon, which was the spring of 536 BCE (Da 10:1–4). As the year following 1 BCE is 1 CE, moving forward 2,500 years from when Daniel received the prophecy points to the year 1965.

7.5.d. The Three Revolutions of the 1960s

So here we are again in the 1960s. The Jews were finally delivered then as three independent revolutions were forming the first wave of the great spiritual awakening.

The first revolution was the societal upheaval that rocked the Western world. The civil rights movement challenged the inequities of biblically justified racism and rolled to legislative victories in 1964 and 1965. Young men and women challenged the biblical mindset of a good spirit battling the evil flesh and dismissed its sexual prohibitions. Souls who could no longer stomach the hellish and guilt-ridden teachings of Christianity began exploring the Eastern religions and New Age spirituality. Last but not least, the peace movement challenged the establishment's Vietnam War and its biblically justified pipeline of external power.

The second revolution was occurring in the Catholic Church with the Second Vatican Council, which met from October 11, 1962, to December 8, 1965. Pope John XXIII (1958–1963) called the council to reform the

Church, better align it with the modern world, and start healing the split with Protestantism.

In the words of Catholic commentators, the Church's "monolithic and absolutist character was forever changed" by this "revolution."[20] More specifically, "the church shifted from seeing itself as a hierarchical institution that organized and ruled people to church as a community of people with co-responsibility."[21]

One of the council's highlights was the Church finally relenting from its intolerant and dominating mindset with the Decree on Religious Liberty, which was bitterly opposed by many bishops. Catholic scholar Eamon Duffy describes what the Church finally embodied:

> Perhaps most revolutionary of all, the Decree on Religious Liberty declared unequivocally that "the human person has a right to religious liberty," and that this religious freedom, a fundamental part of the dignity of human beings, must be enshrined in the constitution of society as a civil right.
>
> This was truly revolutionary teaching, for the persecution of heresy and enforcement of Catholicism had been a reality since the days of Constantine, and since the French Revolution pope after pope had repeatedly and explicitly denounced the notion that non-Catholics had a right to religious freedom. On the older view, error had no rights, and the Church was bound to proclaim the truth and, wherever it could, to see that society enforced the truth by secular sanctions. Heretics and unbelievers might in certain circumstances be granted *toleration*, but not *liberty*.[22]

In sum, to the exact year of the "time, times and half a time" prophecy, the Church finally abandoned its tyrannical mindset of submitting non-Catholics to its dogma. It finally stopped committing the grave sin of trying to coerce free will.

Vatican II was thus a commendable example of institutional growth. Furthermore, the Church under Pope John Paul II (1978–2005) began owning up to and apologizing for many of its past sins. The Church has thus taken some significant steps of spiritual growth in recent decades.

All the while the third revolution of the 1960s was quietly developing in the fringe outposts of science. Historically speaking, scientists had been content to study the natural laws of the universe and steered clear of supernatural questions. Although some rogue scientists made forays onto the well-defended turf of religion before the 1960s, most of those efforts flamed out because their promising leads were not pursued. More importantly, nobody dared stake a scientific claim to matters of religion.

That changed in 1964, though, when a famous psychologist issued a manifesto for an enlarged science to examine the most cherished beliefs, values and experiences of mankind. In doing so, he became the figurehead of an obscure movement that was the third revolution of the turbulent decade. Although most people were unaware of it, this one would prove to be the most dangerous for the holy people and their power.

7.5.e. A Jewish Man Named Abraham

The Western religions began with a Jewish man named Abraham. As it turns out, they will be coming to an end because of a revolution championed by another Jewish man named Abraham.

Abraham Maslow was born in 1908 in Brooklyn, New York. He was the first of seven children of uneducated Jewish immigrants from Russia.

A leader of the humanistic branch of psychology, Maslow made the case for an optimistic view of humanity. He termed it the third force of psychology, which he believed was needed to counterbalance the negative implications of psychoanalytic theory and behaviorism. As he explained, "To oversimplify the matter somewhat, it is as if Freud supplied to us the sick half of psychology and we must now fill it out with the healthy half."[23]

Best known for his model of the hierarchy of needs, he knew we have a fundamental drive for personal growth, the pinnacle of which he termed self-actualization. In the last years of his life, he strove to extend his theory even further into our spiritual nature and potential.

In 1964, he published a landmark book, *Religions, Values, and Peak-Experiences*, that addressed the dichotomized split between science and religion. He challenged both sides to put aside all cherished assumptions so we could arrive at a far greater understanding of the human condition. He wrote:

> I want to demonstrate that spiritual values have naturalistic meaning, that they are not the exclusive possession of organized churches, that they do not need supernatural concepts to validate them, that they are well within the jurisdiction of a suitably enlarged science, and that, therefore, they are the general responsibility of all mankind.[24]

Maslow was not trying to destroy religion and faith. Rather, he was arguing for unbiased truth-seeking into the realm of religion to rescue the baby from the bathwater. The "problems of values, ethics, spirituality, morals," he wrote, "are being taken away from the exclusive jurisdiction of the institutionalized churches and are becoming the 'property,' so to speak, of a new type of humanistic scientist."[25]

He was just as critical of modern science, which was focused on only "the actual and the existent" and was having "nothing to do with the ideal, that is to say, with the ends, the goals, the purposes of life, i.e., with end-values."[26] Science would thus have to be broadened and redefined for us to overcome the failings of religion and tradition and arrive at a deeper understanding of ultimate truth.

Maslow was convinced there was a greater truth about humanity than could be found in our religious and psychological theories. In 1968, he wrote, "I should say also that I consider Humanistic, Third Force Psychology to be transitional, a preparation for a still 'higher' Fourth Psychology."[27] This new field was called transpersonal psychology, a discipline for exploring and including the transcendent aspects of the psyche.

In 1969, he cofounded the *Journal of Transpersonal Psychology* as a forum through which it could develop. Abraham Maslow died in 1970.

7.5.f. The Search for Truth in Religion's Backyard

Maslow did not inspire a wave of other scientists to delve into the core assertions of religion. Yet his visionary thesis heralded a small but far-reaching development that caught fire this time around.

Back in the closing decades of the 19th century, scholars in England and America had formed professional organizations to examine supernatural topics (§2.3.b.). Their effort gathered impressive evidence but fizzled out because hardly any scientists of subsequent generations pursued those openings. The only subject that continued to get noteworthy attention was psi phenomena (§2.5.b.), which posed absolutely no threat to religion.

After 1965, however, maverick scientists began publishing research about lines of inquiry that will be having devastating repercussions for the traditional religions. Here are the most important trailblazing efforts:

- In 1966, Ian Stevenson, MD, published his first set of reincarnation cases (§A.5.).

- In 1975, Herbert Benson, MD, published his research into the physiological effects of meditation in *The Relaxation Response*.

- In 1975, Raymond Moody, MD, published the first study of near-death experiences (§2.5.d.).

- In 1983, M. Scott Peck, MD, published *People of the Lie*, which was a psychological study of evil (§5.2.). His book also delved into spirit possession as other psychiatrists and degreed clinicians began publishing their empirical data about it in the 1980s (§B.2.).

- In the late 1990s, Gary Schwartz, PhD, and Linda Russek, PhD, tested five spirit mediums under laboratory conditions and demonstrated their legitimacy (§2.5.e.).

All these lines of inquiry have been progressing and generating more evidence and insights. Although many pioneers tilled the ground for it, this kind of research did not begin taking root and bearing fruit until the 1960s. Even though it was a grassroots movement without a formal leader, Abraham Maslow unfurled the banner of its arrival. Its findings opened the door for us, and it was only a matter of time before we unraveled the prophecies.

7.5.g. Assessing the Accuracy of the Prophecy

As for the accuracy of the second crown jewel prophecy, keep in mind the original question: "How long will it be before these astonishing things are fulfilled?" (Dn 12:6). Such a question practically dictates the answer will have the condition of "at least" implied with it.

For instance, imagine going back to when the Chicago Cubs had just won the World Series in 1908. Suppose a fan asked a psychic how long it would be before they won another one and was told, "A century." Since the Cubs did not win it again until 2016, it would have been a painfully accurate and impressive reading because the "at least" was implied. But if the Cubs had not won it again until 2067, the reading would have been accurate but not as impressive, for "a century and a half" would have better demonstrated omniscience.

The omniscient angel had just foretold ten centuries of ancient history, the deliverance of the Jews and the great awakening (§7.5.a.). He then indicated how many years would transpire "before" those things had occurred.

Meanwhile, the great awakening would not be a binary condition like a light switch that is either on or off. Rather, it would be a process that transpired over decades. So when should it be deemed fulfilled? When it began firing up in the 1960s? When its occurrence had been proven by the holy people's power having finally been broken?

Consider as well that his unit of measure was a millennium. If we deem the great awakening to have occurred by, say, 2030, was he supposed to have said, "It will be for a time, times, half a time, and 6.5 percent of a time"?

So try not to overthink it. Moving two-and-a-half millennia forward from 536 BCE lands us in the middle of the 1960s and a societal revolution, Vatican II and the onset of the scientific march into the core tenets of religion. The great awakening kicked into gear that decade, and this intangible process will eventually prove itself in the breaking of the holy people's power. The other fulfillment that would have to wait for at least 2,500 years was the deliverance of the Jews, which had its milestones in 1965 and 1967.

All in all, the omniscient angel crushed another towering drive in the spiritual realm's game of home run derby. But given what this prophecy is about and the impact it foretold, we should really call it a grand slam.

7.5.h. The Omniscient Angel's Parting Words

After Daniel said he had heard but had not understood, he asked what the outcome of it all would be. The book that bears his name concludes with the omniscient angel's parting words to him:

> He replied, "Go your way, Daniel, because the words are rolled up and sealed until the time of the end. Many will be purified, made spotless and refined, but the wicked will continue to be wicked. None of the wicked will understand, but those who are wise will understand.
>
> "From the time that the daily sacrifice is abolished and the abomination that causes desolation is set up, there will be 1,290 days. Blessed is the one who waits for and reaches the end of the 1,335 days.
>
> "As for you, go your way till the end. You will rest, and then at the end of the days you will rise to receive your allotted inheritance." (Dn 12:8–13)

Many interpreters believe these statements refer to a forthcoming apocalypse and antichrist. These folks also think the 1,290 and 1,335 days are associated with the 3.5 years that are half of an apocalyptic 70th seven (§7.5.c.).

Trouble is, the Daniel prophecies have nothing to do with an antichrist, and the 70th seven occurred in the first century CE. Moreover, the math does not compute, either, for 3.5 years of a so-called biblical year of 360 days is 1,260 days, and 3.5 years of a solar year of 365 days is 1,277.5 days.

We also know Daniel's prophecies refer to two different abominations. As Appendix H demonstrates, the verse about the 1,290 and 1,335 days was in all likelihood referring to the first "abomination that causes desolation" (ACD-1) that occurred in the 160s BCE. While those numbers would have meant everything to Jews living through that trauma, they are unimportant to us now.

In sum, these verses are best understood as the omniscient angel answering Daniel's question on three different levels. His answer tapers down from the big picture of global history to Daniel's tribe to Daniel himself.

As for the big picture, he revealed nothing more. Instead, he told Daniel to move along because his prophecy would not begin making sense until the "time of the end" had arrived. He also indicated it would take wisdom to unlock the totality of the prophecies.

As for Daniel's tribe, the omniscient angel at least threw the prophet an informational bone about ACD-1 and the traumatic era of Antiochus IV. He disclosed the number of days to comfort those Jews by letting them know the wicked king would be a short-term storm that would soon blow over.

As for Daniel himself, the angel bid him well. The humble receiver of the prophecies was assured that in due time he would be rewarded for his divine work.

7.6. Conclusion

Daniel's prophecies are absolutely astonishing in how accurately they foretold the future, but the spiritual realm did not render them to dazzle us. Rather, it had a far more important agenda while it honored our free will. With the knee-buckling curveball about Constantine, the mystery of "a time, times and half a time" and the two different instances of an "abomination that causes desolation," the prophecies were designed to be unsolvable until we finally started awakening. But once we started seeing through the darkness of our religions, their truth would suddenly be unleashed to affirm our newfound direction.

The "time of the end" was an era in which the Anointed One arrived and proclaimed his revolutionary message. The divine kingdom of freedom, truth-seeking, equality and love was thus born into a world of beastly empires that thrived on hierarchical dominance, conquering invasions, royalty, inequality, coercive submission and slavery.

Although the divine kingdom was destined to triumph over the beasts, it did not happen then. Instead, the Messiah's teachings were subsumed into an unenlightened and deceptive version of Christianity that devolved into an abomination that causes desolation. The Roman Catholic Church collaborated with its totalitarian husbands, and the beastly empires crushed the divine kingdom for the better part of two millennia.

We finally started vanquishing these dark forms of governance a few centuries ago despite the Church's vehement opposition. Obviously, then, there was one more beast that needed to expire.

As the omniscient angel long ago foretold, a great awakening would eventually occur and break the power of the holy people. Pinpointing its origins to the 1960s, this process would fire up with three different revolutions as the Jews were finally delivered from the horrors of Christian demonization.

Heaven knows how long it will take for the world to awaken, for it is still our choice as to when we finally usher in the divine kingdom. Deny and fight the process all you want if you must, but the writing is on the wall for the mainstream Western religions. All that remains to be seen is how soon it transpires.

Chapter 8

Triangulating the Great Awakening

8.1. Introduction

After the omniscient angel foretold the ancient empires (§7.3.g.), he indicated there would eventually be a time of unprecedented distress as the Jews were delivered and a great awakening engulfed the planet (§7.5.a.). These events would be completed sometime after 1965, and the milestone marking their completion would be when "the power of the holy people" was finally broken (§7.5.b., §7.5.c.).

This chapter presents material that triangulates this interpretation. It begins with our societal evolution and the Maya calendar's corroboration. It then delves into the life and messages of Edgar Cayce, which include a fascinating reference to the Daniel prophecies.

The heart of the chapter follows with the ominous prophecy of Saint Malachy. Its unraveling flashes another thunderbolt across the dark religious sky. After presenting what an atheist was told during a near-death experience, the chapter concludes with some dialogue from the *Conversations with God* material.

8.2. Freedom, Prosperity and Mass Communication

We now take religious freedom for granted, but it was a hard-fought victory in recent centuries. Modern democracy finally afforded legal protection as the Church lost its power to dominate the religious landscape. This development was a prerequisite for the widespread communication and adoption of "heretical" beliefs.

Meanwhile, technological and economic growth has made it much easier for many to raise their concerns above the demands of daily survival. In 1840, workers in farm occupations comprised 68.6 percent of the United States' labor force. In 1900, such workers were 37.5 percent of the labor force. In 1960, that percentage was down to a mere 6.1, and it was at 2.7 in 1980.[1] This data reflects how the Western industrialized nations recently became quite adept at fulfilling their most basic needs.

This development has blessed us with more time and money for pursuits beyond life's necessities. More importantly, our collective prosperity has made it much easier to escape the gravity of tribal unity. Until recently, the pressure to conform to group norms had been very high, for it was hard to survive without the acceptance of family and community.

Over the past few centuries, however, people have been nowhere near as dependent upon their families and communities for survival. Also aided by modern transportation, disenchanted individuals can distance themselves from dysfunctional situations.

As Jesus and many subsequent martyrs demonstrated, a greater spirituality could have been lived at any era of history. Yet for almost all people, the fears of torture, death or being disowned by one's family and tribe were far too overwhelming. Fortunately, times have changed, and the massive walls that previously bordered the well-traveled religious roads have been dramatically lowered. Nowhere near as much faith and courage are needed to surmount them to find the narrow gate and path that lead to true life.

In addition, the 20th century ushered in the Information Age and the technologies of mass communication, which has made it possible for shocking discoveries to rapidly canvass the world like never before. There is nothing the Church can do anymore to censor and block the search for truth. All in all, if there was ever an era to be singled out by an ancient prophecy for a global awakening, this would sure seem to be it.

8.3. The Maya Calendar

The ancient Maya were native Central Americans who had an exceptional understanding of astronomy and developed a remarkable calendar. The Maya Long Count calendar tracks extensive periods of time, and monuments bearing calendar markings have been dated as far back as 37 BCE. Comprised of 13 "baktuns" of approximately 394 years each, it measures 5,125 years.

The calendar received considerable attention in doomsday circles because it concluded on the winter solstice of 2012. The Maya apparently back-calculated to begin their calendar in 3114 BCE.

Based on his study of Maya rituals, rites, myths and astronomy, John Major Jenkins articulates a well-substantiated theory that the Maya arrived at their end date by using the dark rift in our galaxy as their primary long-term reference point. This galactic center came into rare alignment with the sun on the winter solstice of 2012 (the calendar's concluding date). Jenkins presented his theory in 1998 with this summary:

> The ancient Maya understood something about the nature of

the cosmos and the spiritual evolution of humanity that has gone unrecognized in our own worldview. This understanding involves our alignment with the center of our Galaxy, our cosmic center and source, and identifies A.D. 2012 as a time of tremendous transformation and opportunity for spiritual growth, a transition from one World Age to another.[2]

The Spaniards came to the Americas and conquered the Aztecs, Maya and Incas in the 16th century. They thoroughly destroyed those cultures and indoctrinated their beloved Catholicism. Will the Church soon be experiencing the karma of its culture-obliterating past? Is it just a coincidence the Maya calendar concluded just before its conqueror's final rites were pronounced?

8.4. The Life and Messages of Edgar Cayce

The channeled messages of Edgar Cayce also touch on the topic at hand, and putting them into context has its own gift as well. His story reflects how challenging life can be when you are called to serve a spiritual purpose. Many people run from their calling, but Cayce did not.

8.4.a. Cayce's Special Talent

Edgar Cayce was born in Kentucky in 1877. He only had a seventh-grade education and was a photographer, devout Presbyterian Christian, Sunday school teacher, husband and father. He realized at an early age that he had a spiritual gift and used it in humble service.

In 1910, an article in the *New York Times* entitled "Illiterate Man Becomes A Doctor When Hypnotized" announced his mysterious ability to the world. Physicians would simply tell him the name and address of a patient and nothing else. The entranced Cayce would report his findings and treatment recommendations as if he had graduated from a prestigious medical institution. The testifying physician stated, "I have used him in about 100 cases, and to date have never known of any errors in diagnosis."[3]

From 1901 to 1944, Cayce delivered an estimated 16,000 readings. While in a hypnotized trance, he would journey into otherworldly dimensions. His stenographer recorded his utterances, as he was unaware of what he had spoken upon returning to waking consciousness. The records of 14,249 of his readings are kept by the Association for Research and Enlightenment. He died in Virginia in 1945.

8.4.b. Cayce's Christianity Challenged

For over two decades, Cayce's readings were dedicated almost exclusively to the health concerns of his clients. In October of 1923, though, Arthur Lammers invited him to Dayton, Ohio, for a different type of reading. Lammers was passionate about exploring the hundreds of different philosophic and theological systems and wanted to pose his questions to Cayce. Cayce agreed and traveled to Dayton with his secretary and stenographer.

Lammers probed the hypnotized Christian about astrology, which Cayce expected would prove to be fake. When Cayce awoke, he was shocked to learn what he had said. Astrology was not only legitimate but also needed to be coupled with an understanding of reincarnation. He replied, "But what you've been telling me today, and what the readings have been saying, is foreign to all I've believed and been taught, and all I've taught others, all of my life. If ever the Devil was going to play a trick on me, this would be it."[4]

Lammers wanted to continue the exploration, but Cayce needed to decide if he did too. He spent the night walking the streets of Dayton and contemplating at a bridge until the morning. He thought about the countless souls who had been given opportunities to serve but fell back and failed because it would have required too much sacrifice. Cayce thought about how he, too, was failing, and all he had to lose. But then he reconsidered. If his family and friends could accept his readings about the body, why not for the soul as well? In the words of biographer Thomas Sugrue:

> Would they not be forced to admit, as he was forced to admit—standing there above the Dayton River, looking at the stars—that what the readings had said that day, what Lammers had said that day, was logical: inescapably, unavoidably, irrevocably logical? They might. They might not.[5]

At the age of 46, Cayce left his career as a photographer and dedicated himself to this bizarre line of work. The life readings he later began giving for some of his clients delved into the past sequence of lives that were influencing the current one. Prophecies about future events and an interpretation of Revelation also came forth, which return us to our primary topic.

8.4.c. Cayce's Foray Into Prophecy and Interpretation

The traditional Western religions are largely built upon the testimony of men who reported what they learned from the Other Side. More recent religions and spiritual conceptions have also arisen from otherworldly sources.

As these teachings are widely divergent, we have to figure out where universal truth has come through and where it has not. We can blindly worship one and deny the others where they diverge, denounce them all and cast our faith with science, or consciously navigate the dilemma via all means of knowing.

The wisest approach is neither blindly embracing nor categorically dismissing information from the Other Side. Instead, we should apply careful and unbiased discernment while integrating all other sources of knowledge.

Only about two dozen of the Cayce readings dabbled in prophecy, yet significant predictions were made therein. Supporters say he successfully predicted numerous future events while critics note how many of his bold claims failed to materialize. Supporters retort that the future is never set in stone and prophetic warnings may alter our behavior and create a different future.

Scholars assess Cayce's track record with future events as being unimpressive at best and even worse with producing veritable information about the past. Comparing his performance here with his other roles as a holistic health advisor, Christian theosopher and esoteric psychologist, scholar K. Paul Johnson summarizes: "The appraisal of Cayce as a clairvoyant time traveler is inevitably much less favorable than in regard to the other three roles addressed in this book. It would be unfortunate if his failures in divining the past and future come to overshadow his genuine contributions."[6]

Cayce and his colleagues also explored Revelation. Generally speaking, his discourses read like a King James Bible scholar had merged with a New Age metaphysician. His otherworldly source was aware that Revelation must be read metaphorically, but the rambling and obtuse explanations are reminiscent of a politician responding to a question he is unable to answer. Rather than admit ignorance, an esoteric reply is given amid a deluge of words.

The Cayce interpretation is far from omniscient. For instance, Revelation describes a beast with ten horns and seven heads that resembled a leopard, a bear and a lion (Rv 13:1–2). From our study of Daniel, we know the animal part of the imagery signifies a mix of the dominant earthly kingdoms. Yet Cayce's source talked about the beast being representative of the human psyche's forces and centers.[7]

Revelation also describes a beast that had two horns like a lamb but spoke like a dragon (Rv 13:11). The true meaning will be disclosed in Chapter 10, but for now it is enough to know the metaphor does not represent what Cayce's source identified it as: "double-mindedness" in the human psyche.[8]

To whatever extent the metaphors have a secondary meaning in agreement with Cayce's source, so be it. However, Cayce's source was oblivious to their primary meaning. In sum, the Cayce material is far from omniscient when it comes to interpreting biblical prophecy. This is to be expected, for the spiritual realm did not want its prophecies to be unraveled until the appointed time.

8.4.d. The Cayce Material Corroborates the End Times

Nevertheless, Cayce's source was apparently tuned in to Daniel's prophecy about the great awakening. In March of 1936, Cayce had a dream where he had been born again in Nebraska in 2100 and lived there in a coastal city. All to the west was presumably covered by the ocean, and water also covered part of Alabama.

He inquired about the dream three months later. The interpretation he received began with a brief sermon to not be afraid. He should follow the Golden Rule, remain humble, and know that God would be with him through every trial. The reading concluded (underlining added):

> That the periods from the material angle, as visioned, are to come to pass, matters not to the soul, but do thy duty TODAY! TOMORROW will care for itself. These changes in the earth will come to pass, <u>for the time and times and half time are at an end</u>, and there begin those periods for the readjustments. For how hath He given? "The righteous shall inherit the earth."[9]

The secondary point is the apparent error in literally interpreting the dream. It is exceedingly rare for a dream to accurately present the surface details of reality, but dreams often conjure up metaphors to represent the underlying nature of a situation.

The primary point is that in discussing the changes from 1936 to 2100, Cayce's source said "the time and times and half time are at an end" and referred to the widespread distribution of power. It is an intriguing piece of corroboration from a source on the Other Side.

8.5. Saint Malachy's Prophecy

Saint Malachy (c. 1094–1148) was an Irish bishop who traveled to Rome in 1140 to meet with Pope Innocent II. While in Rome, he had a heavenly encounter during the middle of the night and was given a detailed prophecy. It was a list of epithets for the next 111 popes, followed by a short paragraph that seemed to pinpoint the end of days to the 112th and final pope.

The bishop tendered his prophecy to the pope. It ended up in the Vatican's subterranean archives until it was uncovered by a new librarian in 1556. It was leaked shortly thereafter, for the first published reference to it was made in a book by Girolamo Muzio in 1570 (*Il Choro Pontificate*).[10]

The prophecy was published in its entirety by historian Dom Arnold Wion in his 1595 book, *Lignum Vitae*.[11] As Wion explained why he was publishing it, "This, as it is short, and so far as we know, has never before been printed, is inserted here, seeing that many people have asked for it."[12]

It has long been believed the succession of popes would come to an end because of a horrifying apocalypse as suggested by the final epithet and Revelation. However, Saint Malachy was just like Daniel in foretelling a future that would arrive in a shocking way because humanity had no idea it would be manifesting this way.

8.5.a. The List of 111 Brief Epithets

Just a few years after Saint Malachy tendered his prophecy to Innocent II, it began doing its supernatural thing when the pope died and a new man stepped into the office. Here are the first five epithets along with their corresponding fulfillments.[13]

1. *Ex castro Tyberis* (From a castle on the Tiber). Celestine II (1143–1144) was born in Citta di Castello, Toscany. *Castello* means castle, and the town is on the shores of the Tiber River.

2. *Inimicus expulsus* (Enemy expelled). Lucius II (1144–1145) had the surname of Cassianemici (drive out the enemy). He led a small army against a revolutionary republic in Rome that was trying to separate the papacy from its sovereign rule over the Papal States. His army was defeated, and he died during the battle. As this pope was defeated and expelled, logic says he was the enemy. It is the prophecy's first clue the spiritual realm does not side with the Church.

3. *Ex magnitudine motis* (From the great mountain). Eugene III (1145–1153) is believed to have come from the Montemagno family, a name derived from *mons magnus* (Latin for great mountain). He was supposedly born in the Gramont (great mount) castle.

4. *Abbas Suburranus* (Suburran abbot). Anastasius IV (1153–1154) was Corrado Demetri della Suburra.

5. *De rure albo* (Of the field of Albe). Adrian IV (1154–1159) was born in St. Albans and later became the bishop of Alba on his path to the papacy.

The prophecy was published during the papacy of Clement VIII (1592–1605), the 77th pope on the list. Wion had previously consulted a Dominican scholar to authenticate and interpret it, so *Lignum Vitae* includes the names of the popes who fulfilled the first 77 epithets along with brief explanations of each fulfillment.

Some 80 years after *Lignum Vitae* brought the prophecy to the world, a Jesuit scholar charged that its accuracy was because it was a forgery, and many other Catholic scholars followed suit. However, the prophecy continued to deliver on its predictions long after its earliest critics had come and gone. As Catholic prophecy expert John Hogue explains in his 1998 book, "Time judges their official rejection by Church authorities as suspect because the mottoes remain remarkably and even chillingly accurate in describing the natures, family arms, and fates of the popes up to the current Vicar of Christ [John Paul II] and perhaps beyond."[14]

So you can judge for yourself how well the last of the brief epithets predicted papal history, here they are.

101. *Crux de cruce* (Cross from a cross). Pius IX (1846–1878) was opposed by King Victor Emmanuel II, whose troops seized Rome and the Papal States and extinguished the pope's sovereign rule in 1870. The unifying king of Italy

came from the House of Savoy, whose coat of arms is a large white cross.

102. *Lumen in coelo* (Light in the sky). Leo XIII (1878–1903) had a coat of arms depicting a comet. The epithet also aptly describes his character.

103. *Ignis ardens* (Burning fire). Pius X (1903–1914) died shortly after World War I had begun and was spreading like a wildfire across Europe. In addition, the Tunguska meteor blast of 1908 was seen by millions over most of North America and Eurasia.

104. *Religio depopulate* (Religion depopulated). Benedict XV (1914–1922) ruled as 35 million Christians died from World War I and the Spanish influenza epidemic. Moreover, 200 million Christians were stripped of their religion by the atheistic Bolsheviks after the Russian Revolution.

105. *Fides intrepida* (Intrepid faith). Pius XI (1922–1939) was a strong-willed pope with high standards who loved mountaineering, so the epithet aptly describes his character.

106. *Pastor angelicus* (Angelic pastor). Pius XII (1939–1958) took a neutral and passive role during World War II, so the epithet aptly describes his character. He also loved and adamantly promoted the philosophy of Saint Thomas Aquinas, who was referred to as the angelic doctor. Moreover, Pius XII commissioned a promotional film about himself entitled *The Angelic Pastor* (although the title probably came from the prophecy).

107. *Pastor et nauta* (Pastor and marine). John XXIII (1958–1963) was previously the patriarch of the marine city of Venice. He also initiated Vatican II, whose badge displayed a cross and a ship.

108. *Flos florum* (Flower of flowers). Paul VI (1963–1978) had a coat of arms displaying three flowers.

109. *De medietate lunae* (From the half-moon). John Paul I (1978) entered the seminary and served as chancellor of the diocese in Belluno (good moon). More importantly, he was elected on August 26, 1978, and died on September 28, 1978, which was from one half-moon (August 25) to another (September 24).

110. *De labore solis* (From the sun's labor). John Paul II (1978–2005). In medieval Latin poetry, an eclipse is referred to as a sun's travail or labor. He was born on May 18, 1920, during a partial solar eclipse (one of only two solar eclipses in 1920). His funeral was on April 8, 2005, during a rare hybrid eclipse (one of only two solar eclipses in 2005).

111. *Gloria olivae* (Glory of the olives). Benedict XVI (2005–2013). A 1969 book commented about *Gloria olivae*, "The order of St. Benedict has claimed by tradition that this pope will come from within the Order…The Order of St. Benedict is also known as the Olivetans, which may well account for another interpretation of the prophecy."[15] Although not from the order himself, this pope's naming choice of "Benedict" glorified the Olivetans. He said he did so

to "remember Pope Benedict XV, that courageous prophet of peace."[16] The olive branch is symbolic of peace. Finally, he had been the cardinal-bishop of Velletri, which has three olive trees on its coat of arms.

The final epithet is a short paragraph. Since it is so different from the others and requires a paradigm shift to interpret, it will be presented later.

8.5.b. Which Came First, the Prophecy or the History Book?

As with Daniel, we will not rest on the laurels of fulfilled prophecy. Rather, we need to address the arguments that it was a 16th-century fabrication.

Skeptics point to a book about the popes that was written by a Vatican historian named Onofrio Panvinio and published in 1557 (*Epitome Romanorum Pontijicum usque ad Paulum IV*). In the few instances where this book is in error, the prophecy appears to make the same mistake.[17] As a few other idiosyncrasies are also mirrored, one of the documents most likely influenced the other. That leaves us with a classic case of which came first, the chicken or the egg?

Skeptics argue that Panvinio's book came first. Somebody who had his history book then fabricated the prophecy—thereby producing the telltale mirroring—before it ended up in Wion's hands for publication in 1595.

There are two major problems with this theory. First, the accuracy of the closing epithets has essentially disproven the idea that the prophecy was fabricated in the 16th century.

Consider *Religio depopulata* (Religion depopulated), which was a very risky and naked prediction. There was no cover if the religion did not suffer a huge loss of people on that pope's watch (Benedict XV, 1914–1922). Moreover, the prediction had an extremely low chance of success, for only one pope in recent centuries would have delivered a hit. Yet the spiritual realm threaded the needle by pinning it to the pope who was presiding when the religion suffered an unimaginable loss in numbers.

Prophecy expert Robert Howells also highlights the epithet for Innocent XII (1691–1700), *Rastrum in porta* (Rake in the door). This pope's family name was Rastrello, which is Italian for "rake," and a rake was depicted in the family's coat of arms. This very specific prediction, Howells comments, "could not have been chance on the part of the author."[18]

Nor has it been a matter of the cardinals electing popes to fit the prophecy, for no evidence has ever been presented to show that any election has ever been influenced by the prophecy. In the case of Innocent XII, the conclave was hotly contested and lasted for five months. Besides, what are the chances there would be an electable cardinal with such an eclectic last name to begin with?

As for the entire list of epithets, Howells observes that "the prophecies post-release are no less accurate than those that came before."[19] He judges there to be, though, a slightly lower rate of such accurate hits after 1595. He understands the arguments for forgery but observes that the theory does not square with reality:

> The accuracy of the later predictions proves that this cannot be a simple case of forgery for political ends. That would require our forger to have been a prophet or have one in their employ, but even this is unlikely in the extreme as seers are not known for being able to focus on anything so specific. The act of receiving visions is like opening to grace: it cannot be directed in such a controlled manner.[20]

The most important and profound point about accuracy pertains to the big picture of the prophecy. As explained later, it is being fulfilled in spades. It was rendered as a long-term chronological yardstick to measure the arrival of the modern end times, and it is proving to be amazingly accurate. So, too, is its cutting awareness of what was destined to come to an end.

The second major problem with the skeptics' charge involves a trio of assumptions about the chicken-or-the-egg dilemma. First, they assume a truth-minded historian would never source from a prophecy while writing a book of history, but a deception-minded forger would surely source from a book of history while fabricating a prophecy. Second, they assume Panvinio was very knowledgeable and did sufficient research to discern fact from fiction. Third, they assume his ultimate motive was producing the most accurate and uniform version of papal history he could.

These assumptions are gravely in doubt, though, because a far more believable explanation exists. Before he became a teenager, Onofrio Panvinio (1530–1568) entered a monastery order called the Augustinian Hermits. At the age of 23, he graduated in Rome with a Bachelor of Arts degree, whereupon he returned to his order to teach for a year. He then went to his order's monastery in Florence and taught theology for a couple more years before accepting the position of corrector and reviser of books at the Vatican Library in 1556.[21]

As he published his history book the next year at the age of 27, he was obviously not a well-seasoned expert. Given how quickly he produced it, exhaustive research was surely not a part of his process either. But what about his ultimate motive?

According to Vatican sources, there is ample evidence that Panvinio found Saint Malachy's prophecy in the Vatican archives in 1556.[22] Thus, it has been argued that he considered the prophecy as a reference source and wrote his history accordingly.[23]

Strangely enough, this scenario makes sense. If this rookie historian indeed discovered the prophecy when he went to work in the Vatican Library in 1556, he would have been astonished by how well it foretold papal history. This lightning-bolt experience probably motivated and guided what he published the very next year. After all, he was first and foremost a religious man, and he would have seen the need for a history book to catch the gravity-defying pitches of Saint Malachy so others could also see this supernatural game.

In line with his assigned duties, Panvinio's book was a correction and revision of a history book about the popes published in 1471 by Bartolomeo Platina (*De Vitis pontificum*).[24] In his first year at the Vatican Library, something motivated this 26-year-old man to immediately update Platina's book of papal history.

Put yourself in Panvinio's shoes in a subterranean Vatican warehouse where you were the only person on the planet who saw and could appreciate this spine-tingling manifestation of the supernatural. His motive for updating and revising Platina's book was to serve up an authenticating source for the prophecy whenever the latter was finally published.

Hence, Panvinio produced a papal history that would allow his readers to easily make the connections. The prophecy thus came first and gave birth to the mirrored idiosyncrasies between the two disparate documents.

For instance, papal historians have always had a thorny issue in dealing with the so-called antipopes (popes who were elected in defiance of an existing pope because of a controversial split in the Church). Panvinio differed from Platina by including the antipope Clement VIII (1423–1429) as a legitimate pope. The prophecy includes an epithet for this antipope.

Skeptics believe this was simply a bizarre choice on Panvinio's part that was later copied by the forger of the prophecy. The oddity of their theory, though, is why the young and unseasoned Panvinio would make such an alteration—seemingly out of nowhere if the prophecy did not yet exist—when Platina had been much closer to that action. Moreover, why would a young Catholic working in the Vatican go against his Church by including an antipope who had already been excluded from its version of papal history?

What makes far more sense, of course, is the prophecy was the reason why the rookie historian included that antipope. Again, his motivation was cobbling together an ordinary catcher of history to play ball with a supernatural pitcher of prophecy.

Another mirrored idiosyncrasy is that Panvinio's book does not always include each pope's coat of arms, but when this information appears in his book, it also appears in the prophecy as a clue for that pope. Skeptics believe a forger had an affinity for the coat of arms. When such information was available in Panvinio's book, he used it for his bogus prophecy. When it was absent in the history book, the forger had to concoct another connection.

Yet the opposite scenario feels much stronger and reinforces the theory that Panvinio wrote his book to complement the prophecy. Since he composed it so quickly, he apparently included such information on an as-needed basis. However, if his motive was being a good historian and the prophecy did not yet exist, surely he would have been equitable and comprehensive and included the coat of arms for all popes. Since his book was not even close to such consistency, it suggests he had the prophecy by his side and it influenced his choice of content.

Now only two mysteries remain. The first is about the so-called historical errors in both Panvinio's book and the prophecy. For instance, the prophecy renders the epithet "*Lupa coelestina*" for Pope Eugene IV (1431–1447), which means "the Celestine she-wolf" or "the heavenly she-wolf" (as *celestine* means "heavenly"). Panvinio said this pope belonged to the order of Célestines, when in fact Eugene IV was from the order of Augustinians.

As skeptics see it, Panvinio made the error out of nowhere, and the forger of the prophecy followed in his folly. Trouble is, historians without ulterior motives do not make wild guesses, and such errors are almost always because they repeated a source that was in error. With no evidence yet presented of a wayward source that Panvinio repeated, this scenario is highly unlikely.

Chances are he had the prophecy by his side and was compiling his history to match it. Per this scenario, he learned from the books at his disposal how most of the pre-1557 epithets had been fulfilled. But what about the remainder for which he could not find an accurate historical connection?

It seems he did not quit on any of the epithets by allowing his book to have a few blanks vis-à-vis the prophecy. He apparently desired a perfect match for them all, trusted the prophecy's accuracy, and got a little loose with his history in those troublesome patches.

All that really matters, though, is the big picture of this scenario. Saint Malachy's prophecy existed and astounded the young historian, who wrote his book so others could eventually see what he was seeing.

The world is now seeing, and guess what else we see? While the skeptics correctly charge Panvinio with a historical error, they wrongly charge the prophecy with one. In fact, a solid fulfillment exists for *Lupa coelestina* (the heavenly she-wolf). Eugene IV had been the bishop of Siena, which quite surprisingly had a female wolf on its banner.[25] This strongly suggests the prophecy came first and got it right by sourcing from the supernatural, but Panvinio sourced from the prophecy and got it wrong by misinterpreting the epithet.

The only remaining mystery is why Panvinio did not also publish the prophecy. In other words, why did he put his ordinary catcher on the field while hiding his superstar pitcher in the clubhouse? This is easily answered.

Panvinio was under a strict hierarchy being ruled by the ruthless Pope Paul IV (1555–1559), and the Vatican has always been the antithesis of disclosing inside information. Especially because Paul IV was the Father of the Roman Inquisition, the Protestant revolution was in full force, and the printing press was a painful and dangerous thorn in the Vatican's side, such secrecy was surely at record high levels.

Again, 1557 was the year when the Church first published the *Index Librorum Prohibitorum* (§7.4.h.). Knowledge is power, and the Church was all about suppressing radical information, not publishing it. How much more so for a prophecy whose final epithet could be used to undermine the Church's authority?

We can safely assume, then, the young historian did not dare ask permission to publish such a powerful secret as Saint Malachy's prophecy. It was probably more than enough for him to do two things. First, he wrote his mirroring history book to ensure the prophecy would be a hit when the latter was finally published. Second, he carefully leaked the prophecy sometime later. Like all leaks are intended by their disclosers from within powerful institutions, it would eventually be published with no indications as to who leaked it.

8.5.c. Spiritual Fingerprints on the Document

For the post-1595 epithets, skeptics have an extraordinarily difficult case to make against their authenticity because the prophecy had been published. Although a few of them are so generalized they could apply to many popes, how do we explain the rest? The skeptics cannot, but they believe something is amiss because of a significant change in emphasis in the epithets after 1595. They believe this is a fingerprint of fraudulence.

A critical error in reasoning has been made, however, by failing to account for the source of the information. As we learned from Daniel, the spiritual realm had a serious agenda that underwrote everything it foretold.

The Daniel and Saint Malachy prophecies have a similar pattern. From a particular point on a timeline of what they predicted—165 BCE for Daniel, 1595 for Saint Malachy—there is a consensus about their accuracy for what had previously transpired. After that fulcrum point, though, the skeptics cry forgery because of shifts in form and content.

Yes, there are definitive fingerprints on the Daniel and Saint Malachy prophecies, but they are not from the hands of charlatans. Rather, they are the markings of a spiritual intelligence that did not want its truth to be fully revealed until a certain time. This infinite intelligence pivoted the Saint Malachy prophecy to coincide with its earthly trajectory. Knowing it would lie dormant for four centuries, the spiritual realm shifted the nature of its epithets to coincide with its publication.

As for the last remaining skeptical argument, some epithets have not been matched with a solid fulfillment or are so general as to be meaningless. For example, what pope is not a "religious man" per epithet #99 (Pius VIII, 1829–1830)? Since most of the duds are post-1595, skeptics deem them to be more evidence of fraudulence.

The duds could be from an error in transmission by Saint Malachy and his scribe or our inability to uncover a valid connection. Chances are, though, the spiritual realm sandbagged them to stir up more doubt until the time was right. After all, it knew this doubt would be erased by the prophecy coming on like gangbusters with the closing popes of the brief epithets and then its grand finale.

Believe it or not, the evidence suggests this is indeed what happened. In addition to the shift in the epithets after 1595 and the six duds among them from 1605 to 1846,[26] we have another obvious case.

The prophecy includes three antipopes who were elected in opposition to Alexander III (1159–1181)—Victor IV (1159–1164), Pascal III (1164–1168) and Callistus III (1168–1178)—but does not include the fourth and final antipope of this set, Innocent III (1178–1180). Unless Saint Malachy and his scribe failed to record the epithet for Innocent III, the spiritual realm deliberately muddied the waters by disclosing only three of these four antipopes. By the way, Panvinio's book mirrors the prophecy's choice of inclusion and exclusion.

Again, the spiritual realm had a much grander purpose than just revealing the future. The prophecies of Daniel and Saint Malachy were designed to allow considerable doubt to swirl until their astonishing truth would suddenly be unleashed like a tsunami.

8.5.d. The Ominous Mystery of Peter of Rome

Speaking of, here is the 112th and final epithet: "During the last persecution of the Holy Roman Church, there shall sit Peter of Rome, who shall feed the sheep amidst many tribulations, and when these have passed, the City of the Seven Hills shall be utterly destroyed, and the awful Judge will judge the people."[27]

This text was included in the 1595 version of *Lignum Vitae*,[28] but there is no guarantee it was part of the original manuscript. It could have been appended before Wion published the prophecy. After all, over four hundred years is a lot of time for something to happen to a document sitting in an underground library.

The text arouses suspicion that it was a later addition. First, it radically deviates from the previous 111 epithets, none of which had more than four words.

Next, an impartial referee would have to rule that Peter of Rome is a prophetic fumble if the play is viewed from a literal perspective. Pope Francis (2013–present) is Jorge Mario Bergoglio, who was born and raised in Argentina. Although his parents were of Italian descent, they both hailed from northern Italy (not Rome).

Connecting Bergoglio and the prophetic football requires quite a stretch.

Apologists argue that having Italian parents makes you a Roman because citizens of the Roman Empire were called Romans, and his papal name of Francis counts for Peter because the saint's full name was Giovanni di Pietro di Bernardone.

Yet the stretch is even weaker than it appears because the saint's full name is often rendered without the Peter. As history has it, the saint's mother originally named him Giovanni (John), but his father, Pietro (Peter) di Bernardone, returned home from business and demanded his son be named Francesco (the Frenchman). According to scholar André Vauchez in a book published before this became an issue of prophecy, "Francesco di Bernardone...is the real name of the one we call Francis of Assisi."[29]

Here, then, is the prophesied identification we are supposed to be impressed with. Jorge Mario Bergoglio is really Peter of Rome because this pope chose the name Francis and that saint's dad's first name was Peter. The only name missing in this connection is Kevin Bacon's.[30] It is hard to imagine how the spiritual realm could suddenly drop the ball on the most important pope of all after being on such a roll.

The final reason Peter of Rome looks like a later addition involves the spiritual realm's nature and intention. The text evokes the dogma of an "awful" God casting down judgment upon all, which contradicts the true nature of God and life (§3.3.e., §3.4.). The text also appears to be ignorant about the endgame of biblical prophecy, wherein a great awakening is the spiritual realm's intention.

In any case, the proof will soon be in the pudding. By the end of Pope Francis's papacy, we will know for sure if Rome (which was known in antiquity as the City of Seven Hills) was "utterly destroyed" or not. In sum, this paragraph is a prophetic fumble from a literal vantage point and hence our suspicion it was a fraudulent addition.

But wait! A red challenge flag has been thrown on the field to review the play from a metaphysical perspective, and the call is being overturned. As we will now see, Peter of Rome was indeed given to Saint Malachy back in 1140 and was spoken with incredible omniscience.

As we learned from unraveling Daniel, the spiritual realm long ago foretold the Roman Catholic Church as the "abomination that causes desolation" (§7.4.d.). The Church would earn the ire of the spiritual realm for many reasons, some of which apply to all branches of mainstream Christianity.

The primary reason for the ire, though, would pertain to power and how the Church would consolidate and wield it with such tyranny and violence. The spiritual realm foresaw how the Church would crush religious freedom and truth-seeking, kill to defend its power, and collaborate with the beastly empires that also opposed the divine kingdom. Therefore, the spiritual realm would not be rendering kind words to Saint Malachy about this ruthless, deceptive and spiritual growth-killing institution.

Just like with Daniel, the spiritual realm shrouded this prophecy in mystery so it would not be understood until the appointed time had finally arrived. The 111 brief epithets were given to mark the passage of time from when the prophecy was rendered. After that long-count calendar had played itself out, the mystery would be simultaneously revealed with the Bible's apocalyptic prophecies.

The spiritual realm never intended for Peter of Rome to represent the next pope. We can infer this from the radical deviation from the brief epithets and the lack of correlation with Pope Francis. Rather, the term was used to identify the office of the papacy as the passage foretold its destiny.

Peter of Rome was a brilliant reference to this seat of tremendous religious power, for the Roman Catholic Church had always claimed the papacy had divine authority because Peter's life concluded in Rome. As the First Vatican Council reaffirmed this doctrine in 1870, "Whoever succeeds to the chair of Peter obtains, by the institution of Christ himself, the primacy of Peter over the whole church."[31] If anyone denied that Christ had instituted this perpetual line of successors of Peter or that the pope was this special ruler, the unbeliever should be "anathema" (excommunicated).

The Church based this argument on four assumptions that have all been refuted (§4.6.e.). Yet this bogus argument became the capstone for siphoning spiritual power from the masses and aggregating it into the papacy's tower of external power. As the First Vatican Council also decreed:

> We promulgate anew the definition of the ecumenical council of Florence [1439], which must be believed by all faithful Christians, namely, that the apostolic see and the Roman pontiff hold a world-wide primacy, and that the Roman pontiff is the successor of blessed Peter…To him, in blessed Peter, full power has been given by our lord Jesus Christ to tend, rule and govern the universal church.[32]

The prophetic reference was thus perfect for calling out the office and its empowering doctrine. The men who had filled the office were a dime a dozen, but the masses submitted to the office because they had been brainwashed that the authority of Peter was channeled into it. The only way the prophecy could have been any clearer was if it had said "Peter the Eternal Roman Pontiff," but that would have been a dead giveaway.

The prophecy foretold that when the truth was finally unleashed, the fallacy of this ancient argument for religious power would be exposed on every level. The papacy would be powerless to save its tower of power, for the masses would begin reclaiming their spiritual power amid the great awakening.

Even the prophecy's "feed the sheep" phrase was carefully chosen to reflect the Catholic justification for religious power. The Church's favorite verse was "You are Peter, and on this rock I will build my church" (Mt 16:18), and its only other biblical reference for its Peter-based authority was from an ambiguous passage in John. After Peter thrice professed his love for Jesus (to atone for having denied his master three times), Jesus told him, "Feed my sheep" (Jn 21:17).

The "feed the sheep" line is another sign the spiritual realm was targeting the basis of the Church's religious power. As for the future, the spiritual realm indicated the papacy will keep on feeding the sheep as the mighty institution collapses. In other words, do not expect any revolutionary changes from the papacy.

As the breaking of the power of the holy people is not an instantaneous event but rather a process that will play out over decades, this final paragraph refers to the office. It refers to the succession of popes who will rule the religious castle as it gets blasted by a tsunami of truth.

Chances are many Catholics will fight the truth as Pope Francis and his successors feed them with the same old tradition and dogma. The prophecy seems to predict this dynamic as the "many tribulations" that will pass as the sheep are fed. Yet the power of Rome (the Church) will be "utterly destroyed" because new generations will not submit themselves to the spiritual stagnation of the old religious dogma and hierarchy.

By the way, the "awful Judge" is not God. The prophecy never said it was. If the spiritual realm wanted to warn us of God's impending judgment and eternal doom, it would have explicitly said "God."

Just like with Daniel, it gave us a mystery that would be impossible to solve until we had made a paradigm shift. In the meantime, we were free to project onto the words what we were expecting to find. Readers thus assumed the "awful judge" would be God (it is hard to imagine Saint Malachy was told to capitalize "judge").

As it turns out, the awful judge is the human ego, which is the king of all judgment. As this process plays out, there will surely be a lot of judging going on as the remaining sheep in the Catholic flock are belittled by outsiders who wield the truth without love.

8.5.e. The Tidal Wave of Truth Was Foretold

The spiritual realm long ago informed us through both Daniel and Saint Malachy of how much time would pass before the great awakening began (§7.5.g.). These independent measures are a divine gift to affirm we are on the right track. Unlike Daniel's encompassing view of this multifaceted process, Saint Malachy's prophecy was focused on its epic milestone: the breaking of the power of the holy people (§7.5.b.).

In 1140, the spiritual realm foretold exactly how many more popes would appear before a tsunami of truth suddenly rose up from a tranquil sea and crashed down upon the hierarchical castle that governs a sixth of the world's population. All would be comparatively smooth sailing through 111 new popes, just a mundane litany of one pope after another. After the last pope in that line, though, the tsunami of truth would suddenly strike.

We now know the exact timing of this fascinating prophecy. The tsunami would strike sometime after Benedict XVI was no longer the pope, which occurred in 2013. It would strike during the reign of the next man to step into the office, whom we now know as Pope Francis.

The papacy—Peter of Rome—would continue ruling with him and an untold number of successors. It would be a hopeless cause, though, as the great awakening kicked into high gear and the mighty Catholic Church petered out over time. The spiritual realm thus lumped all these popes together with an executive summary of what was being executed.

All in all, Saint Malachy's prophecy is a perfect piece of triangulation to Daniel. The great awakening is indeed transpiring in our era, and it will be capped by the breaking of the holy people's power. The Catholic Church will implode as the masses are suddenly able to see through the ancient deceptions and erroneous dogma.

While such a leap in consciousness will probably be too much for a vast majority of Catholics, the truth will be shining too brightly and will ultimately prevail with future generations. Awakening souls will no longer mindlessly submit to this dark institution as they disavow anything that dares get between them and their spiritual growth toward the truth and a God of pure, unconditional love.

8.6. An Atheist Learns About the Spiritual Revolution

In 1985, an avowed atheist and art professor named Howard Storm had a near-death experience in which he had an extended conversation with Jesus and a group of angels. It impacted him so strongly that he thereafter became a minister.

After being told the Cold War would come to an end "in a couple of years," Storm asked what would come next. The luminaries told him, "The world is at the beginning of a major transformation. It will be a spiritual revolution that will affect every person in the world."[33]

So an atheist was told in 1985 that a "spiritual revolution" was on the nearby horizon. How is that for some more remarkable corroboration?

By the way, Storm was also told that God is always the epitome of unconditional love for everybody and never sends anybody to hell. As he learned the hard way, though, hell can be chosen and experienced by rejecting God and the Light (§B.3.c.). When he asked which religion is the best one, he expected to hear a Christian denomination but was told, "The religion that brings you closest to God."[34]

Jesus and the angels instructed him, "God wants you to grow spiritually by trial and error, but not to repeat endless cycles of self-defeating behavior." Just as Peck reasoned, a universe of spiritual growth means God's ultimate objective is obvious (§3.4.c.). As Storm was also informed, "God wants you to become like the Christ."[35]

Moreover, Storm was told that we are here to know and live God's will, which we do by loving others as God loves us. It is our most challenging and important lesson. Storm summarizes what he was told about why we have been failing it:

> Every religion began with revelations of God, and in time we have perverted these revelations and created religious traditions to serve our worst instincts. God has given us a revelation of God's will to affirm the worth of every individual. When we pervert God's will by constructing religious traditions that demean another people, we have horribly distorted the will of God in order to deny God's will…All of heaven is horrified by our use of the name of God to do harm to one another. This is the worst mistake we can make.[36]

Keep this in mind as you read the remaining four chapters, which are a testament to how a perverted version of Christianity repeatedly failed to love and affirm the worth of everybody. Since spiritual growth is the name of the game and domination and violence in God's name is what troubles God the most, is it any surprise our worst mistakes will soon be coming to an end? Is it any surprise the Western religions were the foremost target of the apocalyptic prophecies?

8.7. The "Conversations with God" Material

The Daniel and Saint Malachy prophecies have proven the spiritual realm can see how the future will unfold. As Jesus and the angels told Storm, "God knows everything that will happen and, more important, God knows everything that could happen."[37]

Yet in the *Conversations with God* material, God keeps us focused on the fact that the future is always being created by our ongoing choices in the present. It is yet another paradox in this amazing universe. Even though the spiritual realm can see the future, it has not yet been created and thus determined. God therefore refrains from revealing future events even though a prophetic party trick or two would sure be nice for authentication purposes.

Nevertheless, Walsch's fourth book in the series has God rendering a rather bold prediction for the 21st century. Published in 1999, God is quoted by Walsch as identifying this era as the time for a dramatic awakening:

> As you move into the next millennium, you will plant the seeds of the greatest growth the world has ever seen. You have grown in your science and in your technologies, yet now you will grow in your *consciousness*. And this will be the greatest growth of all, making all the rest of your advances look insignificant by comparison.[38]

Walsch was later informed that a revolutionary change in our beliefs about God could quickly sweep over the planet. Published in 2004, God supposedly told Walsch, "A movement, a radical shift, in humanity's understandings about God could occur rapidly. Easily within your lifetime. Within three decades. Perhaps even faster than that, once the first domino falls."[39]

The primary point is that the *Conversations with God* material corroborates the prophecies of Daniel and Saint Malachy about the era of our awakening. The secondary point is that the material displays impressive omniscience, for there is a very good chance an unprecedented change in religious beliefs will transpire in the next few decades.

8.8. Conclusion

The chapter presented a collection of disparate material that triangulates the interpretation of Daniel's "time, times and half a time" prophecy to the last third of the 20th century. Again, the great awakening and the breaking of the holy people's power is a process that essentially fired up in the 1960s. Having completed the trio of chapters about Daniel, the next chapter explores what Jesus purportedly had to say about the end times.

Chapter 9

The Little Apocalypse

9.1. Introduction

This chapter explores Jesus's prophecy about the end times, which is known as the Olivet Discourse or Little Apocalypse, and explains the unprecedented distress that is accompanying the great awakening (§7.5.a.).

9.2. Guiding Principles

Before delving into the prophecy, a couple of guiding principles need to be discussed.

9.2.a. The Assumption of Omniscience

We will proceed on the assumption that Jesus had the gift of prophecy. As the Daniel prophecies have authenticated him as the Anointed One, he probably did. However, it is by no means guaranteed.

When Christian apologist C. S. Lewis was coming to terms with a glaring error that will be discussed later, he assumed the gospels were trustworthy and concluded that Jesus "clearly knew no more about the end of the world than anyone else."[1] If Jesus was quoted accurately, he was wrong on at least one prediction. If he was also clueless with other parts of his prophecy, the forthcoming interpretation should be dismissed.

9.2.b. A Comparatively Unreliable Prophecy

Even if Jesus could foretell the future, his prophecy is unreliable because its three different versions were not written until many decades after his execution. Some of his spoken words were surely distorted or lost in the process of being remembered by eyewitnesses, retold to others, and eventually penned by the gospel authors (§4.4.). This situation should be contrasted with the prophecies of Daniel and Revelation, which were written by the men who actually experienced the visions.

Furthermore, there could have been confusion about Jesus's esoteric references. Even if he knew about the huge difference in the Daniel prophecies between the "time of the end" (§7.3.h.) and the era of the great awakening (§7.5.a.), his disciples and those who followed in the chains of transmission would have been prone to getting tangled up over what he had said.

More specifically, Jesus may have talked about the "time of the end" in literal terms as he alluded to the forthcoming destruction of the temple. He may have also talked about the great awakening in metaphorical terms as he warned about the "abomination that causes desolation." Can you imagine the textual mess if the human process jumbled and merged his words as referring to the same event? Indeed, this appears to have been what happened.

In any case, the exact text of the Little Apocalypse is unreliable. We have to accept this uncertainty and refrain from locking down conclusions from particular words or phrases. The chapter thus sifts through the uncertain details to surface the accurate undercurrent that is evidently flowing.

9.3. The Little Apocalypse in Mark

We begin with the Little Apocalypse in Mark, as scholars almost unanimously agree this gospel preceded and was a source for Matthew and Luke (§4.4.a.).

9.3.a. Signs of the End Times

As Jesus and his disciples were walking out of the temple, one of them commented on the massiveness of the stones and the magnificence of the buildings. Jesus replied that not a single stone would remain on another, that all of them would be thrown to the ground. The disciples asked when these events would happen and for the sign that they were about to occur (Mk 13:1–4). He replied:

> Watch out that no one deceives you. Many will come in my name, claiming, "I am he," and will deceive many. When you hear of wars and rumors of wars, do not be alarmed. Such things must happen, but the end is still to come. Nation will rise against nation, and kingdom against kingdom. There will be earthquakes in various places, and famines. These are the beginning of birth pains.
>
> You must be on your guard. You will be handed over to the local councils and flogged in the synagogues. On account of me you will stand before governors and kings as witnesses to them. And the gospel must first be preached to all nations. Whenever you are arrested and brought to trial, do not worry beforehand about what to say. Just say whatever is given you at the time, for it is not you speaking, but the Holy Spirit.

Brother will betray brother to death, and a father his child. Children will rebel against their parents and have them put to death. Everyone will hate you because of me, but the one who stands firm to the end will be saved. (Mk 13:5–13)

A prophecy has little meaning or credibility if it is so vague that a fulfillment can be associated with different historical times and events (§2.5.g.). Wars, rumors of war, earthquakes and famines have been a perpetual part of history. They have as much value in predicting a future event as a modern prophet who foretells the existence of taxes, political scandals and hurricanes.

Where the prophecy specifies something of value, though, is with the destruction of the temple. This has basically split Christian interpreters into two camps.

The first believes the Little Apocalypse has not yet been fulfilled. These folks hope the temple will someday be rebuilt so an antichrist can erect the abomination on it, whereupon it can be destroyed again to also fulfill Daniel's "the people of the ruler who will come will destroy the city and the sanctuary" (§7.4.).

The second camp believes Jesus was referring to the events of 70 CE. Regarding the prophetic text so far, this camp is the winner. After all, Jesus was referring to buildings that existed in the first century CE, and the disciples asked about their destruction and requested a warning sign. Such logic, though, gets ignored by the fundamentalists in the first camp because it contradicts their "fire and brimstone" theology.

By the way, this issue has profound ramifications. That is because most Christians have pitched their tents in the first camp, and fundamentalists who promote it are strongly in favor of an Israel that engulfs Palestine. For instance, the Reverend John Hagee has been delivering apocalyptic sermons with his internationally televised ministry for many years, and he founded a political organization that lobbies politicians to empower the Israeli government.

On the surface, it looks like Hagee and the growing swell of Christian Zionists are good for Israel. However, Jeremy Ben-Ami, the president of a pro-Israel organization that is striving for peace and security in the Middle East, begs to differ. The likes of Hagee, he points out, claim the Holy Land was promised to the Jews and Israel should not give back any of the occupied territories to achieve peace.

Ben-Ami, whose father fought for Israel's independence in the 1940s, observes that these Christian Zionists hope Israel's uncompromising quest will trigger a war that cascades into Armageddon and Jesus's second coming. He concluded his point in a 2008 editorial, "Do your ambitions for Israel extend beyond turning it into the fuel for the fire of the 'End of Days'? Then Hagee and company are not—repeat, not—your friends."[2]

9.3.b. The Abomination That Causes Desolation

Jesus supposedly continued:

> When you see "the abomination that causes desolation" standing where it does not belong—let the reader understand—then let those who are in Judea flee to the mountains. Let no one on the housetop go down or enter the house to take anything out. Let no one in the field go back to get their cloak. How dreadful it will be in those days for pregnant women and nursing mothers! Pray that this will not take place in winter, because those will be days of distress unequaled from the beginning, when God created the world, until now—and never to be equaled again.
>
> If the Lord had not cut short those days, no one would survive. But for the sake of the elect, whom he has chosen, he has shortened them. At that time if anyone says to you, "Look, here is the Messiah!" or, "Look, there he is!" do not believe it. For false messiahs and false prophets will appear and perform signs and wonders to deceive, if possible, even the elect. So be on your guard; I have told you everything ahead of time. (Mk 13:14–23)

The "abomination that causes desolation" refers to Daniel. In Matthew's version, "the prophet Daniel" is cited (Mt 24:15). Now we have some leverage for analyzing the Little Apocalypse.

Daniel has two different abominations that cause desolation. The first (ACD-1) was fulfilled back in the 160s BCE by Antiochus IV (§7.3.f., §I.2.). The second (ACD-2) would later be established by the Roman Empire. As Gabriel told Daniel, "he" (the Roman Empire) would "destroy the city and the sanctuary" and "set up an abomination that causes desolation" (Dn 9:26–27). We now know it is a metaphorical reference to the Bible and Roman Catholic Church (§7.4.d.).

If the Little Apocalypse refers to ACD-1, the foretelling of an event that happened two hundred years prior would demonstrate gross ignorance. We would need to charge an error to either Jesus or the authoring process of the gospels. Presuming, then, that Jesus was referring to Gabriel's ACD-2, we bog down in three different scenarios that have their own set of problems.

The first is the popular belief that the Little Apocalypse is a literal and physical event that has not yet occurred. Trouble is, the "he" who sets up the "abomination that causes desolation" is the Roman Empire. This is a big problem because the Roman Empire no longer exists to set it up. Furthermore, there is no support in Daniel whatsoever for the involvement of an antichrist. As Chapter 10 shows, there is no support in Revelation either.

The second scenario is that the Little Apocalypse was fulfilled with the Jewish revolt of 66–73 CE. Trouble is, a physical fulfillment of the abomination is at odds with Gabriel's words (§7.4.d.). In addition, this scenario's "days of distress unequaled from the beginning" has a major chronological conflict with Daniel and its "time of distress such as has not happened from the beginning of nations" (Dn 12:1). The context of the Daniel passage places this era sometime after the demise of the Roman Empire in the fifth century CE (§7.5.a.).

Moreover, the distress of 66–73 CE could not possibly be categorized as unequaled in history. Even if the passage only refers to the Jews, they had already had such an experience when Nebuchadnezzar demolished their temple and exiled them to Babylon. As for the prophecy's birth pains, the revolt produced nothing of epic importance to the totality of history.

The third scenario views ACD-2 metaphorically and will be called the "spiritual awakening" interpretation. When the omniscient angel spoke to Daniel about the "time of distress," he explained that "at that time" many of Daniel's people would be delivered and "multitudes who sleep in the dust of the earth will awake" (§7.5.a.).

Trouble is, the Little Apocalypse makes it all sound like a specific event that posed such an immediate threat that there would be no time to go back to one's house or run back across a field to get a coat. So the Little Apocalypse as written does not align with the spiritual awakening interpretation, which is not transpiring in a particular season of a year or requiring such immediate lifesaving action.

9.3.c. The Rapture

Jesus then supposedly quoted Isaiah:

> But in those days, following that distress, "the sun will be darkened, and the moon will not give its light; the stars will fall from the sky, and the heavenly bodies will be shaken."
>
> At that time people will see the Son of Man coming in clouds with great power and glory. And he will send his angels and gather his elect from the four winds, from the ends of the earth to the ends of the heavens. (Mk 13:24–27)

This passage has fueled the belief that Jesus will be making a supernatural appearance at the end of the world. For instance, Paul described his belief about the rapture:

> According to the Lord's word, we tell you that we who are still alive, who are left until the coming of the Lord, will certainly not precede those who have fallen asleep [physically died]. For the Lord himself will come down from heaven, with a loud command, with the voice of the archangel and with the trumpet call of God, and the dead in Christ will rise first. After that, we who are still alive and are left will be caught up together with them in the clouds to meet the Lord in the air. And so we will be with the Lord forever. (1 Thes 4:15–17; see also 1 Cor 15:51–52)

Fundamentalists concur with Paul and are certain that Jesus talked about a rapture that will teleport them up to meet the Lord in the air. Trouble is, Daniel's prophecies have nothing to do with a rapture. The only text therein that even remotely resembles it is the line about the sleeping multitudes who will awaken. But the omniscient angel's words are a metaphorical reference to a spiritual awakening that coincides with the deliverance of the Jews, and Jesus supposedly denounced the belief in the resurrection of the dead as badly mistaken (§7.5.a.). As we will see later, Revelation has no support for a rapture either.

Furthermore, Paul and other New Testament authors believed the end of the world would occur before they died (Rom 13:11; 1 Cor 7:29; 1 Thes 4:13–18; Heb 10:25; Jas 5:8; 1 Pt 4:7; 1 Jn 2:18; Rv 22:10, 22:20). Since they were wrong about the timing of the second coming, chances are they were also wrong about its nature. They believed Jesus had spoken literally about a physical event, but we have every reason to believe he had really spoken metaphorically about a metaphysical event.

If Jesus actually spoke in metaphors—more parables, if you will—about what would happen during the great awakening, he communicated that it would be a time of jarring disillusionment. Our sacred mental orientations would be rocked so violently that it would be like the sun no longer giving its light and the stars falling from the sky. The firmaments of our religious universe would no longer shine their light to orient our lives.

Yet in the midst of this global trauma, spiritual truth would be filling a sky that had been suddenly vacated of religious orientation. People around the world would suddenly "see" and understand Jesus in a whole new light and what the spiritual life is really all about. The narrow gate would be illuminated, and multitudes would rapidly rise in consciousness to live their earthly lives at a higher metaphysical level.

9.3.d. A Grievous Error

Jesus then supposedly advised learning from a fig tree and how its budding leaves signal the imminent arrival of summer: "Even so, when you see these things happening, you know that it is near, right at the door. Truly I tell you, this generation will certainly not pass away until all these things have happened" (Mk 13:28–30). Almost two thousand years have passed, though, and "these things" have still not happened. C. S. Lewis thus admitted, "It is certainly the most embarrassing verse in the Bible."[3]

Jesus may have been dead wrong. Chances are, though, he preached in one instance about Daniel's "time of the end" (§7.3.h.) and in another about the great awakening (§7.5.a.), but his followers jumbled and merged his words about these two different events into a discourse about one and the same event. If Jesus had spoken literally about the impending doom of Jerusalem and its temple, he was correct. And if he had also spoken metaphorically about an era of great disillusionment when multitudes would suddenly awaken to join him, he was also correct.

Unfortunately, we will never know what he actually said. All we know for sure is the Bible has a grievous error that everything would happen before "this generation" had passed away.

9.3.e. Expect the Unexpected

Jesus then purportedly warned, "But about that day or hour no one knows, not even the angels in heaven, nor the Son, but only the Father. Be on guard! Be alert! You do not know when that time will come" (Mk 13:32–33). After comparing the situation to a man who leaves his home in the care of servants and tells one to keep watch, the Little Apocalypse in Mark concludes: "Therefore keep watch because you do not know when the owner of the house will come back—whether in the evening, or at midnight, or when the rooster crows, or at dawn. If he comes suddenly, do not let him find you sleeping. What I say to you, I say to everyone: 'Watch!'" (Mk 13:35–37).

Since Jesus's sermon was most likely distorted in transmission, we will look beyond its exact words to understand its prominent themes. First, he emphasized being on guard and avoiding deception.

Just as counterfeit money is made to look like the real thing, deception is perpetrated by those who try to look authentic. Christians should thus be on guard in the realm of their religion. Given what this book is revealing, Jesus probably said something to the effect of, "Watch out that no one deceives you. Many will come in my name, claiming, 'I am he,' and will deceive many" (Mk 13:5–6).

Did not the Catholic Church come in his name by declaring the pope was his authoritative representative on earth in his bodily absence ("I am he")? Has not this dark institution deceived many people?

In 2007, the Catholic Church was still proclaiming that only one church was established by Jesus, and it was it. It explained that other denominations are not true churches with the "means of salvation" because they cannot trace their bishops back to the original apostles. The Eastern Orthodox world has legitimate churches, the Church also explained, but they are defective because they no longer recognize the supreme authority of the pope, the Vicar of Christ (a deputy assigned the authority to rule in the absence of Jesus).[4]

In Luke's version, the warning includes an additional phrase that implies the deception would arise from the religion: "Watch out that you are not deceived. For many will come in my name, claiming, 'I am he,' and, 'The time is near.' Do not follow them" (Lk 21:8). Do not countless preachers incite their followers with warnings that the time is so near that the rapture could happen before their sermons are finished? Again, "Do not follow them."

Another theme is that the deception would be accompanied by persecution from the partnership of government and religion. At first glance, the text refers to the earliest assaults upon the Christians. Yet far more pain and death were meted out during the Inquisition and witch hunts, wherein tens of thousands of souls who dared to defy the religious deception were tortured and/or murdered. An omniscient Jesus would have had those abuses in his name foremost on his mind.

He also advised us to expect the unexpected, so here we are. God has suddenly returned with the great awakening, but who is ready to embrace a greater spirituality? The deception has been deeply brainwashed into Christians, and the reaction of many will be to fight this process because of pride, fear, dogma and tradition.

Jesus thus forewarned his followers to be spiritually on guard. If you were metaphysically sleeping and not embracing the wisdom of his teachings, you would be opposing God when this global upheaval finally arrived. Yet if you awaken enough to see the "'abomination that causes desolation' standing where it does not belong," it is time to run like hell from that dark religious town (Mk 13:14).

The final prominent theme is that it would be a time of unparalleled distress. The nature of this distress will be discussed later.

9.4. Additional Perspectives in Matthew and Luke

The Little Apocalypse is very similar in Matthew and Luke. Nevertheless, those gospels have additional text that is worth considering.

9.4.a. On the Nature of the Deception

Right after Matthew mirrors Mark in warning against deception and foretelling the onset of birth pains (§9.3.a.), it reports these statements from Jesus:

> Then you will be handed over to be persecuted and put to death, and you will be hated by all nations because of me. At that time many will turn away from the faith and will betray and hate each other, and many false prophets will appear and deceive many people. Because of the increase of wickedness, the love of most will grow cold, but the one who stands firm to the end will be saved. And this gospel of the kingdom will be preached in the whole world as a testimony to all nations, and then the end will come. (Mt 24:9–14)

Jesus seems to have foretold how far too many Christians would forsake his teachings of loving everybody and instead act from hatred for their fellow man. The "false prophets" of the religious deception would get Christians to conduct the Crusades, Inquisition and witch hunts. Those who lived his teachings while defying the Church were often "persecuted and put to death."

The religious deception would also enable a host of Christian nations to perpetrate atrocities like colonialism, slavery, institutional racism and the Holocaust. In addition, it would teach his followers to hate and condemn gays and lesbians. Yet eventually the true "gospel of the kingdom" would be preached, and the end of the dark religious dominance would suddenly arrive.

9.4.b. Deceptive Vultures and Permissive Carcasses

The next passage in Matthew that does not appear in Mark occurs after the warning to avoid false messiahs and prophets (§9.3.b.). According to Matthew, Jesus supposedly extended his point:

> So if anyone tells you, "There he is, out in the wilderness," do not go out; or, "Here he is, in the inner rooms," do not believe it. For as lightning that comes from the east is visible even in the west, so will be the coming of the Son of Man. Wherever there is a carcass, there the vultures will gather. (Mt 24:26–28)

Fundamentalists believe that when Jesus returns, he will be blazing across the sky as part of the rapture. The spiritual awakening paradigm also believes he will return but differs on the nature of the visibility. He will be metaphysically seen around the world by millions who are awakening to a greater understanding of his teachings and becoming aware of the deception that has convoluted them for so long.

Although Mark lacks that passage, the synoptic gospels concur on the theme. Do not be fooled by holy people who claim to represent Jesus, and do not expect him to make a physical return and appear in a particular place.

The unique part of Matthew's passage is the final sentence about the carcass and vultures. The context is the deceptive versions of Christianity, and a carcass signifies someone who is spiritually dead. The carcasses are those who believe they are unworthy sinners who could never be like Jesus and have not yet embraced a God of pure, unconditional love. They have tendered their spiritual power to the religious authorities, do not search for the truth, and thus allow themselves to be deceived.

Vultures gather where there are carcasses to feed upon, and that is exactly what the Catholic Church and its offspring have been doing. They have been living upon the spiritually dead and holding it all together with fear. Yet when there are no more spiritual carcasses to feed upon, the religious vultures will exist no more.

9.4.c. The Rapturous Reunion

Matthew's version of the Little Apocalypse also includes these supposed words of Jesus:

> As it was in the days of Noah, so it will be at the coming of the Son of Man. For in the days before the flood, people were eating and drinking, marrying and giving in marriage, up to the day Noah entered the ark; and they knew nothing about what would happen until the flood came and took them all away. That is how it will be at the coming of the Son of Man. Two men will be in the field; one will be taken and the other left. Two women will be grinding with a hand mill; one will be taken and the other left. (Mt 24:37–41)

Will millions of Bible-thumpers suddenly disappear as they are snatched up to an external reunion with their Lord and master in the air? Or will millions of lost souls awaken and rise in consciousness toward an internal reunion with their masterful brother and the divine kingdom here on earth?

Ironically, Christians who stubbornly wait for a physical rapture will be the ones left behind. As the great awakening produces the rapid ascension of millions of souls all around them, they will still be working in the field and grinding away because it is not materializing as they had been taught. Anchored by self-righteousness and afraid to grow beyond their unenlightened religion, they will be stuck until they transcend their egoic pride and fear.

Jesus forewarned that the waiting game is for fools. Rather, growth in consciousness is required to metaphysically see and enter the divine kingdom.

As the Gospel of Thomas states, "His disciples said to him, 'When will the kingdom come?' [Jesus said,] 'It will not come by waiting for it. It will not be a matter of saying 'here it is' or 'there it is.' Rather, the kingdom of the father is spread out upon the earth, and men do not see it'" (GTh, 113).[5]

Luke's version of the Little Apocalypse is essentially the same as Mark's and Matthew's. Its only substantial deviation occurs in a passage that mirrors Thomas: "Once, on being asked by the Pharisees when the kingdom of God would come, Jesus replied, 'The coming of the kingdom of God is not something that can be observed, nor will people say, 'Here it is,' or 'There it is,' because the kingdom of God is in your midst'" (Lk 17:20–21).

Two men will be in the field and two women will be grinding hand mills. Two of them will awaken to find the divine kingdom as the other two remain asleep and are left behind.

9.4.d. The End Times Parables, Part 1: The Tyrannical Servant

After Matthew concludes its common text with Mark with an admonition to be on watch and expect the unexpected, it continues with a series of four parables. In the first, Jesus asked who the wise and faithful servant is who has been charged with giving the other servants their food on time. It would be good for him to be doing so when his master returns. But suppose the servant with authority is wicked, recognizes his master is gone for a long time, and begins beating the other servants and eating and drinking with drunkards. The master will return at an unexpected time, severely punish him, and banish him alongside the hypocrites in hell (Mt 24:45–51).

Was the Catholic Church a wise and faithful servant who gave us our spiritual meals at the proper time? Not at all. The servant in charge ignored his master's instructions of love and equality and instead got drunk on hierarchical control and the power of the Roman Empire. As evidenced by the crushing of alternative Christian sects, the Crusades, Inquisition, witch hunts and imprisoning the Jews in ghettos, the tyrannical servant beat his fellow servants.

Now, however, this servant is being caught unaware by his master's sudden return. As the masses learn about the roots of the gospels, the nature of evil and the meaning of the apocalyptic prophecies, they will no longer be deceived by the Church's claim to divine authority and its image of unerring righteousness. The prophetic parable is being fulfilled, and this dark institution will be going the way of all hypocrites in the face of spiritual truth.

9.4.e. The End Times Parables, Part 2: The Ten Virgins

In Matthew's next parable, Jesus said the kingdom of heaven at that time would be akin to ten virgins who headed out to welcome the bridegroom. Five were wise and brought jars of extra oil for their lamps, and five were foolish and took only their lamps. The bridegroom was long delayed, and the young ladies fell asleep.

At midnight came the cry that the bridegroom had arrived. The virgins awoke to go meet him, but their lamps began going out because of the long wait. The foolish ones lacked spare oil, so they asked the wise ones to share. Their request was denied because there might not be enough to spare, and they were told to go buy their own.

While they were away, the bridegroom escorted the wise ones into the wedding banquet. The foolish ones returned to find the door shut and begged to be let in. But the bridegroom told them he did not know them. Therefore, Jesus warned, you should keep watch because you know not when the time will come (Mt 25:1–13).

It may seem mighty un-Christian to disavow sharing. Yet the parable refers to one's readiness to spiritually grow when God calls, and this attribute cannot be begged from or given to another.[6]

As the parable reinforces, the world is metaphysically asleep but is now being abruptly awoken. If you have been living the essence of Jesus's teachings, you are like a wise virgin who was prepared. You may have dozed off from living amid the darkness, but your emphasis on love and spiritual growth has kept you from being completely brainwashed by the religious deception. The revelations will be shocking but not paralyzing, so you will be able to make the journey to the divine banquet.

If you have not been living the essence of Jesus's teachings, you are like a foolish virgin who showed up without any oil. You are a spiritual carcass who is not prepared to transcend your brainwashing, and the religious vultures will continue to feed upon you. Pride and fear will keep you bonded to a religious herd that is still ensnared by the ancient deceptions.

9.4.f. The End Times Parables, Part 3: Investing the Talents

Next up is the Parable of the Talents, which tells the story of three servants whose master gave each of them a lot of money to manage in his absence. Two of them invested it and yielded big returns while the third was afraid of losing his master's money and protected it. The first two servants were rewarded for their work, but the third was punished even though he returned the master's money (§3.6.c.).

Viewing this parable now in context, it drives home the point that God is interested in abundant growth and wants us to manifest our divine nature. Those who fail to comprehend and live this truth will continue to experience the darkness. If you are afraid of being sent to hell, there you already are and will continue to be (for you do not yet know God or who you truly are).

9.4.g. The End Times Parables, Part 4: The Sheep and the Goats

In Matthew's final parable, Jesus said that when he comes, he will divide everybody into two different groups like a shepherd who separates his sheep from his goats. He will welcome the sheep into his kingdom because they fed and gave him drink, invited him in as a stranger, clothed him, looked after him when he was sick, and visited him in prison. The righteous will ask when they ever saw him in such need, and he will reply, "Truly I tell you, whatever you did for one of the least of these brothers and sisters of mine, you did for me" (Mt 25:40).

He will then condemn the goats for failing to do those things for him when he was in need. They will also ask when that was the case, and he will reply that whatever was not done for the least of his brothers and sisters was not done for him. They will be eternally punished while the righteous enjoy eternal life (Mt 25:31–46).

The essence of the parable is the truth that we are all one. Nowhere did Jesus mention that accepting him as an atoning sacrifice is the ticket for entering the divine kingdom. To the contrary, he differentiated the sheep and goats by who is living the truth of unity and love and who is not.

As for the parable's punishment, it is about returning to the physical universe of energy and the crucible of spiritual growth (§7.3.c.). It is about the law of consequences and remaining stuck in a hell of your own creation for as long as you live as a spiritual goat.

9.5. The Unparalleled Distress of the Great Awakening

Echoing the omniscient angel in Daniel (§7.5.a.), the Little Apocalypse reports this era would be marked by "days of distress unequaled from the beginning… and never to be equaled again" (Mk 13:19). Most Christians believe it will come from a supernatural assault of divine retribution. However, a different kind of pain was most likely foretold.

The era of unparalleled distress began with the most destructive war and greatest crime in history (World War II and the Holocaust). The deeper and more pervasive impact, though, would be forthcoming as the great awakening struck at the roots of our wayward societies and psyches that were producing such catastrophes.

9.5.a. The Purpose and Nature of the Pain

The distress will have a positive purpose as it accompanies our spiritual growth. The omniscient angel depicted it as a global awakening (§7.5.a.), and Jesus supposedly referred to it as "birth pains" (§9.3.e.).

Humanity will be experiencing the breaking of some deeply entrenched structures from personal to global levels, which is the only way an enlightened spirituality can break through and prevail. Trouble is, most people run from the turmoil involved with challenging core beliefs and building a more accurate map of reality (§1.2.c). As Peck notes, "The process of making revisions, particularly major revisions, is painful, sometimes excruciatingly painful."[7]

9.5.b. The Upheaval of the 20th Century

Prior to the 20th century, most people were far more burdened by the rigors of physical survival. Energies were poured into long and exhausting days of labor, which bled off whatever angst those folks were feeling. The arduous task of staying alive was also a perpetual distraction from existential emotions. Life was not easy, but its physical demands helped those folks block off and escape its deeper complexities. When exhaustive work was not enough, alcohol helped stave off the inner turbulence.

Moreover, most women were bound to their husbands by survival needs, and multiple generations of families typically lived in close proximity. Long-standing roles and traditions provided structure, order and calming stability in a world that operated on a slower and more natural rhythm. They may not have been wealthy or emotionally fulfilled, but it does not seem those generations were overly distressed.

Nowadays our basic physical needs are being widely fulfilled in the industrialized nations, so desires for deeper fulfillment have been arising with ever greater force. These desires are a natural part of our spiritual development, but they come with a distressing price: the opening of a Pandora's box of issues and emotions.

All in all, our evolution has taken us to the shoreline of the tumultuous waters of emotional transformation. It is a discombobulating swim that no ego wants any part of, yet we have arrived at this inevitable phase of our journey.

Additionally, the onset of movies and television have generated significant distress for a couple of reasons. First, their beautiful actors, adventurous stories and desire-provoking commercials repeatedly drive home the message that who we are and the lives we are living are severely lacking. They promote lifestyles of keeping up with others, improving our images, and acquiring more stuff. We have fallen for the premise that such changes will fill our holes of emptiness, longing and insecurity.

Second, they have raised our awareness to the injustices and suffering in the world. They appeal to our divine nature and compassion, but it is distressing to see what is going on. It is so much easier to live in an unconscious state of ignorance is bliss, but the distress of witnessing reality and stepping up to collective responsibility is an inevitable part of the process.

Meanwhile, these developments are coinciding with a world of information overload that is running at an increasingly frantic pace. Adding to the mounting distress, the great awakening began in the 1960s with a societal revolution,

Vatican II and science's truth-seeking march into the core tenets of religion (§7.5.). It was only a matter of time before the apocalyptic prophecies were unraveled and the global distress jumped to a whole new level.

9.5.c. A Paradigm War

The spiritual revolution will trigger significant distress for those who are entrenched in a Western religion. Many believers will recoil from the deep changes it demands and instead double down on their traditional beliefs as their religious herd circles the wagons to protect itself. Perceiving a world that is going to hell in a handbasket, they will be blind to the self-righteousness and fear that is generating their hell from deep within.

With mass communication fed by millions who are awakening, those who are left behind will surely be hearing about it. A paradigm war over ideologies is inevitable, and the religious ostriches will find it increasingly difficult to keep their heads buried in the sand.

9.5.d. Disillusionment and Deep Fear

In this era of profound disillusionment, the religious maps will no longer render their guidance and assurance. The universe will no longer be what it had been.

Christians who stay present to these developments will probably experience a profound fear of eternal damnation as they consider forsaking the Bible and their traditional beliefs. The truth, though, is that those very fears are blocking their spiritual growth toward salvation (§3.6.). Many will legitimately suffer through those fears and make major revisions to their map of reality. Although such work is painful, these awakening souls will be living the wisdom that the only way out is through it.

9.5.e. Leaving the Religious Herd

Such growth does not occur in a vacuum. Rather, we make choices amid an array of relationships and societal culture.

The deepest place of fear is in the root chakra, or first energy center. Located at the base of the spine, the root chakra is home to energies pertaining to physical survival and our ties to the various tribes we were born into such as family, community, religion and nation. As babies and children, we needed our tribe to survive, and the tribe ingrained us with its beliefs, values and traditions.

Since there is phenomenal power in numbers, safety is built upon conformance to tribal norms. Loyalty keeps the tribe bonded and is thus demanded. Conformity is also driven by primal fears of societal acceptance and physical survival.

If you have not done so already, be forewarned that when you dare to transcend the tribes of your childhood, you will be greeted by these deeply entrenched fears. Challenging a religion of origin includes challenging unconscious loyalty to the family and its larger tribes. Yet Jesus taught the path to spiritual liberation usually entails breaking from religious and family traditions (§4.3.b.).

All in all, such a break requires a journey through immense fear, not to mention the possibility of being ostracized by one's family and community. But at least being burned at the stake is no longer a potential consequence for going against the Church.

9.5.f. Against All Odds

The distress will be compounded by the realization that we are sleeping in a bed that we have been making for thousands of years. We are creative beings of free will, responsibility and spiritual power (§1.3.c.), and because of reincarnation there are no easy ways out of our predicament.

As we awaken and take responsibility for the state of our world, this era will be unparalleled in its distress for three more reasons. First, we are in a state of minimal power right now because we are hampered by the most wounding and fear. As we heal and grow, though, life will get easier.

Second, we are facing powerful institutions that are governed by people who profit by maintaining the status quo. Whether their external power, prestige and/or wealth derive from their prominent positions in governments, corporations or religions, they will not go quietly. Just like our deeply ingrained fears, they will do all they can to keep things the way they are. Be forewarned that deception and preying upon fear are still their primary means of doing so.

Finally, we are going against the grain of our culture. Our hope will be going against every historical and emotional reason people have to be cynical. Living on our planet means living amid mass and gravity, and society's momentum will be extremely difficult to reroute. It will take a tremendous amount of courage, energy and perseverance to shift ingrained patterns and reconstitute a new way of collective living.

9.5.g. The Birth Pains of a New World Order

Nevertheless, thousands of inspired souls have been dedicating their lives to the divine process. Martin Luther King Jr. was one such spiritual warrior, and he also knew what the world was going through. As he noted in 1956, "There can be no birth and growth without birth and growing pains." As he saw it, the global tensions of his day were indicative of a new world order being born as the old order was starting to crack.[8]

The 1960s rocked the religious and political elite, but those power structures withstood the wave of progressive change. We live, though, in a spiritual universe that has an overriding agenda that will not be denied.

Although Christian institutions will be hit the hardest, this process will also be impacting our governments as a critical mass develops among those who have awakened. Stepping into their spiritual power and responsibility, these visionary progressives will become a political force to be reckoned with. For all who prefer or profit from the way the world is currently run, this will be a distressing development as the so-called meek begin inheriting the earth.

9.5.h. The Nature of the Spiritual Path

The ego craves structure and order, for there it finds security and safety. It also defends itself from whatever it deems to be a threat to its well-being. In sum, the ego loves building walls.

Yet divine love will eventually break through everything in the way of our spiritual growth and defenseless unity. Some day and some way, in this lifetime or one to come, life will break us all open. Peck called these agonizing experiences the "grace of breaking moments."[9]

The spiritual path also requires the unearthing and processing of painful emotions. When unconscious fears drive our behavior, they remain hidden and dormant because they are in control and appear to be delivering safety. When we go against the grain of those fears, however, they scream bloody murder from deep within.

So instead of allowing such fears and other emotions to silently dictate their lives, awakening souls have been squaring up to face them. Suffice it to say, it is not an easy process. Spiritual teacher Marianne Williamson describes the dynamic:

> Spiritual progress is like a detoxification. Things have to come up in order to be released. Once we have asked to be healed, then our unhealed places are forced to the surface. A relationship that is used by the Holy Spirit becomes a place where our blocks to love are not suppressed or denied, but rather brought into our conscious awareness.[10]

Such is the path for those who have found the narrow gate and are forging through the emotional pain. They are no longer running away through the use of cigarettes, alcohol and other recreational drugs. They are no longer relying on psychiatric medications to quell their anxiety and/or depression. Instead, they are minimizing the med-escape-tion by delving into and healing the underlying issues that created the painful symptoms in the first place.[11]

They have embraced what Jung called legitimate suffering, which means delving into and transforming through the root issues and emotions that lurk underneath our defenses. Those who avoid this path are at the mercy of what

Jung called neurotic suffering. "Neuroses" used to refer to psychological defenses and the maladaptive patterns of thought and behavior that accompany them. Neurotic suffering refers to the isolation, loneliness, anxiety, depression, addictions, et cetera, that are spawned by our neuroses.

A defining experience of the spiritual path is emotional pain, but it is pain with a purifying purpose. Having recognized there is no escaping the pain (for it will either be legitimate suffering or neurotic suffering), awakening souls chose the pain that disappears when we transform through it instead of the pain that builds the more we run away from it.

So it is these people are no longer denying and hiding how they feel. They are learning how to authentically and vulnerably connect with themselves and others as they forge their way through this unavoidable gauntlet.

Meanwhile, the universe is turning up the heat in our psychological kitchens. Intuitives have been reporting that our world is being flooded by accelerated vibrational frequencies. This quickening of the energetic fabric of life is stirring emotional charges that are buried within our immortal selves from previous lifetimes (§1.4.g.). This emotional density needs to be triggered, processed and released for us to heal and grow to higher levels.[12]

According to a spiritual channel named Rasha, this process will be too intense for some, and "many will choose seemingly violent exits from this lifetime" as they relinquish their physical form.[13] Meanwhile, others will be "seemingly untouched by the process and will opt for the continued experience of an obsolete reality for some time to come."[14] All the while millions of souls will be aligning with the quickening as they advance their awakening.

9.5.i. Swimming Against the Current

Although many will avoid the work until a subsequent lifetime, there is no escaping the birth pains of spiritual growth. The process will eventually get easier as people become more acclimated to swimming and surrendering their way through its turbulent waters. Moreover, our culture will eventually become more understanding and loving of those who are moving in this direction.

In the era of unequaled distress, though, they will be swimming upstream against a strong current. Our culture is still strongly promoting the ascendancy of a man's ego, which sadly comes at the expense of the healing, freedom and connectedness of his soul. It glorifies a man's tough exterior shell—his appearance of having it all together and conquering the world he faces—while it shames his vulnerability and softer emotions as weak and unmanly.

Bishop T. D. Jakes has met with thousands of men from all walks of life. Using the metaphor of a fish that is trapped in an aquarium being heated to ever greater temperatures, he describes the neurotic suffering that men are experiencing as "a silent soul scream that no one can hear as the water around you goes from tepid to warm to boiling-point hot."[15] He continues, "We are being boiled alive by our own fears and insecurities, those thoughts that gnaw at us below the surface of our attempts to look like we have it all together."[16]

As Jakes observes about life in the Christian world, men do not have "the tools they need to become aware of their feelings and handle them effectively. There is no material that helps men work through their pain and maintain their relationships."[17] He continues, "Many men simply don't have the help they need to effectively deal with their emotions. Most men are ashamed to admit that they even need the help."[18] As the ego's dark underbelly is shame, it would rather suffer in silence than allow the soul to reach out for help and healing.

Women and children are suffering, too, as they attempt to live in this culture, relate to its insanity, and recover from the emotional and physical violence it so often produces. All in all, it will take time before it is culturally acceptable for all adults, especially men, to not only be authentic and vulnerable but also be loved and supported through the emotional river instead of being shamed and ridiculed for being in it.

Until then, alcohol and other mind-numbing escapes will continue to bury countless souls in the neurotic suffering of their silent distress. As for those who dare do anything about it, they will be doing so in the shaming glare of our prevailing culture.

9.6. Conclusion

The Little Apocalypse is an unreliable prophecy because it was not written by the man who experienced it. Assuming Jesus had the gift of prophecy but his followers got confused in passing it along, the chapter focused on its themes and found it unravels with uncanny resonance by viewing it with a spiritual awakening paradigm.

Instead of portraying a neurotic and sadistic God who will someday unleash holy hell upon the world, Jesus apparently knew about the Christian institutions that would block the spiritual growth of God's children. He foretold the rampant deception and tyrannical servant who got drunk on external power.

This beastly servant is not expecting the master's sudden return, but God is neither seething with contempt nor destroying the Catholic Church. Rather, this is simply a process of humanity growing in consciousness and no longer partnering with the darkness. The only way this religious vulture and its offspring can survive is to continue preying on the unconscious fear and ignorance that has rendered millions of spiritual carcasses.

The religious vultures will find this increasingly difficult to do with future generations, especially when the world learns that Revelation is also shining a floodlight of consciousness upon their darkness. The next chapter steps through the entire book and shows it yields exponentially more truth and wisdom when viewed with a spiritual awakening paradigm.

Chapter 10

The Vision of Revelation

10.1. Introduction

Near the end of the first century CE, a man named John had a prophetic experience on the Greek island of Patmos. He described it in a letter to the churches of seven cities in what is now western Turkey. His letter was originally known as the Apocalypse of John.

As apocalypse means "revelation," it is now known as the Book of Revelation. Ominously positioned at the end of the Bible, it is filled with horrifying imagery and has been the capstone of Christian theology about the end times. Per this mindset, it foretells the days when God will unleash his wrath upon the earth and Jesus will return with a vengeance to defeat the armies of evil in the battle of Armageddon.

These ideas are widely embraced. For instance, a *Newsweek* poll in 2004 reported 55 percent of American adults believe a rapture will occur and 36 percent believe Revelation is a literally true prophecy about the end of the world. The *Left Behind* novels depict such a future with over 62 million copies sold as of 2004.[1]

In 2015, a thousand American adults were surveyed by YouGov and the *Huffington Post* with the question, "Do you think that the end of the world, as predicted in the Book of Revelation, will happen?" Half of them (52 percent) said "Yes."[2]

This chapter reveals a radically different meaning for the imagery. Revelation is more abstract than Daniel, so some areas are more open to interpretation. However, its paradoxes and precision rule out all other possibilities for its ultimate meaning.

The chapter unravels the mysteries to show how the prophecy rendered an amazing portrait of life. By viewing Revelation with a metaphorical lens of a spiritual awakening paradigm, we witness an almost infinitely more believable and coherent painting than with a literal lens that foresees a cataclysmic destruction. This is strongly corroborated by the omniscient angel in Daniel, who declared that his epic prophecy would be completed with the breaking of the holy people's power, not with the world's annihilation (§7.5.b.).

Revelation's symbols and mysteries produce a complex lock that only one key can open. The spiritual awakening paradigm carves out the grooves and fills in the nooks that open the book's vault of secrets.

By the way, what we believe about the book reveals what we believe about God. For if we believe it foretold our awakening from the darkness, we glorify God as supremely loving through it all. But if we believe it foretold God's explosive vengeance against the heathens, we deem God to be light years away from unconditionally loving. We also deem God to be more genocidal than the Nazis, who attempted to do what God is expected to do in purging the planet of the non-Christians who were believed to be the problem.

10.2. Guiding Principles

Before delving into the prophecy, a few guiding principles need to be discussed.

10.2.a. Caution About the Information

Just because information comes from the Other Side does not guarantee it is correct (§8.4.c.). Recall as well how an angel was in the dark about what a prophecy meant and had to ask the omniscient angel (§7.5.b.).

With Revelation, John twice fell to the feet of an angel who had been escorting him. The angel told John not to worship him, as he was a "fellow servant" (Rv 19:10, 22:8). Trouble is, this fellow servant was mistaken on at least one matter of fact. He told John the time was near and Jesus was "coming soon" (Rv 3:11, 22:7, 22:12, 22:20). Almost two thousand years later, though, the world is still waiting.

Meanwhile, we do not know how much a person's beliefs and emotions will influence the reception of otherworldly information. A television signal may be sharp and pure, but the picture will be distorted if the television is faulty. We also need to consider memory errors and the assimilating influences of the prophet's paradigm. John apparently received all the information in one fell swoop, and it would only be natural if he inadvertently contorted some of it as he documented what he had experienced.

In sum, we should naturally be wary of any prophecy. Revelation demonstrates legitimacy, but we should not expect John's descriptions to be a flawless report of what the spiritual realm actually projected onto his mind.

10.2.b. John Inserted His Interpretations

Daniel only recorded what he had seen and heard and did not try to interpret his prophecies. Unfortunately, that is not the case with Revelation, for John elaborated on his experience with biblical quotes and paraphrases. It would all be fine and well if an angel had spoken the bonus material, but that does not appear to be the case given John's penchant for diligently quoting what the angels actually told him.

Scholars have calculated that almost 70 percent of Revelation's verses contain one or more allusions to Old Testament passages.[3] The correlation is often the result of John's synthesizing commentary. A good example comes from his account of the beast that he saw come out of the sea (annotated with the verses that most likely engendered his words):

> [**PART 1**] It had ten horns and seven heads, with ten crowns on its horns, and on each head a blasphemous name. The beast I saw resembled a leopard, but had feet like those of a bear and a mouth like that of a lion. The dragon gave the beast his power and his throne and great authority. One of the heads of the beast seemed to have had a fatal wound, but the fatal wound had been healed. The whole world was filled with wonder and followed the beast. People worshiped the dragon because he had given authority to the beast, and they also worshiped the beast and asked, "Who is like the beast? Who can wage war against it?"
>
> [**PART 2**] The beast was given a mouth to utter proud words and blasphemies and to exercise its authority for forty-two months. [Dn 7:8, 7:11, 7:20, 7:25] It opened its mouth to blaspheme God, and to slander his name and his dwelling place and those who live in heaven. It was given power to wage war against God's holy people and to conquer them. [Dn 7:21]
>
> [**PART 3**] And it was given authority over every tribe, people, language and nation. All inhabitants of the earth will worship the beast—all whose names have not been written in the Lamb's book of life, the Lamb who was slain from the creation of the world. [Dn 12:1; Mt 25:34; Jn 1:29; Phil 4:3]
>
> Whoever has ears, let them hear. [Mt 11:15] If anyone is to go into captivity, into captivity they will go. If anyone is to be killed with the sword, with the sword they will be killed. [Jer 15:2] (Rv 13:1–10)

In part 1, the text gives us confidence that John reported what he actually saw and heard. Although sharing a variety of traits with Daniel's terrifying beast (§7.3.b.), John's beast has many unique details that differentiate them. As will become clear later, both the similarities and differences are essential parts of the metaphor.

In part 2, however, it seems John believed he had basically seen the same beast as Daniel and tried to synchronize his vision with his predecessor's. Since he meticulously quoted the angels and the text does not say, "I heard an angel say this beast would rule for 42 months," he most likely gleaned this information from Daniel.

In any case, part 3 is comprised of commentary from verses that John deemed to be relevant. It exemplifies how he tried to enrich and explain his visions for his fellow Christians.

As far as timing issues are concerned, he apparently took the liberty of making some calculations for his readers. To see it, we need to briefly diverge to a previous part of Revelation where two different verses in close proximity are most likely talking about the same event.

Discussing a metaphorical woman in heaven, John tells us she "fled into the wilderness to a place prepared for her by God, where she might be taken care of for 1,260 days" (Rv 12:6). After describing a heavenly battle between angels and a dragon, John tells us this same woman was given the wings of an eagle "so that she might fly to the place prepared for her in the wilderness, where she would be taken care of for a time, times and half a time" (Rv 12:14).

John's reiteration of the length of time the woman would be cared for in the wilderness produces four possibilities. Scenario A: an angel told John both "1,260 days" and "a time, times and half a time." Scenario B: an angel told John the period would be "1,260 days," but John rehashed Daniel for the second mention. Scenario C: an angel told John the timeframe would be "a time, times and half a time," but John calculated it to be 1,260 days for the first mention. Scenario D: John was told neither and recorded both timeframes from his interpretation of Daniel.

Scenario A is the least likely to have occurred, for John did not quote an angel on the matter as he habitually did throughout the rest of his letter. Moreover, it defies all sensibility for an angel to render a mystery after having already given the answer of 1,260 days. The most troublesome part of scenario A, though, is the answer is an erroneous interpretation of the mystery given to Daniel.

The scenario that actually occurred, then, is most assuredly B, C or D. Since John's handiwork appears in all three of them, the point is proven that John included his interpretation.

Now let us return to the main passage, part 2, where John said the beast was given a mouth "to exercise its authority for forty-two months" (Rv 13:5). As just discussed, John most likely wrote part 2 from what he had gleaned from

Daniel. If so, we have another case where he made a chronological calculation, for the measure of time given to Daniel was not 42 months but rather the mysterious "a time, times and half a time" (Dn 7:25).

Based on John's mistaken understanding of Daniel's 70th seven, he figured the relevant timeframe was 3.5 years = 42 months = 1,260 days. Since we now know the solution of the mysterious equation (§7.3.d.), we also know that John jumped to an erroneous conclusion. In a textbook case of circular logic, modern Christians have followed in his folly by referencing Revelation to decode Daniel (§7.5.c.).

All in all, Revelation is filled with John's extraneous commentary and calculations. We thus have to discern where the prophetic information ends and where his interpretations begin.

10.2.c. Dreaming in Metaphors: The Story of Our Evolution

Spiritual visions are often mistaken to be literal predictions, and Revelation is another case of material that must be interpreted metaphorically. As it turns out, it is like a meaningful dream that depicts the real-life dynamics in which the psyche is immersed. With Revelation, though, the symbolic reflection is about our collective psyche and the story of our spiritual evolution.

To comprehend it, wisdom is needed about the conflict between good and evil. So let us review how we arrived at our current paradigm and are awakening to an enlightened understanding.

For as far back as archaeology can discover, humanity has been trying to make sense of our difficult existence and polarities such as life and death, growth and decay, and creation and destruction. The devastating power of storms, floods, earthquakes, famines and plagues were persistent dangers in a world of wild animals, poisonous reptiles and opposing tribes and kingdoms that invaded, raped and pillaged with reckless abandon.

With minimal control over these forces, our ancient predecessors were swimming like goldfish in the blender of life. Undoubtedly influenced by otherworldly experiences, they imagined all kinds of gods as the creators and controllers of earthly events and tried to figure out how to win their favor.

The birth of monotheism was a landmark development, but the paradigm was far from enlightened and was further darkened by an explanatory appendage. To have only a single deity who was good and account for life's tragedies, a theology arose that God must be engaged in a cosmic war with an ultrapowerful archenemy.

We have recently learned, however, that nature is not operating at the whim of one or more deities. Rather, the universe is humming along to a symphony of elegant laws. We are also beginning to understand the nature of evil and how it relates to an unconditionally loving God who granted us free will. Moreover, we are learning about our eternal immersion in a process of spiritual evolution.

If good is synonymous with consciousness, wisdom, honesty and love and evil is synonymous with unawareness, ignorance, deception and fear, then good has been battling with evil throughout history. Nevertheless, God is not battling an evil insurrection that has challenged his supremacy. To the contrary, God created the battlefield of polarities and granted all souls the freedom of creating amid this spectrum however we wish.

Since all beings are intertwined with God and God designed life for spiritual evolution, we will eventually manifest our divine nature. The outcome of the conflict between good and evil was never in doubt, and God is not fighting any kind of war over it. Rather, a process was long ago created and is playing itself out in accordance with free will. Even though our world is still immersed in the darkness, the Light will eventually prevail.

This is the grand story of the universe that is transpiring across billions of years in billions of galaxies. As for life on our planet, John was given a prophetic glimpse of this amazing process. Revelation's metaphors simply depict our spiritual evolution through the gauntlet of polarities and the oppressive bastions that have stonewalled our spiritual growth. The eventual result of it all will be heaven on earth.

10.3. Global Story, Slice #1: Darkness and Awakening

Like a holographic image, the spiritual realm presented the complex story from four different angles. This section presents the first slice of the global story of Revelation.

10.3.a. The Seven Messages to the Seven Churches

After a prologue and greeting, John's letter includes specific messages to each of the seven churches being addressed (Rv 1–3). Generally speaking, the messages commend, critique and encourage each church as part of a call for substantial improvement. Each message includes a specific promise that he who overcomes will be greatly rewarded. Instead of preaching for believing in a savior, the spiritual realm was calling for spiritual growth.

10.3.b. Worthy to Open the Scroll

John was then guided to witness a throne in heaven, and so began the vision of Revelation (Rv 4). God was seated on the throne and holding a scroll with seven seals. A lamb that looked like it had been slain took the scroll amid praise from a multitude of angels (Rv 5).

The slain lamb does not mean Jesus was a human sacrifice. Rather, it symbolizes a pure and innocent person with no physical means of attack or defense who was slaughtered at the whim of a powerful authority. He was allowed to open the scroll because he had overcome the darkness.

A heavenly elder concurred that this spiritual lion had triumphed and could thus open the seven seals (Rv 5:5). Jesus was allowed to reveal the story of our existence by breaking the seals that represented how it had been kept secret.

10.3.c. Seals #1 to #5: Life in the Metaphysical Darkness

John wrote:

> I watched as the Lamb opened the first of the seven seals. Then I heard one of the four living creatures say in a voice like thunder, "Come!" I looked, and there before me was a white horse! Its rider held a bow, and he was given a crown, and he rode out as a conqueror bent on conquest.
>
> When the Lamb opened the second seal, I heard the second living creature say, "Come!" Then another horse came out, a fiery red one. Its rider was given power to take peace from the earth and to make people kill each other. To him was given a large sword.
>
> When the Lamb opened the third seal, I heard the third living creature say, "Come!" I looked, and there before me was a black horse! Its rider was holding a pair of scales in his hand. Then I heard what sounded like a voice among the four living creatures, saying, "Two pounds of wheat for a day's wages, and six pounds of barley for a day's wages, and do not damage the oil and the wine!"
>
> When the Lamb opened the fourth seal, I heard the voice of the fourth living creature say, "Come!" I looked, and there before me was a pale horse! Its rider was named Death, and Hades was following close behind him. They were given power over a fourth of the earth to kill by sword, famine and plague, and by the wild beasts of the earth. (Rev 6:1–8)

A horse symbolizes our animal nature—our bodies, instincts and emotions. A rider symbolizes our human nature—our thinking minds that make choices and direct our bodies. Just as the horse is a dutiful servant of humanity, the body is a dutiful servant of the mind. The metaphor of a horse and its rider, then, provides a powerful tool for conveying the human condition.

So what has been pulling on humanity's reins and where has it been leading us? Our wills have not been aligned with God's will of love. Instead, powerful desires and emotions have been riding us and commandeering our collective choices, and life has been a hellish stampede.

The rider of the white horse represents the kings and rulers of the earth. As most people believe their nation is good, monarchs, dictators and presidents command populaces of self-perceived purity—a white horse. Crowned with the power to make decisions for the masses, they often direct their nations into war to conquer others. The bow represents fighting without having to be in the thick of it. Without an arrow, the rider's weapon is only for show.

As for the second seal, the fiery red emotions of anger and revenge become primal motivators when nations are attacked or slighted by others. The lust for vengeance has a long history of taking peace from the earth and making men slay each other. Warmongering hawks have always found it ridiculously easy to stir their nations into avenging attacks. The resulting cycle of violence feeds on itself.

The third seal invokes a pair of scales to represent commerce and trade, and the rider of the black horse symbolizes greed and economic exploitation. In John's era, a day's wages could have purchased ten times the offered amount of wheat or barley, so the spiritual realm was depicting jobs with ridiculously low compensation with corresponding pressure for quality work. As companies have long exploited the hunger of the masses to maximize profit, there has been minimal compassion or conscience. The associated color is therefore black.

[Note: People in poverty have no choice but to work for dirt-cheap wages when the only other legal option is watching their families starve. The desperate masses of third-world countries have been competing for slave-like jobs while the Western democracies collude with local governments so corporations can keep capitalizing on their fight for life and we can keep purchasing low-cost products. This cruel dynamic is why the Western democracies developed labor-protection laws at home and why they should demand the same kind of worker protection and wages for any company that does international business.]

As for the fourth seal, overwhelming fear will make you pale, and fear has been perpetually riding humanity. As the United States demonstrated with Iraq in 2003, fear leads populations into wielding the sword for reasons that are neither in self-defense nor to preempt an imminent attack. The pale horse of fear also shuts down sharing and thus enables famines. Moreover, it weakens immune systems and makes us more vulnerable to plagues. Finally, wild animals attack when they sense fear.

Most Christians believe the four horsemen of the apocalypse are warrior-angels who will someday unleash hell upon the earth. No such thing is forthcoming, though, for we have already been living in it for thousands of years. The spiritual realm's depiction of the core dynamics is exceptional. John continued:

> When he opened the fifth seal, I saw under the altar the souls
> of those who had been slain because of the word of God and

> the testimony they had maintained. They called out in a loud voice, "How long, Sovereign Lord, holy and true, until you judge the inhabitants of the earth and avenge our blood?" Then each of them was given a white robe, and they were told to wait a little longer, until the full number of their fellow servants, their brothers and sisters, were killed just as they had been. (Rv 6:9–11)

John was shown how the true messengers of God would continue to be executed "under the altar" of religion. Whether the killing of ancient prophets by Judaic authorities or heretical Christians by the Church, the fifth seal refers to how the so-called houses of God have been opposing the true will of God.

All in all, the first five seals render a phenomenal summary of our metaphysical story. History has been driven by the root motivations of the first four seals: conquest, revenge, greed and fear. Meanwhile, the Western religions continue to engender fear, hatred and conflict while keeping the masses blinded about our collective predicament. This is the great tribulation of life that all who hope to follow in the path of Jesus will also have to overcome.

10.3.d. Seal #6: A Revolutionary Breakthrough

Despite the dominance of the darkness, the divine kingdom would eventually prevail. John wrote:

> I watched as he opened the sixth seal. There was a great earthquake. The sun turned black like sackcloth made of goat hair, the whole moon turned blood red, and the stars in the sky fell to earth, as figs drop from a fig tree when shaken by a strong wind. The heavens receded like a scroll being rolled up, and every mountain and island was removed from its place.
>
> Then the kings of the earth, the princes, the generals, the rich, the mighty, and everyone else, both slave and free, hid in caves and among the rocks of the mountains. They called to the mountains and the rocks, "Fall on us and hide us from the face of him who sits on the throne and from the wrath of the Lamb! For the great day of their wrath has come, and who can withstand it?" (Rv 6:12–17)

The opening of the sixth seal depicts the revolutionary breakthrough of truth, which will strike the dark pillars of our civilization like an earthquake. Hundreds of millions of people will be disillusioned amid the great awakening as their stars of religious orientation and guidance no longer hold firm (§9.3.c.).

It is finally happening as the darkness of controlling hierarchies, especially those of religious institutions, is being exposed. This dynamic was shown to John in the mountains being removed from their places, which reiterates Isaiah's prophecy of the valleys being filled and the mountains being leveled (§7.3.a.). As for those of all social classes who scurry for cover, Jesus purportedly explained that light had come to the world, but evildoers would hide to prevent their deeds from being exposed (Jn 3:19–20).

By the way, literal interpreters of Revelation cannot explain how every mountain will be removed yet so many will be running for cover into the rocks of those mountains. Moreover, a star would immediately obliterate the earth if they ever collided.

In sum, the Messiah's revolutionary paradigm shift was missed two thousand years ago, but it has suddenly returned to finish the job. Our consciousness is rapidly growing to recognize the cloaked darkness of egoic pride and the spiritual illness of "righteous" people like Job and "infallible" institutions like the Catholic Church. With the unearthing of erroneous assumptions and the unraveling of the apocalyptic prophecies, bedrock paradigms are being cracked wide open.

In the grand sweep of history, this illuminative breakthrough will look like a flash of lightning. As the Daniel prophecies long ago foretold, we are living in the era when the power of the holy people will finally be broken (§7.5.). Amid these societal birth pains, the time of unparalleled distress is at hand (§9.5.).

10.3.e. The Sealing of 144,000 and the Great Multitude

John then saw four angels who were preparing to unleash wrath upon the land and sea. Another angel appeared and asked for a timeout to place seals on the foreheads of 144,000 servants from all the tribes of Israel (Rv 7:1–8).

The sealing of the 144,000 parallels the mark placed on Cain to protect him even though he had just murdered his brother Abel and been banished from his homeland (Gn 4:15). It evokes the theme of a loving God who is still reaching out to his wayward Jewish servants despite their rejection of spiritual correction.

The symmetrical tally of an even 12,000 for each of the 12 tribes strongly suggests it is symbolic. More importantly, it is a literal impossibility because ten of the tribes vanished thousands of years ago. As Jeff Booth summarizes his extensive research, "The ten lost tribes were conquered, and, like almost every other conquered people in the ancient world, lost their separate identity and were assimilated away into the sands of history." Meanwhile, the "belief that the Jews represent all 12 tribes is an erroneous Christian doctrine" with no justification whatsoever from ancient or modern Jewish experts.[4]

In any case, there will be millions of others who awaken and make the spiritual journey home. "After this," John reported, there before him was "a great multitude that no one could count, from every nation, tribe, people and language, standing before the throne and before the Lamb. They were wearing white robes and were holding palm branches in their hands" (Rv 7:9). An elder explained that these are the ones who made it through the "great tribulation" (Rv 7:14).

As the next few subsections reveal, however, Revelation affirms common sense that despite the widespread communication of spiritual truth, far more people will avoid it. With their souls buried under energetic layers of lifetimes in the darkness, they will need something more to awaken.

10.3.f. Seal #7: The Global Awakening

When the seventh seal was opened, all was silent in heaven for approximately half an hour. John also saw seven angels who received seven trumpets. He continued:

> Another angel, who had a golden censer, came and stood at the altar. He was given much incense to offer, with the prayers of all God's people, on the golden altar in front of the throne. The smoke of the incense, together with the prayers of God's people, went up before God from the angel's hand. Then the angel took the censer, filled it with fire from the altar, and hurled it on the earth; and there came peals of thunder, rumblings, flashes of lightning and an earthquake. (Rv 8:3–5)

Lord knows how many earthly years are represented by half an hour in heaven. What we do know is that Revelation canvasses the history of Western civilization. As the sixth seal is suddenly striking in the early 21st century, the brunt of the seventh seal is forthcoming.

Meanwhile, we need not fear a giant fireball crashing down from the sky. To the contrary, the metaphor of fire is often used to represent God (§7.3.c.), and the fire of heaven could very well be manifesting in accelerated vibrational frequencies (§9.5.h.). The divine fire will be making it all the more difficult for the masses to avoid the process. As Jesus was quoted by the Gospel of Thomas, "I have cast fire upon the world, and see, I am guarding it until it blazes" (GTh, 10).[5]

10.3.g. Trumpets #1 to #4: Environmental Agony

For those who believe in a vindictive God, the visions of the sounding trumpets depict the spiritual realm annihilating the world. Nothing could be further from the truth, though, as to who is unleashing the damage. As a wise saying from an old comic strip puts it, "We have met the enemy, and he is us."[6]

The imagery simply represents the process of karma and how the pain of sleeping in a bed of our making will be spurring our awakening. Yes, the seventh seal portends a crucible of spiritual growth for those who remained asleep during the sixth seal. It is about the escalation of natural consequences that will spur us into a more aware and harmonious way of life with the rest of life. Even though we will always have free will, it may feel as if we have no choice but to grow up or perish.

The spiritual realm's intention is for a global illumination, not a fascist domination. For if you want people to fall in line and march in a mindless parade, brandish some weapons and pound on a drum. But if you want to wake them up, greet them with your bugle corps at the break of dawn. John's vision continues along those lines:

> The first angel sounded his trumpet, and there came hail and fire mixed with blood, and it was hurled down on the earth. A third of the earth was burned up, a third of the trees were burned up, and all the green grass was burned up.
>
> The second angel sounded his trumpet, and something like a huge mountain, all ablaze, was thrown into the sea. A third of the sea turned into blood, a third of the living creatures in the sea died, and a third of the ships were destroyed.
>
> The third angel sounded his trumpet, and a great star, blazing like a torch, fell from the sky on a third of the rivers and on the springs of water—the name of the star is Wormwood. A third of the waters turned bitter, and many people died from the waters that had become bitter.
>
> The fourth angel sounded his trumpet, and a third of the sun was struck, a third of the moon, and a third of the stars, so that a third of them turned dark. A third of the day was without light, and also a third of the night. (Rv 8:7–12)

Nobody in John's era could have ever imagined what the "hail and fire" was about, much less the inclusion of blood with the contradictions of cold/hot and water/fire. But now many people know that global warming will be creating not only more scorching heat but also more powerful storms. The heat is the essence of the problem, though, and thus the depiction of global warming with the burning of the earth, trees and grass.

The blood confirms the spiritual realm is not unleashing this destruction. Rather, it is metaphorical DNA that implicates humans as the perpetrators of this ecological crime. The prophecy thus agrees with a nearly unanimous consensus of climate scientists who have been actively publishing in peer-reviewed journals. As the National Aeronautics and Space Administration (NASA) recently summarized, 97 percent of them concur that "Climate-warming trends over the past century are very likely due to human activities."[7]

For instance, the ice sheets of Greenland and Antarctica have given scientists an amazing record of the earth's climate for the past 800,000 years. By drilling into and extracting cylindrical cores from their giant domes of ice, which built up for all those years like tree rings, scientists have yearly data of both temperature and the amount of carbon dioxide (CO_2) in the atmosphere. The temperature data comes from the ice's chemistry and the CO_2 data from trapped bubbles of air.

The data clearly shows that temperature and CO_2 are highly correlated. When one goes up, the other is usually in pretty close proximity, and the same dance continues when one goes down. Causation is easily explained by the greenhouse effect, as CO_2 does an incredibly good job of trapping heat like an invisible blanket wrapped around the earth.

In all that time and despite natural variability, atmospheric CO_2 has never been less than 180 parts per million and until recently never more than 300. The closest it previously came to this ceiling was over 300,000 years ago.

With the Industrial Revolution and the population explosion, we have been releasing an incredible amount of CO_2 into the air while decimating forests that breathe in and reduce CO_2. So guess how much CO_2 is in the atmosphere now? In 2018, it was at 407 parts per million. In the past 60 years, CO_2 increased at a rate about a hundred times greater than the previous spikes in the data (such as the rapid warming after an ice age).[8]

While the first trumpet signifies damage to the atmosphere, the second trumpet draws our attention to fertilizers, insecticides, herbicides, plastics, pollution and other waste products that drain or are dumped into our oceans. "Something like a huge mountain" refers to the raw materials that are being mined from the earth, and the blazing fire represents their transformation into the various chemicals and other products that we spew into the air and onto the earth. A lot of this stuff is eventually washed away by rain and rivers into the oceans.

The prophecy's blood in the sea represents our culpability, with the end result being the loss of sea life and thus the decimation of fishing fleets. So how does that compare with reality and where we are heading?

Excessive chemical nutrients from agricultural runoff and other waste pouring into the oceans are the primary culprits of low oxygen areas that suffocate most marine life.[9] Almost 500 of these dead zones now exist and span more than 245,000 square kilometers (equal to the surface area of the United Kingdom).

Plastic debris kills more than a million seabirds and 100,000 marine mammals each year. In 2006, scientists estimated that if all the pieces of floating plastic were spread equally across the oceans, every square mile would contain 46,000 pieces of debris. Ocean currents, though, have concentrated five massive garbage patches called gyres. The North Pacific Gyre is twice the size of Texas.[10]

Meanwhile, about 26 percent of the CO_2 we release into the atmosphere gets absorbed by the oceans. Although global warming would be much worse without this mitigating dynamic, it is acidifying the oceans (because the dissolution of CO_2 in seawater creates carbonic acid). Ocean acidity has risen 30 percent since the Industrial Revolution began, and it is already devastating coral reefs around the world. It may also be severely harming many species of plankton and zooplankton, which comprise the critical bottom rung of the oceanic food chain.[11]

In sum, we are conducting a gargantuan experiment on our oceanic ecosystem that is already greatly alarming marine scientists. Revelation apparently foretold what the world will eventually learn the hard way as the interrelated effects begin impacting us in horrific ways.

The "great star" of the third trumpet is the shining allure of science and technology, which humanity has put so much faith in as our guiding light to well-being. The rivers and springs represent our life source, for fresh water is the basis of all land-based food. The "great star" crashing into and polluting our life source is the perfect metaphor for what we started experiencing in the past century.

Appendix M ("The Crashing of the Great Star") describes how the reckless application of science and technology has been having a devastating impact on our health. For instance, roughly one in six Americans has an autoimmune disease. While genetic susceptibility plays a substantial role, the key driver of an autoimmune attack is environmental exposure to toxins and chemicals.

The spiritual realm named this "great star" of science and technology that we thought would light the way to our salvation but has instead been wreaking havoc with our environment and health. Is it just a coincidence that Chernobyl—the site of the world's first nuclear meltdown in the old Soviet Union back in 1980—translates into the herb named Wormwood?[12]

Chances are it is not. The spiritual realm apparently selected this name so it would remain a mystery until an accident made it the perfect symbol for the nature of our self-inflicted damage.

The fourth trumpet foretold how humanity would react to our awakening karma. It depicts the world's impaired ability to see with clarity. Once again, a dastardly result is not being caused by the spiritual realm. Rather, our partial blindness is being caused by the ego's darkness.

Egoic forces are obfuscating the issues and confusing people about the truth of what is really going on. For instance, conservative organizations have been spending upward of a billion dollars a year to get the public and our elected officials to reject what scientists are learning about global warming.[13] Their dubious "experts" have been using sophomoric tricks to derive bogus conclusions from the data.[14] Their deception is driven by political ideology, economic greed, denial of this challenging reality and arrogance that our way of life supersedes everything and we need not take any responsibility to adapt.

Darkness appeals to darkness, and the masses are allowing this deception to justify their own ignorance, denial and fear. Meanwhile, thousands of elected officials are ducking the issue of global warming and behaving as political prostitutes who are selling out the long-term health of their nations and planet to get reelected.

These dark dynamics are also in play with our reckless application of science and technology (§M.2.c.). Until we awaken and stop playing the ego's wicked games, we will suffer the escalating consequences.

In sum, the first four trumpets forewarned that damage to our environment and health would be waking us up, but that awakening would be thwarted by egoic darkness. The industrial age is only a few centuries old, and we are already seeing what our disdain for the environment is doing to our collective home and long-term health. Do we really want to keep traveling down this godforsaken road to experience a self-created hell on earth?

10.3.h. Trumpet #5: A Psychological Sting

At the epicenter of the great awakening is the conflict between the darkness and the Light. Indeed, the egoic fight against our spiritual growth pervades the fourth through sixth trumpets. John wrote:

> The fifth angel sounded his trumpet, and I saw a star that had fallen from the sky to the earth. The star was given the key to the shaft of the Abyss. When he opened the Abyss, smoke rose from it like the smoke from a gigantic furnace. The sun and sky were darkened by the smoke from the Abyss. And out of the smoke locusts came down on the earth and were given power like that of scorpions of the earth. They were told not to harm the grass of the earth or any plant or tree, but only those people who did not have the seal of God on their foreheads. They were not allowed to kill them but only to torture them for five months. And the agony they suffered was like that of the sting of a scorpion when it strikes. During those days people will seek death but will not find it; they will long to die, but death will elude them.
>
> The locusts looked like horses prepared for battle. On

> their heads they wore something like crowns of gold, and their faces resembled human faces. Their hair was like women's hair, and their teeth were like lions' teeth. They had breastplates like breastplates of iron, and the sound of their wings was like the thundering of many horses and chariots rushing into battle. They had tails with stingers, like scorpions, and in their tails they had power to torment people for five months. They had as king over them the angel of the Abyss, whose name in Hebrew is Abaddon and in Greek is Apollyon (that is, Destroyer). (Rv 9:1–11)

The star that fell to the earth represents our collective consciousness, and its fall symbolizes the first half of our eternal journey. It began a long, long time ago when we descended from heaven to experience life in a polarized universe as spirits of the Light who were in the world but not of it.

The key to the shaft represents free will to unlock anything in this realm of opposites to experience, and our opening of the Abyss symbolizes how we chose the enticements of the darkness. We all went astray from a God of pure, unconditional love and fell into the great trap of the ego.

More specifically, we all got fooled by the illusion of the physical world and its trump card of death, felt deeply alone in a dangerous place, and have had many traumatic experiences of feeling like God has forsaken us (Mk 15:34). As all hell continued to break loose, our individual sparks of consciousness became increasingly consumed by the ego's fearfulness, woundedness, defensiveness, greed and selfishness.

These energetic patterns have continued to mount through countless lifetimes and further bury our souls in a cocoon of pain, isolation and darkness. Most of us have been going deeper into this bottomless pit by choosing (creating) from arrogance, ignorance, shame and fear.

Whether we call the result of our metaphysical fall the ego or the false self, it thrives by repressing and denying what psychologists call the authentic self. The authentic self is an aspect of our psyche that embraces humility and equality while vulnerably revealing the truth about all aspects of the self.

On the other hand, the false self lives defensively and believes itself to be superior to and more valuable than others as it hides the truth about all aspects of the self. At its worst, the false self believes itself to be perfected already and beyond even God's reproach. This narcissism is closely related to the Teflon defense of egoic pride (§5.2.). Egoic pride is the devil inside and a master of deception.

The prophecy symbolizes egoic pride with the smoke pouring out of the Abyss. The deceptiveness of egoic pride smokes out the light of divine love, truth and awareness. So it is that conquest, revenge, greed and fear have been allowed to run rampant as we ravage the earth.

Nevertheless, the spiritual realm will not be denied. As the Light penetrates the deceptive smoke, the egoic darkness from which it spews is being exposed. The awakening people of the earth will no longer be deceived about the hows and whys of our collective creations. Although political and religious leaders have long been hiding behind an image of goodness as their enabling citizens and followers delude themselves with "I'm not responsible" innocence, this well-hidden darkness will become increasingly visible.

Since no damage was to be done to the earth, nor were any humans to be killed, the nature of the locust attack is clearly psychological. Psychologists have observed that one of the most painful emotional wounds in human existence is anything that strikes at the core of narcissism. The literature often describes the "narcissistic wound" as the feeling that the self has been severely stung.

Indeed, few among us are truly comfortable with criticism or other forms of reproach to the self, and we often denigrate ourselves to prevent the job from being done by others. For those with narcissism in spades, though, any such rebuke is intensely painful, an agony "like that of the sting of a scorpion."

A narcissistic wound is acutely painful because the false self is the ultimate defense and compensation for a deep cesspool of unconscious fear and shame about an inferior and defective self. A narcissistic wound is felt when something pierces the defense and triggers these buried emotions, and narcissistic rage is the typical reaction.

Awakening souls are immune to such stings because they are no longer attached to their images. Living authentically and transparently, they accept all aspects of themselves as they process and release their fear and shame. They simply choose to heal and grow when life reflects their places of inner darkness.

The locusts symbolize the power of a group to swarm and sting, which is exactly what image-oriented (shame-based) people do to one another. The dark polarity of superior image and repressed shame moves in a circle of protective lies and destructive exposures and is judged by a societal rank-ordering of greater-than and lesser-than.

As the prophecy so graphically depicts, the nature of the swarming locust stings is altogether human. The gold crowns represent an attitude of innate royalty and superiority, and the women's hair and the prominent teeth vividly refer to obsession with image and beauty. The breastplates of iron symbolize stalwart psychological defenses, and the sound of their wings evokes the use of external power. Clearly such a culture is not born of love, nor does it produce a joyous experience of life. It is a culture of vanity.

The king of it all is an angel whose name simply means "destroyer." Just like a swarm of locusts consumes all vegetation in a gross ecological imbalance that cannot persist for long, our false selves have forsaken an equitable balance with others and the environment to appease their compensating desires. The result has been a gross cultural and ecological imbalance that is headed for destruction.

Speaking of destruction, this culture of vanity will gladly turn on itself with the piercing arrows of truth. These arrows will be fired by those who find it easier to attack the darkness out there than to address the darkness within.

Meanwhile, those who are strongly identified with their religion will be gravely challenged by the great awakening. The religious pride of Jews, Christians, Muslims and atheists will be sharply stung by the process. Many of them will find it too difficult to go from the intoxicating heights of religious superiority to the sobering ground of a far different reality.

It should come as no surprise, then, that many fundamentalists will resist our spiritual evolution as they wage an ideological war against it. As it turns out, this is a perfect segue to the next trumpet blast. After all, when you fire an arrow of truth at a dark and mighty dragon, it is going to roar back.

10.3.i. Trumpet #6: Paradigm Wars

Ever since Jesus heralded the divine kingdom, it has been stifled by the Western religions. These massive manifestations of egoic pride believe their teachings about God and life could not possibly be in error. Instead of encouraging their followers to engage in a no-holds-barred search for truth, they have demanded unquestioning submission to their beliefs and have killed to enforce them.

Daniel's two crown jewel prophecies and Revelation's fifth seal have already shown the spiritual realm is taking dead aim at them (§7.4., §7.5., §10.3.c.). The sixth trumpet brings them back into the crosshairs by foretelling how they would react to the great awakening. John continued:

> The sixth angel sounded his trumpet, and I heard a voice coming from the four horns of the golden altar that is before God. It said to the sixth angel who had the trumpet, "Release the four angels who are bound at the great river Euphrates." And the four angels who had been kept ready for this very hour and day and month and year were released to kill a third of mankind. The number of the mounted troops was twice ten thousand times ten thousand [200 million]. I heard their number.
>
> The horses and riders I saw in my vision looked like this: Their breastplates were fiery red, dark blue, and yellow as sulfur. The heads of the horses resembled the heads of lions, and out of their mouths came fire, smoke and sulfur. A third

of mankind was killed by the three plagues of fire, smoke and sulfur that came out of their mouths. The power of the horses was in their mouths and in their tails; for their tails were like snakes, having heads with which they inflict injury. (Rv 9:13–19)

The text has to be interpreted metaphorically. Otherwise, do we really believe that someday some 200 million soldiers will mount horses that are like fire-breathing dragons with snakes for tails, and the riders will do nothing as their mounts massacre over two billion people by belching out their plagues?

What would precede this? Will the killer horses magically appear at the doors of millions of Christians with a red, blue or yellow suit of armor draped over their backs and a nonverbal look of, "Put this on, dude, and let's ride"?

Since horses and riders of flesh and blood are out of the question, literal interpreters have to imagine an army of apparitions. Now the quandary is how nonphysical entities could belch out plagues that kill a third of mankind. Or are these plagues nonphysical, too, and over two billion people will die from what would be deemed a global hallucination if not for the grisly aftermath?

To understand the metaphor, a little perspective is needed. The great awakening began in the 1960s (§7.5.). In 1996, philosopher Mark Woodhouse articulated the zeitgeist with his book *Paradigm Wars: Worldviews for a New Age*. In his introduction, he explained how many reviewers felt its title was counterproductive.

He agreed about the value of emphasizing peace and finding common ground but pointed out that professional lives were hinging on "profound disagreements around current paradigm conflicts." For people who were trying to upend or defend the prevailing worldviews, he commented, "wars" was imminently appropriate. "The transition to a new worldview," he noted, "is never entirely peaceful, despite our efforts to make it so."[15]

As for the prophetic text, it is referring to the same conflicts but on an exponentially larger scale. The sixth trumpet portends a paradigm war that will engulf the world. Its outcome is of the utmost importance because our future will be created by our choices, which are driven by our beliefs.

By itself, this passage does not paint an undeniably clear picture. Bear with the following interpretation, though, for it will be solidly corroborated later.

The four angels symbolize the heavenly image and astounding power that the four great Western religions have been granted by their believers, and being bound to the Euphrates refers to their common roots and ancestral birthplace. Judaism, Christianity and Islam trace back to the heart of ancient Mesopotamia (where they believe the Garden of Eden existed), and their dogma led to the countermovement of science that hardened into scientism.

The angels being released means these religions will unleash their power in a fight for their lives. Nothing will be held back as they try to counter the revolutionary breakthrough of truth (§10.3.d.).

The four angels are indeed symbolic, for John's vision quickly transitioned into a more practical representation of these entities and what they are commanding. Interestingly enough, the tally of two hundred million troops is an impressive reflection of the modern world. That is, only a decided minority of the Western religions are fundamentalists who will reactively fight against the New Spirituality.

"This very hour and day and month and year" refers to the appointed and comparatively sudden eruption of the great paradigm war. As the Light pierces the religious darkness, watch what rages back. John saw horses and riders, yet it was the horses that bellowed the plagues of fire, smoke and sulfur. With a rider symbolizing human consciousness and a horse symbolizing our bodies, instincts and emotions (§10.3.c.), the prophecy foretold a knee-jerk reaction from these religions.

The red, blue and yellow breastplates depict how fundamentalists will defensively and proudly display their true colors. They will not integrate into the all-inclusive spirituality of white but rather remain defiantly exclusive.

The horses' lionlike heads predict a loud and prideful roar from these reactionaries. Straight from the horses' mouths will come words and energies that are symbolized by fire, smoke and sulfur. In this case, fire represents the lashing flames of self-righteous anger and messages of burning in the fires of hell. Smoke signifies the deception of egoic pride and its refusal to be wrong.

Sulfur is translated as "brimstone" by the King James Version—hence, the cliché about a "fire and brimstone" sermon. With the exception of Revelation, the word appears only once in the New Testament amid a recollection of how "fire and sulfur rained down from heaven and destroyed" the cities of Sodom and Gomorrah (Lk 17:29). Sulfur thus symbolizes teachings of divine vengeance.

In sum, the plagues from the reactionaries will be brimming with self-righteous anger and threats of burning in hell (the fire), coming from religious deception and egoic pride (the smoke), and forewarning divine vengeance (the sulfur). The plagues will "kill a third of mankind" because they will be imbibed by moderately religious folks who are too brainwashed to escape the darkness. The metaphor portends spiritual deaths for those who succumb to these teachings and fail to awaken in this lifetime (§9.4.b.).

The tails with heads like snakes refer to the sly ways in which fundamentalists will lash out from their darkness to inflict injury. The symbology is also an identifying feature. As both John the Baptist and Jesus purportedly named it, the religious leaders were a "brood of vipers" (Mt 3:7, 12:34, 23:33).

John then wrote that the folks who survived the plagues did not repent from worshipping demons or their hand-created idols. They also did not repent from murders, magic arts, sexual immorality and thefts (Rv 9:20–21).

This passage came from John's erroneous interpretation that the survivors of the plagues were the target of God's wrath. He figured they had not repented, so he added some commentary that is rife with Old and New Testament phrases. Trouble was, he was blind to the spiritual realm's agenda and what his visions were really portending, and his misguided worldview and commentary are painfully apparent.

10.3.j. Trumpet #7: Not Yet

John then saw an angel come down from heaven with a little scroll in his hand. The angel proclaimed, "There will be no more delay! But in the days when the seventh angel is about to sound his trumpet, the mystery of God will be accomplished, just as he announced to his servants the prophets" (Rv 10:6–7).

The angel presented the scroll to John and told him, "Take it and eat it. It will turn your stomach sour, but in your mouth it will be as sweet as honey" (Rv 10:9). John ate it and was then told he had to prophesy again about numerous peoples, languages, kings and nations (Rv 10:10–11).

The next chapters in Revelation have tasted very sweet to Christians like John. These literal-minded folks believe this material foretells how God will unleash even more wrath upon the heathens. However, this "fire and brimstone" theology is gravely mistaken and incapable of making sense of the bizarre imagery. Moreover, the spiritual realm forewarned John that the forthcoming revelations would be quite revolting to what his gut desired. For those who hunger for divine vengeance, the truth would be upsetting medicine.

10.4. Global Story, Slice #2: The Divine Kingdom

The spiritual awakening paradigm naturally expects the seventh trumpet to herald the triumph of the divine kingdom over the darkness. Indeed, that is exactly what it is about. Before sounding it, though, the spiritual realm wanted to tell the global story of Revelation from a different angle. The second slice is quite different from the other three, for it is brief and presents little imagery. Yet it is at the heart of the drama and casts its light upon the other three. It was quickly presented before the upsetting medicine was dispensed in the third and fourth slices.

10.4.a. The Two Witnesses

Revelation continues with John's testimony of what he saw and heard:

> I was given a reed like a measuring rod and was told, "Go and

measure the temple of God and the altar, with its worshipers. But exclude the outer court; do not measure it, because it has been given to the Gentiles. They will trample on the holy city for 42 months. And I will appoint my two witnesses, and they will prophesy for 1,260 days, clothed in sackcloth." (Rv 11:1–3)

As John dutifully recorded what he actually saw and heard, the next passage seems to be marred by his commentary and is at best a glossed report of a vision:

> They are "the two olive trees" and the two lampstands, and "they stand before the Lord of the earth." If anyone tries to harm them, fire comes from their mouths and devours their enemies. This is how anyone who wants to harm them must die. They have power to shut up the heavens so that it will not rain during the time they are prophesying; and they have power to turn the waters into blood and to strike the earth with every kind of plague as often as they want.
>
> Now when they have finished their testimony, the beast that comes up from the Abyss will attack them, and overpower and kill them. Their bodies will lie in the public square of the great city—which is figuratively called Sodom and Egypt—where also their Lord was crucified. For three and a half days some from every people, tribe, language and nation will gaze on their bodies and refuse them burial. The inhabitants of the earth will gloat over them and will celebrate by sending each other gifts, because these two prophets had tormented those who live on the earth.
>
> But after the three and a half days the breath of life from God entered them, and they stood on their feet, and terror struck those who saw them. Then they heard a loud voice from heaven saying to them, "Come up here." And they went up to heaven in a cloud, while their enemies looked on.
>
> At that very hour there was a severe earthquake and a tenth of the city collapsed. Seven thousand people were killed in the earthquake, and the survivors were terrified and gave glory to the God of heaven. (Rv 11:4–13)

Christians who expect a fulfillment in the future are probably waiting for a couple of Billy Grahams to take the world by storm in ancient clothing, perform astounding miracles, torment the heathens with their sermons, and become a public spectacle after their deaths. Trouble is, humanity has grown quite accustomed to the "fire and brimstone" sermons. What else could be preached that has not already been broadcast far and wide?

A vital clue is obtained by wondering why John was told to measure the temple with its worshippers. The answer is simple yet profound: it still existed.

The spiritual realm was alerting us that it had taken John back in time to an earlier era. The trampling of the holy city for 42 months refers to when the Romans would later assault Jerusalem and destroy the temple during the revolt of 66–73 CE, which is a milestone event in the apocalyptic prophecies.

[Note: John had not seen an otherworldly temple, for a few paragraphs later he differentiated the temple to be measured from God's temple he saw in heaven (Rv 11:19). He had not seen a rebuilt temple in the 21st century or beyond either. If he had, surely he would have commented about the bizarre nature of the worshippers' clothing and all that surrounded it such as cars, paved roads and streetlights. Yet his letter gives us no indication he saw anything abnormal from the ancient way of life.]

In this ancient era when the Jews were offering sacrifices in their temple, God was trying to redirect his wayward people. As Ezekiel quoted him, they were stubborn and obstinate, a rebellious nation whose fathers had been revolting against him all the way up to the present (Ezk 2:3–4).

The Jews were striving for God but were gravely askew from him. Nevertheless, he had promised them an Anointed One (§4.2.), and Jesus eventually arrived to guide them home. For testimony to be valid, two witnesses were needed (Dt 19:15; Mt 18:16). The first was John the Baptist, who supposedly testified to Jesus's divine identity (Jn 1:34). The second was Jesus himself, who supposedly said the Father's work he was doing was testifying that he had been sent by God (Jn 5:36).

This is the heart of the story of the spiritual realm and Judaism. Revelation referred to it with the two witnesses who would "prophesy for 1,260 days" while "clothed in sackcloth."

Sackcloth is a thick garment made of goat or camel's hair, and John the Baptist wore clothing made from camel's hair (Mt 3:4; Mk 1:6). Camel's hair was the expected clothing of Jewish prophets (2 Kgs 1:8; Zec 13:4). It was also worn to demonstrate mourning and penitence. Jesus purportedly wept over Jerusalem and how it could not recognize the time of God's coming (Lk 19:41–44).

In addition, only one person in the Bible is credited with having the "power to shut up the heavens so that it will not rain" (Rv 11:6). That person was the prophet Elijah (1 Kgs 17:1). Since Jesus was twice quoted as having said that John the Baptist was Elijah (§A.2.a.), the Revelatory passage about preventing rain is a fascinating reference to the soul who walked the earth as Elijah and John the Baptist.

Revelation's two witnesses had supernatural abilities, prophesied for three and a half years, were killed in Jerusalem, had their dead bodies involved in a public spectacle, yet were resurrected some three days later. Moving beyond the expectation that both witnesses had (or will have) exactly the same talents and experiences, John the Baptist and Jesus were in all likelihood the men portrayed by the prophecy. Between the two of them, they essentially fulfilled all the impossible requirements.

John of Patmos did not recognize his Lord because he was not the disciple John from six decades prior. Moreover, the vision was probably abstracted and vague because of the spiritual realm's agenda. Now that we are awakening, though, we know where to look and can identify the two witnesses from the police sketch. The spiritual realm highlighted them in the precursor to the seventh trumpet because of their monumental roles but in a way that would remain a mystery until the appointed time.

10.4.b. Trumpet #7: The Manifestation of the Divine Kingdom

The seventh angel then sounded his trumpet. John heard loud voices proclaim that the divine kingdom had prevailed on earth and would rule forever (Rv 11:15). This corroborates the spiritual awakening paradigm and our identification of the two witnesses who first heralded it.

All in all, this brief slice of prophecy has just two milestone events. The first is the birth of the divine kingdom, which occurred a long time ago with the two witnesses. The second is when it finally triumphs over the darkness, which is in the future and will be celebrated with the seventh trumpet.

John also quoted the worship of 24 elders in heaven. Their praise includes a noteworthy statement that the time had come to judge the dead, reward the dutiful, and destroy those who destroy the world (Rv 11:18). Again, there is only one source of earthly destruction in Revelation: wayward humans.

John continued, "Then God's temple in heaven was opened, and within his temple was seen the ark of his covenant. And there came flashes of lightning, rumblings, peals of thunder, an earthquake and a severe hailstorm" (Rv 11:19). With this abrupt termination of John's vision, we have been alerted that the prophecy is shifting gears. Having just shown us the divine seeds that would eventually bloom into the seventh trumpet's everlasting kingdom, the spiritual realm transported him back on the timeline to witness another view of history.

10.5. Global Story, Slice #3: Religion's Dark Reign

The next slice of prophecy foretold why there would be such a long gap between the two witnesses and the seventh trumpet. This topic should sound familiar, for it was also a big part of Daniel's prophecies (§7.3.i.).

10.5.a. Understanding Beasts With Multiple Heads and Horns

We need to first understand the foundational metaphor of a beast with seven heads and ten horns, for three different variations of it appear in Revelation. As we learned from Daniel, a horn represents one or more kings who have power over the masses. This power primarily pertains to matters of the body and what people do, hence the more animalistic symbol of a horn and its connotation of physical domination. With Revelation's panoramic view of history, the ten horns symbolize a series of monarchs in one or more empires.

In the first two variations of the foundational metaphor, a head represents a religious leader such as a high priest or pope who has power over the masses. This power primarily pertains to matters of the mind and what people believe, hence the more human symbol of a head and its connotation of mental domination. Multiple heads represent a religious institution and its continuity from one leader to another. In these two cases, seven heads were depicted to pinpoint a particular religion.

With the last variation, the spiritual realm abstracted things out to get the widest-angle view of history. In this case, each head represents a religion.

We never see a beast with only heads and no horns. That is because religion cannot dominate the masses if it is not backed by rulers, laws and soldiers. Herein lies the deadly power of the beasts of Revelation. Here, then, is the core meaning of the metaphor.

<u>A beast with seven heads and ten horns represents a dominating partnership of government and religion that lords over its subjects</u>. Such a beast generates its power over the masses by ruling both the body (via laws and force) and the mind (via deceptive teachings and fear). This is the essence of the metaphor. Now it is simply a matter of examining the details of each appearance to understand what the spiritual realm wants us to see.

10.5.b. The Woman and the Red Dragon

Returning to the prophecy, John continued:

> A great sign appeared in heaven: a woman clothed with the sun, with the moon under her feet and a crown of twelve stars on her head. She was pregnant and cried out in pain as she was about to give birth. Then another sign appeared in heaven: an enormous red dragon with seven heads and ten horns and seven crowns on its heads. Its tail swept a third of the stars out of the sky and flung them to the earth. The dragon stood in front of the woman who was about to give birth, so that it might devour her child the moment he was born. She gave birth to a son, a male child, who "will rule all the nations with

an iron scepter." And her child was snatched up to God and to his throne. (Rv 12:1–5)

The twelve stars represent the original tribes of Israel, and the woman represents the Jewish people. From them was born a son—Jesus of Nazareth—whose spiritual teachings will eventually govern the world (§7.3.c.). The Anointed One had an archenemy, but it was not the mythical devil. As seen in Chapter 4, the mighty force that had it out for him was his religion of origin. Yes, the red dragon represents the ancient institution of Judaism.

Although it has directed moral behavior and countless acts of goodness, the ancient institution is represented as a dragon because the prophecy is about our spiritual evolution. It had gained enormous power by having indoctrinated a slew of erroneous and deadly beliefs, and it would rather kill spiritual teachers than grow toward higher understandings.

Preaching the fallacy that God is exclusively male, the dragon cursed women to subservience in its Garden of Eve deception. Per the dragon, God plays favorites and wanted his chosen people to invade their promised land and slaughter its inhabitants. Per the dragon, God is a jealous and insecure deity who demanded the execution of any man, woman or child who dared to explore another religion. Per the dragon, homosexual acts were to be punished with death. Per the dragon, God is a neurotic and wrathful deity who required animal sacrifices to atone for sin.

Prior to the sixth century BCE, both the heads (high priests) and horns (Judaic kings) were united in a Jewish theocracy. The spiritual realm could have used any number of heads to signify a procession of religious leaders, but seven were shown because it is the signature number of Judaism (§7.4.b., §K.4.c.). The crowns are on the heads because the dragon's power was primarily derived from religious beliefs, not monarchical authority. For instance, the Jews often lived under the rule of Judaic law even when other empires were their overlords.

When the Messiah appeared, the force-wielding state was the Roman Empire and thus the symbolism of ten horns (§7.3.b.). The dragon's religious leaders (the high priest and Sanhedrin) collaborated with its governing rulers (local Jewish kings like Herod and Roman procurators like Pilate) to enact its intentions.

As Judaism believes it is comprised of God's chosen people at the exclusion of others, it is steeped in narcissism. Denying the need for spiritual growth as an institution, it is steeped in egoic pride. When its Anointed One came with spiritual correction, the dragon was red with narcissistic rage. It eliminated him, and thus the woman's sacred son was snatched up to God. John then wrote:

The woman fled into the wilderness to a place prepared for

her by God, where she might be taken care of for 1,260 days.

Then war broke out in heaven. Michael and his angels fought against the dragon, and the dragon and his angels fought back. But he was not strong enough, and they lost their place in heaven. The great dragon was hurled down— that ancient serpent called the devil, or Satan, who leads the whole world astray. He was hurled to the earth, and his angels with him.

Then I heard a loud voice in heaven say: "Now have come the salvation and the power and the kingdom of our God, and the authority of his Messiah. For the accuser of our brothers and sisters, who accuses them before our God day and night, has been hurled down. They triumphed over him by the blood of the Lamb and by the word of their testimony; they did not love their lives so much as to shrink from death. Therefore rejoice, you heavens and you who dwell in them! But woe to the earth and the sea, because the devil has gone down to you! He is filled with fury, because he knows that his time is short."

When the dragon saw that he had been hurled to the earth, he pursued the woman who had given birth to the male child. The woman was given the two wings of a great eagle, so that she might fly to the place prepared for her in the wilderness, where she would be taken care of for a time, times and half a time, out of the serpent's reach. Then from his mouth the serpent spewed water like a river, to overtake the woman and sweep her away with the torrent. But the earth helped the woman by opening its mouth and swallowing the river that the dragon had spewed out of his mouth. Then the dragon was enraged at the woman and went off to wage war against the rest of her offspring—those who keep God's commands and hold fast their testimony about Jesus. The dragon stood on the shore of the sea. (Rv 12:6–13:1)

Michael is the angel who protects the Jewish people (§7.5.a.). A servant of God who desires the spiritual growth of his flock, his nemesis was the Messiah's nemesis: the ancient institution of Judaism. His out-of-the-blue appearance here confirms we are in sync with the spiritual realm.

The dragon is not an indestructible entity of eternal life. Rather, it is only a creation of collective belief that will exist only as long as the Jews empower it by embracing its dogma. It had a place in heaven as a valid stage 2 religion, but like the dinosaurs it was not destined to live forever. Because of an eternal truth and divine process that has a far greater intention for humanity, it was cast out of heaven.

Since free will is honored, it was free to exist on earth as long as the Jews wanted it. Yet it would not be given a free ride to blind them forever. It would have to deal with the Messiah as the darkness suddenly had to contest with the Light.

Contrary to John's commentary that he had just witnessed the devil, his vision simply reflects the metaphysical story of the Jews and their religion. As for his quoting of the loud voice in heaven also using the devil word, either that being was also uninformed or John overlaid his understanding while documenting what he remembered. Chances are it was the latter.

Because the dragon rejected the Messiah's spiritual correction, everyday Jews were put to the test. One option was breaking from family and cultural traditions to embrace the Messiah's teachings. The other was avoiding the inner and outer conflicts and remaining in the dragon's domain.

Most Jews naturally opted for the latter as indicated by the woman fleeing into the wilderness, which is a desolate place that represents being lost and far away from one's spiritual home. In a more physical sense, the dragon motivated their revolts that resulted in their diaspora and desolate existence away from their homeland.

The dragon thus survived and continued spewing its teachings that appealed to deep emotion (for which water is the classic metaphysical symbol). But the earth swallowed up the torrent, which represents the truth that nothing could ultimately harm these wayward souls. Just like Cain wandering through the wilderness, the Jews would always remain divinely protected and loved despite their dance with the dragon (§10.3.e.).

John was most likely informed that the physical aspect of their sojourn in the wilderness would be for the mysterious "time, times and half a time"—which is how he wrote it the second time around—but he erred by calculating it to 1,260 days for the first mention (§10.2.b.). As we now know from Daniel, the phrase refers to the prophetic period that concluded in the 1960s. Revelation concurs that the Jews would have a desolate experience until their deliverance at that time (§7.5.).

During the Messiah's brief ministry, the dragon only had a tiny fraction of the coercive force the Church would later wield with its partnering empires. Nevertheless, the Judaic religious leaders "went off to wage war against the rest of her offspring" who dared break from their orthodoxy. This was exemplified by Saul and his fellow zealots persecuting the Jews who had embraced Jesus and were forsaking the law.

Because of its subsequent revolts, the dragon lost the last vestiges of coercive force it derived from collaborating with Rome. This dynamic was depicted by the woman being "out of the serpent's reach" and the dragon standing ominously but harmlessly on the shore of the sea.

10.5.c. The First Beast

The spiritual realm's next target for illumination was the Roman Catholic Church and its offshoots, which would wield the power of numerous empires to crush truth-seeking and spiritual growth for well over a thousand years. Symbolizing the totalitarian beast of church and state in its many forms was far more challenging, but the spiritual realm was up to the task. The prophecy continues:

> And I saw a beast coming out of the sea. It had ten horns and seven heads, with ten crowns on its horns, and on each head a blasphemous name. The beast I saw resembled a leopard, but had feet like those of a bear and a mouth like that of a lion. The dragon gave the beast his power and his throne and great authority. One of the heads of the beast seemed to have had a fatal wound, but the fatal wound had been healed. The whole world was filled with wonder and followed the beast. People worshiped the dragon because he had given authority to the beast, and they also worshiped the beast and asked, "Who is like the beast? Who can wage war against it?" (Rv 13:1–4)

[Note: These verses were previously presented (§10.2.b.). Parts 2 and 3 of that passage have not been repeated because they are far less relevant and a litany of John's commentary.]

In Daniel, each of the animals represents a different empire (§7.3.b.). This time the spiritual realm showed a blended beast with ten horns and traits of a leopard, bear and lion to signify an aggregation of empires. The secular side of this wide-ranging beast manifested as the Roman Empire, the Holy Roman Empire that ruled the heart of Europe from 800 to 1806, the Byzantine Empire (the eastern half of the old Roman Empire) that ruled from Constantinople until 1453, and various European monarchies such as England, France and Spain.

Ten horns are depicted because Daniel's terrifying beast of ten horns foretold the Roman Empire (§7.3.b.) and Revelation's first beast came into being when the Roman Empire empowered Catholicism. The crowns are on the horns to highlight the power of the collaborating empires to subjugate the masses with laws and soldiers. After all, Christianity was a state religion that routinely called on this force to crush heretical movements. Moreover, the Catholic hierarchy glorified and crowned the rule of monarchies instead of deflating them.

Meanwhile, the seven heads represent the religious side of this monstrosity and its Judaic roots. They are not signifying Judaism, though, for Judaism is symbolized by the dragon. The seven heads are exclusively Christian, and the lion's share of the religious side of the beast was the Roman Catholic Church.

The blasphemous names on the heads refer to the headlining deceptions of the ecclesiastical rulers. From papal titles like the Holy Father and Vicar of Christ to claims like salvation only coming through the Church, they were all telling the big lie that they were flawlessly teaching the truth and ruling with God's authority.

Fortunately, the spiritual realm could foresee this dark future. To ensure the success of the great awakening, it gave us plenty of confirmation for this identification.

For instance, the "dragon gave the beast his power and his throne and great authority" refers to how Christianity was an extension of Judaism. The new religion was based on the Jews' Messiah and derived its pedigree and legitimacy from their ancient scriptures and validating prophecies. It also claimed the dragon's throne as the king of monotheism.

Meanwhile, the fatal head wound signifies the damage that was originally inflicted upon this religion. Although Nero executed Christians as scapegoats for the fire of Rome, they were generally free from an emperor's persecution for their first two centuries. Nevertheless, they were occasionally attacked in local pogroms and put on trial by local authorities for refusing to appease the Roman gods.

Beginning with Decius (249–251), though, the Roman Empire began systematically crushing Christianity. State laws were enacted that imposed penalties for being a Christian (including executions), although Rome relented in 260. The harshest persecution of all occurred when Rome tried to extinguish Christianity with a new wave of draconian laws during an especially brutal eight years of assault from 303 to 311.

Because the Roman Empire was splitting its Christian head wide open with an ax, the world was astonished when it suddenly reversed itself and made Christianity its official and exclusive religion by the end of the century. The fatal head wound was indeed dramatically healed.

Recall Gabriel's prophecy that foretold how the Roman Empire would set up the Catholic Church and its Bible on the Jewish scriptures (§7.4.). The masses thus worshipped the dragon via the dogma that its Messiah and the Old Testament were divinely authoritative. They also worshipped the beast, which waged war against heretical Christians for well over a thousand years. Indeed, nobody could stand against the totalitarian monster that was the perpetual marriage of church and state.

10.5.d. The Second Beast, Part 1: Mirroring the First Beast

The Church was an essential part of the first beast but took on a beastly life of its own when the popes ruled the Papal States of Italy from 756 to 1870. Because it was also a well-disguised beast, the spiritual realm gave it a special metaphor. John wrote:

> Then I saw a second beast, coming out of the earth. It had two horns like a lamb, but it spoke like a dragon. It exercised all the authority of the first beast on its behalf, and made the earth and its inhabitants worship the first beast, whose fatal wound had been healed. And it performed great signs, even causing fire to come down from heaven to the earth in full view of the people. Because of the signs it was given power to perform on behalf of the first beast, it deceived the inhabitants of the earth. It ordered them to set up an image in honor of the beast who was wounded by the sword and yet lived. The second beast was given power to give breath to the image of the first beast, so that the image could speak and cause all who refused to worship the image to be killed. (Rv 13:11–15)

John gives the impression that the second beast looked like an innocent lamb. If so, it was a perfect metaphor for the Church presenting an image of being like Jesus. In any case, the lamblike beast spoke like a dragon with its arrogance and dominating authority.

After the Church married the Roman Empire in the fourth century, it "exercised all the authority of the first beast" to eradicate its religious competitors. It returned the favor by ensuring Christians were also dutiful subjects of the state because its Bible dictates submission to the governing authorities (Rom 13:1; Ti 3:1; 1 Pt 2:13–14). The Church thus made the masses "worship the first beast" (the marriage of church and state).

The two horns depict the Church's split into its Roman Catholic and Eastern Orthodox branches in the 11th century. At the heart of the schism was the West's belief the bishop of Rome (pope) had primacy over everybody versus the East's belief the bishop of Constantinople was equal in power to him.

Meanwhile, some Catholics were able to perform "great signs, even causing fire to come down from heaven to the earth in full view of the people." The fire represents the divine, and the Church has always been enamored with documenting and promoting miracles. To be deemed a saint, one must be credited with at least one miracle.

Scholar Keith Thomas notes that the Church itself did not claim miraculous powers, "But it reaped prestige from the doings of those of its members to whom God was deemed to have extended miraculous gifts."[16] These reports became imbedded in various rituals and holy objects that purportedly offered supernatural benefits, and they were especially prevalent in prayerful invocations. Thomas explains how the worshipping of saints "depended upon the belief that the holy men and women of the past had not merely exemplified an ideal code of moral conduct, but could still employ supernatural power to relieve the adversities of their followers upon earth."[17]

The Church and its offshoots indeed "deceived the inhabitants of the earth." Jesus foretold the religious deception and how this servant would behave as a tyrant when it got drunk on external power (§9.3.e., §9.4.d.). Its lamblike facade reflects his saying, "Watch out for false prophets. They come to you in sheep's clothing, but inwardly they are ferocious wolves. By their fruit you will recognize them" (Mt 7:15–16). More of this fruit will be observed later.

The second beast ordering the masses to set up an "image of the first beast" refers to their submitting to the monarchy of the papacy. The Church first began mirroring the Roman Empire with the monarchical bishop. It completed its beastly makeover with the papacy and thereby fashioned its own emperor who was also revered as a demigod.

At the heart of this image is *the* image of being a king. Until 1978, new popes were crowned with the papal tiara (an ornately bejeweled three-tiered crown). They still dress in royal attire to look like a king.

With the papal throne indoctrinated as the Vicar of Christ, the second beast spoke through this image as a supreme religious authority. As history sadly documents, those who did not submit to and thereby worship the monarchical Church were often killed.

10.5.e. The Second Beast, Part 2: Mark, Name and Number

The second beast's identity is already obvious, but the spiritual realm pinpointed it even more:

> It also forced all people, great and small, rich and poor, free and slave, to receive a mark on their right hands or on their foreheads, so that they could not buy or sell unless they had the mark, which is the name of the beast or the number of its name.
>
> This calls for wisdom. Let the person who has insight calculate the number of the beast, for it is the number of a man. That number is 666. (Rv 13:16–18)

Being marked means being a Catholic. The Jews were the largest religious minority in Europe during the Middle Ages, lacked the mark, and could not freely participate in commerce. They were widely prohibited from owning land and severely restricted in their professional options. They were essentially forced into socially inferior occupations like tax collecting and money lending, which were off limits to Christians because usury (charging interest on a loan) was prohibited.

Moreover, Jews were banished from England in 1290, France in 1306, Switzerland in 1348, Hungary in 1349, Austria in 1422, Spain in 1492, Lithuania in 1495 and Portugal in 1497. Many Germanic territories also expelled them from the 14th through 16th centuries. To buy or sell in Europe's most powerful kingdoms, you had to be there. Submitting to the Church and being marked as one of its own was the price of being there.

In numerous European cities where Jews had not been expelled, ghettos were established in the 15th and 16th centuries, most notably the ghetto of Rome established by Pope Paul IV in 1555. Having been walled off from the Catholic social and business world, Jews were thus severely restricted in their freedom to buy and sell.

The classic mark of Catholicism is the sign of the cross. Although it was a prominent symbol in numerous cultures of antiquity, it was not a significant part of Christianity's first three centuries. Scholar Graydon Snyder observes, "The universal use of the sign of the cross makes more poignant the striking lack of crosses in early Christian art scenes, especially any specific reference to the event on Golgotha."[18] He adds, "The cross symbol, as an artistic reference to the passion event, cannot be found prior to the time of Constantine."[19] It is interesting how the cross did not become the quintessential sign of Catholicism until the Church had married the Roman Empire.

The spiritual realm had to code this exceptional identifier so it would remain a mystery. Had the cross been directly foretold, the Church would have ducked its biblical badge of darkness by establishing something else. The spiritual realm thus rendered a three-sided mystery whereby the identity of the mark would also be the "name of the beast" and the "number of its name."

This mystery attracted all kinds of answers over the centuries, but they all fail to fulfill the three interrelated sides (not to mention the rest of the prophecy's correlated clues). With the insights of the great awakening, though, the mystery has been unraveled.

As for the mark of the beast being on the foreheads of Catholics, Tertullian (c. 155–230) attested to its presence when he wrote, "Whatever employment occupies us, we mark our forehead with the sign of the cross."[20] Saint Augustine (354–430) wrote, "In no secret place do I keep the Cross of Christ, but bear it on my forehead…Let me not have a bare forehead, let the Cross of my Lord cover it."[21]

More importantly, the cross is also marked physically. During the annual ceremony of Ash Wednesday, it is marked on foreheads with the ashes of burned palm branches.

As for the mark of the beast on the right hand, the prophecy foretold the traditional greeting process between the laity and clergy in the Eastern Orthodox branch of Catholicism. A modern book explains:

> When we approach an Orthodox Presbyter or Bishop (but not a Deacon), we make a bow by reaching down and touching the floor with our right hand, place our right hand over the left (palms upward), and say: "Bless, Father" (or "Bless, Your Grace," or "Bless, Your Eminence," etc.). The Priest or Bishop then answers, "May the Lord bless you," blesses us with the Sign of the Cross, and places his right hand in our hands. We kiss then his hand.[22]

The clergy's sign of the cross is not directed only at the layman's right hand. However, the right hand is at the center of this marking ritual.

As for the next part of the mystery, the mark of the beast (the sign of Jesus being crucified) is also the beast's name: "crucifier of Christ." From a spiritual perspective, this name indeed reflected the Church's behavior.

Jesus taught that whatever was done to the least of humanity was done to him (Mt 25:40). The Inquisition tortured or executed tens of thousands of people who did not conform to Catholicism, and the witch hunts murdered even more. Most prominently, though, the Church's demonization and persecution of the Jews ultimately resulted in the Holocaust. Pope John XXIII (1958–1963) acknowledged this history when he prayed, "Forgive us the curse which we unjustly laid on the name of the Jews. Forgive us, that with our curse, we crucified Thee a second time."[23]

For the final side of the mystery, 666 is the number of the beast's name, which is synonymous with its mark. Any interpretation for the 666 that does not triangulate with the beast's name and mark must be rejected.

In both ancient Hebrew and Greek, numbers were recorded with letters from their alphabets. Just like the Roman system, each letter has a corresponding numerical value. This opens the door for a slew of solutions. According to the most popular one, the Hebrew version of "Neron Caesar" adds up to 666. However, this interpretation fails on five counts.

First, it is preposterous that a Christian author writing in Greek would suddenly and without warning revert to Judaism's Hebrew to communicate a Christian message to Greek readers in western Turkey. Second, the solution is jury-rigged with the "n" appended to Nero's name. Third, the rules of Hebrew numbering hold that the second time the letter *nun* ("n") appears in a word, its value is 700. "Neron Caesar" thus adds up to 1316, not 666.[24] Fourth, a reference to a Roman emperor would be applicable for the first beast with ten horns and seven heads but not for the second beast with the lamblike horns. Finally, it fails the triangulation test.

In the 180s CE, Irenaeus proposed an ironic solution with *Lateinos*, the ancient Greek word for "the Latin-speaking man." The bishop figured it was referring to the Roman emperor. What little did he know that Latin would later become the official language of the Church and its papal monarch. Anyway, a handful of other letter-summation solutions have been proposed over the centuries, including *Italika Ekklesia* (the Italian Church). However, they all fail the triangulation test of being synonymous with the beast's mark and name.

The true solution resides in a different approach. Acrostics were often used by ancient religious sects to protect secrets from outsiders. In an acrostic, each letter stands for a word or phrase that begins with that letter.

The number 666 is recorded in Revelation by the Greek letters *chi* (value of 600), *xi* (value of 60) and *stigma* (value of 6). So what secret is imbedded in an acrostic of these letters?

Chi is the first letter of *Christos*, which is the Greek word for "the Anointed One." *Xi* is the first letter of *xulon*, which means wooden substance or tree and is used five different times in the New Testament for the cross of Jesus's crucifixion (Acts 5:30, 10:39, 13:29; Gal 3:13; 1 Pt 2:24). *Stigma* is an obsolete Greek letter that by itself has the meaning of "a hole, or mark, made with a pointed instrument."[25] The plural of *stigma*, by the way, is *stigmata*, which is the phenomenon of wounds that suddenly appear and resemble a crucifixion.

A compelling acrostic for 666, then, is "Christ, cross, pierced."[26] These words clearly point to the crucifix, which is the preeminent symbol of Catholicism. Most importantly, this impressive solution joins the beast's mark (the sign of the cross) and name (crucifier of Christ) in a powerful triangulation of cohesive meaning that aligns with the rest of Revelation.

[Note: There is nothing inherently evil about the crucifix or cross. The spiritual realm simply pointed it out for identification purposes only. Any symbol is what you make of it. If the cross represents your commitment to living the teachings of Jesus no matter what the world does to you, it is an enlightened symbol.]

10.5.f. Remembering the Crusades, Inquisition and Witch Hunts

When Daniel's "abomination that causes desolation" was revealed to be the Catholic Church, the verdict was backed by an illumination of its darkness (§7.4.). Revelation has added some amazing corroboration that Catholicism unwittingly perpetrated the greatest deception of all time.

For those who find it hard to accept the Church is the second beast of

Revelation and a signature part of the first beast as well, another serving of historical fruit is in order. Appendix N ("The Wolf in Sheep's Clothing") summarizes the Crusades, Inquisition and witch hunts.

While most people have heard about those gruesome events, few know much at all about the crusade against the Cathars ("the pure ones," from the Greek *katharos*) in southern France. In 1209, the Church launched a war against these peaceful and ascetic Christians who had abandoned the opulent wealth and power of the Catholic hierarchy. In this case, we do not need to see through the wolf's disguise. Rather, the wolf openly and viciously attacked a flock of defenseless sheep. The massacres morphed into a senseless war between Catholic nobles and resulted in a death toll of about two million people (§N.2.b.).

The spiritual realm foretold how the second beast would mark foreheads with the sign of the cross. Now consider how, as Catholic scholar James Carroll summarizes, the Spanish Inquisition operated: "Repentant heretics were reconciled to the Church by being signed with the cross on the forehead, as the friar intoned, 'Receive the sign of the cross, which you denied and lost through being deceived.'"[27] We now know the deception was working in the polar opposite direction.

10.5.g. Keeping Things in Perspective

Since another biblical prophecy is shocking the Judaic and Catholic faithful, perhaps more commentary is in order (§7.4.i.). We have all been fooled by the illusion of the physical universe and its mistaken paradigms. But we are all destined to awaken, so leverage this awareness to challenge your beliefs and leave the darkness behind.

Meanwhile, the Eastern Orthodox, Anglican/Episcopalian and Protestant churches are in no position to gloat. They are all branches of a Catholic tree whose New Testament trunk is badly twisted from errors, deceptions and wayward Old Testament roots.

Nevertheless, Judaism and Christianity have many wise teachings. So let us draw out the best and discard the rest.

10.5.h. The Lamb, the Firstfruits and the Three Angels

John then saw before him the Lamb standing atop Mount Zion along with 144,000 who had the Lamb's name and God's name on their foreheads. John heard a sound from heaven that was like roaring waters, pealing thunder and harpists strumming their harps. The 144,000 were singing a new song to the throne and its heavenly attendees that nobody else could learn. These folks had kept themselves pure on earth and been redeemed from it. They were offered up as firstfruits to the Lamb and God (Rv 14:1–5).

At first glance, the passage refers to the same group of 144,000 who came from the twelve tribes of Israel (§10.3.e.). Upon closer examination, though, it is most likely a different group that John mistakenly assumed were the same folks in a different setting.

The first group was identified as exclusively Jewish, John was explicitly told 144,000, the setting was on the earth, they were not in front of the Lamb, and seals had been placed on their foreheads. However, this second group's ethnicity was not specified, John did not record having been told a total, the setting is in heaven, they were singing before the Lamb, and the names of Jesus and God were written on their foreheads. Chances are John guessed that there were 144,000 in this heavenly multitude.

In any case, the passage's details are unimportant. What matters is staying in tune with the spiritual realm's song. The third slice of Revelatory history just finished with the way things have been and is transitioning toward the great awakening. Revelation once again jumps forward in time because the spiritual realm had nothing else to foretell here besides the divine kingdom being crushed by the dark beasts but eventually triumphing.

The heavenly view of firstfruits is at the end of the era of beastly dominance. These leading-edge souls found the narrow gate and did their transformative work despite having little guidance or support from the world at large.

The passage is concurrent with the fifth seal from the first slice of Revelatory history. The last of the five seals depicting life on our planet features righteous souls who had been slain because of religion—the beasts we just saw—and were told to wait awhile longer (§10.3.c.). We know from the sixth seal that the next big event would be the widespread breakthrough of spiritual truth (§10.3.d.). So are we singing in key? John wrote:

> Then I saw another angel flying in midair, and he had the eternal gospel to proclaim to those who live on the earth—to every nation, tribe, language and people. He said in a loud voice, "Fear God and give him glory, because the hour of his judgment has come. Worship him who made the heavens, the earth, the sea and the springs of water."
>
> A second angel followed and said, "Fallen! Fallen is Babylon the Great, which made all the nations drink the maddening wine of her adulteries."
>
> A third angel followed them and said in a loud voice: "If anyone worships the beast and its image and receives its mark on their forehead or on their hand, they, too, will drink the wine of God's fury, which has been poured full strength into the cup of his wrath. They will be tormented with burning sulfur in the presence of the holy angels and of the Lamb. And

> the smoke of their torment will rise for ever and ever. There will be no rest day or night for those who worship the beast and its image, or for anyone who receives the mark of its name." This calls for patient endurance on the part of the people of God who keep his commands and remain faithful to Jesus.
>
> Then I heard a voice from heaven say, "Write this: Blessed are the dead who die in the Lord from now on."
>
> "Yes," says the Spirit, "they will rest from their labor, for their deeds will follow them." (Rv 14:6–13)

The first angel's "eternal gospel" of spiritual truth affirms we are singing with the heavenly choir, which means this passage parallels the sixth seal and is occurring in the 21st century. This angel flying in midair signifies how these revolutionary insights will reach "every nation, tribe, language and people" in record time (thanks to our political and technological evolution in prior centuries). By the way, the "eternal gospel" is not the biblical gospel, which has already been preached around the world and is a gross distortion of the "eternal gospel."

Although the angel advocated fearing God, the essence of the message is to have great awe and reverence for our spiritual evolution and go all in with it. The "hour of his judgment has come" refers to the appointed time of the great awakening and the end of the line for the religious beasts and their descendants.

As for the nature of the judgment, the heavenly side of God will not be doing the judging. Rather, the God that is the individuated souls of each one of us will be deciding their fate. As lost souls enter through the narrow gate, the religious institutions they leave behind will be collapsing. These developments are a perfect segue to the announcements of the next two angels.

The full meaning of the second angel's "Fallen is Babylon the Great" will be explained later in the final slice of Revelatory history. It refers to the end of the long era of empires.

Thanks to democracy's freedom of religion and distribution of power, the first beast of ten horns and seven heads is essentially dead. Although the second beast with two horns has ducked its date with destiny, the second angel's mystery was that the final empire would finally fall.

The third angel's warning is simple. If you continue to worship the second beast and its image (the papal monarchy pretending to be a divine authority; §10.5.d.) and receive its mark (the sign of the cross; §10.5.e.), you will continue to suffer. It primarily refers to Catholicism but includes all versions of biblical Christianity.

In a tragic case of being so close yet so far away, these folks "will be tormented with burning sulfur in the presence of the holy angels and of the Lamb."

As the sulfur represents teachings of divine vengeance (§10.3.i.), the passage identifies Christians who are still embracing their misguided religion. Afraid of burning in hell, they are afraid to spiritually grow beyond their religious authorities and the Bible.

The spiritual realm could not have been more direct in a prophecy that needed to remain a mystery. Those who continue to embrace biblical Christianity will be in their churches seeking the divine and will thus be in the presence of the holy angels and Jesus. Trouble is, they will not experience true communion with God until they clear out the false beliefs and fears that gum up that channel.

"There will be no rest day or night for those who worship the beast and its image" refers to how biblical Christianity fosters psychological pain. In addition to the consequences of embracing false beliefs about the nature of us and God (§3.6.a.), a believer's psyche is torn between the "good" spirit and the "evil" flesh. This polarization generates unnecessary suffering by barring the believer from a healthy integration of mind, body and soul.

For instance, psychiatrist M. Scott Peck detailed his treatment of a tormented young Catholic woman who felt horrible guilt about her sexual desires and feared divine punishment. He reported Kathy's case so extensively, he said, "because it is so typical of the relationship between religious upbringing and psychopathology. There are millions of Kathys."[28]

As for the "the dead who die in the Lord from now on," the dead are those who are still asleep in the dust of the earth (§7.5.a.). Their egos are alive and kicking, but their souls are buried by the fears and deceptions of the darkness. They are spiritual carcasses being fed upon by religious vultures (§9.4.b.).

Those who "die in the Lord" are those who suffer through the deaths of their egos to embark upon the journey home to God. When they die this way, they will truly begin to live (Mt 16:24–25; Mk 8:34–35; Lk 9:23–24).

The spiritual realm has a special metaphor for this process, which the third angel introduced as drinking "the wine of God's fury." It is a perfect segue into the next passage of prophecy, wherein we find more heavenly confirmation that we are in sync with the truth.

10.5.i. The Great Harvest

John continued:

> I looked, and there before me was a white cloud, and seated on the cloud was one like a son of man with a crown of gold on his head and a sharp sickle in his hand. Then another angel came out of the temple and called in a loud voice to him who was sitting on the cloud, "Take your sickle and reap, because

the time to reap has come, for the harvest of the earth is ripe." So he who was seated on the cloud swung his sickle over the earth, and the earth was harvested.

Another angel came out of the temple in heaven, and he too had a sharp sickle. Still another angel, who had charge of the fire, came from the altar and called in a loud voice to him who had the sharp sickle, "Take your sharp sickle and gather the clusters of grapes from the earth's vine, because its grapes are ripe." The angel swung his sickle on the earth, gathered its grapes and threw them into the great winepress of God's wrath. They were trampled in the winepress outside the city, and blood flowed out of the press, rising as high as the horses' bridles for a distance of 1,600 stadia [180 miles]. (Rv 14:14–20)

For many Christians, this predicts the days when millions of heathens will be plucked from their whereabouts and jammed into a colossal meat grinder. Trouble is, literal interpreters have no choice but to read this passage metaphorically, for those were grapes being gathered and thrown into a winepress, not people.

So why did the spiritual realm use this metaphor? If God is really going to slaughter humanity, why the grapes of wrath? But if something else is going on, why the harvest of grapes getting pressed into blood?

It should be obvious by now that our future will never involve divine vengeance. To understand the passage, we turn to the life and teachings of Jesus.

The Anointed One purportedly told his disciples to open their eyes and see the fields as ripe for harvesting. He alluded to himself as a reaper who was harvesting the crops for eternal life (Jn 4:35–36). According to another gospel, he had compassion on the helpless and harassed masses. The harvest was plentiful, he told his disciples, but the workers were few (Mt 9:36–37). His metaphor of harvesting was not referring to a divine annihilation but rather leading folks to the joy of divine reunification.

The process of life, our evolution to date and the widespread breakthrough of truth are rendering millions of souls ripe for harvest. The great harvest, then, is at the heart of our global awakening. It foretells how this process will be reaping the masses and breaking open their egoic shells (the grape skins) so they, too, selflessly pour out their life force (their blood) for a greater purpose.

Unfortunately, this will all be too much for much of the world. Still buried by the darkness both inside and out, these folks will hunker down in what they were taught as they cope with their neurotic suffering. Hence, there is more to the story of what it will take for our planet to awaken.

10.5.j. The Bowls of Wrath

Before continuing, we need to take a step back to see the big picture. As we journey through the third of Revelation's four holographic views, we are witnessing their overlapping nature. In other words, it is a grave mistake to expect these prophecies to be fulfilled in one incredibly long sequential order.

Their message is that the divine kingdom will overcome the darkness. The second slice presents an overview with its two witnesses declaring its inception and the seventh trumpet celebrating its improbable triumph (§10.4.).

As for the details, the first slice began with the first five seals depicting life in the darkness (§10.3.c.). The third slice began by depicting the beasts that would crush the divine kingdom for so long (§10.5.b.–§10.5.e.). After these slices reflected our dark history in different ways, they parallel one another more clearly and render corroborating views of the great awakening.

Here is the overlap we have seen so far. The first slice's souls who were slain "under the altar" and told to "wait a little longer" in heaven (seal #5; §10.3.c.) are concurrent with the third slice's firstfruits in heaven who had been redeemed from the world (§10.5.h.).

The first slice then depicted the disillusionment of the sudden and widespread breakthrough of spiritual truth (seal #6; §10.3.d.). The third slice mirrored it with the first angel proclaiming the "eternal gospel" to "every nation, tribe, language and people" (§10.5.h.).

Finally, the first slice showed a "great multitude" in heaven from "every nation, tribe, people and language" (§10.3.e.). The third slice mirrored it with the "eternal gospel" and Great Harvest (§10.5.i.), which show how the "great multitude" of the first slice would be produced.

For the first slice of Revelatory history, its next event was the opening of the seventh seal amid all kinds of smoke at the golden altar (§10.3.f.). It was followed by the first six trumpet blasts, and the seventh trumpet was eventually sounded.

Resuming now with the third slice of Revelatory history, John saw seven angels who had seven plagues that would complete God's wrath. The temple in heaven opened, and the seven angels emerged from it and were each given a golden bowl to pour out on the earth. Meanwhile, the smoke of God's glory filled the temple (Rv 15:1–8).

The continued symmetry strongly suggests more overlapping with the first slice. We can thus expect the seven bowls to mirror the seven trumpets. As it turns out, they are remarkably similar.

As we delve into the seven bowls of wrath with this orienting insight, remember that the seven trumpets were sounded because the widespread breakthrough of spiritual truth would not be enough to awaken the world. A planet of lost souls will need something more to begin embracing and living in the Light.

Remember as well that this is not the spiritual realm initiating wrathful things upon us. To the contrary, we are doing it to ourselves, and the prophecies simply foretold this awakening karma (§10.3.g.).

The winepress of the Great Harvest will be breaking open egoic shells at high gear, for a global breaking point is fast approaching that will awaken the world to a sobering truth. What we do to our environment, we do to ourselves. Because of reincarnation, there is no escaping our creation. The only way out is through the darkness of our egos and the self-righteous religions that have blinded us for so long.

10.5.k. Bowls #1 to #4: Environment and Ego, Revisited

Just like the first four trumpets (§10.3.g.), the first four bowls target the environment and reflect the dark reaction of egoic pride:

> The first angel went and poured out his bowl on the land, and ugly, festering sores broke out on the people who had the mark of the beast and worshiped its image.
>
> The second angel poured out his bowl on the sea, and it turned into blood like that of a dead person, and every living thing in the sea died.
>
> The third angel poured out his bowl on the rivers and springs of water, and they became blood. Then I heard the angel in charge of the waters say: "You are just in these judgments, O Holy One, you who are and who were; for they have shed the blood of your holy people and your prophets, and you have given them blood to drink as they deserve."
>
> And I heard the altar respond: "Yes, Lord God Almighty, true and just are your judgments."
>
> The fourth angel poured out his bowl on the sun, and the sun was allowed to scorch people with fire. They were seared by the intense heat and they cursed the name of God, who had control over these plagues, but they refused to repent and glorify him. (Rv 16:2–9)

With the first trumpet, "hail and fire mixed with blood" was "hurled down on the earth" (Rv 8:7). Here the first bowl was poured out on the land, so the common ground is both actions targeting the land.

With the second trumpet, "A third of the sea turned into blood" and "a third of the living creatures in the sea died" (Rv 8:8–9). Here the second bowl also hit the sea, turned it to blood, and killed its creatures.

With the third trumpet, a third of the rivers and springs of water turned bitter and led to many deaths (Rv 8:10). Here the third bowl also hit the rivers and springs of water.

With the fourth trumpet, the sun, moon and stars were all struck, which rendered them, the day and night partially dark. It is a metaphor for the darkness of egoic pride that would keep the world from seeing what we have been doing. Here the fourth bowl also hit the sun and told a similar story of egoic pride. Amid the obvious truth of global warming and its consequences, humanity got angry and refused to repent.

While the first four trumpets and bowls are not identical, they focus on the same aspects of the environment and the avoidance of egoic pride. This is far beyond coincidence and suggests the two different visions are of the same future. Perhaps the spiritual realm wanted to keep the holographic story from being unraveled until the appointed time. Perhaps the distorting effects of John's paradigm and memory led to the differences.

In any case, the symmetry becomes even more impressive with a little mixing and matching. The global warming of the first trumpet matches the sun's scorching heat of the fourth bowl, and the chronic diseases caused by the reckless application of science and technology in the third trumpet match the "ugly, festering sores" of the first bowl. After all, how else would you visually depict a chronic disease?

The interpretation of the first four bowls of wrath, then, is the same as the first four trumpet blasts (§10.3.g.). The self-inflicted pain from our assault upon our collective home will eventually wake us up.

10.5.1. Bowl #5: A Psychological Sting, Revisited

Trouble is, that process will be opposed by the devil inside of egoic pride. As the fifth trumpet foretold, egoic pride would darken the world with its deceptive smoke (§10.3.h.). As for the fifth bowl, John wrote: "The fifth angel poured out his bowl on the throne of the beast, and its kingdom was plunged into darkness. People gnawed their tongues in agony and cursed the God of heaven because of their pains and their sores, but they refused to repent of what they had done" (Rv 16:10–11).

Here is yet another matching parallel with a corresponding trumpet. Although the first four trumpets and bowls target the environment with allusions to egoic pride, the fifth ones zero in on the darkening impact of egoic pride.

The fifth bowl's "throne of the beast" is the power structure of the Catholic Church. At this point, the masses will at least be aware of the breakthrough of spiritual truth. With the Catholic kingdom being "plunged into darkness," the fifth bowl depicts them continuing to be deceived. It predicts the Church will oppose the great awakening and be supported by those who succumb to their own egoic pride and remain submitted. The darkness will still be bonded with the darkness.

The fifth trumpet highlights the psychological sting that is felt when the truth pierces the Teflon defense of egoic pride (§10.3.h.). The fifth bowl refers to a similar thing but emphasizes the reaction of the unrepentant ego. Here we see it doubling down on its neurotic suffering and angrily defending its position instead of embracing the legitimate suffering of spiritual transformation.

Although the prophecy calls out the Church, it applies to all versions of biblical Christianity that refuse to square up to the truth and spiritually grow. In any case, expect a horde of fundamentalists to circle the wagons and oppose the divine process. If you remember the sixth trumpet, you know what comes next.

10.5.m. Bowl #6: Paradigm Wars, Revisited

John's next passage seals the deal about the synchronization of trumpets and bowls:

> The sixth angel poured out his bowl on the great river Euphrates, and its water was dried up to prepare the way for the kings from the East. Then I saw three impure spirits that looked like frogs; they came out of the mouth of the dragon, out of the mouth of the beast and out of the mouth of the false prophet. They are demonic spirits that perform signs, and they go out to the kings of the whole world, to gather them for the battle on the great day of God Almighty.
>
> "Look, I come like a thief! Blessed is the one who stays awake and remains clothed, so as not to go naked and be shamefully exposed."
>
> Then they gathered the kings together to the place that in Hebrew is called Armageddon. (Rv 16:12–16)

With the sixth trumpet, four angels were released from "the great river Euphrates" (§10.3.i.). Of all the things in the world the sixth bowl could possibly involve, it just so happens to be the same river. Go figure.

Moreover, both the sixth trumpet and bowl refer to a massive war. Christians have long believed it would be a physical war fought by armies of unprecedented size, but now we know better. As explained earlier, this monumental conflict will be a paradigm war that is primarily waged intellectually and emotionally.

"The kings from the East" are not the rulers of Russia or China. After all, neither of these military powers would need a river in Iraq to dry up to "prepare the way" for invading the Middle East. Instead, the reference is to the spiritual truths of the Eastern religions that will eventually be integrated into the Western paradigm. By the way and as will be confirmed later, Revelation occasionally uses "king" to signify a religion (for a religion indeed governs its followers).

The Euphrates represents the genesis of the Western religions. Their soul-quenching water will stop flowing because they no longer fulfill disillusioned Westerners. In fact, the Western religions have already been losing their ability to satisfy the populace's thirst for the divine, and hence the rapid rise of Eastern teachings that began in the 1960s. For instance, meditation and yoga are now common practices in the West. As the errors and deceptions of the Western religions become common knowledge, exponentially more Westerners will welcome the spiritual insights of the East.

With the sixth trumpet, John saw how the traditional Western religions would fight a reactionary paradigm war against the great awakening (§10.3.i.). The sixth bowl fully concurs. Since Revelation is currently focused on religion's last stand, the impure spirits who are looking for a fight are easily unmasked.

As these agitators come "out of the mouth" of each unsavory character, they represent the unenlightened teachings of the traditional Western religions. Their froglike appearance symbolizes a less-evolved life form and the repetitious croaking of the same old thing. Recalling the "great signs" from the second beast (§10.5.d.), their "signs" are yet another sign of their strong but unevolved religious essence.

Because the dragon's religious authority is Judaism (§10.5.b.), the impure spirit coming out of the dragon's mouth represents traditional Jewish dogma. Because the beast's religious authority is Christianity (§10.5.c.), the impure spirit coming out of the beast's mouth represents traditional Christian dogma.

The third impure spirit represents traditional Islamic dogma, and the spiritual realm dropped another future-foretelling bombshell by having it come out of the mouth of the "false prophet." After all, the religion was created by a single prophet—Muhammad—in the seventh century CE.

Islam may appear to be outside of Revelation's scope, but rest assured it is not. The sixth trumpet also includes it as one of the mainstream Western religions (§10.3.i.), and the fourth and final slice of Revelation encompasses Islam as well. Moreover, the term "false prophet" is not used anywhere prior.

[Note: In a later passage, John fingers the pope as the "false prophet." Although we no longer put much stock in his commentary, it undercuts the power of the prophecy. As for the quote about staying awake and keeping your clothes on, we are once again treated to his commentary and another scriptural paraphrase (Lk 12:35–40).]

Whether or not the "false prophet" foretold Islam, the writing is also on the wall for that religion. See Appendix O ("The Impact on Islam") for the explanation.

In any case, both the sixth trumpet and bowl foretold a paradigm war that will be waged against our spiritual evolution. The irony is that Judaic, Christian and Islamic fundamentalists who are so confident that they are the good guys will be acting from egoic pride and filling the ranks of the dark side.

10.5.n. Bowl #7: The Divine Kingdom Manifests, Revisited

John continued:

> The seventh angel poured out his bowl into the air, and out of the temple came a loud voice from the throne, saying, "It is done!" Then there came flashes of lightning, rumblings, peals of thunder and a severe earthquake. No earthquake like it has ever occurred since mankind has been on earth, so tremendous was the quake. The great city split into three parts, and the cities of the nations collapsed. God remembered Babylon the Great and gave her the cup filled with the wine of the fury of his wrath. Every island fled away and the mountains could not be found. From the sky huge hailstones, each weighing about a hundred pounds, fell on people. And they cursed God on account of the plague of hail, because the plague was so terrible. (Rv 16:17–21)

It should come as no surprise that the seventh trumpet and bowl attend to the same topic. When the seventh trumpet sounds, "the mystery of God will be accomplished" (Rv 10:7). Here the seventh bowl has the divine proclamation, "It is done!" The imagery is also remarkably similar, for the seventh trumpet will be accompanied by "flashes of lightning, rumblings, peals of thunder, an earthquake and a severe hailstorm" (§10.4.b.).

The collapsing cities and nonexistent mountains reflect Isaiah's prophecy about everything being leveled amid the glory of the Lord being revealed (§7.3.a.). The religion-based pillars of Western society will not be able to withstand the shockwaves, and the hailstorm of life will be crushing egoic shells that resist our spiritual evolution.

With the completion of the seven bowls and trumpets, we have reached the synchronous conclusion of the first three slices of Revelatory history. Amid the thrill of arriving at the triumph of the divine kingdom, we need to remain attentive. Did you notice anything missing from all we have seen?

Although the battle of Armageddon was prefaced, its details were skipped in the sixth and seventh bowls. Why? It was only a paradigm war, and its outcome was a foregone conclusion.

However, mainstream Christians think Revelation foretells an unbelievably massive war involving 200 million enemy troops (§10.3.i.). As famed evangelist Billy Graham said, "The Bible plainly forecasts the coming of yet another great war. It will be a war to eclipse anything the world has ever seen. It will embrace most of the nations of the world."²⁹

We now know these beliefs about the end times are pure fantasy, and the true nature of the conflict is further illuminated by the final slice of Revelatory history. The next section of prophecy long ago foretold how the truth would slice and dice the mainstream Western religions.

10.6. Global Story, Slice #4: Physical Seductions

The fourth and final slice of Revelatory history began when an angel arrived to show John the great prostitute and her punishment. After saying the kings of the world had committed adultery with her and the masses were intoxicated from her adulteries, the angel carried John away in a spiritual way to a wilderness (Rv 17:1–3). The spiritual realm thus made it clear that John was going on another magic carpet ride and what he saw next was not to be misconstrued as sequential to the previous material.

10.6.a. The Woman on the Scarlet Beast

John continued:

> There I saw a woman sitting on a scarlet beast that was covered with blasphemous names and had seven heads and ten horns. The woman was dressed in purple and scarlet, and was glittering with gold, precious stones and pearls. She held a golden cup in her hand, filled with abominable things and the filth of her adulteries. The name written on her forehead was a mystery:
>
> BABYLON THE GREAT
> THE MOTHER OF PROSTITUTES
> AND OF THE ABOMINATIONS OF THE EARTH.
>
> I saw that the woman was drunk with the blood of God's holy people, the blood of those who bore testimony to Jesus. (Rv 17:3–6)

Again, a beast with seven heads and ten horns represents a dominating partnership of government and religion that lords over its subjects (§10.5.a.). We will explore the scarlet beast in the next subsection.

The mystery indicates the woman's identity would not be easily recognized. Thanks to our enlightened paradigm, though, the solution is easy when we ask the right question. What rides and directs the beast of human dominance? In other words, what has driven our secular and religious rulers?

The answer is all that is craved by the physical side of human nature. The woman's purple represents royalty and external power, her scarlet represents the sultry appeal of sex, and her gold and gems represent wealth. Secular and religious authorities have perpetually sold out a higher path of equality, honesty, freedom and integrity in hot pursuit of these intoxicating pleasures.

Yet the greatest of lusts for the rulers of the earth was having the greatest empire. This seduction was signified with "BABYLON THE GREAT." To be the greatest you had to conquer other kingdoms and eventually the reigning champion, which is why "GREAT" is a crucial part of the title. Kings lusted for this ultimate treasure she had to offer, and they regularly invaded other nations to expand their empires when they thought their armies could win without suffering excessive losses.

Babylon was named because it was the opening greatest empire in the apocalyptic prophecies. It was coveted and eventually conquered by Cyrus, whose empire was coveted and eventually conquered by Alexander, whose empire was coveted by his successors, and so on and so forth. Since the mystery is all about the desire to become the greatest empire, the label perfectly signified the coveted treasure that would tempt such violence. This history-shaping desire for conquest was also depicted in the first seal as one of the signature aspects of life in the darkness (§10.3.c.).

Technically speaking, the metaphorical woman is not a prostitute. As she represents the desires of our physical nature, she is the "MOTHER OF PROSTITUTES" who gives birth to countless prostitutes across all races, genders and social classes. Her seductions govern those who sell out their souls for greater empires, external power, wealth, security, societal approval, sex and fame.

Practically speaking, though, she is the great prostitute as she was first introduced. As the mother of all prostitutes, she is essentially the greatest of them all who also gives birth to the "ABOMINATIONS OF THE EARTH." These nations and institutions are created and run by prostitutes who sell out their souls to satisfy their base desires.

The spiritual realm was most concerned about the monstrosity of church and state that would wield its terrifying power against alternative Christian truth-seekers. John was thus shown that "the woman was drunk with the blood of God's holy people" who truly lived like Jesus.

10.6.b. The Seven Heads of the Scarlet Beast

John said he was greatly astonished when he saw her. The angel replied:

> Why are you astonished? I will explain to you the mystery of the woman and of the beast she rides, which has the seven heads and ten horns. The beast, which you saw, once was, now is not, and yet will come up out of the Abyss and go to its

> destruction. The inhabitants of the earth whose names have not been written in the book of life from the creation of the world will be astonished when they see the beast, because it once was, now is not, and yet will come. (Rv 17:7–8)

Some folks think the scarlet beast is the first beast (§10.5.c.), but the metaphors are distinctly different. Nothing is riding the first beast, and its body resembles a leopard. It has a blasphemous name written on each head, crowns on each of its horns and an apparently fatal head wound. It does not go in and out of existence. However, a woman is riding the scarlet beast of that homogenous color. It has blasphemous names written all over, is devoid of crowns or head damage, and goes in and out of existence.

The metaphor was previously used to implicate Judaism (§10.5.b.) and Christianity (§10.5.c.), but now it represents a more encompassing perspective. The scarlet beast entails the big picture of Western civilization.

Seen in this panoramic context, Christianity is an extension of Judaism. After all, Jesus was the Jewish Messiah, and the Tanakh comprises over 70 percent of the Bible. The spiritual realm also saw Judaism and Christianity as intertwined when it foretold the red dragon giving the first beast its power and authority (§10.5.c.).

Although the historical lens has been zoomed out, it is still focused on the Judeo-Christian aspect of the epic saga. The beast "once was" in existence with the theocracy of the ancient Jewish kings. It thrived until the kingdom split in 930 BCE and was conquered in subsequent centuries (the northern kingdom of Israel in 722 BCE and the southern kingdom of Judah in 586 BCE). For John in the first century CE, then, the beast "now is not" in existence as a dominating state religion.

As the angel foretold, though, this beast "will come up" to great external power again, which it did with the Church's marriage to the Roman Empire a few centuries later. The pagan world would be astonished by the spectacular ascent of the Judeo-Christian paradigm, for it had long been emasculated from governing power and was embraced by just a small minority of the populace.

Revelation once again foretold the same history from a different perspective. The purpose of the multiple holographic views was to deepen our understanding while ensuring the prophecies could be interpreted in no other way. The angel continued: "This calls for a mind with wisdom. The seven heads are seven hills on which the woman sits. They are also seven kings. Five have fallen, one is, the other has not yet come; but when he does come, he must remain for only a little while" (Rv 17:9–10).

We need to be careful and not get our minds bound up like a pretzel in trying to perfectly decipher these passages, for they are marred by a logical contradiction. How can a beast with seven different heads not exist, yet at the same time its sixth head (king) exists? Rather, we need to be in sync with the spiritual realm's intent to convey numerous meanings through the same metaphor. We are thus informed that we will need some insight.

With the passage's first symbolization, the seven heads are Rome because it was known as the City of Seven Hills. The second symbolization involves the metaphor of a beast with seven heads and ten horns (§10.5.a.). In this panoramic context, each head/king represents a religion.

In the sixth bowl, Revelation uses "king" to represent an Eastern religion (§10.5.m.). Moreover, the Church established a kingship with the papacy and its coronation ceremony (§10.5.d.). The current passage corroborates both the use of "king" for a religion and the meaning of the Church setting up an image of the first beast.

The five kings that have fallen refer to state religions prior to the first century CE. They are the Judaism of Israel/Judah (the monotheistic Yahweh), the pantheon of the Assyrian Empire (supreme god Ashur), the pantheon of Babylon (supreme god Marduk), the Zoroastrianism of the Persian Empire (the monotheistic Ahura Mazda), and the pantheon of Greece (supreme god Zeus).

The religious king in John's era was the pantheon and emperor cult of the Roman Empire. Rome was surprisingly tolerant of other religions, so the sixth king was comparatively benign and minded its own business. Therefore, the sixth king existed at the time, but the Revelatory beast of religious domination did not exist in the first century CE, especially because the spiritual realm was emphasizing the beast's Judeo-Christian manifestation.

As the panoramic prophecy saw Christianity as an extension of Judaism and did not count it as one of the seven, we all know the identity of the seventh religious king that would later arise. Islam (the monotheistic Allah) would indeed remain for a little while (as viewed from a spiritual perspective).

In sum, both of the symbolizations point to Rome. The angel was referring to how the great whore's seductions were pulling on the reins of power structures that were centered in the city that would later empower Christianity.

The angel then further confirmed our understanding is correct by explaining about that religion, "The beast who once was, and now is not, is an eighth king. He belongs to the seven and is going to his destruction" (Rv 17:11). The paradoxical mystery is conclusively resolved as we witness again the emphasis on Christianity's beastliness.

10.6.c. The Ten Horns of the Scarlet Beast

The angel continued:

> The ten horns you saw are ten kings who have not yet received

> a kingdom, but who for one hour will receive authority as kings along with the beast. They have one purpose and will give their power and authority to the beast. They will wage war against the Lamb, but the Lamb will triumph over them because he is Lord of lords and King of kings—and with him will be his called, chosen and faithful followers. (Rv 17:12–14)

Revelation's first beast is a conglomeration of different kingdoms over many centuries, and the scarlet beast is even broader. The ten kings are therefore not a literal tally, for the scarlet beast would have needed hundreds of horns if the spiritual realm was bent on historical precision. Rather, it is conveying numerous meanings through the same metaphor and expects us to follow its lead.

The angel's point was forthcoming Roman emperors and Christian monarchs of other empires would be of minimal significance except for one aspect. They would empower the Church's war against religious competitors and rarely grant religious freedom. The angel dispensed more clues to accentuate and isolate the only acceptable solution to the mystery:

> The waters you saw, where the prostitute sits, are peoples, multitudes, nations and languages. The beast and the ten horns you saw will hate the prostitute. They will bring her to ruin and leave her naked; they will eat her flesh and burn her with fire. For God has put it into their hearts to accomplish his purpose by agreeing to hand over to the beast their royal authority, until God's words are fulfilled. The woman you saw is the great city that rules over the kings of the earth. (Rv 17:15–18)

This passage renders more proof that we are witnessing a panoramic view of history. The woman and her scarlet beast were sitting on a wide range of ethnicities and nations.

The scarlet beast was manifesting in John's era as the Roman Empire and was equated with Rome in a prior passage (its "seven heads are seven hills on which the woman sits"; §10.6.b.). For this part of the future-looking prophecy, though, the essence of the scarlet beast would be the Roman Catholic Church. This is how "the great city" of Rome would continue to rule despite the empire's collapse in 476. Subsequent European empires and their dime-a-dozen monarchs would dutifully grant "their royal authority" to their state religion.

In prior passages, the great whore was not Rome. As she was riding the scarlet beast, she was sitting on Rome. Nevertheless, the latest passage equates her with "the great city that rules over the kings of the earth."

The spiritual realm thus engendered another contradiction by altering what the woman was symbolizing. It once again wanted to convey as much meaning and illuminating value as possible while ensuring the prophecies could be interpreted in no other way. So why and how would the scarlet beast leave the woman naked and in ruins while cannibalizing and burning her?

The spiritual realm symbolized this history with another double entendre. The first meaning has to do with the woman representing traditional Roman culture. After the scarlet beast reared its Christian head (the eighth king that belongs to the seven) in the fourth century, the Church had the Roman Empire destroy Rome's beloved paganism.

Just as the angel had foretold, the ten horns served the Church's intolerant agenda. The late Roman emperors were the first kings to empower the assault on Roman paganism, and subsequent monarchs of other European lands also submitted their native religions to Catholicism.

Eating the prostitute's flesh foretold how the Church would incorporate numerous pagan symbols and rites to win those folks over while overrunning their religions and cultures. After all, to eat something is to both kill it and make it a part of you. A textbook on medieval Europe summarizes:

> The most striking feature of medieval Europe was that there was but one religious explanation available, from which no serious deviation was tolerated. That religion we call Christianity, but we must never forget how obstinately classical and barbarian paganism survived, and how many of its elements were incorporated into the new cult. If by Christianity we mean the teachings of Christ and nothing else, we are almost bound to call the new religion paganized Christianity—if it was not, as some have claimed, rather Christianized paganism.[30]

Perhaps the greatest incorporation of paganism occurred when the Judeo-Christian day of rest was changed in 321 from the Sabbath to, as Constantine ordered it, "the venerable day of the Sun" (§G.4.d.). As for burning the prostitute with fire, the prophecy foretold how the scarlet beast would later burn tens of thousands of suspected witches (pagans) at the stake (§N.2.d.).

The second meaning has to do with the prostitute's metaphysical essence. As for ruining her and leaving her naked, the Church tried to defeat the sources of temptation that the mother of all prostitutes was using to ride humanity. By exalting poverty and banning usury, it tried to strip the great whore of her power to seduce with wealth. By denouncing sexuality and later demanding celibacy of its clergy, it tried to strip the great whore of her power to seduce with sex.

Trouble was, the Church would not have an answer for her appeal of power.

So although it would bring the great whore to ruin in so many respects, she would still be a force to be reckoned with. Church leaders would ignore the teachings of Jesus as they fell for her greatest seduction: expanding and defending a great empire. Just as the metaphor began and despite the Church's assault upon the so-called evils of the flesh, the mother of all prostitutes would still ride the dominating beast that was riding humanity.

10.6.d. Fallen Is Babylon the Great

By understanding our spiritual evolution and Revelation, we know what comes next. The onset of democracy and the great awakening would finally end the long era of empires. Indeed, John saw a different angel descend from heaven who emanated great authority and shouted mightily:

> Fallen! Fallen is Babylon the Great! She has become a dwelling for demons and a haunt for every impure spirit, a haunt for every unclean bird, a haunt for every unclean and detestable animal. For all the nations have drunk the maddening wine of her adulteries. The kings of the earth committed adultery with her, and the merchants of the earth grew rich from her excessive luxuries. (Rv 18:2–3)

This new angel's appearance and more synchronization indicate the prophecy has once again jumped into the 21st century and beyond. In the third slice of Revelatory history, the tyrannical portrait of Christianity was followed by the firstfruits in heaven and the first angel's "eternal gospel" of spiritual truth. The second angel followed with "Fallen! Fallen is Babylon the Great, which made all the nations drink the maddening wine of her adulteries" (§10.5.h.).

Here the tyrannical portrait of Christianity is also followed by an angel's proclamation of "Fallen! Fallen is Babylon the Great!" and the corresponding "all the nations" that "have drunk the maddening wine of her adulteries." Although the fourth slice of Revelatory history skips over the eternal gospel, it is clearly paralleling the third slice.

Both slices foretold that sometime after the breakthrough of spiritual truth, the whore would no longer ride the scarlet beast of human dominance. Although her seductions are many, her greatest is the allure of a great empire (§10.6.a.). She will not fall because secular and religious rulers forever renounce such aspirations. Rather, awakening souls will no longer surrender their power to them. In other words, you cannot be a secular or religious king when people no longer see you as superior and take their share of responsibility for collective actions.

The West has already dumped its kings and dictators into the dustbin of history, and only one empire remains. When its subjects see through its ancient deceptions and embrace a greater spirituality, the whore of Babylon's beastly ride will finally come to an end.

The eulogy in Revelation's 18th chapter thus makes perfect sense as another voice in heaven joined in, "Come out of her, my people, so that you will not share in her sins, so that you will not receive any of her plagues" (Rv 18:4). This continues the parallel with the third slice of Revelatory history and the third angel who warned that those who still worshipped the religious beast would be "tormented with burning sulfur in the presence of the holy angels and of the Lamb" (§10.5.h.).

Poetic commentary follows about how the merchants and shippers who profited from her empire-expanding seductions would be shocked and stricken with grief (Rv 18:9–20). This is primarily a reference to Christianity's enabling of colonialism and slavery, but it also hearkens forward to when the exploitation of third-world countries is no longer countenanced.

Another angel stated that the nations had been led astray by the whore's spell. He concluded the eulogy, "In her was found the blood of prophets and of God's holy people, of all who have been slaughtered on the earth" (Rv 18:24). The desire for great empires has been the greatest cause of killing for thousands of years as secular and religious rulers enabled their collaborating partners' conquering agendas.

10.6.e. The Rider on the White Horse

In previous slices of Revelatory history, the great awakening builds to a crescendo with the paradigm war of the sixth trumpet and bowl. We are thus prepared to understand what John wrote next after witnessing a great celebration in heaven:

> I saw heaven standing open and there before me was a white horse, whose rider is called Faithful and True. With justice he judges and wages war. His eyes are like blazing fire, and on his head are many crowns. He has a name written on him that no one knows but he himself. He is dressed in a robe dipped in blood, and his name is the Word of God. The armies of heaven were following him, riding on white horses and dressed in fine linen, white and clean. Coming out of his mouth is a sharp sword with which to strike down the nations. "He will rule them with an iron scepter." He treads the winepress of the fury of the wrath of God Almighty. On his robe and on his thigh he has this name written: KING OF KINGS AND LORD OF LORDS. (Rv 19:11–16)

The rider on the white horse is Jesus, who was earlier presented as the progeny of the Jews who would "rule all the nations with an iron scepter" (§10.5.b.). But in his long-awaited second coming, will he really slay millions of heathens with a magic sword? If so, will he really be wielding it from his mouth?

The answer to both questions is absolutely not. Millions of enemy soldiers will not be firing machine guns at angelic apparitions, and Jesus will not be cutting off heads and limbs as his angelic wingmen cheer him on. A literal interpretation makes a mockery of the great teacher of forgiving love and a God of pure, unconditional love.

We are clearly witnessing another insightful metaphor. Yes, there will be a massive conflict that embroils the world, but it will be a paradigm war where the divine kingdom finally shreds the darkness that has blanketed our planet. Jesus's teachings will be returning as the world sees him in a whole new light. Since his weapon against the darkness is a metaphysical sword of truth, it was depicted as coming out of his mouth.

As he said while wielding it in the first century CE, he had not come to bring peace but rather a sword (§4.3.b.). Trouble was, his revolutionary teachings did not make their intended impact because they were enveloped by the Judaic paradigm and hybridized into biblical Christianity. The Church eventually came to absolute power and reigned supreme as the totalitarian beasts continued their dominance.

Revelation foretold how his wisdom would suddenly resurface, slice through the religious deception, and strike down the remaining towers of external power. As he supposedly said, the meek (humble people without external power) would inherit the world (Mt 5:5). The next metaphor is thus a dead giveaway:

> And I saw an angel standing in the sun, who cried in a loud voice to all the birds flying in midair, "Come, gather together for the great supper of God, so that you may eat the flesh of kings, generals, and the mighty, of horses and their riders, and the flesh of all people, free and slave, great and small." (Rv 19:17–18)

By the way, the small people who get sliced up by the truth are not the meek who inherit the earth. Rather, they are those who keep fearfully conforming and ducking the truth. The meek who inherit the earth are those who humbly step through the narrow gate and reclaim their spiritual power.

10.6.f. Religion's Last Stand (Armageddon)

John continued with the rehashing of the great paradigm war:

> Then I saw the beast and the kings of the earth and their

> armies gathered together to wage war against the rider on the horse and his army. But the beast was captured, and with it the false prophet who had performed the signs on its behalf. With these signs he had deluded those who had received the mark of the beast and worshiped its image. The two of them were thrown alive into the fiery lake of burning sulfur. The rest were killed with the sword coming out of the mouth of the rider on the horse, and all the birds gorged themselves on their flesh. (Rev 19:19–21)

Because of John's lack of specificity, we have to deduce which beast he saw. We can rule out the scarlet beast because it subsumes Judaism (the dragon), Christianity (the first and second beasts) and Islam (the false prophet) within its seven heads. For John to have seen the scarlet beast, there could not have been any other religious characters on the stage. Because the false prophet is back in play and the next passage welcomes back the dragon, John most likely saw the first beast (or its metaphorical enhancement in the lamblike second beast).

Ultimately, though, it hardly matters if we are correct. Since the scarlet beast is an abstracted integration of the three remaining religions, its demise is concurrent with their demise. The scarlet beast is thus not to be seen again in Revelation, which further corroborates our entire interpretation.

This will not be a physical war where armies are slaughtered by a levitating Jesus and his magic sword. To the contrary and as already foretold by the sixth trumpet and bowl, religious fundamentalists will wage a reactionary fight against the Light as they refuse to spiritually grow (§10.3.i., §10.5.m.).

Think about how not a single fighter will be killed by anything other than "the sword coming out of the mouth of the rider on the horse." Either Jesus will slaughter billions with a sword jutting out of his mouth while the "armies of heaven" fail to rack up a single kill, or something metaphorical is transpiring.

The traditional Western religions are abstract entities that have no will of their own, so in and of themselves they can do nothing. The billions of people who promote and believe them, though, make them incredibly powerful forces. We know the beast and false prophet symbolize Christianity and Islam, and the passage depicts their fate.

The "kings of the earth" symbolize their highest religious leaders, and their armies are the clergy, clerics and fundamentalists who are also entrenched in those religions. These leaders and followers will vehemently defend their beliefs, but the sword of truth is too sharp and will cut through it all like a hot knife through butter. The truth will resonate with many awakening souls who suddenly rise in consciousness and leave behind their religious corpses—their old beliefs and identities—as food for society's crows.

Although the exodus will significantly deflate the religions, they will face a much graver problem with carrying on their traditions. As new generations refuse to buy into the debunked beliefs, the beast and false prophet will eventually collapse.

The beast and false prophet being tossed "into the fiery lake of burning sulfur" means their remaining members will be stewing in their "fire and brimstone" worldview of self-righteousness, judgment and anger (§10.3.i.). They will not be at peace with what is washing over the world, and their only remaining hope will be for a cruel and unusual apocalypse that never happens. With their wicked fantasy that God will violently purge the world of its darkness, they will be blind to their own darkness and fail to awaken.

Although this paradigm war may be waged for centuries, it is of no major concern to the spiritual realm. A warm spring has arrived on our planet, and the religious snowmen are doomed.

10.6.g. Doubt About the False Prophet

As the last passage suggests its beast marked foreheads and projected a royal image, that beast would have to be the lamblike second beast—the Catholic Church (§10.5.d., §10.5.e.). Since the passage says the false prophet performed signs on its behalf, the false prophet would have to be the pope. A face-value reading of this passage thus contradicts our previous identification of the false prophet (§10.5.m.).

There are three problems with this accounting. First, we were previously told the performer of the "great signs" that "deceived the inhabitants of the earth" was the lamblike second beast, not a false prophet who was never mentioned at the time (§10.5.d.). The face-value reading is thus at odds with the detailed description of the lamblike second beast.

Second, the pope has never been considered a prophet nor has he tried to act like one. To the contrary, he has only refined dogma that was extrapolated from the Bible. Calling him a false deputy or a false apostle would have squared with historical reality, but not a false prophet.

Finally and most importantly, the face-value reading contradicts the sixth bowl. Given the sixth bowl's focus on religion's last stand, its false prophet surely refers to Islam (§10.5.m.). Moreover, Islam's appearance with the sixth bowl is corroborated by its inclusion in the scarlet beast (§10.6.b.).

Remember that John had no idea what his visions portended, and he inserted misleading commentary on multiple occasions. The spiritual realm most likely rendered the false prophet as a reference to Islam, but John tried to interpret this figure in the last passage and bungled it.

If the false prophet was indeed foretelling Islam and John had not added his ignorant commentary, Muslims would have had an amazing clue—rendered over 500 years before their religion was born—that it would be wise to challenge some core assumptions. As it is, though, the prophetic reference has been tarnished with doubt.

10.6.h. The Dragon's Imprisonment and the Millennium of Peace

John continued:

> And I saw an angel coming down out of heaven, having the key to the Abyss and holding in his hand a great chain. He seized the dragon, that ancient serpent, who is the devil, or Satan, and bound him for a thousand years. He threw him into the Abyss, and locked and sealed it over him, to keep him from deceiving the nations anymore until the thousand years were ended. After that, he must be set free for a short time. (Rv 20:1–3)

For mainstream Christianity, this passage renders a peculiar interlude to the cosmic war between God and Satan. Why did God struggle with Satan for thousands of years when a rank-and-file angel was able to imprison the archenemy like a mischievous dog being banished to the backyard? In addition, why does Satan need to be released to torment the world again when his millennial timeout is over?

We now know a much different reality is transpiring. The dragon refers to ancient Judaism (§10.5.b.), and the passage signifies the end of its deceptions. This will happen when its scriptural teachings (such as God requiring sacrifices to atone for sins) are no longer widely embraced as divine truth.

Notice how the prophecy distinguishes between the fates of the dragon, beast and false prophet. Since Christianity and Islam have exponentially more members and far more appeal to outsiders, a paradigm war impacting billions would have to transpire for the divine kingdom to triumph. Since that is not the case with Judaism, the dragon was not shown in the battle scene.

Yet the ancient Judaic beliefs about God are at the root of all three religions, so the dragon received special attention. Its imprisonment represents the sequestering of the Judaic paradigm from Western consciousness.

Meanwhile, John's unenlightened commentary is yet again present in his discourse about the dragon being the devil. We can only wonder where he got the idea that the dragon would be locked in solitary for a thousand years and then released on parole. Anyway, John continued:

> I saw thrones on which were seated those who had been given authority to judge. And I saw the souls of those who had been

> beheaded because of their testimony about Jesus and because of the word of God. They had not worshiped the beast or its image and had not received its mark on their foreheads or their hands. They came to life and reigned with Christ a thousand years. (The rest of the dead did not come to life until the thousand years were ended.) This is the first resurrection. Blessed and holy are those who share in the first resurrection. The second death has no power over them, but they will be priests of God and of Christ and will reign with him for a thousand years. (Rv 20:4–6)

The first death is bodily death. The "second death" is far more impactful to the soul's eternal journey and refers to those who did not awaken amid the world's many deceptions. This metaphorical death keeps them from divine reunification as they instead keep meandering through the darkness with endless reincarnations.

The symbolism of the thousand years probably signifies how numerous souls will go through numerous lifetimes without awakening. After all, the illusion of the physical world seems incredibly real, and layers of energetic and egoic disconnection can make spiritual truth seem incredibly unreal.

10.6.i. Integrating the Vision of Another Prophet

John continued:

> When the thousand years are over, Satan will be released from his prison and will go out to deceive the nations in the four corners of the earth—Gog and Magog—and to gather them for battle. In number they are like the sand on the seashore. They marched across the breadth of the earth and surrounded the camp of God's people, the city he loves. But fire came down from heaven and devoured them. And the devil, who deceived them, was thrown into the lake of burning sulfur, where the beast and the false prophet had been thrown. They will be tormented day and night for ever and ever. (Rv 20:7–10)

A literal reading of this passage is absurd. What could possibly be the point of releasing God's archenemy for one more great battle before finally dispensing of him? Only a sadistic God would order or allow Satan's release so more death and destruction could be inflicted upon the world. Moreover, the giant fireball from the sky reads like a comic-book fantasy.

If John indeed saw into the 31st century or beyond, it was surely a metaphorical vision that apparently predicts a resurgence of Old Testament ideas. However, the passage is in all likelihood his exposition. After all, John did not report seeing any of this or hearing from an angel about it either.

Perhaps his vision of the dragon's imprisonment was not a satisfactory conclusion. Believing the dragon was Satan, perhaps he figured something far more climactic had to happen. No surprise, then, if he assumed there was more to the story that needed to be sourced from another prophet. As an avid Old Testament reader (§10.2.b.), it is obvious who he believed had seen this part of the future.

Ezekiel chapters 38 and 39 are a prophecy against Gog from the land of Magog (Ezk 38:2). John figured it was about the end times, for it said Gog would be the leader of a vast coalition of nations that would invade Israel with an army so massive it would appear to blanket the land (Ezk 38:9–16).

After their attack had begun, though, God would unleash torrents of burning sulfur upon Gog's army from above (Ezk 38:19–22). God said he would send fire on Gog's land, and all would know that he was the Lord. It was coming, God declared, and would surely occur. It would be the day that he had spoken of (Ezk 39:6–8).

Moreover, God also ordered Ezekiel to tell the birds and wild animals, "You will eat the flesh of mighty men and drink the blood of the princes of the earth…At my table you will eat your fill of horses and riders, mighty men and soldiers of every kind" (Ezk 39:18–20). Notice how similar this is to what John had previously written (§10.6.e., §10.6.f.).

John apparently believed this prophecy was a missing puzzle piece about the end times and integrated it into his letter. Trouble is, there is nothing in Ezekiel's prophecy that suggests God was foretelling the end times or a final victory over Satan. To the contrary, God supposedly explained why he would destroy Gog's armies when they invaded. Israel would subsequently know that he was their God as the other nations understood that the Israelites had gone into exile for being unfaithful to him (Ezk 39:22–23).

In any case, the uncertainty about this passage will eventually get answered. After the world enjoys a millennium of peace, it will get to see if a massive army suddenly musters and marches against Jerusalem but gets destroyed by a giant fireball from the sky.

10.6.j. The Great White Throne Judgment

John continued:

> Then I saw a great white throne and him who was seated on it. The earth and the heavens fled from his presence, and there was no place for them. And I saw the dead, great and small,

standing before the throne, and books were opened. Another book was opened, which is the book of life. The dead were judged according to what they had done as recorded in the books. The sea gave up the dead that were in it, and death and Hades gave up the dead that were in them, and each person was judged according to what they had done. Then death and Hades were thrown into the lake of fire. The lake of fire is the second death. Anyone whose name was not found written in the book of life was thrown into the lake of fire. (Rv 20:11–15)

Here we have more evidence that the previous passage about Gog and Magog was fabricated. After all, remove that material and we go seamlessly from John's prior vision of "thrones on which were seated those who had been given authority to judge" (§10.6.h.) to the great white throne judgment and an explanation of the "second death."

This passage contradicts the heart of biblical Christianity, which maintains that your fate regarding heaven or hell only depends on whether or not you have been saved by Jesus's atoning sacrifice. What John saw, though, is that it all boils down to what each person "had done."

How we direct our energies in every moment of life impacts the universe and is recorded by it. Having it all documented in a book is an apt metaphor. After bodily death, a comprehensive review takes place in the loving illumination of the Light, but God does not render any judgment. Rather, each soul reviews its life and judges for itself how it lived.[31]

This spiritual teaching is being validated by the research of near-death experiences (NDEs; §2.5.d.). NDErs often report that a life review occurs wherein they have a much greater awareness of how their choices impacted others. As one woman described it, "My actions were not judged by others; I judged myself…Gently I was encouraged to understand how my mistakes hurt others by experiencing what others felt as a result of my actions."[32]

The NDE research strongly suggests the Golden Rule (do unto others what we would have them do unto us) is a visceral reality. As Kenneth Ring, PhD, explains, "If these accounts in fact reveal to us what we experience at the point of death, then what we have done unto others is *experienced* as done unto ourselves."[33]

This research has time and again shown how the life review is completely free of divine judgment or condemnation. To the contrary, NDErs are loved unconditionally and treated with total compassion. As Ring emphasizes, "*You are already forgiven. You are only asked to look at your life, and to understand*…In the life review, you need never fear being judged by a force outside yourself."[34] Underscoring the life review's purpose as the "ultimate teaching tool," Ring summarizes the findings:

> The being of Light holds you, as it were, in arms of unconditional love in order to allow you to see yourself truly—without guilt, and objectively—so that you can become a *clear-eyed judge of yourself.* For make no mistake about it, you still have to face yourself and learn from your actions. The life review does not let you off the hook, but merely suspends you from it so that you can see and understand your life as a totality. And NDErs, of course, understand this—and are plain to say that while the being of Light never judges, *they themselves do.*[35]

The earth and sky fled from God's presence because the physical world is an illusion and immaterial to the soul's agenda of spiritual growth. Those of us who fail to transcend the darkness (the "second death") will return to the "lake of fire"—which symbolizes the crucible of divine energy that comprises the physical universe (§7.3.c.)—for as many lives as it takes to awaken and grow through it. The process will eventually transform us all and cleanse away every impurity.

10.7. The Grand Future

Revelation foretold how the bastions of domination and deception that have crushed the divine kingdom would eventually meet their doom, whereupon we will finally be on our way to creating heaven on earth. Its closing chapters foretell this storybook ending.

10.7.a. The Wellspring of Divinity for Those Who Overcome

John wrote, "Then I saw a new heaven and a new earth, for the first heaven and the first earth had passed away, and there was no longer any sea" (Rv 21:1). He saw a new Jerusalem descending from heaven and heard a voice say that God's dwelling was now with men. God would live with them, and "There will be no more death or mourning or crying or pain, for the old order of things has passed away" (Rv 21:4).

God said to John, "It is done. I am the Alpha and the Omega, the Beginning and the End. To the thirsty I will give water without cost from the spring of the water of life" (Rv 21:6). Those who overcome, God added, will inherit this and be his son, but those who do not will be in a burning lake of the second death (Rv 21:7–8).

The "first earth" is our violent, deceptive and exploitative world of fear-driven egos who rape and poison our collective home. The "first heaven" is the wayward paradigm of a neurotic, judging and wrathful God.

Those who thirst for God will forge through the gauntlet of spiritual growth. Those who overcome the darkness will drink from the wellspring of divinity as they unite with their God of pure, unconditional love in the here and now. As the masses release false beliefs and entrenched fears, the "new earth" will arise. It will be a peaceful, truthful and supportive world of love-driven souls who revere and purify our collective home.

As an ocean usually symbolizes the emotional cauldron of the unconscious, John's vision portends an awakened planet ("no longer any sea"). Although bodies will still die, an awakened planet knows the truth about eternal life ("no more death"). When we mature into this state, "the old order of things" will have certainly passed away.

10.7.b. An Enlightened Civilization

John then summarized the vision of Jerusalem coming down from heaven. He described the city as being made with jasper and gold and adorned with all kinds of precious jewels (Rv 21:9–21). He did not see a temple, though, because God and the Lamb comprise it. The city also had no need for the sun or moon because its light came from God's glory. The nations will bring their honor and glory into this city as they walk by God's light. Nobody will act shamefully or deceitfully, he added, as nothing impure enters the city (Rev 21:22–27).

John did not see a temple in the transformed city because a synagogue, church or mosque is not a special home for God, for God is everywhere and everything is holy. Humanity will finally perceive the divine kingdom being spread out upon the earth (§9.4.c.).

10.7.c. The River and Tree of Life

John continued:

> Then the angel showed me the river of the water of life, as clear as crystal, flowing from the throne of God and of the Lamb down the middle of the great street of the city. On each side of the river stood the tree of life, bearing twelve crops of fruit, yielding its fruit every month. And the leaves of the tree are for the healing of the nations. (Rv 22:1–2)

More commentary follows of how wonderful it will be as the city's divine servants rule forever. Revelation then concludes with some closing words and a warning from John to anyone who alters his letter (Rv 22:3–21).

The "healing of the nations" is further proof that the spiritual realm has an unconditionally loving intention and heaven is meant to manifest on earth. "The river of the water of life" is the wellspring of divinity and is no longer hidden by the physical illusion. With the "tree of life" that bears continual fruit and essential healing for our planet, the story of the Judeo-Christian paradigm comes full circle to its disillusioning end.

According to Genesis, our troubles began with "the tree of life and the tree of the knowledge of good and evil" (Gn 2:9). The Old Testament God wanted us to remain unaware of good and evil, but Adam and Eve ate the forbidden fruit from its tree and became self-conscious and aware. An aggravated God declared, "The man has now become like one of us, knowing good and evil. He must not be allowed to reach out his hand and take also from the tree of life and eat, and live forever" (Gn 3:22). So God banished them from the Garden of Eden and installed cherubim and a flaming sword to block them from returning.

One of the great biblical shams was that God commanded Adam and Eve not to grow in consciousness. The ancient Hebrew authors invented the story and its dictate of blind obedience to win a cultural war and gain priestly control (§3.3.b.). As this and many other deceptions were indoctrinated as God's truth, the holy people entrenched their power as the darkness sunk its hooks more deeply into humanity.

Fortunately, though, the will of God would not be denied. We were deeply inspired to search for the truth, see things clearly, and gain the knowledge of good and evil. By doing so, we have become aware of the darkness of the mainstream Western religions. As Revelation long ago foretold, it was the biggest step in our awakening and the manifesting of the divine kingdom.

Genesis had also told a monstrous lie that God abhorred the idea that we might partake in the tree of life. However, we learn at the very end of the Bible that humanity was meant to feed upon the tree of life and its perennial fruit, and "the leaves of the tree are for the healing of the nations." The fallacy of an infallible Bible has come full circle.

10.8. Conclusion

The spiritual awakening paradigm delivers an almost infinitely superior answer to the bizarre imagery and mysteries of Revelation than the cataclysmic destruction paradigm. It provides a coherent explanation for just about every prophetic detail. With the exception of the Gog addition, all the jagged, weird and paradoxical pieces of the puzzle fit seamlessly into a big picture that reflects a deeply loving God and elegant universe.

The same does not hold true for the mainstream Christian view. Unless we believe our universe will suddenly morph into the cosmos on LSD and slaughter billions in the strangest of ways, this wrathful perspective cannot explain a long list of paradoxes and peculiarities. It is a blasphemous interpretation of bad faith, for it implies that God is an insecure and genocidal deity who is anything but a God of pure, unconditional love.

As the chapter has shattered the delusion that Revelation is pointing to our planet's annihilation, Christians should ask some penetrating questions. For instance, where is Paul's "left behind" rapture? One would think that over a billion Christians meeting Christ in the air would have been the signature event in an apocalyptic prophecy, but it is curiously absent in both Daniel and Revelation. We should not be surprised Paul was mistaken, though, for he was also convinced the end would occur with his generation (§9.3.c.).

Where is the proof of a forthcoming antichrist? It is not to be found anywhere in the Old Testament and especially not in Daniel. In addition, the beasts of Revelation represent the institutions that usurped the freedom and spiritual power of humanity. The collusions of heads and horns—the marriages of religion and government—wielded their terrifying power to crush the spiritual growth of a planet still mired in the darkness.

It would be nice if these mistaken ideas about the end times were as irrelevant as believing in Santa Claus. Unfortunately, the apocalyptic delusion has been having a very real impact by driving America's foreign policy with the Arab-Israeli conflict. Because fundamentalist Christians are unilaterally supporting the right-wing Israelis who are striving to reclaim the so-called Holy Land (go, Armageddon!), Washington is collaborating.

The United States keeps vetoing the global community at the United Nations and enabling Israel's ongoing construction of permanent settlements on Palestinian land. This horrible injustice is the primary instigator of the region's violence. Moreover, our complicity with this blatantly illegal crime has angered Muslims across the Middle East and fueled terrorism against us.

Why has America behaved like a crooked cop who turns a blind eye to organized crime? Our leaders will not dare hold Israel accountable because they do not want to be politically beheaded by a massive voting bloc of Christians.

The apocalyptic mindset is also hindering our spiritual evolution toward being a community of nations that never again opts for war to resolve a conflict. To achieve this, America will need to move beyond the law of the jungle (where might is right) and submit itself to the rule of international law.

[Note: Even though America has become the king of the jungle, it is in our best interests to lead the nations into a legitimate version of a new world order. Consider how and why our 50 different states have lived in peace for so long. For example, California does not resolve water conflicts with Arizona by bullying or invading its weaker neighbor. Rather, the most powerful state is submitted to resolving such conflicts under the rule of law. The glaring exception was the Civil War, which was triggered by the Southern states refusing to remain submitted to the rule of law. Fearing it was about to abolish slavery, they seceded before it could happen.]

Trouble is, many Christians believe the ten horns of the scarlet beast will manifest as a coalition of nations led by the antichrist (Rv 17:12–14), so there is reactionary opposition to even the mere suggestion of a stronger version of the United Nations. This paranoia was popularized by the bestselling book *The Late, Great Planet Earth*. Published in 1970, it sold over 35 million copies and was a springboard for the *Left Behind* novels.

Despite Jesus having supposedly said the peacemakers are God's children (Mt 5:9), many Christians denounce efforts to create a peaceful global system as the work of the devil. For instance, Tim LaHaye, who coauthored the *Left Behind* novels and is deemed an expert on biblical prophecy, calls the United Nations a "monstrosity on Manhattan Island" that has "already deceived the American people."[36]

There indeed has been a monstrous deception, but it is working in the polar opposite direction. Remember, "By their fruit you will recognize them" (Mt 7:16). Mainstream Christianity has been enabling injustice and empowering the law of the jungle. It has therefore been perpetuating violence while sabotaging our spiritual evolution on all levels. This is poisonous fruit, and the religion is unaware of its ignorance and deception as it keeps sowing seeds of fear in biblical proportions.

Anyway, the apocalyptic prophecies were a spiritual gift to help us see through the religious darkness that has led billions of people astray. We have all paid and are continuing to pay the price. To further prove the point, the book now shifts gears to show how Christianity sowed and watered the killing fields of the Holocaust.

Chapter 11

The Broad Road That Led to Destruction

11.1. Introduction

We have seen how the hybrid religion was founded upon a faulty paradigm and justified with deception. We have also seen how the apocalyptic prophecies foretold its demise amid the great awakening.

To corroborate these shocking truths, the final two chapters travel a third independent path to the same destination. This path leverages Jesus's advice for seeing through the deceptions of false prophets. As he was quoted, "A good tree cannot bear bad fruit" and "by their fruit you will recognize them" (Mt 7:18–20).

Recognizing this religious tree's poisonous fruit has a fascinating correlation with another Jesus quote from just a few verses prior: "Wide is the gate and broad is the road that leads to destruction, and many enter through it" (Mt 7:13). While this destruction obviously manifested with the Crusades, Inquisition and witch hunts (§N.2.), humanity also traveled the broad road of Christianity to the horrors of Nazi Germany.

This chapter explains the dynamics that resulted in the Holocaust and how the Catholic Church and its Protestant offshoots were critical forces in creating and enabling it. With greater awareness of how we are creating our collective nightmare, we will know what we need to change to produce far better results.

11.2. The Formative Undercurrent of Hatred and Fear

Science is moving toward agreement with spiritualists that the universe is essentially unified. Physicists have been shocked to learn how interconnected and malleable everything really is, even the seemingly independent dimensions of space and time. Moreover, a wide range of disciplines have been embracing a systems perspective that recognizes such interrelatedness. As a popular saying explains it, a sneeze in China impacts the weather in San Francisco.

When it comes to human behavior, societal patterns routinely induce people into manifesting their collective energy flows. Since it is simply a matter of going with the flow, mass movements easily arise when powerful undercurrents converge and flare up with the right set of circumstances. To blame only the lost souls who ride these dark waves into infamy is to see only the surfers and not the powerful waves they rode.

When we address the underlying issues, far fewer bad apples will fall from society's tree. More importantly, though, lost souls who come to an enlightened planet will not find any strong currents to ride and produce widespread destruction.

The case of Nazi Germany exemplifies the point and illuminates the formative undercurrent that the Christian world would rather ignore. We begin with the energetic tsunami that Adolf Hitler and the National Socialists (Nazis) aligned with and surfed.

11.2.a. The Power of Hatred and Fear

Paranoia is a dangerous flaw in thinking that arises from unconscious fear that is not surfaced and addressed. The antisemitic paranoia that engulfed Europe was spawned by a raging undercurrent of hatred and fear that had been flooding European psyches for hundreds of years.

The Catholic Church and its Protestant offshoots generated the torrent by spewing and reinforcing centuries of venomous hatred against the Jews. The Christian world had little to fear, though, because the pervasive marriages of church and state had all the power. European society was thus comparatively stable.

However, the Enlightenment of the 19th century produced rapid and immense societal change with the onset of democracy and liberation of the Jews. This turbulence was exacerbated by explosive population growth, extensive industrialization, wild economic cycles and international competition.

The breakthrough of liberty and equality was met with a reactive backlash from Christianity. As the dominant religion fought against our spiritual evolution, centuries of animosities were suddenly supercharged by a slew of fears. All the while many Jews were greatly benefiting and being cast as villains for all that ailed Europe. These emotionally appealing theories harmonized with Christian ideologies and proclaimed a malignant "Jewish problem" that had to be resolved.

As political parties jousted for power, many of them flaunted antisemitic platforms in the closing decades of the 19th century. The Catholic Church played an especially dark role in fueling the political antisemitism that later became Hitler's calling card.

A scientific dimension also opened up that century with the discovery of genes and theory of evolution. Antisemites integrated them into an overarching racial explanation that resonated with the continental emotions. All in all, Europe was swimming in hatred and fear of the Jews as Christian authorities encouraged the masses to join the political fight against them.

After World War I, conspiracy theorists amplified the paranoia with a sensational claim: wealthy Jews in European financial circles had schemed for the war to produce windfall profits and increase their power from the continental destruction and reconstruction. Meanwhile, the demise of the Russian Empire in 1917 had given conspiracy theorists a fact they waved before the world as a smoking gun: the leadership of the Bolshevik Revolution was disproportionately filled with men of Jewish origins. Antisemites were sounding the alarm that the Jews hoped to crush Western society with atheistic communism as they had just done in Russia.

These passions were even more inflamed in Germany as antisemites blamed the Jews for their nation's defeat. Another treacherous dynamic was shaped by the Treaty of Versailles that ended the war in 1918. The Allies blamed Germany for it, stripped the nation of vital territory and natural resources, and saddled the new democracy with devastating economic burdens.

Critics deemed the Allies' vengeful approach at Versailles to be shortsighted and predicted that emasculating Germany would produce economic hopelessness and pave the road for political extremism. This was especially true for a country that was getting its first taste of a full-fledged democracy after a painful military defeat.

The Weimar Republic (1919–1933) had no reasonable chance of handling its debts of war, costs of reconstruction and reparations. The resulting hyperinflation of the early 1920s destroyed the accumulated wealth of millions of Germans. Less than a decade later their recovering economy was struck by the global depression and the highest unemployment rate in the world.

The undercurrent in Germany was thus a churning blend of national humiliation, economic despair, surging antisemitism and a rampant fear of communism. Although the Nazis had failed to make any political headway in the 1920s, the dire situation of the early 1930s led the good people of Germany into an act of desperation. The Nazis would be given a chance to restore their dignity and economy.

11.2.b. The Politics of Arrogance and Fear

Hitler made reprehensible choices that a person of higher consciousness would not have made. Like most other people on our planet, he was a lost soul. But if we also call him a bad apple, we have to admit he was produced by a continental tree of economic exploitation and ethnic hatred.

This ambitious man actually had good intentions to protect the poor working men who were being ground up and spit out by the capitalistic machine.

When he landed in the especially turbulent waters of postwar Germany, he also had good intentions to unify his people and lead them out of the storm.

Trouble was, Hitler had fallen for the popular belief that the Jews were the primary cause of society's problems. During his early adult years in Vienna (1907–1913), he succumbed to the antisemitic press of Austria that offered an appealing explanation. He embraced the conspiracy theory that the Jews were secretly undermining Western society through exploitative capitalism and liberal democracy.

A decorated and frustrated corporal in World War I, he knew how to capitalize on the situation to achieve his otherwise good intentions. Having observed in Vienna that religiously themed antisemitism was formidable, he figured that racially themed antisemitism that was properly framed would generate tremendous political power.

Hitler believed the weak democracy of the Weimar Republic was evidence of the Jews' well-cloaked assault. He also embraced the prevailing idea that life is a competitive fight to survive, so races and nations should not shrink from this Darwinian reality. He therefore rallied his people to regain the glory and power of the Second Reich under the Prussian monarchy (1871–1918) and to fight, as life demanded of any creature that wished to survive, against the Jews and other races that would have the Germans under their boot.

Hitler was a gifted orator and power-savvy politician, but he was not a magician who brainwashed these beliefs into millions and created hatred out of thin air. Rather, he simply tapped into and channeled the prevailing undercurrent. With stellar insight into political sociology (§L.2.e.), he appealed to the emotions of the masses. Millions of Germans were unable to rise above those primal feelings to see through the politics of arrogance and fear, thereby enslaving themselves to being played like a fiddle.

Hitler crested and rode the rising tsunami by stoking national anger about the Schandvertrag (Treaty of Dishonor), hyping the overblown threat of communism, promoting an Aryan utopia, and unifying his nation against its enemy. He seduced the populace with the easy way out: surrender your divisive liberties by uniting for a glorious return of the Fatherland, offload your shame by casting blame for Germany's ills upon the Jews, and ease your pain by venting your rage against the perceived cause of your distress.

He came to power because millions of Germans were blind to the darkness of Nazi ideology and the politics of arrogance and fear. Because the masses then completely submitted to his authority with their corresponding avoidance of collective responsibility, his will was allowed to run rampant.

Without this dark collusion, Hitler would have been hard-pressed to have invaded a synagogue. But relieved by a rapidly improving economy and the intoxicating resurgence of national pride, millions went along for the consensual ride. Their destination was one of the most gruesome episodes of history, as German conquests in World War II allowed the Nazis to enact their murderous intentions upon European Jewry (only 2.4 percent of the Holocaust victims were from Germany; 70 percent of them were from Poland and the Soviet Union).

11.3. The Convergence of the Darkness

The Holocaust emerged from three lethal dynamics that converged over Germany like a perfect storm.

11.3.a. Evil at the National Level

The first dynamic was evil that was enacted at the national level (§5.2.b.). The Hitler regime had no higher authority beyond itself—neither God nor German law—as its will banished the nation's conscience to achieve its dominating aspirations and glorify itself.

To block the light of self-examination, the regime prohibited free speech and silenced all voices of political dissent with surveillance, imprisonment, terror and murder. It also thrived upon propaganda and deception. It had no qualms about deliberately lying, thereby serving its egoic will instead of being truthful and serving something greater than itself. As Hitler asserted, there was no lie he would not tell for the sake of Germany.[1]

Moreover, Nazi Germany refused to meet its Shadow while projecting its repressed and unacceptable qualities upon the Jews (§5.2.c.). As historian Yehuda Bauer explains, "When one reads Nazi sources, it is almost impossible to avoid a centrally important conclusion: the Jews were, in Nazi eyes, *the* central enemy, the incarnation of the Devil."[2]

11.3.b. The Dark Power of Antisemitism

The Nazis never could have polarized the national psyche against the Jews by themselves. They were successful only because they channeled a strong current that was already flowing in the same direction. The second converging dynamic, then, was a deeply ingrained antisemitism.

This powerful undercurrent of hatred and fear had been flooding European minds for centuries. The Nazis leveraged it with a hopeful vision of national glory and racial supremacy. Since Nazi ideology was dressed in traditional Christian themes and prevailing scientific theories, the movement was very seductive. The independent dynamics of institutional evil and a pervasive antisemitism converged and unified Germany in polarized opposition to what it perceived to be its irredeemable cancer.

A chilling characteristic of evil is that it sees itself as entirely good as it crusades against the evil it has projected onto the world. It believes its salvation will come from eliminating the evil it sees "out there."

Believing that salvation is to be found in an external change in worldly conditions and not in an internal change of personal conditions is a spiritual error that is as old as humanity. For instance, the ancient Jews had hoped for a warrior-king Messiah, and modern Christians expect God to unleash an apocalyptic purification of the planet.

The Nazis believed they were on a heroic crusade to address the problem of global evil. For instance, even when Nazi leaders were being condemned at the postwar trials in Nuremberg, Hermann Göring predicted there would be statues of himself all over Germany in 50 or 60 years. Bauer explains:

> For the Nazis, the "Jewish problem" was not a German or even a European issue but a global problem of the greatest magnitude. The delivery of humankind from the Jews was conceived in pseudo-religious, messianic terms. On the "solution" of the problem depended the future of humankind.[3]

Hitler had announced this ideology in *Mein Kampf* while discussing why the Christian Social Party in Austria had ultimately failed with its antisemitic platform a few decades prior. Because it had based its antisemitism upon religion instead of race, the movement looked like another go-round of converting the Jews. Having thus alienated the intelligentsia and others who were repelled by such religious squabbling, its struggle lacked "the conviction that this was a vital question for all humanity, with the fate of all non-Jewish peoples depending on its solution."[4]

Historian Saul Friedländer terms the Nazi worldview a "redemptive anti-Semitism," noting that "Hitler relentlessly repeated a story of perdition caused by the Jew, and of redemption by a total victory over the Jew."[5] Since the regime demonstrated in 1934 that wholesale murder was an acceptable means for fulfilling its will (§L.2.k.), the decision to implement the Final Solution is hardly a mystery.

Again, a primary trait of evil is that the will has completely dominated the conscience. Eliminating the Jews was perceived to be like eliminating parasites, bacteria or cancerous cells to save a life. Even Catholic scholars of the early 20th century used this argument to defend the Inquisition (§7.4.g.).

In the Nazi worldview, the Jews had to be eliminated to protect their nation and save humanity. No small wonder, then, that the Gestapo appealed to the Japanese government to exterminate 18,000 Jews in a Shanghai ghetto (the request was denied).

11.3.c. The Abdication of Spiritual Power and Responsibility

The third and final dynamic was how millions of Germans abdicated their spiritual power and responsibility. This is one of the two greatest lessons of the Holocaust. <u>We are spiritually responsible for not only our own actions (even if we were ordered by a general or president) but also the actions of the organizations and nations that we have empowered with our association or participation</u> (§1.3.c.).

Failure to live this truth allows bureaucratic machines to launch unjustified wars or commit atrocious crimes. Although tendering spiritual power and offloading responsibility to national leaders has been par for the course throughout history, this pervasive culture is of the darkness.

After the Nazis built a thunderous political tribe and were granted dictatorial power in March of 1933, they entrapped Germany in a societal centrifuge. They quickly spun up their totalitarian vortex by silencing all sources of opposition while appealing for national unity and loyalty. By August of 1933, the regime had imprisoned almost 27,000 citizens in concentration camps (almost all were political opponents).

The German populace and its elected representatives had freely bestowed dictatorial power and then failed to check the behavior that opened the door for much greater evil. Unaware of the need to preserve a free press and individual rights to organize and publicly protest should their government ever contravene their values and standards, German citizens had blindly surrendered their power and consented to being blindfolded.

It was a fatal metaphysical error that put astronomical power in the hands of a few, blanketed public awareness, and gagged the expression of the national conscience. It was a crucial reason that evil was later able to prevail.

Meanwhile, every institution in Germany faced the conforming pressure of the Gleichschaltung (switching into the same gear) to align for the common good. The centrifugal force for obedience also gained strength from the national resurrection. The Nazi beast ruthlessly protected its hard-earned power while controlling the flow of information, indoctrinating its narratives, and escalating its bureaucratic assault upon the Jews.

With the onset of World War II, the totalitarian vortex became even stronger because the populace was driven by a deeper layer of fear to remain obedient. After all, the primordial energies pulling the individual into tribal compliance can be overwhelming when the tribe is demanding loyalty for its survival. Nobody wants to be ostracized, branded a traitor or to blame for the tribe's demise. By the way, this is a textbook example of root chakra energies (§9.5.e.).

To live the path of spiritual power when the rest of your tribe is marching together in the other direction is as great a spiritual challenge as there is, especially when your life is on the line. So it was in Nazi Germany as the nation fought for its life and its emasculated citizens toed the line for their collective survival.

So even though most Germans were only mild to moderate antisemites who did not subscribe to the radical antisemitism of the Nazis, they remained silent, trusted their highly revered Führer, and did their jobs despite the rampant rumors and Nazi boasts and insinuations about the slaughtering in the East.[6] Their surrender of spiritual power was cemented by the psychological defense of compartmentalization (§5.2.a., §L.3.e.). For instance, railway officials sent Jews to death camps with the same administrative techniques for sending German youth to summer camps. The circle of darkness was complete.

11.3.d. The Perfect Storm Unleashes Hell on Earth

Unaware of the overwhelming darkness that had enveloped them for so long, far too many Germans were convinced the Jews were irredeemably evil and a dangerous enemy. By the time the war was raging, even prominent church leaders had swallowed Nazi propaganda and were promoting the utter fiction that the Jews were responsible for it.

No small wonder, then, that after centuries of antisemitism compounded by years of Nazi indoctrination of blame upon the "evil" Jews, far too many Germans were willing to murder for their tribal leaders as they perceived their killing as a selfless duty for the common good that had an imminently justifiable cause.[7] Tens of thousands of Germans thus slaughtered almost six million Jews in less than four years. Over a million of the victims were under the age of 13.

While the goal was complete elimination, the projection of shame and venting of rage upon the defenseless Jews was often taken to the lowest level of human depravity. Unable to see Jewish men, women and children as fellow human beings who were deeply suffering, German guards, soldiers and executioners routinely treated them with brutality, cruelty and humiliating domination. The Germans even inflicted pain and misery until the very last hours of the war with their torturous death marches.

Neither antisemitism nor subservience to a bureaucratic machine can fully explain how such an abomination could arise from an otherwise respectable nation. That is because the Holocaust was born from the womb of evil. <u>The other great lesson from the Holocaust, then, is a better understanding of the nature of evil, for it deceptively arises from the last place self-righteous crusaders ever think to find and address it: within.</u>

To reiterate, the Holocaust can be explained only by integrating three independent dynamics. First and foremost was the choice for evil at the national level. The unsubmitted will of the Hitler regime repressed its conscience and silenced anybody who attempted to illuminate its darkness. The *Triumph of the Will*, as an extremely successful Nazi documentary was aptly titled, meant that nothing would get in the way of claiming more *lebensraum* (living space and resources) and cleansing the demographic map of Europe (the Nazi machine and its accomplices also murdered millions of non-Jewish Poles, other Slavic people, the gypsies and others who were deemed inferior or undesirable).

Second, Germany had long been immersed in the raging undercurrent of antisemitism that had flooded Europe for centuries. The Nazis were able to polarize a national consensus about racial good and evil and progressively act upon their ideology as circumstances permitted only because millions of Germans already viewed the Jews as religious opposites and dangerous influences on their government, economy and society.

Third, ordinary Germans surrendered their spiritual power, consented to being blindfolded, and compartmentalized their standards and values. Ordinary Germans thus partnered with, empowered and enacted evil. If you take any of these three elements out of the equation, the Holocaust would not have happened.

11.4. The Churches Empower the Nazi Regime

We now turn to a critical dimension that has not yet been integrated. The three formative dynamics were all created or enabled by Christianity, which was the greatest reason that evil flowed from the heart of Germany. After all, an enlightened religion never would have generated the devastating undercurrent of antisemitism, nor would it have allowed the manifestation of national evil and perpetration of the Holocaust.

The masses were never taught the dynamics of evil or the imperative of owning your spiritual power and responsibility for collective behavior. They instead took their cues from their religious authorities.

11.4.a. The Vatican Sells Out the German Catholics

Going back to when the Nazi storm clouds were first billowing on Germany's horizons, it is important to understand why a more enlightened set of teachings did not blow them away in the minds of the masses. As 95 percent of the populace belonged to a Christian church (per a 1939 census), religious leaders could have easily kept the governing sky clear of the Nazis. All that was needed was awakening their congregations to the movement's true colors and demanding political opposition.

This is exactly what the German Catholic Church, the formidable Catholic Center Party and hundreds of Catholic publications had been doing in the early 1930s. They saw the evils of Nazism and campaigned vigorously against it, but they were undermined and then silenced by their masters in Rome. As detailed in Appendix L, the Vatican sold out both the German Catholic Church and one of the nation's most powerful political parties to serve its own totalitarian agenda (§L.2.).

The Vatican had always lusted for autocratic regimes (§7.3.i.). Its latest marriage had come from assisting Benito Mussolini's rise to absolute power in Italy during the 1920s, which culminated in 1929 with a treaty that greatly enriched and empowered the Vatican (§L.2.c.).

The Vatican had been on a quest since 1920 for a Reich Concordat (a treaty with Germany) to gain more authority over German Catholicism. Trouble was, democratic politics in the more Protestant nation had made it impossible. The Vatican needed a right-wing regime to get its holy grail, and it pleaded with the Catholic Center Party to reverse course and form a governing coalition with the Nazis. Although the Center Party remained united with the Social Democrats in their political battle against the Nazis, the Vatican got its wish when President Paul von Hindenburg appointed Hitler as the chancellor in January of 1933.

Although the Vatican had nothing to do with the appointment, its agenda and influence played a crucial role in Hitler gaining dictatorial power in March of 1933. Had it backed the staunch opposition of German Catholicism, the new chancellor's stab at absolute power would have been defeated in the Reichstag (German parliament). But Hitler got the votes he had to have from the Center Party—which betrayed its constituents to serve the Vatican—by most likely promising a Reich Concordat in return (§L.2.h.).

The Vatican immediately negotiated its holy grail. Formally signed in July of 1933, the treaty with Nazi Germany lawfully forced the German Catholic Church into political silence and obedience. The Vatican not only terminated what had been a boisterous Catholic fight against the Nazi movement but also committed the clergy to always supporting the Hitler regime.

In 1998, the Vatican would denounce Christians who did not raise their voices in protest of the Holocaust. Although this monstrous hypocrite did not disclose what it had done back in 1933, the point for now is how the Church had long indoctrinated Europe with a hierarchical paradigm of unifying obedience.

How can anyone expect German Catholics of the 1930s and '40s to have suddenly followed their highest inner guidance when for so many centuries they had been taught to obey their religious and secular authorities? If Catholic authorities did not lead a moral charge against Nazi criminality, how can anybody expect a powerless Catholic to have stuck his neck out to do so (with no protection at all from a deportation or execution)?

Instead, Catholic Germany—over a third of the populace—dutifully followed its "holy father" in Rome and the strategic partnership between the Vatican and Nazis. As Catholic sociologist Gordon Zahn summarizes:

> At no time was the German Catholic population released from its moral obligation to obey the legitimate authority of the National Socialist rulers under whom those Catholics were placed by the 1933 directives of their spiritual leaders; At no

time was the individual German Catholic led to believe that the regime was an evil unworthy of his support.[8]

11.4.b. The Protestants Joyfully Submit

Protestant Christianity fared no better in guiding its German constituents, largely because of a theological and structural demarcation between religion and politics. Unlike the unified Catholic Church, there were 28 regional Protestant churches in Germany in the early 20th century. These independent churches were either Lutheran, Reformed or a union depending upon the province.

Stemming from the protection of German princes during the Reformation, they were each aligned with their province's ruling prince, who was the titular head of each church until 1918. In a harmonious relationship referred to as the "altar and throne," most churches received excellent support from their princes.

In stark contrast with the Middle Ages when Catholicism and royal governance were intertwined, Protestant pastors stayed away from political issues and princes stayed away from religious issues. All in all, the decades before World War I were a golden era of order and prosperity for the Protestant churches amid the prominence of the Second Reich.

The Great War ended the beloved monarchy and threw the Protestant churches into the maelstrom of the new democracy. In 1922, the 28 provincial churches sought to develop political power by forming a loose-knit federation known as the Evangelische Kirche in Deutschland (German Evangelical Church, though sometimes translated as the Protestant Church in Germany).

Although Protestant pastors did not oppose the democracy, they generally longed for the return of a strong, conservative and nationalistic monarchy. So when the Nazi movement suddenly caught fire in 1930, many of them ecstatically jumped on board. These Protestants were known as the German Christians and officially organized in 1932. They strongly supported Nazi ideology and embraced Hitler as a divine blessing. As one pastor expressed the sentiment, "Christ has come to us through Adolf Hitler."[9]

On January 30, 1933, Hitler was sworn in as the chancellor. On March 23, the Catholic Center Party took its well-orchestrated dive as the Reichstag granted him dictatorial power (§L.2.). On April 1, the Nazi government alarmed the world with its militant boycott of Jewish businesses. Two days later the German Christians concluded their first national conference with this resolution: "God wills that I should fight for my Germany. War service is in no case a forcing of the Christian conscience, but obedience before God…Adolf Hitler's State appeals to the Church, the Church must obey the appeal."[10]

While the Nazis were negotiating the Vatican's complicity in the spring of 1933, the German Christians persuaded Hitler to help them unify the 28 Protestant churches under a single leader—a Reich Bishop—who would govern the German Evangelical Church in line with the State's agenda. The candidate of choice for Hitler and the German Christians was Ludwig Müller, a military chaplain and fervent Nazi, but Müller was soundly defeated in a church election in May of 1933.

With trademark Nazi interference and political machination, though, a different voting result was achieved later that summer to eventually sweep Müller into the office of Reich Bishop. At a national synod in September of 1933, a church leadership now stacked with German Christians passed a resolution prohibiting non-Aryans from being pastors or church officials.

Alarmed at the German Evangelical Church's headfirst slide into Nazism, a dissenting faction of roughly 10 percent of the Protestant clergy split off to form a competing structure to Müller's authority. But the Confessing Church, which was led by Pastor Martin Niemöller, was neither a political protest against Hitler nor a moral stand against the flaming antisemitism. To the contrary and as expressed in its Barmen Declaration of 1934, the Confessing Church was only protesting the German Christians' bastardized theology and the submission of church doctrine to the State's ideology and authority.

Hitler was keenly aware of the polarization that was developing and the danger he faced if it flourished. So within a handful of months of having thrown the weight of the Nazi Party behind the German Christians, he quickly withdrew all such support. He thus left the Protestants to bicker among themselves and eliminated the possibility that a powerful Reich Bishop might someday lead a moral protest against him.

Hitler thus ditched his hope of controlling the Protestant churches for a far better strategy of getting what he really wanted. First, he emphasized a policy of doctrinal and denominational indifference. Second, his regime strongly suppressed any attempt by either Protestants or Catholics to engage in political interference. The widely proclaimed maxim was, "Politics do not belong in the Church."[11]

Hitler's primary tool for enforcing this policy was the Gestapo (the secret state police), whose mission was to combat any potential threat to the State. By Nazi law not accountable to the German judicial system, the Gestapo could deport citizens to concentration camps without a trial.

The operative goal was beating down the churches as much as possible without provoking a backlash. The Nazis quickly crushed church organizations that had anything to do with politics, funneled these folks into a similar Nazi organization, and punished those who did not voluntarily join in these moves toward national unity.

As the Nazis drove the politically minded pastors and priests back to the religious confines of their churches, they allowed Germans to worship wherever they wished. Hitler was thus able to deviously promote his regime as never having persecuted anybody in Germany for religious reasons. With regards to politics, though, he proclaimed that the State would "ruthlessly bring to their senses any priests, who, instead of serving God, think it is their mission to vilify our present Reich, its institutions, or its leaders."[12]

In sum, the Confessing Church proved to be inconsequential, as it had little outside support and was undercut from within by theological disputes and political considerations. Its most damaging problem, however, was that the Gestapo arrested over a thousand of its more defiant pastors and laymen before any type of coordinated resistance could be mounted (e.g., Niemöller was imprisoned from 1937 to 1945).

Those Protestants were the outliers, though, and not the norm. As instructed by their Bibles, the vast majority of pastors were dutifully subservient to the Hitler regime. Moreover, the German Evangelical Church was deeply ingrained in a Lutheran tradition of respect for ruling powers and had historically refrained from political issues. As historian J. S. Conway notes, "The popular image of the pastor in German society was one of loyal support to the ruling classes, never of discontent or opposition."[13]

For so many reasons, then, Protestant pastors were lost in a hierarchical version of Christianity and carrying water for a murderous Caesar. Even more disturbing was their failure to recognize Jesus amid the outcasts of Germany.

The mass deportation of Germany's Jews to the concentration camps of the East began in October of 1941. By December of 1941, rumors were already buzzing through the populace about mass executions.

Meanwhile, seven provincial leaders of the German Evangelical Church issued a joint declaration that, as Nazi leaders had "irrefutably proved by numerous documents," the Jews were responsible for the global war. These church leaders affirmed the "Reich police regulations of marking the Jews as the born enemies of the world and the Reich" and cited Martin Luther's call for "the strictest measures against the Jews and their expulsion from German territories."[14]

The church leaders then proclaimed the Jews were biologically incapable of being redeemed by baptism and terminated all relations with Jewish Christians. As their pronouncement was made on December 17, 1941, it could have easily been read as a tacit endorsement of the Final Solution.

The bottom line is best summarized by the Northern Protestant State Church of Germany. In 2001, it began a three-year traveling exhibition to show in graphic detail, according to a local newspaper account, the "unbelievable extent to which the churches of the region had participated in the Holocaust. [The exhibit] declares courageously 'the majority of the church supported the persecution of the Jews.'"[15]

11.4.c. The Fallacy of a Grassroots Protest Fantasy

Nowadays the conversation about the Holocaust is often about how ordinary Christians failed to speak out against it. Such a hypothetical protest is irrelevant, though, because the Holocaust could not have been stopped by a grassroots effort.

The Nazis had long been in totalitarian control of Germany, and the Gestapo had been scrutinizing the populace and silencing opponents. Courageous individuals who had criticized the regime had already been banished to concentration camps. Any grassroots attempt to organize a movement would have been crushed before it could get off the ground.

With the exception of a military coup, the Nazis could have been challenged from within only if two conditions were met. First, a significant part of the populace needed to embrace more universal values that surpassed all hatred and fear of the Jews and were also so cherished that they could trump the compulsion to obey authority, the gravity of mass conformity and the instinct of self-preservation.

Second, an enlightened organization needed to exist whose leaders were willing to pay the ultimate price, if need be, to appeal to those values in the face of the regime's retaliation. The organization would also have to be strong enough to survive the Nazi backlash as it generated support for the cause.

For instance, consider the regime's euthanasia program of Germans who were incapacitated by an incurable condition such as a severe mental illness. This secretive program began right after World War II started for reasons of eugenics (purifying the gene pool) and freeing up hospital resources. After terminating what Hitler had termed a "useless mouth," the next of kin would get a death notice with a fabricated medical explanation.

In August of 1940, Cardinal Adolf Bertram protested on behalf of his fellow bishops to the head of the Reich Chancellery. Cardinal Michael von Faulhaber objected to the minister of justice a few months later. Cardinal Faulhaber defended his violation of the Reich Concordat, "I have deemed it my duty of conscience to speak out in this ethico-legal, non-political question, for as a Catholic bishop I may not remain silent when the preservation of the moral foundations of all public order is at stake."[16]

Those protests and more were behind closed doors, and the regime did not waver despite the program being an open secret. Although German citizens were not banding together to protest it, deeply cherished values and emotions were being stirred. Yet no organizational power went public with its protest as the program continued. By August of 1941, roughly 70,000 invalids had been eliminated.

Everything changed that month when a Catholic bishop named Clemens Graf von Galen raised his voice in public protest. He called the program an act of murder and its perpetrators criminals. He compared it to dispensing with machines that no longer run and beasts of burden that no longer produce anything, thereafter stating, "They now want to treat humans the same way."[17] Copies of his sermon quickly flooded the country and even reached soldiers on the front lines (who feared they might be next if they returned home seriously disabled).

The Führer was incensed and wanted to dispose of the Catholic rebel. He was at the peak of his war success but feared making a martyr out of Galen, triggering a cultural war with the Catholic Church, and suffering a loss of public morale his nation could not afford. He officially ended the program because of the bishop's public protest.

So what was different about the elimination of the Jews? The churches and their members had placed a higher value upon and felt more compassion for their incapacitated brethren than they did for the Jews. The Jews were not valued as fellow human beings because they had long been debased as the religious and political enemy and demonized as the murderers of Christ. As Bauer explains:

> The prevalent latent or overt nonmurderous antisemitic attitudes in the general population, the result of Christian antisemitism that had sought to dehumanize the Jews for many centuries—though never translated into a genocidal program by Christian society—prevented any serious opposition to the Nazis once they had decided to embark on the murder of the Jews.[18]

In sum, criticizing ordinary Christians for failing to speak out is like criticizing bystanders for not pouring their bottled water on a raging ten-story inferno. Although it is hard to imagine that everyday Christians were glad to see the fire, their Bibles had taught them such fates often needed to play themselves out. The accursed Jews were getting their due for the ancient blood on their hands, and some bleeding-heart liberals who may have tried to put out the fire would not have generated much help. After all, who cries when their enemy dies?

Yet had enough Christians felt in their hearts that God wanted them to defend the Jews instead of allowing him to mete out biblically ordained punishment, the bigger problem would have been tactical. Without some kind of organizational support or protection, such Germans were powerless to do anything about the Holocaust, and they knew it.

11.4.d. The Heart of the Matter

So where were the firemen who had the power to put out the inferno? Even more importantly, why did it erupt in the first place?

The moral firemen who the masses trusted to battle the flames of evil were the great institutions of Protestantism and Catholicism. Their ancient training manual had left them woefully unprepared, though, so they failed miserably when life put them to the test.

An enlightened set of churches never would have allowed Hitler to drive them out of Germany's political discourse, and they would have confronted the Nazi regime every time it crossed a moral line. They would have held their national behavior accountable to the same values and standards they had for personal behavior.

Trouble was, Protestantism had previously surrendered its power to the Nazis, and it was far too late to reverse the emasculation once the Holocaust had begun. Without a higher church authority outside of Germany who could defend them, protesting pastors were banished to concentration camps before they could build a following.

Once the Holocaust was blazing, the only firemen who could have put it out were the leaders of the so-called greatest moral power on earth, the Catholic Church. Considering what a single bishop was able to do against the euthanasia program, imagine what could have happened had the pope rallied every Catholic against the Holocaust.

Hitler despised how entrenched Germany was in its religious beliefs and thus the regime's efforts to eradicate denominational schools and indoctrinate the youth in Nazi ideology. He was hyperaware that if a cultural war ever fired up for the minds and hearts of a nation of Christians, he would have lost.

He knew how the Iron Chancellor, Otto von Bismarck, had been defeated by the pope and a steadfast Catholic populace in the Kulturkampf (cultural struggle) of the 1870s and '80s (§L.2.e.). He still felt the wounds of how the German Catholic leaders and their Center Party had solidly opposed the Nazis in the democratic years of the Weimar Republic, during which the Nazis had never been able to garner a majority of the popular vote.

Hitler had backed down to a single Catholic bishop because he knew the highest allegiance of German Catholics. As his propaganda chief Joseph Goebbels later explained, "The population of Münster could be regarded as lost during the war, if anything were done against the bishop, and in that fear one safely could include the whole of [the state of] Westphalia."[19]

Had the pope ever challenged Hitler for the allegiance of German Catholics, the masses would have seen it as God's deputy versus the boisterous Austrian, the Bible versus *Mein Kampf*, and centuries of tradition and entrenched holy teachings versus the recent spate of Nazi propaganda. Hitler would have had to immediately bow to the Vatican's pressure if he wanted to preserve German unity and keep his war effort from collapsing.

The Führer had nothing to fear, though, because the Vatican was turning a blind eye to the darkness it was enabling. Pope Pius XII (1939–1958) was also oblivious to the power he possessed if he really wanted to do something about the Holocaust. A private threat of boldly leading all of Catholicism in a moral crusade against it would have surely bullied Hitler into halting it (§L.3.). But the pope wanted to remain neutral, so the moral firemen never left their stations.

Moving on now to the utmost question of why the fire erupted, we arrive at the wisdom of a German Jew, Albert Einstein, who had moved to America in 1932: the problem could not have been solved at the same level at which it had been created. Here, then, is the heart of the matter. <u>The unenlightened churches and the teachings and values they had previously ingrained were the reason the Nazi problem existed in the first place</u>.

An enlightened holy book would have produced teachers and followers who would have rejected the ideology of racial superiority and the demonization of the Jews. As it was, though, far too many Christians embraced the Nazi preaching because their holy book and religion had long ago indoctrinated these perspectives and emotions.

What would have happened had their Bible only comprised the teachings of Jesus and not any verses of hatred, collective guilt or eternal curses? A nation of 95 percent Christians never would have demonized their Jewish neighbors, nor would they ever have shot or gassed a defenseless man, woman or child.

Over the course of centuries, though, Christianity's Bible-based teachings had produced a much different mindset. So when the Nazis asked Germany to dance in the early 1930s, millions of Protestants jumped right into bed with them. Credit the German Catholic leaders for warning against the darkness that would arrive by voting for the Nazis, but they were betrayed from above by the Vatican's totalitarian agenda and lust for a Reich Concordat.

The Vatican was unable to see the darkness in the Nazis' hatred of the Jews, disdain for democracy and repression of individual freedom because it was looking at a mirror image of itself. It believed totalitarian governance was part of the divine order of things, and the Catholic Church was the historical master of debasing the Jews and coercing a false unity (§L.3.b.). The Vatican thus formed a strategic partnership with its metaphysical soul mate just as it had done with Fascist Italy.

Some might argue that what we have seen so far were only errors of biblical interpretation. However, this apology is easily exposed as one of base denial. First, any textbook that fails to convey vital lessons to the vast majority of its diligent and intelligent students must be considered below average at best. Second, the Bible is clearly at fault for the next errors, which are linked to the previous ones like train boxcars still tangled together at the scene of a crash.

Whereas Catholics were sold down the river by the Vatican, Protestants were led astray by their Bibles. Christian marching orders were unmistakably rendered in Paul's letter to the Romans: "Let everyone be subject to the governing authorities, for there is no authority except that which God has established. The authorities that exist have been established by God" (Rom 13:1; see also Jn 19:11; Ti 3:1; 1 Pt 2:13–14).

Per the so-called word of God, Adolf Hitler was established by God. However, an enlightened populace never would have chosen or allowed Hitler as its governing authority. So did God really establish Hitler's authority, or did a nation of misguided Christians? The truth is obviously the latter, which obviously invalidates the Bible, which obviously empowered Hitler's bureaucratic machine.

This leads to another tangled-up boxcar, which is the religion's myopic focus on saving souls at the detriment of addressing societal injustices. This lack of integration and wholeness in Christian theology is buttressed by the Bible demanding submission to governing authorities and stating that God metes out horrible fates upon people and races who have been cursed. Meanwhile, the Bible also fails to articulate the truth of spiritual power and responsibility (§1.3.c.).

Because of what the Bible does and does not teach, Christians have habitually ignored certain injustices. Centuries of antisemitic atrocities were accepted and rationalized as an ancient curse and modern consequence. As will be seen in the next chapter, the same dynamic transpired in America with the Negroes and slavery.

Moreover, the churchmen allowed themselves to be easily driven out of the political arena. Stuffed back in the caboose of the German train and powerless to offer their political input, they idly gazed at the passing scenery as Hitler steamed it into World War II and the Holocaust. All the while and for all the above reasons, the churchmen had fallen for the darkness of submission and compartmentalization. The behavior of a group of people (the German nation) was not held to the same Christian standard applied to a single person. Even worse, the group was held to no standard at all!

<u>The primary driver of the Holocaust, though, was the raging undercurrent of antisemitism, and the originating source of this continental hatred was the Bible</u>. As seen back in Chapter 4, the gospel authors embellished their accounts with caustic words about the Jews. Trouble was, their words were later deified and worshipped as inerrant.

The deadliest impact was caused by the reports of Pilate's stratagem for washing the blood from his hands. Most Christians have fallen for his trick that a crowd's decision about a pardon would absolve him of responsibility for ordering the execution, but that is beside the point.

What especially condemned the Jews to centuries of Christian hatred and persecution was the idea that they were collectively and eternally responsible for Jesus's crucifixion. Again, the author of Matthew went far beyond his primary source (Mark) to attest that a crowd of Jews had chosen for Jesus to die instead of Barabbas with the cry, "His blood is on us and on our children!" (§4.4.h.). The next deadliest verse was Jesus telling the Jews, "You belong to your father, the devil" (§4.3.b.).

The Church perpetually promoted these beliefs and passions and thereby instigated centuries of hatred and violence against the Jews. So it was that not a single high-ranking Catholic ever protested against the genocide of the Jews. Cardinal Faulhaber, who felt a "duty of conscience" to oppose the euthanasia program, did not feel such a duty to oppose the Holocaust. Bishop Galen, who spoke out against the murder of Germany's invalids because they were human beings, did not speak out against the murder of Germany's Jews.

Instead, Catholic leaders in Germany and Rome idly watched as the biblical curse played itself out. Only after the Holocaust did they start waking up to the darkness of their doctrine.

The Protestants were also spellbound by the biblical deceit. As the Northern Protestant State Church of Germany sadly recalls, churchmen "eagerly emulated" the regime's antisemitic policies in the 1930s. The church of one particular state even declared it would "joyfully" aid in the pursuit of racial purity.[20]

All in all, the churches submitted to the darkness and enabled the darkness because they, too, were the darkness. Had they been of the Light, they never would have allowed the darkness to come to power. If it had somehow come to pass that way, they would have stood for spiritual truth every step of the way and held their ground at every turn. But, alas, the churches were unenlightened because their holy book is unenlightened.

Had only the true teachings of Jesus been taught throughout the ages, the Nazi horrors *would* never have transpired because they *could* never have transpired. Truth is, there was and is something terribly askew with the guidance rendered by the totality of the Bible. The churches were simply unable to rise above it.

11.5. Christianity Creates the Energetic Tsunami

Although the Bible was the originating source of the Holocaust's antisemitism, the Catholic Church and its Protestant offshoots made a bad situation even worse. Instead of downplaying the deadly verses and emphasizing love and forgiveness, they inflamed the collective hatred of the Jews for nearly two thousand years.[21]

This section summarizes their antisemitism and how it expanded into societal, political and racial aspects. This sordid history shows the many ways in which Christianity created the energetic tsunami that Hitler later crested and rode into infamy.

11.5.a. Religious Antisemitism

Antisemitism predates Christianity, but Christian antisemitism arose from the religious quarrel that began with the revolutionary rabbi from Nazareth. The passions stirred by conflicting beliefs were a textbook recipe for a highly charged and polarized relationship. Had the population and power been more equally distributed, there probably would have been centuries of conflict akin to what is now occurring in the Middle East.

The history of Jewish-Christian relations, though, was shaped by two crucial differences. First, the Christians eventually gained absolute power and an exponentially greater population.

Second, the Tanakh and Bible have much different messages about the other religion's members. Because the Jewish canon was already closed by the time of Jesus, the Tanakh had nothing to say about Christians. The New Testament had plenty to say about the Jews, though, because it was written after his execution.

Generally speaking, two different routes were available for the religions. Enlightened leaders could have led their followers to honor the multiplicity of paths to God and the equality and unity of humanity. But a lower consciousness was dominant, and institutional growth was rejected, so dogma and animosity drove the polarization of Jews and Christians and the course of Western history.

Reinforcing cycles of hatred are fueled by perceived injustices and retaliation and can only be deflated by forgiveness and love. Jesus taught this great truth and supposedly demonstrated it amid the agony of crucifixion (Lk 23:34). Unfortunately, his proto-orthodox followers somehow missed the memo.

After his execution, the Jews were the more numerous and powerful side that persecuted and drove away the earliest Christians (§4.5.a). According to Josephus, the Sanhedrin later had Jesus's brother James and some of his companions stoned to death in 62 CE.[22] But this era of persecution ended with the revolt of 66–73 CE and the crushing of centralized Judaism.

The Jewish persecution of Christians briefly returned amid the revolt of 132–135, during which Simon ben Kosiba was believed to be the Messiah. As Christian Justin Martyr summarized a couple of decades later in a letter to Rome, the Jewish warrior "gave orders that Christians alone should be led to cruel punishments, unless they would deny Jesus Christ and utter blasphemy." Justin wanted Rome to understand that the Jews "count us foes and enemies; and, like yourselves, they kill and punish us whenever they have the power."[23]

As Rome had throttled both sides, the conflict between Jews and Christians was practically nonexistent. The situation changed dramatically, though, in the fourth century. With a spiteful Church in possession of absolute power and far greater numbers, the Jews were doomed to centuries of oppression and widespread hatred.

The Church harangued the Jews with the charge of deicide (the murder of God) as it stoked the hatred with its Easter passion plays. The Jews were also demonized by propaganda such as the infamous blood libel, which claimed they were murdering Christian infants to draw blood for their rituals. In addition, they were prohibited from owning land, forced into socially inferior trades, expelled across Europe, terrorized and murdered by the Crusades and Inquisition, blamed and assaulted for the Black Plague, and walled into ghettos.

All in all, the Jews were despised and treated as subhuman. As historian Daniel Goldhagen summarizes, "The Catholic demonology about the Jews made it second nature for many Catholics, at all levels of society, to blame the Jews for any natural or human calamity."[24]

The Church's hatred and oppression did not dissipate with the Reformation or Enlightenment. To the contrary, the popes of the 16th to 19th centuries kept the Jews walled up in their Italian ghettos and forced them to wear yellow patches to announce their deplorable status.

When Napoleon's troops invaded Rome in 1798, they tore down the ghetto gates and granted equal rights to all. But papal rule was eventually reestablished, the ghetto gates were rebuilt, and the Jews were ordered to return. Napoleon recaptured Rome in 1809 and again destroyed the ghetto gates and granted equal rights. But his defeat allowed the pope to reclaim the Papal States, and the Jews were driven back into the ghetto.

An Italian nationalist uprising in 1848 drove the pope from Rome and once again freed the Jews, but Austrian and French troops restored the pope to power. The Jews were returned to the ghetto in Rome, which lasted until the pope's governance of the city finally ended for good in 1870.

On April 1, 1933, the Nazis conducted a national boycott of Jewish businesses that included physical assaults and the burning of Jewish shops. They also enacted a trio of laws within the next two weeks that banned Jews from being attorneys, drove them out of civil service jobs, barred them from being teachers or judges, established a max quota on their attendance at universities, and terminated benefits to Jewish veterans and the families of over 32,000 Jewish German soldiers who had been killed in the Great War. On April 26, Hitler told a Catholic bishop how his actions were aligned with Catholic history:

> The Catholic Church considered the Jews pestilent for fifteen hundred years, put them in ghettos, etc., because it recognized the Jews for what they were. In the epoch of liberalism the danger was no longer recognized. I am moving back toward the time in which a fifteen-hundred-year-long tradition was implemented. I do not set race over religion, but I recognize the representatives of this race as pestilent for the state and for

> the church and perhaps I am thereby doing Christianity a great service by pushing them out of schools and public functions.[25]

The Church had supercharged biblical antisemitism into the powerful undercurrent that was cresting in Nazi Germany. The vicious oppression of the Jews was built upon century after century of blaming all Jews in all places and times for the crucifixion of Jesus. So when the Nazis came calling for them, Catholic authorities saw divine justice unfolding. As a German archbishop wrote in 1941 after blaming them for the death of Jesus, "The self-imposed curse of the Jews, 'His blood be upon us and upon our children,' has come true terribly until the present time, until today."[26]

Believe it or not, the Church did not renounce this lethal doctrine until 1965.[27] Sadly and shockingly, the Holocaust was needed for the Church to finally drop one of its signature teachings.

Meanwhile, the Protestant antisemitism in Germany was a continuation of its biblical and Catholic origins. Martin Luther simply opened the floodgate for this branch of the current.

After breaking from the Church, he originally defended the Jews from its oppression and misguided teachings. As he wrote in 1523, "If I had been a Jew and had seen such dolts and blockheads govern and teach the Christian faith, I would sooner have become a hog than a Christian."[28] He argued that forbidding the Jews from respectable professions was not doing them any good, nor was treating them like dogs and isolating them from fellowship with Christians. "If we really want to help them," he concluded, "we must be guided in our dealings with them not by papal law but by the law of Christian love."[29]

However, Luther later returned to his Catholic roots. In 1543, he published his searing antisemitic tract *On the Jews and Their Lies*. In addition to his theological argument against Judaism, he denounced them with statements like, "Such a desperate, thoroughly evil, poisonous, and devilish lot are these Jews, who for these fourteen hundred years have been and still are our plague, our pestilence, and our misfortune."[30]

He cited the Old Testament to advocate the burning of Jewish synagogues, schools and homes (Dt 13:12–16; 1 Sm 15:23). He also pressed for the confiscation of all Jewish books and Talmudic writings. If the authorities were unwilling to use force to restrain the Jews, he argued, the Jews should be expelled from German lands.[31]

Luther was a greatly revered hero in Germany, and his writings were embraced like a secondary Bible. His legacy was a substantial part of the antisemitism that fueled the Holocaust, and his words were used to justify Christian support for antisemitic politics. For instance, Protestant pastors formed a right-wing organization in the early 1920s to promote German nationalism. Conway explains, "They repeatedly stressed Luther's anti-semitic statements and his abhorrence of democracy."[32]

Consider as well the violence and destruction of Kristallnacht. On the evenings of November 9 and 10, 1938, roughly 100 Jews were killed, another 30,000 were shipped off to concentration camps, 276 synagogues were burned and demolished, and the storefront windows of roughly 7,500 Jewish stores and businesses were shattered. A Protestant bishop thereafter published a collection of Luther's antisemitic discourse, noting therein how the synagogues were burning on Luther's birthday (November 10) and that Germans should heed the writings "of the greatest antisemite of his time, the warner of his people against the Jews."[33]

Martin Luther had simply perpetuated the antisemitic animosity of his Catholic training. As scholar Franklin Sherman notes about his 1543 treatise, "Much of his theological argumentation is borrowed from earlier Christian polemics against Judaism."[34] His "more favorable attitude toward the Jews as expressed in the early 1520's is to be understood as a temporary modification of the underlying negative stereotype which characterized his earlier statements, and to which he returned in his later treatises."[35]

Amid defending the Jews, Luther chastised Catholic priests for stoking the fires of hatred during Easter week: "Passion preachers do nothing else but exaggerate the Jews' misdeeds against Christ and thus embitter the hearts of the faithful against them."[36] Tragically, the great reformer eventually became what he had earlier denounced.

In sum, Protestant antisemitism was inherited from its Catholic parents. This branch of Christianity did not mature enough in its first four centuries to heal the deicidal blame and hatred of its Catholic DNA.

A grim example of this can be seen in a letter from a Protestant pastor to the Nazi newspaper *Der Stürmer* in 1935. After expressing enthusiastic support for the Nazi struggle against the Jews and their friends, the pastor wrote: "We will fight alongside you and we will not give up until the struggle against all Jewry and against the murderers of Our Savior has been brought to a victorious end, in the spirit of Christ and of Martin Luther. In true fellowship, I greet you with Heil Hitler!"[37]

Although the Vatican continues to deny the Church had any role in fostering the antisemitism that fueled the Holocaust, other Catholic leaders have been able to confess the truth. In a 1994 letter that was read throughout his diocese, Bishop Christopher Budd owned up to the obvious:

> The death of Jesus and the death of millions of Jews this century are tragically and inextricably linked. For centuries Jews have been pilloried, persecuted and blamed for the death of

Jesus. The charge of deicide or killing God was leveled against them—this was the fertile soil in which the evil of Nazism took root with such catastrophic effect.[38]

In their "Declaration of Repentance" in 1997, French bishops also told the truth about the Church's role:

> It is a well-proven fact that for centuries, up until Vatican Council II [in the 1960s], an anti-Jewish tradition stamped its mark in differing ways on Christian doctrine and teaching, in theology, apologetics, preaching and in the liturgy. It was on such ground that the venomous plant of hatred for the Jews was able to flourish.[39]

11.5.b. Societal and Political Antisemitism

The Catholic Church and its Protestant offshoots reinforced the religious hatred by also driving the societal and political antisemitism of the 19th and early 20th centuries. This subsection shows how the Church indirectly created and then directly promoted this outgrowth of religious antisemitism.

The Church repeatedly condemned usury from the 4th through 12th centuries and forced the Jews into disreputable jobs like money lending and tax collecting. As an archbishop in Cologne documented for the Jewish community in the 13th century, "If we find a Christian doing money exchange, he must leave the city: that business is yours."[40]

Not surprisingly, then, some Jews generated wealth and influence through the wonders of capitalism. As Martin Luther complained, "With their accursed usury they hold us and our property captive. Moreover, they mock and deride us because we work and let them play the role of lazy squires at our expense and in our land."[41] He also reported "the Jews donate large sums of money and thus prove beneficial to governments" but argued the money came from plundering and robbing lords and subjects via usury.[42]

Nevertheless, the Vatican had tremendous power across Europe and wielded it to suppress them. That eventually changed when the American and French revolutions sparked the onset of democracy and religious freedom, and one government after another followed suit and cut ties with the Church. This devastating blow to the Vatican was highlighted by its loss of sovereignty over the Papal States by 1870. Meanwhile, the Jews were being emancipated across Europe and granted their political rights and equality despite the papacy's opposition.

As historian David Kertzer explains, the Vatican responded in subsequent decades by bitterly opposing what it termed "modern" ideas, which included the freedoms of religion, speech and publishing, the separation of church and state, and the liberalism of Jews having the same legal rights and privileges as Christians. The Jews naturally became a tangible representation for Vatican officials of the advancing world they despised.[43]

No surprise here, but the Church was fighting against the Light. Instead of championing equality, it tried to repress the Jews back to an inferior status. Instead of advocating the distribution of power, it tried to keep Europe submitted to monarchical-papal rule. Instead of promoting a range of human freedoms, it tried to throttle them.

Since the Vatican was no longer privy to the power of the sword, it fought back with the power of the pen. Kertzer explains:

> It was in the Catholic press that the Church's battle against liberalism came for a time to focus on the Jews, who were painted as evil conspirators—in cahoots with the Masons—doing the devil's work. And it was in no small part through the press, as we shall see, that traditional Church hostility toward the Jews was transformed into modern anti-Semitism.[44]

At the heart of this effort was a journal founded in 1850 by Pope Pius IX. *Civiltà cattolica* was produced by the Jesuits on a biweekly basis and always reviewed before publication by the secretary of state and often the pope himself to ensure it was sending proper messages. *Civiltà cattolica* and the Vatican's daily newspaper, *L'Osservatore Romano*, were considered to be the most authoritative sources for Vatican opinions on current events, and Catholic publications around the world constantly quoted from *Civiltà cattolica*.

Beginning in December of 1880, the journal embarked on a 40-month campaign against the Jews with a series of 36 articles that Kertzer describes as "fiercely anti-Semitic."[45] In a recent book commemorating the 150th anniversary of *Civiltà cattolica*, a Jesuit historian admitted the journal had regularly charged the Jews with ritually murdering Christian children, almost controlling governments with their vast political power, and having great wealth and economic influence that they were wielding to harm Christianity and its adherents.[46]

Many other Catholic publications followed suit and also made these accusations. Of special note is how the Church still promoted the inflammatory propaganda of the blood libel despite numerous Jews being put on trial for this charge in the 19th and early 20th centuries. Although the trials spawned sensational news coverage and pogroms against Jewish communities, the popes refused to denounce the myth despite urgent pleas from a few outspoken cardinals and other powerful lay Catholics.

All in all, the Church was engaged in a relentless antisemitic campaign to incite political action against the Jews. For instance, the *Civiltà cattolica* was so effective that it was applauded in the 1930s as an antisemitic model by the Nazi and Italian Fascist newspapers *Der Stürmer* and *Il Regime fascista*.

Ironically, the Church was spewing a bowling ball of poisonous messages to knock down societal and economic bowling pins that it had previously set up. Because of its prohibition of usury and shaming of financial services, these lucrative domains had been left wide open for the Jews. The royal courts and aristocrats of Europe had disdained this work and turned to Jews for these services.

In the 19th century, Jews played a major role in the evolution of the modern system of international finance and banking. For instance, the Rothschild family business helped develop the international bond market, and their offices across Europe were the primary loan providers for many governments. The Rothschild sons who ran the London and Paris offices were Europe's richest men in the middle of the 19th century, and even the Vatican negotiated for much-needed loans from them to prevent bankruptcy in 1831 and 1850.

Jews never comprised more than about 1 percent of Germany's population in the late 19th and early 20th centuries, yet they had an extremely disproportionate presence in numerous businesses. For instance, Jews ran about 40–50 percent of the banks in Germany in the late 19th century. They also owned many of Germany's major daily newspapers, and they dominated ownership of the large department stores.

In the Austrian side of the Austrian-Hungarian Empire, more than 50 percent of the major banks were owned by Jews, and Jews in the Hungarian side had an even greater economic presence. In France, Jews comprised less than 0.2 percent of the population but owned over 20 percent of its major financial institutions.

Some Jews had obviously capitalized on their special advantage to become wealthy. But the Church was no more justified in hating the Jews for their financial power than the United States would be if it had banned all white people from Wall Street and then got angry at African Americans for their wealth.

Although the statistical aberration had been created by the Church's architecting of the societal landscape, a far deadlier dynamic was amplifying it. The economic aggravation was being mirrored by the polarization of religion, which the Church had long been characterizing with salvation on one side and demonization on the other. To the masses who were being taught the financial score, the wealthy beneficiaries were not "good Christians" but rather "evil Jews."

Antisemites thus had an easy time with perpetuating the Church's stereotype and marking the Jews as both a religious and societal cancer. Because the Jews were also such a tiny minority amid the newfound democracies, political parties capitalized on the power of antisemitic politics. To these folks, the Jews were the root cause of society's problems. This message was quite attractive to the massive Christian majority in the late 19th century, especially during economic downturns.[47]

As already summarized, the Vatican was pouring gas on the fire of political antisemitism. Antisemitic parties were the Vatican's allies as the Church tried to salvage political power amid its 19th-century freefall.

Although the political appeal of antisemitism receded at the turn of the century, it flared back up again after World War I. All the while the Church kept driving the societal fight while trying to keep it from becoming violent.

As but one example from just before Hitler came to power, an Austrian bishop reminded Catholics of the Vatican's distinction between good and bad antisemitism. In a letter translated and published throughout Europe, he condemned racial bias and violence against the Jews. Without skipping a beat, though, he wrote, "It is beyond any doubt that many Jews, unrelated to any religious concern, exercise an extremely pernicious influence in almost all sectors of modern civilization." After detailing his case and linking "degenerate Judaism" to international capitalism, socialism and communism, the bishop concluded with this chilling encouragement:

> Not only is it legitimate to combat and to end Judaism's pernicious influence, it is indeed the strict duty of conscience of every informed Christian. One can only hope that Aryans and Christians will increasingly come to recognize the dangers and troubles created by the Jewish spirit and to fight them more tenaciously.[48]

After German Catholicism's opposition to the Nazis abruptly ended in 1933, the masses were free to embrace a movement that had much in common with their religion. Just like the Nazis, Catholics were far more conservative and totalitarian than liberal and democratic, and they also vehemently opposed communism and the Jews. In 1934, a German priest hailed the Führer as "the tool of God, called upon to overcome Judaism."[49]

The Nazis continued to purge Jews from German society. The most prominent of their post-1933 policies were the Nuremberg Laws of 1935, which revoked the citizenship of all Jews and criminalized marriage and sexual relations between Jews and Aryans.

The Vatican, though, did not proclaim any moral issues in these disturbing developments. To the contrary, the *Civiltà cattolica* published an article in 1936 that explained how the Church's opposition to the Nazis' glorification of race should not be misconstrued as a rejection of antisemitism. Rather, the article implored Christians to defend themselves against the Jewish threat by suspending their civic rights and hastening them back into the ghettos.⁵⁰

In the latter half of 1938, Italy enacted a series of racial laws against its Jews. The laws expelled Jews from Italy who had become citizens after 1918, barred them from attending schools, prohibited them from working in a wide range of professions, and confiscated their property and businesses. Pope Pius XI (1922–1939) only protested a small and very specific part of the new laws. He was upset about the prohibition against marriages between Catholics when one of the parties was a converted Jew.⁵¹

The Catholic Church did not protest the antisemitic laws in Germany and Italy because it had a long history of doing so itself. As an Italian bishop explained to his constituents, it had also never denied a government's right to limit or impede the influence of the Jews, nor had the Church ever done or said anything in defense of the Jews.⁵²

The Jews were thus being vilified as a monstrous societal problem, and their financial prowess was being perceived by a Christian mindset that abhorred capitalistic income, equality and free thinking (which was another charge in the clergy's rhetoric against the Jews). The result was even more Christian hatred arising from fear, envy and the projection of repressed greed (for we despise in others what we deny and cannot accept about ourselves).

The societal dimension of antisemitism was a big part of the fury being stirred up against the Jews. In a boisterous speech to the Reichstag in January of 1939, Hitler rehashed the charge that Jewry had been exploiting the working classes and needed to "adapt itself to productive work like any other nation." Referring to himself as a prophet, Hitler disclosed what he had in mind: "If international finance Jewry inside and outside Europe again succeeds in precipitating the nations into a world war, the result will not be the Bolshevization of the earth and with it the victory of Jewry, but the annihilation of the Jewish race in Europe."⁵³

11.5.c. Racial and Redemptive Antisemitism

The most radical solution to the Jewish problem was not Hitler's brainchild. Rather, it had been gestating in European consciousness for quite some time. For instance, Martin Luther's tract against the Jews included the surprising consideration, "We are at fault in not slaying them."⁵⁴ Yet the Christians of his era had everything under control with their expulsions, ghettos and oppressive laws.

Everything changed when Europe embraced democracy and the Jews were granted freedom and equality. As Jewish wealth was also thriving with capitalism, the Jewish problem was becoming far greater than it had ever been before. Antisemitic political parties thus arose in Austria, France and Germany to oppose this development, and they were strongly encouraged by the Church's antisemitic campaign. All the while the conspiracy theory (that the Jews were aiming to dominate the world and dismantle Christian society) was proliferating across Europe.

All in all, the antisemitic tsunami was rapidly approaching its historical collision with the Continent. Like ocean waves that do not begin flaring up until they hit the rising floor of a beach, this massive energy flow was beginning to rise up like a cobra from the backlash of Christianity.

Meanwhile, new scientific insights helped converge and intensify the wave. Theories about genetics and evolution gave the antisemitic movement a powerful and easily communicated master concept that synthesized the religious charges of deicide and apostasy with the societal charges of economic exploitation and destructive intentions.

The onset of racial antisemitism was morphing the perception of the Jewish problem from religious beliefs that could be changed to hardwired biology that could not. Fed by theories of social Darwinism (competition between races for supremacy or extinction) and eugenics, solutions naturally followed.

In Germany, where Jews had finally gained civic equality by 1871, racial antisemitism merged with nationalistic fervor in the polarizing conception of "good Germans" and "evil Jews." The former were moral Christians while the latter were a race of economic parasites who were incapable of rehabilitation.

These views were strongest among the German elite and intellectuals and especially popular in the universities. Amid the turmoil of unprecedented societal change, advocates began advancing more extreme solutions. According to scholar Klemens Felden, antisemitic writers who proposed "merciless persecution and annihilation were by far in the majority and their appeal increased from decade to decade." Felden analyzed the writings of 51 prominent antisemitic authors in Germany from 1861 to 1895, finding that of the 28 who proposed solutions to the Jewish problem, 19 advocated for physical extermination.[55]

In the late 1890s, the antisemitic political parties fell out of favor in Germany. During the first decade of the 20th century, it looked like the previous century's vitriol had just been a reactionary phenomenon whose time had passed. Nevertheless, the antisemitic movement persisted through various associations, organizations and cultural groups. On the eve of World War I, antisemitism in Austria, France and Russia was more extreme than in Germany.[56]

World War I propelled the wave out of its trough and crested it to new heights as antisemites across Europe linked the war with the previous century's emancipation of the Jews. Conspiracy theorists claimed the Jews had schemed for the war to profit economically and politically. In Germany, antisemites blamed the Jews for their nation's defeat. As the widespread myth declared it, the German army had been "stabbed in the back" by secret Jewish complicity with the Allies.

The conspiracy theory was also amplified by a supposedly secret text, *Protocols of the Elders of Zion*, that articulated the Jewish strategy for controlling the world. Fabricated in the 1890s by the Russian secret police to combat liberalism within the empire (where the Jews had not been liberated), it spread rapidly across Europe in the wake of the empire's collapse. Widely revered as proof of the fiendish Jewish agenda, 33 German editions were published before Hitler came to power, and countless more were published thereafter.

The Bolshevik Revolution also energized the paranoia. As an English historian wrote in 1921, "It is this apparent absence of motive, this seemingly aimless campaign of destruction carried on by the Bolsheviks of Russia, that has led many people to believe in the theory of a Jewish conspiracy to destroy Christianity."[57]

Meanwhile, the Catholic Church validated and promoted the paranoia. For instance, the *Civiltà cattolica* ran a feature article in October of 1922 entitled "The World Revolution and the Jews." It claimed they had hidden their real identities and actually comprised 447 of the highest 545 officials of the Bolshevik regime despite comprising less than 5 percent of Russia's population. It also claimed the Jews were scheming to duplicate such revolutions around the world.[58]

[Note: The revolution apparently had a higher percentage of Jews than the general population, but it did not carry over into Lenin's government. In the mid-1920s, only 6 percent of the 417 members of the Soviet Union's highest leadership councils had Jewish backgrounds. This tiny fraction would drop sharply thereafter under Stalin, yet *Civiltà cattolica* continued to deceptively warn as late as 1938 that almost all Soviet leaders were Jewish.[59]]

In Germany, the devastating hyperinflation of the early 1920s had given the middle and working classes strong reasons to embrace the antisemitic fervor of the conservative elite. For all the above reasons and more, German antisemitism was at a fever pitch in those years.

Numerous government reports documented a public hatred of the Jews that was bordering on being explosive. As the president of a district government noted in 1920, "One hears everywhere that 'our [Germany's] government is delivering us over to the Jews.'"[60] In 1921, a police situation summary stated, "Reports agree that the mood for Jewish pogroms is spreading systematically in all parts of the country."[61] In 1922, a police situation summary stated, "The fact cannot be denied that the antisemitic idea has penetrated the widest levels of the middle class, even far into the working class."[62]

The situation was even more volatile in Austria, yet the Church kept propelling the antisemitic wave across Europe while halfheartedly attempting to keep it from cresting into violence. Church representatives even suggested the crime that would later be committed. For instance, a Polish priest wrote in

1923, "If the world is to be rid of the Jewish scourge, it would be necessary to exterminate them, down to the last one."[63]

That disturbing message pales in comparison, though, to what the Vatican published while the Nazi noose was encircling the German Jews. In 1937, *Civiltà cattolica* laid out not only the option of "expulsion" for handling the Jewish problem but also the "clearly hostile manner" of "destruction." As Goldhagen summarizes, the journal "discussed the annihilation of the Jews as an actual thinkable option."[64]

German Protestants were just as agitated by the Jewish problem. An estimated 70–80 percent of pastors during the 1920s supported the very conservative, pro-monarchy and openly antisemitic German National People's Party (DNVP).[65]

After the Nazis caught fire and the German Christians were swooning over Hitler (§11.4.b.), some Protestants were also discussing extermination. For instance, one of Germany's leading theologians and biblical scholars, Gerhard Kittel, posited it as a possible solution in a 1933 speech.[66] That he rejected the option because of logistical feasibility instead of morality is further proof of the deeply ingrained antisemitism in European Christians.

International correspondence among Protestant leaders in the early Nazi years speaks volumes as well. The American chairman of an international council of Protestant churches sent a letter of protest to the council's representative in Germany.

The American indicated he was writing because "colleagues of mine were assured this summer in Berlin by official representatives of the churches that the [German] policy could be described as one of 'humane extermination.'" Christians in America, he explained, could not conceive of any extermination of any people as "humane," nor could they understand how any Christian in any nation in any era could possibly lend credence to such an idea. It forced the Americans to observe, he continued, that even when freedom of speech still existed in Germany, not a single protest from German Protestants against Nazi antisemitism had reached them.

The German official's response proves that it was not a misunderstanding. Rather, the two men had an irreconcilable difference of opinion that was no longer worth discussing.[67]

In sum, Hitler did not invent the Final Solution but rather manifested what had been in the making for almost two thousand years. Christianity had brainwashed antisemitism for centuries and energized this powerful current as it expanded in political and racial directions. It was a continental phenomenon as also evidenced by how the governments of Romania, Hungary, Poland and Italy enacted antisemitic laws in 1937 and 1938.

This tidal wave crested and crashed down upon humanity after it churned into the unique coastline of postwar Germany. Amid national humiliation, overwhelming economic burdens, a global depression, the fear of communism and Christian disdain for liberalism, surfing conditions were suddenly perfect for the Nazis.

Hitler capitalized on the moment with redemptive antisemitism. As he framed it in *Mein Kampf* back in 1925, if the Jew triumphed over the races, the world would be like it was thousands of years prior when humanity did not exist. Because nature always avenges the violation of her laws, "I believe that I am acting in accordance with the will of the Almighty Creator: *by defending myself against the Jew, I am fighting for the work of the Lord.*"[68]

He was only able to crest the dark tidal wave to absolute power because he had the complicity of Protestantism and Catholicism. He was able to thereafter surf his Christian nation into World War II and the Holocaust because the churches partnered with and enabled the darkness.

If it still boggles the mind as to why Hitler and tens of thousands of Germans attempted to massacre the entire Jewish race, remember that they had come to believe the Jews were the ultimate source of evil in the world. Can believers in an infallible Bible really be so surprised? After all, it says Jesus called the Jews the offspring of the devil.

The Nazis ensured their Christian nation was fully aware of this biblical teaching. For instance, their propaganda included an illustrated book with the poem, "The Father of the Jews is the Devil." Another popular book, *The Poisonous Mushroom*, was geared for children and also illustrated this biblical fact.

Yet the greatest single contributor to antisemitism and the Holocaust was the charge of deicide that Christianity and its Bible had leveled against an entire race. No small wonder, then, that so many churchmen passively watched as Hitler—an authority established by God according to their Bibles—meted out an Old Testament version of divine justice.

In the final analysis, it is painfully obvious that while the Catholic Church and its Protestant offshoots did not pull the Holocaust trigger, they had long ago painted a red bull's-eye on the Jews and loaded the gun with centuries of emotional ammunition. They energized and supported the politics that helped a hate-mongering despot gain possession of the weapon and then looked the other way as the genocide was staged and committed.

We teach our children that sticks and stones may break our bones but words can never hurt us. Unfortunately, that is not always true, for words in the Bible and from its teachers led to the murder of six million Jews.

11.6. A Fiendish Impact and a Devilish Denial

There is only one explanation as to how a nation of 95 percent Christians could have ever hated and murdered as it did. The Catholic Church and its Protestant offshoots had failed to properly guide them.

In other words, the Holocaust was a horrific result of the blind leading the blind. If the German people had been taught how to recognize and deal with evil or the imperative to live with spiritual power and responsibility, their nation could not have committed the Holocaust. But the Bible had struck out on those two aspects of the perfect storm, thereby leaving its believers in the dark and prone to enacting evil.

Nevertheless, its teachers still could have prevented the Holocaust by properly dealing with the other aspect. After all, just one hit out of three would have been enough to win this particular game. Although two of the three dynamics were out of the Bible's league, antisemitism was a pitch that its students could have handled.

Trouble was, the message of love was not so clear when it came to the Jews, for it was obscured by words of collective blame and demonization. The churches were misguided by the totality of the Bible and failed to live what Jesus had highlighted as one of his two greatest commandments: "Love your neighbor as yourself" (Mt 22:39). That teaching leads us to connect the dots one final time to further understand how Christianity created and enabled the Holocaust.

11.6.a. The Politics of Hating Your Neighbor

Returning to the Vatican's encouragement of societal and political antisemitism, we will zoom in to see what it looked like in the heavily Catholic nation of Austria. We begin with a vignette about a papal nuncio (ambassador) to Austria named Luigi Galimberti, for it is a microcosm of the politics of hating your neighbor.

In 1889, an Austrian bishop introduced the nuncio to a Jewish landowner who had generously given to Catholic charities. The nuncio commended the donor, and the meeting was reported in the newspapers. Three other Austrian bishops took issue with it, though, and protested to the pope about the nuncio's public praise for a Jew. They asked for disciplinary action against Galimberti.

The Vatican's secretary of state chastised him for giving ammunition to the Jewish press that would weaken the antisemitic movement in Austria and instructed him "to abstain from pronouncing such words of praise."[69] The Catholic Church could not abide the chance that a little goodwill might thwart its dark will.

As the world's oldest institution was continuing to flood Europe with hatred, guess what else happened in Austria that year? Adolf Hitler was born on April 20, 1889.

While the infant was being raised in the backwoods of Austria, a powerful antisemitic movement was roiling in Vienna. Founded two years prior, the Christian Socialist Organization and its charismatic leader, a resolute Catholic named Karl Lueger, had struck a resounding chord with the masses with political attacks on the Jews.

That the heavily Catholic nation harmonized with such diatribes should come as no surprise. After all, the long history of Catholic antisemitism had been reinforced and amplified in the early 1880s by the fiercely antisemitic campaign of the *Civiltà cattolica* (§11.5.b.).

In 1891, Lueger's organization became the Christian Social Party. This political party marked the Jews as the enemy and received the enthusiastic support of the Austrian clergy until the fever started getting too hot. Kertzer summarizes the Vatican's involvement under Pope Leo XIII (1878–1903):

> The Vatican Secret Archives offer dramatic evidence of the active role played by the Pope and his secretary of state in nurturing the Christian Social party's anti-Semitic campaign. Most striking of all is evidence that they undermined efforts by the Austrian Church hierarchy to distance the Church from Lueger and his movement.[70]

The Christian Social Party was extremely successful with its antisemitic campaign during the 1890s. As the party increased its feverish antisemitic rallies, Austria's high society ratcheted up its pressure on the Vatican to condemn the popular movement.

Archbishops from Vienna and Prague made a joint plea to the pope about the party's radical antisemitism, Austrian aristocrats voiced their protest, and newspapers chastised the Vatican for supporting the movement. Even the Austrian prime minister pleaded with the Vatican to withdraw its support, but these appeals fell on deaf ears. To the contrary, Leo XIII responded by sending a letter to Lueger that expressed his sympathy for the party's agenda and his personal blessings for the party's leader.

In 1897, the *Civiltà cattolica* published an article strongly praising the "vigorous counterattack" of the Christian Social Party against Jewish economic and political interests. The journal praised the party as a model for freeing "the Christian countries from their slavery under the emancipated Jews' yoke" and repelling the "evil invaders."[71]

Although Lueger's party had triumphed in Vienna's city council elections of 1895 and selected him as the mayor, his appointment was opposed by the Austrian prime minister and emperor. Only after Leo XIII intervened on Lueger's behalf did the master of political antisemitism finally take office in

1897. Lueger remained the mayor until he died in 1910.

We now turn to the development of Adolf Hitler and his conception of the world. He wrote in *Mein Kampf* that neither his parents or school taught him to think any differently about the Jews, nor did he have any meaningful personal experiences with them while growing up. To the contrary, he used to have a "mild distaste" when he heard unfavorable remarks about them.[72]

So how and when did he learn to hate the Jews? At the age of 18 in 1907, he arrived in Vienna and lived there until moving to Munich in 1913.

He was initially opposed to the venomous discourse of the antisemitic press because of his code of human tolerance, and he continued to reject religious attacks as he did in other cases. He felt the tone of these publications was not appropriate for a great nation with such a rich cultural tradition. He was also bothered by what had happened in the Middle Ages and did not want that history to be repeated.

He then described how he disdained the major newspapers of Vienna because of their over-glorified coverage of the Austrian court, criticism of the German Kaiser and high praise of France. So he turned his patronage to an antisemitic newspaper. He did not agree with its strong antisemitic tone, but he occasionally considered its arguments.

Meanwhile, he was learning about the leader and movement that were ruling Vienna at the time: Dr. Karl Lueger and the Christian Social Party. Upon first arriving there, Hitler said he viewed them as reactionary and opposed them. He continued to tell his story in *Mein Kampf*:

> My common sense of justice, however, forced me to change this judgment in proportion as I had occasion to become acquainted with the man and his work; and slowly my fair judgment turned to unconcealed admiration. Today, more than ever, I regard this man as the greatest German mayor of all times.
>
> How many of my basic principles were upset by this change in my attitude toward the Christian Social movement!
>
> My views with regard to anti-Semitism thus succumbed to the passage of time, and this was my greatest transformation of all.
>
> It cost me the greatest inner soul struggles, and only after months of battle between my reason and my sentiments did my reason begin to emerge victorious. Two years later, my sentiment had followed my reason, and from then on became its most loyal guardian and sentinel.[73]

11.6.b. The Unintended Consequences of Unenlightened Choices

Hitler had thus been converted to the belief that the Jews were the foremost cause of society's problems. He had also learned the best way to develop a solid base of political support was inciting hatred and fear of them, and he saw how Catholic and Protestant authorities were supporting such a platform. Nothing would be in his way except for the bleeding-heart liberals and the human proclivity for kindness when times are good.

The politics of antisemitism were thus an express-lane ticket to power when times were bad. Hitler went all in with his ticket and just needed to wait for the skies in Germany to darken before he could cash it in with the Nazi platform of arrogance and fear.

The Catholic Church could not possibly have known what its antisemitic crop was going to yield when the storms of life struck. How were its leaders to know what dominant personalities were growing amid their Austrian fields and what they might eventually do? Yet ignorance of universal laws is no excuse for violating them, and unintended consequences are a natural part of an interconnected and nonlinear universe. What is always predictable, though, is that we will eventually reap the metaphysical essence of what we sow.

So maybe someday the leaders of the Catholic Church and its Protestant offshoots will awaken and own up to how much fear and hatred they planted in the minds and hearts of humanity. Maybe someday they will understand why Jesus placed so much emphasis on flowing love and forgiveness and why he implored his followers to address the inner darkness of fear, anger, hatred and worry.

Maybe someday the Christian masses will awaken and realize that they have been spiritually blind and following the blind on the broad road that leads to destruction. Maybe someday they will address their inner darkness as they embrace their spiritual power and responsibility for what we collectively create.

11.6.c. The Devilish Denial of Egoic Pride

All in all, it is supremely tragic how an unenlightened version of Christianity created or enabled the Holocaust's three formative dynamics. The sickest part of it all, though, is that the Vatican has continued to deny that it had any responsibility whatsoever for the Holocaust.

Its official assessment of the Holocaust, which took over a decade to produce, was finally released in 1998. The document "We Remember" would have us believe the Vatican had nothing to do with Hitler's rise to power and that Pope Pius XII protested the genocide and did all in his power to save the Jews from the Nazi onslaught. The cold, hard facts of history prove this to be a hypocritical and gutless deception (§L.2., §L.3.).

But the current emphasis is on the antisemitism that fueled the Holocaust, and "We Remember" specifically states the Holocaust's "anti-Semitism had its roots outside of Christianity."[74] In other words, the Vatican would also have us believe European minds and hearts were a blank slate in the late 19th century, but a purely secular movement was able to convince an overwhelmingly Christian nation to forsake Jesus's teachings of neighborly love and so bitterly hate the Jews that the Holocaust could be committed.

The only reasonable assessment of such a claim is that it was written either by a committee whose intelligence and historical knowledge could be easily surpassed by a teenager or one that deviously avoided stating the truth to protect its beloved Church. This is yet more deception, and it was created by a master of deception whose master is not God but rather the self-exalting and self-protecting devil of egoic pride.

11.7. Conclusion

The Holocaust was a perfect storm of three independent dynamics that converged over Germany after World War I. Each of them was created or enabled by the Catholic Church and its Protestant offshoots.

As for the Holocaust's antisemitism, its originating source was the Bible. According to the gospels, Jesus had called the Jews the offspring of the devil, and they had cursed themselves for killing him (§11.4.d.). The Church could have defused these caustic words by emphasizing love and forgiveness, but it did the opposite and flooded this hatred into European psyches for well over a thousand years.

With the Church having also forced the Jews into financial professions while keeping the Christians at bay, the Jews were uniquely positioned to dominate finance and banking and thus had a leg up on owning other businesses. They became easily targeted scapegoats for the dark side of capitalism.

As humanity progressed with the enlightenment of the 19th century, the Church's reactionary backlash was highlighted by decades of venomous publications against the Jews that further empowered the politics of antisemitism. Amid the mushrooming paranoia that engulfed Europe, antisemites mixed in the new ingredients of genetics and evolution to cook up a nourishing argument for their appetite for destruction.

As for the national evil that the Nazis enacted, both Protestantism and Catholicism were blind to it. The churches failed to understand the nature of evil, illuminate it, and withdraw their empowerment of it. Instead, they actively supported it because they were in the dark themselves from having been taught by an unenlightened holy book.

[Note: The German Catholic Church originally sniffed out the evil of Nazism but lacked clarity about those dynamics. Since it was oblivious to the darkness within, it was easily eclipsed from above by the Vatican and the Reich

Concordat of 1933. It thereafter colluded with the darkness in silence.]

As for the countless Germans who enabled or contributed to the genocidal machine, humanity was not yet aware of the truth about free will, spiritual power and responsibility. The Bible had not only failed to teach these truths but had also done the opposite by ordering the masses to always submit to their authorities. With its curse on the Jews and decree that Hitler was God's duly established authority, the Final Solution appeared to be the Jewish destiny. What was really destined, though, was that the broad road of Christianity would lead to destruction.

To create a heavenly future, we have to change the dynamics that have been generating our living hell. Hopefully, an enlightened version of Christianity will soon begin teaching the painful lessons of the Holocaust.

First, awakening Christians will understand why Jesus so greatly emphasized love and forgiveness and that the only way to consistently flow these energies is by addressing our inner darkness. When we sow the seeds of fear, we eventually reap a deadly harvest.

Second, awakening Christians will drop the fallacy of the Bible's infallibility. The unenlightened textbook failed Germany and humanity—and failed them horrifically.

Third, awakening Christians will learn to see through the politics of arrogance and fear, which demonize others and polarize issues so that intelligent discourse becomes improbable and enlightened resolutions impossible. Awakening Christians will prioritize the unity of the human race and the divine call of justice for all.

Fourth, awakening Christians will no longer compartmentalize their nation's behavior from their morals and values. They will no longer abdicate their spiritual power and personal responsibility for collective behavior.

Finally, awakening Christians will better understand the nature of evil and how to address it (§5.2.). They will begin shining the light upon the last place self-righteous crusaders ever think to find and address it: within.

Enough light is now shining for us to wake up from our collective nightmare. We thus move on to the concluding chapter, which synthesizes the book's insights and motivates the next step of our challenging journey through this spectacular universe.

CHAPTER 12

THE TIME IS NOW

12.1. Introduction

The truths of an enlightened spirituality have broken through the deceptions of the entrenched darkness. After thousands of years of suffering through a collective nightmare, the morning dawn has finally arrived on our planet. To accentuate the great awakening, the final chapter recaps the spiritual thesis, offers more guidance for the difficult path ahead, and shows how America also traveled the broad road of religion to destruction.

12.2. The Spiritual Thesis About the Western Religions

Our journey has uncovered some shocking insights. This section elevates our perspective to see the forest of those trees.

12.2.a. Challenging Paradigms and Faulty Assumptions

Paradigms are deeply ingrained ways of understanding life and have an amazing ability to beguile consciousness. Usually based on unchallenged assumptions, their blinding power can only be observed in hindsight. Courage and penetrating insight are required to free the mind for perceiving the universe anew.

Paradigm shifts have allowed scientists to solve previously insurmountable problems (§2.3.b.), and the book has added two more examples. As for the first, conclusively dating Daniel was not a simple problem, but it was not extraordinarily difficult either (Appendix D). It had remained unsolved only because of erroneous assumptions in the two competing paradigms.

Most critical scholars were immersed in the mindset of scientism. Believing long-range prophecy to be impossible, they figured Daniel had to be a fabrication. On the other side, the remaining scholars were committed to the fundamentalist creed about the Bible's inerrancy. Hence, they were unable to acknowledge the errors and additions that were introduced long after Daniel was written.

The far greater example, though, comes from the unraveling of the apocalyptic prophecies. Anybody could have interpreted Daniel's prophecies, for they were abstract summaries of what became well-documented history. The biggest piece of the puzzle was the different king who defeated three kings, Constantine the Great.

Critical scholars did not even try to decode them, for they had already concluded the material was bogus. Meanwhile, the last place fundamentalists ever thought to look was at the first emperor to champion their religion. Moreover, many were determined to find proof of an antichrist in text that was only foretelling the exploits of the Roman Empire. Yet once a new way of seeing things was explored, Daniel's prophecies fell like dominoes, and Revelation was easily unraveled too.

Much can be learned from the blinding power of paradigms. Rather than waiting for pain to spark a move toward greater awareness, wise souls proactively scrutinize their perceptions and conclusions. They become clear as to what is really known and what is assumed to be true.

This awareness is not to be found in the world's religions, all of which are firmly entrenched in their core assumptions. As God supposedly pointed out to Walsch, the state of the world proves we have missed something. The only way we will find solutions is by doing what all great scientists do when something is not working—we have to reexamine our assumptions:

> All great discoveries have been made from a willingness, and ability, to *not be right*. And that's what's needed here.
> You cannot know God until you've stopped telling yourself that you *already* know God. You cannot hear God until you stop thinking that you've already heard God.
> *I cannot tell you My Truth until you stop telling Me yours.*[1]

When it comes to religion, our planet desperately needs a paradigm shift. Physicists of the 20th century stepped through a couple of them as they discovered our universe is far more amazing and breathtaking than our minds can possibly grasp. The paradoxical mystery and mathematical beauty by which it operates has led to the title of "The Elegant Universe."[2]

All fields of knowledge have grown far beyond their antiquated conceptions except for religion. The time has come for us to mature beyond those simplistic and mistaken understandings.

12.2.b. The Spiritual Illness Resides Within

Only egoic pride can stonewall the universal love that is fostering spiritual growth and our creation of heaven on earth. It steadfastly maintains, "I am free from error; I am perfect as I am; I have nothing to change." It has been telling its truth to God and the world for far too long, and we have suffered immeasurably.

Egoic pride is the devil inside. At its worst, it is malignant narcissism, which is an unyielding will that has repudiated its conscience and is solely driven to serve and save itself.

Religions are massive manifestations of egoic pride, for they steadfastly refuse to challenge their root assumptions. Since they are built upon and defined by their core beliefs, their survival depends on driving out all doubt. They are thus monoliths of self-righteousness whose ultimate goal is saving and propagating themselves.

Each of the stage 2 religions is thus afflicted by not only egoic pride amid their leaders and followers but also an egoic pride that pervades the institution itself. Just as the force of gravity exists between two different bodies of mass, so it is with the bonding between believers and their religious institution. A strong, dark force pulls for unity around their beliefs.

The result is a metaphysical black hole that has entrapped billions of souls. As a religious institution is incapable of forsaking its life for the sake of its followers, there is only way to escape it. One must search for the truth and forge through the centrifugal fear of the black hole. The key to salvation is recognizing the spiritual illness within.

12.2.c. The Writing on the Wall for Judaism and Christianity

The Judeo-Christian paradigm was built upon a couple of deeply flawed assumptions. First, the Tanakh or Bible is God's authoritative and inerrant communication to mankind that supersedes all other perceived messages. Second, the character and nature of God is a reflection of human traits.

Inerrancy never even made it out of the gate, for the two creation stories in Genesis are marred by a glaring contradiction. Moreover, the latter story depicts God as a bald-faced liar. When the facts of the goddess-worshipping past are brought to light, it becomes clear why the tale of Adam and Eve was invented.

Meanwhile, the ancient Hebrews projected all kinds of human characteristics upon God. As a ruler above their patriarchy, he was an authoritative male. As a father looking to guide, he was generally loving but would dispense harsh punishment in moments of anger. As a neurotic needing control, he demanded sacrifices for imperfect behavior. As a lover all alone, he was jealous and barred his subjects from worshipping other deities.

All in all, the ancient Hebrews perceived the great truth of "God created mankind in his own image" but missed it 180 degrees (Gn 1:27). By looking at humanity to understand the hidden nature of God instead of vice versa, their ancient tales pinned the theological tail on the wrong end of the donkey.

Another big mistake was believing that God plays favorites. They once again perceived half of a paradoxical truth by viewing themselves as God's chosen people. Trouble was, they failed to comprehend that their Gentile neighbors were also God's chosen people.

They were lost in mistaken dogma and tribal narcissism, so God tried to call them home. Trouble was, they were expecting their Anointed One to be a great warrior who would restore the Judaic kingdom. They had no idea his kingdom would be spiritual, not physical.

Jesus strove to uproot numerous tenets of Judaism to help those lost souls find the path of spiritual growth back home. But as egoic pride naturally does when it is threatened, it defends itself. At its worst, it tries to destroy whatever or whoever is shining light upon its darkness, which it did with the revolutionary rabbi.

A fierce debate ensued within the land of the Jews as the gospel authors tried to prove that Jesus was the Anointed One. Although they may have recorded a lot of accurate material, their books were marred by numerous alterations and inventions.

Nevertheless, the Daniel prophecies have conclusively answered the Messiah question. Penned in the 6th century BCE, they foretold the Anointed One would arrive during the rule of the Roman Empire, in the era of its first ten emperors and between 27 and 34 CE. They also indicated he would make his brief appearance before the temple was destroyed in 70 CE.

There was also debate among believers about what Jesus had communicated, and various forms of Christianity sprouted and grew. As evidenced by the Gospel of Thomas, there were many who heard Jesus's teachings in a mystical way. However, Paul's sacrificial-lamb theology was the version that outgrew and later destroyed the others.

Paul's theology was believed because it fit the prevailing paradigm and his letters were backed by deliberate deceptions in John. That gospel's author incorporated Thomas's mysticism while trashing Thomas's character with invented tales. Since the synoptic gospels were contradicting Paul's theology, the author of John also invented quotes of Jesus and John the Baptist to legitimize it. Similar fabrications were appended to Mark and inserted in Luke to hide the glaring problem at the heart of the proto-orthodoxy.

Although the lies became the public's truth, it was not the truth. The masses had no idea the sacrificial-lamb theology was just a new branch from an old Judaic tree that Jesus had come to uproot.

The theology arose because Paul and his like-minded colleagues failed to grasp all that Jesus had done and taught. So instead of joining their Messiah in rejecting the tenets of Judaism, they built their new religion on the same foundation of a neurotic and wrathful God who required blood sacrifices to atone for sins. They figured that Jesus must have been God's great gift of sacrifice to atone for the sins of humanity.

Although the earliest proto-orthodox Christians lived the truths of equality and collegiality, their communities succumbed to the prevailing paradigm of hierarchies, curses and divine favoritism. Per the Old Testament blueprint that framed the New Testament letters, God wanted submission to his authorities and obedience to his rules and teachings. The monarchical bishop thus arose in the early Church to deliver that conformity. Meanwhile, men were still superior to women (thanks to the curse of Eden), whites were still superior to other races (thanks to Noah's curse), and heterosexuals were still superior to homosexuals (thanks to the Torah's condemnations).

Other Christian movements differed mightily with Catholicism during the first few centuries. Everything changed in the fourth century, though, when Constantine won a brutal civil war and sought to unify the Roman Empire through paganism and Catholicism. The Catholic bishops took full advantage of the absolute power and joined their beloved emperor in destroying their Christian counterparts.

Catholicism soon became the exclusive religion of the Roman Empire, whereupon the totalitarian beast of church and state eradicated paganism. The Church later completed its beastly makeover by mirroring the Roman Empire and morphing into a papal monarchy that projected the image of royalty.

The Roman Catholic Church was the antithesis of the teachings of Jesus and a bastion of darkness. In cahoots with the European monarchies, this beast ruled with unchecked authority for over a thousand years until the courageous reformers began leading humanity to religious, political and intellectual freedom. However, the Church's reactionary backlash empowered the politics of antisemitism and greatly amplified the hatred and fear it had long been indoctrinating. It all culminated in the Holocaust.

Fortunately, this historical sweep was witnessed by a spiritual realm that is not bound to the past-present-future of linear time. So Gabriel disclosed to Daniel back in the sixth century BCE what the spiritual realm already knew would transpire: the Roman Empire would "set up an abomination that causes desolation" upon Judaism and the Old Testament (Dn 9:27). This abomination was the Roman Catholic Church and the Bible.

Its oppressive reign was also foretold by Jesus and Revelation, but the problem extends far beyond the institution. This all meant that a massive revolution still needed to occur and would occur.

The misguided religion also misunderstood the timing and nature of this prophesied future. Paul and his fellow travelers believed the end would occur during their generation, and subsequent Christians were convinced it would be a physical manifestation of supernatural destruction. All in all, mainstream

Christianity was one faulty concept built upon another.

Who knew the destruction would be wrought upon all that separated God from her beloved offspring? Who knew it would be unleashed upon the towering walls of the traditional Western religions?

Now we know, and the time is now. As if it were happening in the middle of the sky for all to see, millions of lost souls will suddenly rise in consciousness toward their God of pure, unconditional love. As they reclaim their spiritual power, they will no longer feed it to the religious beasts, which will eventually implode from the great awakening.

12.2.d. The Writing on the Wall for Islam and Scientism

The writing is also on the wall for Islam, which also posits a hierarchical and vengeful God who demands obedient submission, condones theological coercion, has instructed his followers to kill for his sake, will cast the nonbelievers into an eternal hell, and will eventually destroy the world. In sum, Islam has a different set of stripes but was born in the same litter of metaphysical beasts.

Just like its older siblings, Islam was built upon a couple of critical assumptions. First, Gabriel revealed the ultimate truth to Muhammad. Second, the angel's messages were accurately preserved in the Quran. Spiritual truths demonstrate that at least one of the assumptions is greatly mistaken (§O.3., §O.4.).

While it is possible that Gabriel never visited Muhammad, another theory should be considered. As the angel delivered the amazing prophecy to Daniel that would help uproot Judaism and Christianity, he was probably involved with Islam as well. Because Catholicism was on its way to tyrannical domination, he apparently tempered its global power by establishing a competing religion that would not get overrun.

If so, the angel did so with an admirable set of teachings to suit the spiritual needs of both stage 2 and stage 4 believers. But just like the production of Christianity's holy book, distortions surely occurred with Islam's. Moreover, Islam also deified the unenlightened writings of early champions and anonymous pretenders (§O.4.).

In any case, it is fascinating to consider the timing of Gabriel's involvement with Daniel and then Muhammad in comparison to the beginning of Jesus's ministry, which is the historical landmark Gabriel used for his signature prophecy. The angel first appeared to Daniel in the third year of Belshazzar's reign over Babylon, c. 551–550 BCE (§7.3.e., §D.3.f.). The strongest scholarly case for the beginning of Jesus's ministry is in late 29 or early 30 CE (§K.3.). Gabriel visited Muhammad in 610 CE.

As the year 1 CE follows 1 BCE, 580 years elapsed from 551 BCE to 30 CE. Another 580 years elapsed from 30 CE to 610 CE! Go figure. The astounding symmetry suggests Gabriel indeed appeared to Muhammad and his involvement was linked to his signature prophecy.

Stage 2 religion has been a developmental necessity. Like a massive rocket propelling a spacecraft into orbit, it helped us escape the gravity of our animalistic roots. It helped bring morals, order and civility to a vicious stage 1 world. But like any effective rocket, it needed to be balanced in its thrust. Islam was a countervailing institution that kept the Roman Catholic Church from having a monopoly on religious power across the Western world.

We have flown these religious rockets as far as they can take us, and the time has come to jettison them. We can hold on to the security of what we have always known and plummet to our doom, or we can release what is now dead weight and continue our voyage to our divine destiny.

As for the truth-seeking process of pure science, it is a vital part of a healthy spirituality. However, the stage 3 religion of scientism is also doomed, for it is built upon assumptions that the scientific process has been rejecting. Empirical data is clearly reflecting a spiritual reality, and the case has now been bolstered by the apocalyptic prophecies and their incomprehensible foreknowledge of history.

12.2.e. The End Times Are Now

We have begun a paradigm shift of the greatest magnitude. We are living amid what will probably be recounted in forthcoming centuries as the most tumultuous and significant era of our spiritual evolution.

We took huge strides in the past few centuries to set the stage for it. Because of political freedoms and technological advances, the truth can be widely communicated without the defending institutions being able to muzzle or eradicate it. Just as importantly, truth-seekers put enough pieces of the universal puzzle together to enable the paradigm shift, so our moment of truth with the breakthrough of truth has finally arrived.

The halfway point of our spiritual evolution is now appearing on the horizon. The history of the world has been generated by the dictates of physical evolution. With survival at all costs the ultimate principle, we have been primarily driven by fear. However, we will eventually embrace our divine nature and primarily live from love.

How long will it take before we are living more from soul-expanding love than ego-protecting fear? Time will obviously tell, but at least we can see that future is approaching.

12.3. Taking the Next Step

A thousand-mile journey begins with a single step. To spiritually grow, we have to trust the process and keep taking the next one.

12.3.a. The Divine Paradox: Free Will and God's Will

You do not have to and can instead hunker down and stay where you are. Be forewarned, though, that you will not be creating an enjoyable future.

To illustrate how we are perpetually creating ourselves and our world, consider the decision to lie or tell the truth. There will never be any divine judgment or punishment for lying, but you will be creating yourself and your future either way you go.

You create from fear when you lie, for you feared a particular outcome and lied to avoid it. You testify to and further energize a core belief that you are a weak and unacceptable being who has reason to be ashamed if vulnerably seen. Lying denies your essential nature and further distances you from your soul, God and others.

This devolved and painful state of who you have created yourself to be continues for subsequent lifetimes and is also acted upon by the law of attraction (which will draw similar people and events into your life). Furthermore, lying reinforces your defenses and adds to the deception and darkness in the world. It breeds mistrust and defensiveness in others and influences them to choose from self-protective fear as well.

You create from spiritual power and love when you compassionately tell the truth, for you were not concerned about how such honesty would impact you. You testify to and further energize a core belief that you are an immortal being who is worthy of acceptance, forgiveness and love. Telling the truth dissipates egoic pride, embraces your essential nature, and brings you closer to your soul, God and others. It breeds trust and integrity in relationships and encourages others to do likewise.

God will never force us to make a particular choice. Our free will is always honored, and we are allowed to create and experience whatever we wish. Nevertheless, the omnipotent force of divine love will not let you stay lost in the darkness forever. It will eventually wake you up, and those who have awoken this way will be quick to testify that it is not a pleasant process.

Welcome to the paradox of free will and God's will. We have unequivocal free will, yet the will of God will eventually manifest. We are living in a universe explicitly designed for our spiritual growth, and divine love will eventually break through to us all. It may take many more lifetimes, but rest assured that it will.

Walsch's first book quotes God explaining the paradox in action: "My most powerful messenger is experience, and even this you ignore. *Especially* this you ignore." Our world would not be so messed up if we had paid attention to our experiences. Instead, we have fated ourselves to endlessly reliving them, "For My purpose will not be thwarted, nor My will be ignored. You *will* get the message. Sooner or later." Yet we will never be forced or coerced, for we have been given free will that will never be taken away. So God will keep sending us the same messages until we finally embrace them.³

In Walsch's 2004 book, God says humanity could drop its traditional beliefs about God within 30 years (§8.7.). His book later quotes God again discussing how quickly we might comprehend God as God truly is. With sufficient commitment and dedication to ending our collective nightmare and getting on track with our destiny, we will make the paradigm shift in three decades or less.

It will undoubtedly happen, God informs us, but when and why it happens remains to be seen. Will this enlightened understanding "emerge before life as you know it all but disappears, or as a result of that occurrence?" God reiterates that it all depends on us and how committed we are to living in an earthly paradise. "If you have no commitment to that, you could experience your planet as a far more unfriendly place, and your life as a far more limited expression, in the near future."⁴

As corroborated by Revelation, the process of awakening the hard way has already begun. The prophecy foretold how our reckless application of science and technology would be having a devastating impact on our planet and health (§10.3.g.). Exponential population growth has amplified everything, and global warming is but the most visible of a slew of environmental catastrophes that are in the making if we do not quickly right the ship.

The devastation of our environment is being enabled by the traditional Western religions. For instance, the Bible says God commanded, "Be fruitful and increase in number; fill the earth and subdue it" (Gn 1:28). It also teaches that God is separate from us and Mother Nature.

This is all fine with most believers while they gut life out and get what they can until they die. They deny or avoid our collective problems because their holy book does not teach them that they will be returning to sleep in the bed we are making. So they empower their nations and corporations to bludgeon our ecosystem for maximum material gain with minimal concern for the long-term consequences.

As for the directive to multiply like rabbits, it may have been a good idea thousands of years ago but not anymore. After all, our global population was three billion in 1959, doubled to six billion by 1999, and surpassed seven billion in 2012. Yet the Catholic Church prohibits birth control because the Bible could not be wrong. Meanwhile, the population explosion threatens to devastate our earthly home as it also suffers those who are caught in its wicked cycle of poverty.

Retired Episcopalian Bishop John Shelby Spong sees the systemic causality. Our biblical understanding of God, he points out, "is a primary factor in the destruction of our ecosystem and ultimately of our world."⁵

So will we wake up and act just in time to prevent catastrophic damage to our collective home? Or will we need a more painful experience to realize we are missing something?

12.3.b. Breaking From Deeply Entrenched Fears

Embracing a new paradigm about God and life requires stepping through some deeply ingrained fear. If you were raised in a religious family, you will meet these fears when you dare to transcend your tribal programming (§9.5.e). You will encounter an emotional backlash from deep within and loved ones around you, but there is no other way to spiritually grow than to break through these repressive bonds.

Until recently, entering through the narrow gate had almost invariably meant being alone and rejected by society. Even Jesus was publicly despised and had precious few people supporting him in his final hours. As centuries passed, many more courageous souls accepted society's scorn and punishment rather than renounce the truth and divine connection they had found.

Times have changed, though, and the religious freedoms of many nations have made the path much easier. Now that the narrow gate has been illuminated, stage 4 spirituality may soon become the world's most popular paradigm.

If so, our children will be raised in these truths and spiritual growth will no longer require an agonizing trek through the deeply ingrained fears of a religious upbringing. The darkness will be rapidly dissipating as self-opening love becomes more prevalent than self-protecting fear. A cynical world of egotistical caterpillars will be transforming into a hopeful world of divine butterflies, and war will become a relic of our history books.

Such a reality is off in the distance, but so it will remain as long as we maintain our current beliefs. Our theological arrogance has perpetuated our spiritual ignorance, stifled our growth, and kept us in the dark. The New Spirituality is illuminating the situation and encouraging the world to take the next step.

So what do you choose? What do you wish to create for yourself and the world in which you live (and will live in again and again)? Are you ready to face everything within that blocks the narrow gate?

12.3.c. No Emotional Exemptions

Our world loves to deify its spiritual heroes as having been granted an exemption from the emotions faced by the rest of us. That actually dishonors them, for their greatness came from being human and achieving what they did despite how they felt. They followed God's will through the depths of their sadness, aloneness and fears. They trusted and followed this guidance and kept taking the next step.

For instance, Jesus agonized in the garden at Gethsemane the night before his crucifixion. He thrice prayed that his impending fate be averted, yet he chose to live out the path of his spiritual power (Mt 26:36–44).

In another example, Martin Luther King Jr. is remembered for his magnetic leadership and soul-stirring speeches, yet how he navigated his emotional challenges is a further measure of his greatness. His colleague Marian Edelman recalls:

> [He was] someone able to admit how often he was afraid and unsure about his next step…It was his human vulnerability and his ability to rise above it that I most remember. He didn't pretend to be a great powerful know-it-all. I remember him discussing openly his gloom, depression, his fears, admitting that he didn't know what the next step was. He would then say: "Take the first step in faith. You don't have to see the whole staircase, just take the first step."[6]

There are no emotional exemptions on the spiritual path, and the only way out is through it. Are you ready to take the next step even though it means leaving the stability of dry land to set sail on the emotional high seas?

12.4. Healing Ourselves and the World

By embracing a path of spiritual growth and facing the darkness within, we actualize Gandhi's wisdom of being the change we wish to see in the world. We can also join with other awakening souls in transforming our communities, nations and planet.

To do so, we will need wisdom (knowledge of universal truths), awareness (a deep comprehension of the current situation) and love (the will to nurture spiritual growth). This is like a surgeon needing wisdom about effective procedures, awareness of a patient's unique situation and loving action to achieve a healing result.

12.4.a. Wisdom and Awareness About Energetic Pairings

If you are partnered with a person, institution or government that has traits of the darkness, look within to find a complementary version of the spiritual illness (§1.3.d., §5.2.d.). After all, it takes two to tango.

The complementary illness may be an <u>unawareness</u> of the partner's darkness, which could be the result of metaphysical blindness, denial or the partner's deception. This lack of consciousness is not as innocent as it appears. As King observed how otherwise innocent people cooperate with evil, "Nothing in all the world is more dangerous than sincere ignorance and conscientious stupidity."[7] The great reverend thus had an uncanny sense for the psychological mortar of evil, what Peck would later call "militant ignorance" (§5.2.b.).

It may be a <u>lack of self-worth</u>. Although this is especially prevalent in abusive relationships, it is also laced within stage 2 believers who do not think they are innately equal to Jesus.

It may be allowing <u>fear</u> to dictate the choice of staying in the pairing, such as the fear of physical harm, societal scorn, being alone or having to live without the benefits of the relationship. Such fears underlie the avoidance of responsibility, such as suspending one's conscience to follow orders from above or suspending one's thinking to embrace dogma from above.

Last but not least, it may be <u>spiritual ignorance</u>, such as believing the dark relationship is God's will. This issue typically goes hand in hand with denial, a lack of self-worth or an avoidance of responsibility.

If you are in such a pairing, the choice of love is to address your affliction so you can take action on behalf of yourself or others who are being harmed by your partner (especially if it is an institution or nation). If a healthier bonding cannot be created, love will withdraw the empowerment of the dark partner. To do so, align with God and decide that no matter what your body may have to endure, you will no longer tarnish your soul by continuing to live such an existence.

It takes supreme courage, but it is an act of supreme love for all involved. Many have had to give of their lives to challenge oppressive religions and governments, and such is the cross that many will still have to bear.

12.4.b. The Choice to Love, Part 1: Patience and Service

Although the flaws of the Western religions are now readily apparent, there will surely be many folks who refuse to see. The path of love is to encourage them to open their minds and move beyond their fears, yet always honor their free will by accepting whatever they choose.

Be patient with the process by appreciating its beauty and perfection. Know the divine is within all beings, and be ready to guide them to a new understanding when the pain of their mistaken ways finally wakes them up. Be quick to forgive, and help them heal and grow so they can live from a higher consciousness.

Rest easy in the truth that all paths lead to God. Some routes are as the eagle flies while others snake through deserts and around mountain ranges on the long way home. Remember that every soul will eventually get there, for God loves us all far too much to allow any of us to remain lost forever. Tap into the universal love that is driving it all, and let not the clamoring of their egoic pride deter you from your truth and path.

Meanwhile, integrate that patience with being of divine service. Allow God to use you as a messenger of truth and a contributor to our global awakening. Lord knows how many tormented souls are nearby who have been searching for the way home but have not been able to find it. You may be the beacon who helps them find their path.

That said, there is a more vital imperative for speaking the truth: the children. Stage 2 religion is perpetually striving to indoctrinate them. If nothing else, the New Spirituality encourages parents to raise their children with open minds and hearts so they can find what is true and right for them as they mature. If our children experience human love and know of a God of pure, unconditional love, few will fall for the nonsense of the stage 2 religions.

Far more important than proclaiming the truth, though, is living it. If we wish to create a field of dreams on earth, start building it, and they will come.

12.4.c. The Choice to Love, Part 2: Action for Transformation

Mainstream Christianity is afflicted by a trio of flaws regarding spiritual power and responsibility (§1.3.c.). These flaws have paved the broad road that has led to destruction.

First, it teaches neither the dynamics of power nor personal responsibility for collective behavior. Instead, it orders blind submission to all authorities. "Heil Hitler!"

Second, it fails to teach that the behavior of nations, churches and corporations should be held to the same set of standards that are expected of individuals. Instead, it allows Christians to compartmentalize their groups' behaviors from their personal morals and values.

Third, the religion fails to teach that we will eventually experience the essence of our creation. Instead, it is silent about reincarnation and the law of attraction as its leaders and followers spew venomous energies that culminate in destruction.

When enough people have embraced an enlightened spirituality, their nations will no longer condone unjust wars (which are collective acts of mass murder) or systemic injustices. Since group choices are the consolidation of many individual choices, awakened souls apply their values to and own their collaboration with all forms of group behavior.

Nations and corporations are massive machines through which we consolidate and collectively create. When these entities no longer represent who we are nor produce what we value, it is incumbent upon us to change them. God is quoted by Walsch: "Politics is your spirituality, *demonstrated*. Economics is your spirituality, *demonstrated*...*Your* life is *your spirituality, demonstrated*."[8]

A compartmentalized life is for those in the darkness. An integrated life is for those who have seen the Light. The path of spiritual power and responsibility entails being an agent of positive change amid the intimidating culture of massive institutions.

The first step is developing awareness. Will we be aware of what our groups are doing and why they are doing it, or will we remain ignorant, deceived and in denial?

If you are a citizen or employee of a nation or corporation that behaves in ways that you do not agree, you can conform and be an accomplice, withdraw your empowerment of it, or direct your spiritual power into a movement to effect its transformation. You are either part of the problem or part of the solution.

This is where the spiritual path really heats up, for the unconscious dragons of fear will flare up to block your path. Living in integrity sounds nice, but it means walking a path of legitimate suffering. Instead of running away through denial or compartmentalization, it means feeling your crisis of conscience and various forms of fear as you take appropriate action. If you are wise, you will allow this crucible of spiritual growth to forge your transformation.

Bold action that is rooted in spiritual truth has a magical way of attracting others. Critical mass can develop rapidly and observable results may follow. Yet it may be that at this stage of our evolution, the best you can do is withdraw your empowerment of your dark institution as you help enlighten others. Yet no matter what comes to pass, you will grow tremendously and feel an incomparable level of soul satisfaction. You will, as Jesus taught, find your life. As the signature line from *Braveheart* expresses it, "Every man dies, not every man truly lives."

The key to institutional change is developing awareness, so lovingly speak the truth about what is happening. Judgment is neither required nor recommended. Simply help others become conscious of what is being done and why it is being done. Shine light upon the true state of affairs, and ask if such decisions properly represent what the good men and women of the institution are about. Would they want their children to be the downstream recipients of their collective actions?

In other words, appeal to the Golden Rule. It is a timeless truth that will forever yield good fruit, but we need to apply it to collective behavior.

As for putting this wisdom into practice, Americans are encouraged to see through a veil of deception and the politics of arrogance and fear. Please learn the facts about how our nation has been a textbook case of evil that has been spewing its darkness upon the world. The forthcoming book *Illuminating the Reinforcing Cycle of Darkness: The Path to Reclaim the Soul of America* is dedicated to that task. Will you help enlighten others so we can reclaim the soul of our great nation and have a far better experience from our collective creation?

12.5. Martin Luther King Jr., Christianity and Slavery

The book's penultimate section begins with a modern leader who embodied the New Spirituality. Martin Luther King Jr. (1929–1968) was not just an advocate for transcending racism. Rather, his declared mission was to also heal America of war and poverty.[9]

Even though the civil rights movement was successful, his greater gift to humanity was what he taught by example. Like his role model Mohandas K. Gandhi (also called Mahatma, which means "great soul"), King demonstrated the only means by which our societal problems can ever be solved. We must live with wisdom, awareness, love and spiritual power.

12.5.a. Addressing Racism, War and Poverty

Most everybody is familiar with King's dream, yet far less are aware of how the civil rights movement placed far more emphasis on illuminating the current state of affairs. Both Gandhi and King built their strategies upon the truth that mankind is fundamentally moral and good. Their tactics were designed to raise injustices to the light of consciousness so our proclivity for morality would compel societal change.

The movement lit up the moral ugliness of racial oppression and segregation for the world to see. Opponents like Alabama Governor George Wallace and his sheriffs openly displayed their culture's sickness in words and deeds. Since blatant injustices were being defended by local governments, they could be quashed from above with the Civil Rights Act of 1964 and Voting Rights Act of 1965.

In 1966, King moved to Chicago to bring his campaign against racism and poverty to the North. But the movement floundered there, for it no longer had such easy targets to illuminate. It was facing a social, political and economic system whose leaders were outwardly sympathetic amid a populace that was viciously polarized. As his colleague Jesse Jackson explained, "Here the enemy was not only the redneck, sometimes it was the black face. It was all those forces that represented the self-interest in perpetuating the evil machine."[10]

The movement thus bogged down in the dark marsh of the American psyche and system. The effort had encountered a society, government and economy that were built and running upon energies that no political solution could ameliorate: the core emotions of fear and hatred, the core motivation of self-interest, and the slick deception of egoic pride.

Meanwhile, the same dark elements were on display at the national level as the United States was waging war in Vietnam with the fearful and delusional justification of national security. King had been critical of the war for over a year and took his opposition to the national stage in the spring of 1967. Despite rendering an impeccably rational and spiritual case against the war, he was condemned by the vast majority of newspapers and magazines across the country. In alignment with spiritual truth, though, he counseled that if young men believed the war was dishonorable and unjust, they should not consent to fight in it.[11]

12.5.b. On the Trail of the Deeper Systemic Roots

King was assassinated in April of 1968 at the age of 39, so he did not have the opportunity to more fully examine the systemic roots of the issues. His writings demonstrate, though, that he was close to unearthing the lynchpin that was holding it all together.

At the beginning of the civil rights movement, he realized the two-sided nature of unhealthy systems. While contemplating the plan to boycott segregated buses in Montgomery in 1955, he had an epiphany. Those who were passively accepting evil were participating in it as much as those who were perpetrating it. Being true to God and one's soul left the righteous no alternative but to no longer cooperate with the darkness.[12]

In his 1963 letter from a Birmingham jail, he was responding to eight white clergymen who had published a critical statement about his activism in their city. He politely expressed how the white church and its leaders had greatly disappointed him. Before the Montgomery bus protest, he wrote, he believed the white clergy would be very strong allies of the freedom movement. Although a few stood with him as expected, his dreams were shattered by the outright opposition of some and the cautious silence of many.

Nevertheless, he had come to Birmingham with high hopes that its white religious leaders would understand and support the cause with moral conviction. He was once again disappointed. Amid glaring injustices and an epic struggle to end them, he had heard far too many ministers declare, "Those are social issues, with which the gospel has no real concern."[13]

Before arriving in Birmingham, King had hoped the lack of white religious support in Montgomery was just a matter of inept local clergy. Yet Birmingham proved the religious problem was more pervasive and systemic, and the young minister learned his version of Christianity was exceedingly rare.

Just like Montgomery, the Birmingham campaign forced the local white churches beyond their facade of words to render some fruit from their tree. The unsuspecting King tasted the sour mash of a religion that had been allowing millions of white Christians to condone and cooperate with institutionalized racism.

This should not have come as a complete surprise, for he knew at some level the systemic problem went far beyond the white clergy of Alabama. As he stated elsewhere in a sermon, the church was badly failing Christ in the area of racial justice. Abysmally silent and indifferent, its failure was even more pronounced in how it had participated in the formation of the race-caste structures.

Colonialism, he observed, never would have survived had the church opposed it, and South Africa's apartheid system was being defended by the Dutch Reformed Protestant Church. Slavery in America never would have perpetuated for so long without the church's sanction, and the ongoing discrimination and segregation was because the church had been silently and often vocally supporting it. Time and again, he lamented, the church was lagging behind the Supreme Court and secularism instead of leading humanity to higher ground.[14]

Since the noxious fruit of misguiding and colluding churches had been dropping from the tree of Christianity throughout history, what in the world's living hell was happening? What systemic roots were producing one toxic church after another?

The son, grandson and great-grandson of preachers, King was entrenched in a paradigm that would have to be challenged if that question was to be answered. Given the immense challenge he faced, he was in no position to also consider a revolution in religion. Yet an insight from his seminary years suggests he was close to the grand epiphany. He wrote, "Any religion which professes to be concerned about the souls of men and is not concerned about the social and economic conditions that scar the soul, is a spiritually moribund religion only waiting for the day to be buried."[15]

12.5.c. Recognizing the Fruit From the Tree

Jesus supposedly taught us to identify false prophets by their fruit (§11.1.). Given everything else we also know about Christianity and its authoritative source (the Bible), the time has come to uproot this decrepit tree. It is time to extract the wisdom of Jesus from the biblical sludge that has muddied the river of truth.

This misguided religion has guided America astray and asunder. For instance, had our Christian nation followed only the teachings of its beloved Jesus, there never would have been slavery in our democracy of freedom and equality. Instead, the Civil War was required to eradicate the abomination, and the civil rights movement was needed a century later to dispel its institutional remnants.

The Bible has long been America's moral compass, and it provided defenders of slavery with an abundance of powerful arguments. The great Jewish patriarch Abraham was a slaveholder, and it dictated slavery to be the spoken will of God. For instance, God supposedly instructed Moses that their slaves were to come from the surrounding nations, could be bought, would be your property, could be willed as an inheritance, and could be made slaves for life (Lv 25:44–46).

Moreover, Exodus provided rules for owning slaves, especially when it came to striking them. Moses's God was kind enough to grant freedom to any slave who lost an eye or a tooth from the blows (Ex 21:26–27), but masters were otherwise sanctioned to inflict nonlethal beatings because slaves were their property (Ex 21:20–21).

Yet the most prominent biblical support for slavery and racism came from the Genesis story of Noah and his three sons. As it declares, Noah got drunk and passed out naked inside of his tent. One of his sons, Ham, saw him in the nude and told the brothers. When Noah awoke and learned what had happened, he cursed Ham's son Canaan and his descendants to slavery (Gn 9:18–27).

Abolitionists in colonial America documented that they were being countered as far back as the 1670s by the "curse of Ham" as a moral justification for black enslavement.[16] Abolitionist Theodore Weld later observed in 1837, "this prophecy of Noah is the *vade mecum* [a handbook for ready reference] of slaveholders, and they never venture abroad without it."[17] Moreover, none of the Old Testament prophets condemned slavery, a so-called negative form of biblical approval.

While the Old Testament poured slavery's theological foundation, the New Testament nailed together its framing in Christian doctrine. As Paul instructed, slaves should obey their masters with fear and respect and serve with sincere hearts as if they were obeying Christ (Eph 6:5–8; see also Col 3:22–4:1; 1 Tm 6:1–2; Ti 2:9–10). Peter concurred that slaves should submit to their masters with full respect even if their masters were harsh (1 Pt 2:18). Most importantly, nowhere in the gospels was it recorded that Jesus condemned slavery.

Amid the fiery debate of the 18th and 19th centuries, slavery was most strongly defended by preachers of the Bible. Consider what historian Larry Tise discovered when he researched the authors' biographies of 279 pro-slavery publications: "ministers wrote almost half of all defenses of slavery published in America."[18]

[Note: For that study, Tise only examined the pro-slavery publications listed by William S. Jenkins in the bibliography of *Pro-slavery Thought in the Old South*. Tise comments, "At least 130 of the publications there listed, and perhaps more, were definitely the products of clergymen."[19]]

Going far beyond Jenkins's bibliography, Tise also produced an astounding list of 275 clergymen who published a defense of slavery. Many of them were Northerners. He explains his criteria for the list:

> Each man had to be ordained in one of the recognized religious denominations in America before or during the Civil War or to serve the functions of a clergyman in one of them. Each also had to publish either in a book, a pamphlet, or a periodical article a defense of slavery which argued in favor of the indefinite perpetuation of servitude.[20]

Given the biblical directives to uphold slavery, these historical facts should not be surprising. The pro-slavery clergymen were simply being true to their marching orders. They had no clue their underlying assumption about the Bible's infallibility was dead wrong.

Yes, there were also many ministers who ignored the totality of the Bible, prioritized the teachings of Jesus, and supported the abolitionists. However, because hundreds of clergymen published arguments that it was morally right to enslave people of African descent, had been raised on both sides of the Mason-Dixon Line, and had to override the "love everybody" teachings of Jesus to maintain their positions, one conclusion is undeniable. The Christian defense of slavery was not because a few morons did not know the Bible. Rather, the Bible produced a flood of preachers who did not know the true intentions of God. The Christian abolitionists who took their principled stand did so not because of the Bible but in spite of it.

12.5.d. The Bible and the Politics of Slavery

All in all, the Bible kept the young democracy from stepping up to its founding values of freedom and equality. Rather than properly guiding America's spiritual growth, the Bible was a defective moral compass that hung like a massive millstone around the nation's neck. When it came to rising above the ancient traditions of slavery and social and racial hierarchies, the Bible anchored America in the darkness.

Politics did not drive the Christian defense of slavery. Instead, the Bible allowed slavery to take root in America and then drove its religious and political defense. Without such solid biblical support, the politics of slavery would have been as effective as the politics of gouging your eye out with a stick.

It appears the first person to publish a written defense of slavery in America was a Massachusetts judge and slaveholder named John Saffin. He argued in a 1701 pamphlet that since Abraham had owned slaves, imitating him in this "Moral Action" was as warranted as having his exemplary faith. Tise summarizes and quotes the rest of Saffin's Bible-based defense of slavery and inequality:

> Saffin argued that God had intentionally "set different Orders and Degrees of Men in the World" and that any push toward equality would be "to invert the Order that God had set." Phrasing a sentiment that was repeated endlessly in proslavery literature on the eve of the Civil War, Saffin wrote that God had ordained "some to be High and Honourable, some to be Low and Despicable; some to be Monarchs, Kings, Princes and Governours, Masters and Commanders, others to be Subjects, and to be Commanded; Servants of sundry sorts and degrees, bound to obey; yea, some to be born Slaves, and so to remain during their lives."[21]

This Christian worldview originated with the story of Noah and Ham. As explained by a Puritan minister in a 1703 sermon, "All Servitude began in the Curse."[22]

The Bible was America's authority about what God wanted. Although many Americans felt slavery was morally wrong, those sentiments were no match for the Bible's arguments as to why God created it that way. These justifications were endlessly parroted as America's holy book was deified by the same closed-minded thinking that is commonly spoken in modern churches: "The Bible said it, I believe it, that settles it."

All American colonies hosted slavery until each of the original northern states abolished it from 1777 to 1804. Deeply ingrained in the agricultural South, though, its political leaders even claimed the moral high ground on the paramount issue. For instance, in a speech to the House of Representatives in 1836, Congressman James Hammond of South Carolina proclaimed, "The doom of Ham has been branded on the form and features of his African descendants. The hand of fate has united his color and destiny. Man cannot separate what God hath joined."[23]

In a speech to the Senate in 1850, Mississippi Senator Jefferson Davis argued that despite his biblical fate, the African had been blessed by the slave trade to be serving the Christian servants of God:

> It brought him from a benighted region, and placed him in one where civilization would elevate and dignify his nature. It is a fact which history fully establishes, that through the portal of slavery alone, has the descendant of the graceless son of Noah ever entered the temple of civilization. Thus has been made manifest the inscrutable wisdom of the decree which made him "a servant of servants."[24] (Gn 9:25, KJV)

Later in that speech, Davis rendered a justification for slavery that was stamped from the template of American conservatism. The senator based his position upon the Bible and tradition:

> It is enough for me elsewhere to know, that it was established by decree of Almighty God, that it is sanctioned in the Bible, in both Testaments, from Genesis to Revelations; that it has existed in all ages; has been found among the people of the highest civilizations, and in nations of the highest proficiency in the arts.[25]

Fearing Abraham Lincoln and Congress would abolish slavery, the Southern states seceded from the Union shortly after his election. Southerners were convinced from their biblical indoctrination that they were in the right. In Davis's inaugural address as their president in February of 1861, he expressed the

Southern morality in his conclusion: "Reverently let us invoke the God of our fathers to guide and protect us in our efforts to perpetuate the principles which by His blessing they were able to vindicate, establish, and transmit to their posterity."[26]

The Confederacy's vice president, Alexander Stephens, gave a speech in March of 1861 that described their ideological conflict with the Union. He first explained how Thomas Jefferson and most of America's founding fathers believed enslaving Africans "was in violation of the laws of nature" but was "an evil they knew not well how to deal with."[27] Stephens declared, "Those ideas, however, were fundamentally wrong. They rested upon the assumption of the equality of races. This was an error."[28]

He then explained the Confederate position: "Our new government is founded upon exactly the opposite idea; its foundations are laid, its cornerstone rests, upon the great truth that the negro is not equal to the white man; that slavery—subordination to the superior race—is his natural and normal condition."[29]

Stephens explained how the abolitionists were "warring against a principle. They were attempting to make things equal which the Creator had made unequal."[30] He proclaimed the Confederacy was "the first government ever instituted upon the principles in strict conformity to nature."[31] He thereafter argued his case by citing the Bible:

> With us, all of the white race, however high or low, rich or poor, are equal in the eye of the law. Not so with the negro. Subordination is his place. He, by nature, or by the curse against Canaan, is fitted for that condition which he occupies in our system...It is, indeed, in conformity with the ordinance of the Creator. It is not for us to inquire into the wisdom of His ordinances, or to question them. For His own purposes, He has made one race to differ from another, as He has made "one star to differ from another star in glory."[32] (1 Cor 15:41, KJV)

The Confederacy was so convinced it was following God's will that it put the Latin motto *"Deo Vindice"* on its official seal, which means "God will defend us" or "God will vindicate us." Trouble was, the South believed the Bible was the infallible word of God and was thus gravely mistaken.

The Civil War erupted in April of 1861. The moral error about white supremacy and slavery resulted in the mortal price of over 600,000 deaths—more than all other American wars combined—and can thus be directly charged to the dark guidance of mainstream Christianity and the Bible.

Yet even as the Civil War was ravaging America, countless ministers continued to preach the moral goodness of slavery in having brought the Negro out of Africa and into a "civilized" culture and eternal salvation. In 1864, the General Assembly of the Presbyterian Church in the Confederacy proclaimed:

> The long continued agitations of our adversaries have wrought within us a deeper conviction of the divine appointment of domestic servitude, and have led to a clearer comprehension of the duties we owe to the African race. We hesitate not to affirm that it is the peculiar mission of the Southern Church to conserve the institution of slavery, and to make it a blessing to both master and slave.[33]

12.5.e. The Biblical Lynchpin

Lincoln and the Union ended slavery by winning the Civil War, but the South's biblically based culture perpetuated and gave birth to more abominations. Its Negroes went from the frying pan into the fire while the racial domination continued for another hundred years. As they struggled to survive amid rampant injustices, they also had to cope with terror from the mob violence of thousands of lynchings.

These vigilante executions were often promoted in advance by local newspapers, attended by thousands, and commemorated with photographs, postcards and souvenir body parts from the deceased. Often accompanied by gruesome torture or burning the victim alive, they were not just unleashed upon those who were believed to have committed serious crimes. Rather, lynchings of blacks were often incited by allegations of a petty crime, getting into a fight with or challenging a business injustice from a white man, or daring to cavort with a white woman.

Vicious expressions of collective fear, hatred and rage, they were an integral part of a cultural fight to maintain political, economic and social dominance in the caste system of the South. Sometimes the terror drove blacks by the tens of thousands to seek refuge in the North, which sometimes motivated Southern newspapers to make desperate appeals to curtail a recent wave of lynchings so enough labor would stay to harvest the crops.

Local police were powerless to halt the lawless terrorism, and seven different presidents asked Congress to pass legislation to quell it. Upward of 200 bills were introduced, but Southern legislators were opposed. Nevertheless, three bills were passed by the House of Representatives, but conservative Southern senators used their filibuster power to block them.

Although the wickedness of this phenomenon cannot be adequately summarized, a particular case exemplifies some of the dynamics. In May of 1918, a white farmer was killed in his Georgia home by somebody shooting from outside. His wife was only wounded by the attack, and she named the murderer. A lynch mob quickly formed but could not find the accused black man, so it exacted revenge on several other blacks in the area.

One of the victims was a man named Haynes Turner. His wife, Mary, was eight months pregnant. Infuriated by the killing of her husband, she demanded justice. Historian Philip Dray describes what happened next:

> As *The Atlanta Constitution* reported, she protested what had occurred too vehemently and "made unwise remarks…the people were angered by her remarks, as well as her attitude." The sheriff placed her under arrest, probably for her own protection, but then gave her up to a mob that took her away into the woods near the Little River at a place called Folsom's Bridge. There, before a crowd that included women and children, Mary was stripped, hung upside down by the ankles, soaked with gasoline, and roasted to death. In the midst of this torment, a white man opened her swollen belly with a hunting knife and her infant fell to the ground, gave a cry, and was stomped to death. The *Constitution*'s coverage of the killing was subheadlined: "Fury of People is Unrestrained."[34]

From the 17th to 20th centuries, the institutions of white supremacy—slavery, segregation, a slew of governing injustices and the terrorism of lynching—were held together by the lynchpin of Christianity. Walter White, a mostly Caucasian man who led the National Association for the Advancement of Colored People from 1931 to 1955, observed this dynamic as he tried to make sense of the horrific public spectacles. As he wrote in 1929, "It is exceedingly doubtful if lynching could possibly exist under any other religion than Christianity."[35]

Again, the Bible is at the root of a deadly religious tree that keeps producing toxic fruit around the world. As for another interrelated example, it prohibits interracial marriage because God supposedly barred the ancient Hebrews from intermarrying with other tribes (Dt 7:3; see also Ex 34:15–16; Nm 36:6). All this material and more produced the conclusion that God's will was for racial segregation. Historian Fay Botham explains:

> Though the story of "Noah's curse" remained an important and familiar explanatory paradigm for racial hierarchy after the Civil War, white Americans revised their interpretations of the Genesis stories once the peculiar institution ended and enslaved persons were emancipated. Indeed, following the

Civil War, a localized strain of white southern Protestantism emerged that offered an explicitly biblical rationale for racial segregation. These whites asserted that in Genesis 10–11, God had "dispersed" the human races to separate continents, thus demonstrating God's desire for racial groups to remain separate.[36]

Antimiscegenation laws, which barred interracial marriage and often made a felony out of interracial sex, were first enacted in the late 1600s in Virginia and Maryland, and 41 of the 50 states had such a law at some point. The California Supreme Court struck down its state's version in 1948, and 13 more states followed suit in the next two decades. Yet 16 states in the southeastern corner of the country still had them when the US Supreme Court finally declared them unconstitutional in 1967.

This deeply ingrained taboo did more than just create and defend such laws. It was the primary trigger of countless lynchings, for white men were mortified at the thought of white women having sex with black men. Many a Negro's life came to a sudden and horrific end for daring to cross this biblical line in the cultural sand.

Another outgrowth of the Southern culture of white supremacy and segregation was the Ku Klux Klan (KKK), which never could have developed if America's holy book was comprised of only the teachings of Jesus. As it was, though, the KKK fought to uphold the Southern way of life. Indoctrinated through the centuries because of the Bible, this Christian culture was proudly defended and declared by the KKK with every cross it set ablaze.

Jesus would have his followers commit random acts of kindness. The Bible led its followers into committing random acts of violence.

Modern Christians have their defense. They say the hundreds of clergymen who published their justification of slavery, the presumably thousands more who preached its morality, and the countless preachers since the Civil War who continued wielding the Bible to justify or ignore institutional racism and violence were ignorant of how to properly interpret the Bible.

Yet if the Bible really is God's inerrant communication to humanity, we have to conclude that God is one hell of an incompetent deity. Why? Because so many intelligent people who were so intent on serving him could not understand what should have been the simplest of instructions.

So how about a little help for God when he writes another one of these things for another planet: "Slavery is morally wrong. Everybody is innately equal, for you are all my children, so terminate the practice wherever you find it." How difficult was that? What do you think history would have looked like if the Bible's only commentary on slavery was something like that?

When a high percentage of diligent and intelligent students are failing a self-study class, it is time to replace the textbook. Bishop Spong eventually acknowledged this truth:

> At first I convinced myself that the problem was not in the Bible itself, but in the way the Bible was used. That, however, was a defensive and ultimately dishonest response. I had to come to the place where I recognized that the Bible itself was often the enemy. Time after time, the Bible, I discovered, condemned itself with its own words.
>
> This was certainly true in the battle to overcome the racism and segregation that so deeply affected my childhood church in North Carolina. Quotations from the Bible were frequently employed in the racist battle to maintain segregation in which I, as a white person, was judged to be of greater worth than a black person.[37]

The Bible has clearly been a bastion of inequality as also evidenced by the case of women's suffrage. Women were denied the right to vote because Judaism's patriarchy had perpetuated in the New Testament (1 Cor 11:3, 11:8–9, 14:34; Eph 5:22–24; Col 3:18; 1 Tm 2:11–14; 1 Pt 3:1). When God once again inspired us to break through more chains of the darkness, the Bible once again had its adherents fight against the Light. As scholar Betty DeBerg notes, "Antisuffrage statements in popular fundamentalist periodicals outnumbered prosuffrage statements by a ratio of more than ten to one."[38]

After seven decades of struggle, American women finally got the right to vote when the 19th Amendment was ratified in 1920. The Light once again triumphed not because of the Bible but in spite of it.

In sum, the Bible has authored one dark fight after another against our spiritual evolution. To awaken, we need to see the Bible for what it is, what it has done, and what it continues to do.

Speaking of, it has taught its adherents to abhor homosexuality and thus deny equal marital rights to gays and lesbians (Lv 18:22, 20:13; Rom 1:26–28; 1 Cor 6:9–10). As theologian James Cone has been trying to especially awaken the black churches on the issue, they have assumed the same role as the white Christians who enslaved them because of a literal reading of the Bible.[39] Christian fundamentalists are once again on the wrong side of history as they self-righteously oppose God's will of justice, equality and unconditional love for all. Just as they condemned love between people of different races, so they still condemn it between people of identical sexes.

12.5.f. Revisiting Jesus to Revise the Theology

The blind religion has been leading blind Americans down the broad road to destruction. Having also led Germany to a similar destination, this religion and holy book have been bedeviling us all.

Although its errors are numerous, Christianity's biggest gaffe is the polarizing split it makes between its followers and Jesus. This error was destined for indoctrination with the author of John's fabrications (§4.5.). So instead of teaching Christians about their inner divinity and guiding them to be like their masterful brother (Gospel of Thomas), this religion chastises them as evil sinners who are incapable of ever being like Jesus and thus need his saving redemption (Gospel of John).

No small wonder, then, that men like Martin Luther King Jr. are its phenomenal exceptions instead of the norm. No small wonder that King was compelled to write about Gandhi, "It is ironic, yet inescapably true that the greatest Christian of the modern world was a man who never embraced Christianity."[40]

Paul's theology that a belief in Jesus will deliver you into the kingdom has already been debunked. Yet even more support for this conclusion comes straight from Jesus. As quoted in Matthew, he concluded his Sermon on the Mount by making four intertwined points that feel chillingly prophetic in light of what we now know.

First, he differentiated stage 4 spirituality from stage 2 religion by contrasting the narrow gate and road that only a few could find with the wide gate and broad road that leads to destruction (Mt 7:13–14). Second, he elaborated on his advice, "Watch out for false prophets. They come to you in sheep's clothing, but inwardly they are ferocious wolves. By their fruit you will recognize them" (Mt 7:15–16). We now recognize that deceptive appearance and poisonous fruit in the Catholic Church and its biblical offshoots. Third, he said that only those who actually live his teachings are on the right path:

> Not everyone who says to me, "Lord, Lord" will enter the kingdom of heaven, but only the one who does the will of my Father who is in heaven. Many will say to me on that day, "Lord, Lord, did we not prophesy in your name and in your name drive out demons and in your name perform many miracles?" Then I will tell them plainly, "I never knew you. Away from me, you evildoers!" (Mt 7:21–23)

Finally, Jesus reiterated his previous points with a parable about wise and foolish creators. Those who hear and put his words into practice are like a man who wisely constructed his house on a rock. Those who hear but do not are like a man who foolishly built his home on sand (Mt 7:24–26).

Christians have heard a distorted and invented version of Jesus's words and been preaching them to people near and far. Having embraced a mistaken paradigm built upon erroneous and devious material, they have failed to put his true words into practice.

Good fruit does not appear when you repress truth-seeking with unenlightened dogma. Good fruit does not appear when you coerce obedience and mindless conformity with the soul-constricting fear of a punishing God. Good fruit does not appear when you indoctrinate the masses into believing they are evil sinners who could never be like Jesus. Good fruit does not appear when you teach them that they are split between a good soul and an evil body and thus torment them in the inner crossfire of a polarized war.

You cannot expect people to grow to be like Jesus when you teach them a belief in him is all it takes to enter the kingdom. And you surely cannot expect heaven to manifest on earth when you compartmentalize his teachings on Sunday lest you dare challenge his followers to put them into practice on Monday.

12.5.g. The True Christian Path

How much more horror do we need to live through before we awaken and see through the great deception? The book has hopefully preempted the need for more pain to bring this to our attention.

We have traveled down three independent paths that have all arrived at the same destination. First, we learned Christianity is a hybrid religion that was built upon erroneous tenets from ancient Judaism. Its New Testament is also marred by spins, contradictions and numerous cases of deliberate deception. Next, we learned the apocalyptic prophecies are also proclaiming that the religion based upon the man who came to uproot Judaism must itself be uprooted. Finally, we examined the poisonous fruit being produced by this religion.

It is therefore high time we render this religion its final rites and awaken from our nightmare. Or will we keep succumbing to egoic pride and fear as we keep creating from that darkness?

If you want to be a Christian, engage a path of growth to be like Christ. If not, it is an acceptable choice in the eyes of God as well. But let us not keep deluding those who sincerely wish to be Christians with a bastardized set of teachings that have failed to properly guide mankind. Moreover, let us not keep deluding these folks into thinking they have found a magical ticket to salvation when it is actually a parking ticket on the journey of spiritual evolution.

If you wish to follow the teachings of Jesus to achieve divine wholeness (salvation), the essentials are interrelated and simple:

1. Know that you are an immortal soul and extension of God who is

unconditionally and eternally loved by God. So is everybody else, and we are all intertwined as one.

2. Love God by loving all that is God, embracing the divine intention of spiritual growth, and living for a greater purpose than your ego's miserable cravings.

3. Love your neighbor (everybody on this planet) as yourself.

4. Honor the equality of all people and seek not to rule over them but to empower them.

5. Know that it is far better to make choices that lead to societal rejection, physical pain or death than to make choices that denigrate your spiritual integrity and pollute your eternal soul. Then align with God to help you call forth the love and spiritual power to act accordingly.

6. Keep searching for the truth, go within, and allow the spirit of truth to guide you into all truth.

7. Spiritually grow by healing the darkness within so you can live the above more radiantly, lovingly and powerfully.

Transcending our collective hell can only be achieved by collective spiritual growth. What set of teachings will guide us to that blessed place of being and living? Certainly not the ones that led us into our spiritual wasteland.

Reverend Jesse Jackson Sr. noted in a 2005 speech, "It's easy to admire Dr. King. It's a challenge to follow him."[41] It's a challenge because Dr. King put Jesus's words into practice and thereby followed his masterful brother. Again, Jesus did not give us the easy way of only following him in prayer. Rather, he gave us no other way but following him in practice (Mt 16:24–25; §4.5.j.).

12.6. Conclusion

The New Spirituality has the keys to the divine kingdom, but it cannot be embraced and lived until religious dogma has been challenged and dropped. Although many religious authorities and believers will continue to fight against the Light just as they have for centuries, the eternal river of truth and love will eventually blast through everything in its way.

Punctuated by Martin Luther's posting in the 16th century, the courageous reformers and scientists broke the Church's stranglehold on Europe. In the late 18th century, America introduced the modern world to democracy and freedom of religion. France quickly followed suit and triggered the Enlightenment of Europe.

Early in the 19th century, England led the colonial world by first outlawing the trading of slaves and then abolishing slavery throughout its empire. America later experienced its bloodiest war ever to do the same. In 1893, New Zealand became the first nation to grant women's suffrage. In the 20th century, women gained the right to vote in almost every nation where men have it. Meanwhile, dozens of nations won their freedom from colonialism.

In the early 1960s, the Catholic Church finally decreed religious liberty and stopped condemning the Jews for Jesus's crucifixion. But most importantly and as heralded by Abraham Maslow in 1964, maverick scientists began exploring all matters of religion. It was only a matter of time before we unraveled the apocalyptic prophecies and learned the onset of the great awakening was foretold to the 1960s.

As for that signature decade, the eternal river of truth and love surfaced and crashed into the status quo of a religious superpower. With graphic footage from the new era of mass communication, Americans could see what was happening at home and abroad. The civil rights movement steamrolled institutional racism with its legislative victories. Peace activists challenged the establishment's Vietnam War. Younger generations rocked their religions as Eastern teachings began flooding the West.

The entrenched systems of religion and government were staggered but regained their familiar order. Pope John Paul I was cut down in 1978 before he could enact any more Vatican reforms (§L.4.), and his successor tacked the Church back toward its conservative roots. The Western democracies were doing likewise, and all was well again for the well-to-do as the West continued empowering the law of the jungle and exploiting the third world.

Yet as Bob Dylan expressed it back in 1964, "the times they are a-changin'." The eternal river of truth and love is once again breaching the surface of our collective consciousness. Back then the cresting water was warm with love but light on the truth, so it was ultimately repelled. This time, however, the spiritual torrent contains an astronomical mass of undeniable truth and is thus hitting with the explosiveness of a tsunami.

Since the Western religions are backed by centuries of inertia and deeply entrenched fear, the world will be swimming in an incredible amount of turbulence for quite some time. Yet the spiritual flood of truth and love will eventually blast away their towering walls.

Bear in mind as this happens that Jesus was not a conservative but rather a social and spiritual revolutionary who wielded a sword of truth against the darkness. Our loving God wants us to progressively grow toward a greater future, not to conservatively entrench in a backward past.

Bear in mind, too, that the right-wing version of Christianity that rejects socialism has been one of history's greatest hypocrisies. After all, the gospels clearly depict Jesus as a communal person who taught and lived a message of neighborly love and support. He expects us to live it too.

All is not lost for Western conservatives, though, for they are aligned with the truth that every soul creates and is responsible for its own future. They are also aligned with the truth that love neither entrenches dependency nor erases the growth-inspiring results of foolish living. The more compassionate among them understand that you truly serve people with a hand up, not a handout.

Trouble is, tough-talking conservatives fail to acknowledge the truth on the other side of the coin. We are all responsible for our collective future, and what impacts one eventually impacts us all. We live in a win-win universe, so helping others become wiser, healthier and more responsible makes for a better society.

Awakening nations will tailor their systems to render more equitable opportunity and embrace both the challenging and supportive sides of love. Neither the traditional left-wing agenda of "big government is the solution" nor the traditional right-wing agenda of "you're on your own" is anywhere close to optimal.[42] They will also live with fiscal discipline while taking exceptional care of the environment to better serve their children.

We are creating our world, and our beliefs are guiding what and how we create. For instance, the New Spirituality always supports the flow of love and honors the equality, diversity and uniqueness of all. However, homosexuality is condemned by the same Bible that had America defend slavery and deem women as lesser citizens. We should thus take another step of spiritual growth by rejecting another biblical prejudice and granting homosexual couples the same honor, rights and privileges enjoyed by the heterosexual majority.

The divine process of spiritual evolution has been spurring humanity forward since the beginning. Fearfully and self-righteously fight it if you must, but know that you are serving the darkness by doing so. Also know that defending traditional religious beliefs is a lost cause, for the universal force of love that is fostering spiritual growth cannot be stopped.

Truth and love are here to heal this godforsaken wasteland in which we have been living. It is not God who has forsaken us, though, but we in our devilish religious pride who have forsaken the truth about ourselves and God.

The time has come to awaken. The narrow gate has been illuminated, and your unique path of spiritual growth is calling you home. You have come so far already. Do you have the courage to take the next step?

Your individual and our collective futures hang in the balance. In the privacy of your own thoughts and fears, you will eventually come face to face with your own abyss. Bedrock paradigms will be crumbling as your orienting stars are falling from your sky. Amid your disillusionment, though, the opportunity beckons.

The book therefore closes with words of wisdom from a Native American initiation to offer guidance for this sacred moment. "As you go the way of life, you will see a great chasm. Jump. It is not as wide as you think."[43]

Postscript

In his 2004 book, Neale Donald Walsch quotes God foretelling how our religions would be exposed by the great awakening: "In the very near future, humans will observe with greater clarity, objectivity, and honesty the role of religious teachings and doctrines in the creation of the many Cultural Stories that are producing continuing distrust, hatred, violence, and killing on your planet."

God elaborates, "Humanity will soon become aware" that we have been betrayed by the individuals and institutions we have trusted to guide us. "Humanity will soon understand" that we have been undermined by religious beliefs that we have hoped would free us from our limitations and suffering.

Furthermore, we will soon be awakening from a deep sleep and noticing it is time to create anew. We will be collectively deciding if we wish to experience even worse calamities or the beginning of our brightest future.

God continues, "In the years just ahead millions of individuals will be catapulted to the edge of their consciousness, to the limit of their understanding, perhaps even to the brink of despair." But the magical choice of the soul will still be possible, and those whose hearts are still open will act with exceptional power and speed to reclaim our future. When this happens, we will be grateful to the true God of pure, unconditional love we have awakened to find, for this God will have inspired it all.[1]

www.ingramcontent.com/pod-product-compliance
Lightning Source LLC
Chambersburg PA
CBHW030901080526
44589CB00010B/97